Film, Politics, and Gramsci

Film, Politics, and Gramsci

Marcia Landy

Foreword by Paul Bové

University of Minnesota Press

Minneapolis

London

Published by the University of Minnesota Press
2037 University Avenue Southeast, Minneapolis, MN 55455-3092
Printed in the United States of America on acid-free paper

Library of Congress Cataloging-in-Publication Data

Landy, Marcia, 1931–
    Film, politics, and Gramsci / Marcia Landy : Foreword
by Paul Bové.
        p.   cm.
    Includes bibliographical references and index.
    ISBN 0-8166-2390-2 (alk. paper)
    ISBN 0-8166-2391-0 (pbk. : alk. paper)
    1. Gramsci, Antonio, 1891–1937.   2. Communism and culture.
    3. Politics and culture.   4. Motion pictures.   I. Title.
    HX289.7.G73L36   1994
    335.43'092—dc20   93-43616

The University of Minnesota is an
equal-opportunity educator and employer.

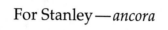
For Stanley — *ancora*

Contents

Contents

Foreword

Paul A. Bové

Marcia Landy echoes Stuart Hall, Joseph Buttigieg, Edward W. Said, and others by insisting that we must think as Gramscians. All these intellectuals are quick to point out that this does not mean that we should simply apply Gramscian notions in analysis of contemporary realities or that we should entertain certain notions simply because they carry the imprimatur of Gramsci. Rather, we should think *like* Gramsci, work *as* he did in trying to understand his own realities better in order to transform them and, later, to understand his own political defeat and that of his movement. We can find in Landy's book an excellent example of how one thinks as a Gramscian. She does set out, by comparison with Derrida, Lacan, and others, to clarify the greater value Gramsci might have for rethinking (and perhaps establishing) socialism in a conservative age such as our own. She transfers to our time the evocative modes of Gramsci's questioning and lucidly adapts certain remnants of his project to the present age. Along the way, she sets the record straight about those who, claiming progressive positions, would better understand the complicities of their positions if they did, indeed, despite their claims, actually think as Gramsci has shown us to think.

Like Gramsci, of course, Landy is primarily a political, historical thinker, and, like Gramsci, as Edward Said maintains, Landy is equally a spatial thinker. Said sees that geography and territory define Gramsci's political terms; one need think only of "The Southern Question" or the contrast between "war of position" and "war of maneuver" to have a sense of Said's perception. Space controls Landy's thinking as well, but it does not take the form of defining geographical categories; it does not derive from essential and given territorial or national differences.

x   There is no "Southern Question" underlying her work. Rather, Landy is
a mapper, perhaps more akin to Deleuze and Foucault in this regard
than to Gramsci. (Deleuze figures most importantly in this book after
Gramsci.)

Gramsci, too, maps in many ways: he theorizes the differences between north and south, between America and Europe. He traces lines of
historical influence and transition: the pressures of the past on present
formations (one thinks of his meditations on intellectuals) need to be
sketched so that the material forces of persistent cultural and political
formations might figure in accounts of the present—indeed, they are
essential in producing accounts of and for the present. Most important,
Gramsci maps this present not only as it has been formed but as it
"now" functions, as it produces itself and its futures. Taken together, all
these mappings create an analytic palimpsest, elucidating how what is
comes from what has been, how what is is and functions, and how in its
function and being it produces the future. Despite the fragmentary and
reiterative nature of the notebooks, Gramsci's thought aspires to produce such a map in detail—how else to read his frequent laments that in
prison he cannot do the complete and thorough work he would like.

Marcia Landy updates and contributes to the completion of Gramsci's
project. She limns our past; she traces the formation of various media;
she details the modifications necessary to use Gramsci's terms again in
our own time. In so doing, she gives us various maps of our time; of its
economic and cultural forces; of its assigned intellectual tasks of production (one should see the bold chapter on the Taviani brothers); and of the
various ways in which, as she says in her early pages, cultural analysis
can become more than simply another commodified form of intellectual
consumption. Just as it would be wrong to read Gramsci as having produced a grand theory of his or any society—that many have done this
makes it no less wrong—one would misread Landy hoping to find a
global thesis about contemporary culture or its specific forms. It is essential to Gramscian thinking that specificity displaces dogma and that
multiple determinations, complexities, and overlapping valences remain
the focus of thought. In culture, then, Gramscians find the traces of
power and negotiation, the plastic relations not only between dominant
and subaltern but the compromises and resistances that define the subaltern in its multidimensional relations. Gender and class, race and ethnicity, as well as place in the chain of value production, access to language
and sign systems, the anonymous forces of capital that determine these
in all their relations—all of this and much more make up the nature of

economics, culture, and politics as they intersect in postmodernity.
Landy's thesis is that Gramscian thought provides the best access to the
current moment; it uniquely presents what is in all its complex materiality, and thus supersedes the potential for ineffective abstraction associated with other, less comprehensive, less "worldly" forms of thought.

One would not exaggerate if one said that Landy's most important
contribution — among many in this book — to advanced academic critique is a unique effort to prevent cultural analysis from assuming a
commodified position within consumption. Indeed, one could say that
Landy determines that the field recently established as "cultural studies"
must be at least revised and perhaps replaced. Throughout this book,
Landy lets us see that she has absorbed the essential aspects of almost all
current critique, from Lacan to Negri to composition studies, and so on.
Her work builds on and usefully places whatever she finds of value in
such critique, yet that placing is always done in the name of thinking
like Gramsci and, in effect, corrects even the best of it for its partiality
and for its complicity with the commodity. Indeed, one judges that
Landy's reservations about Jameson — who usefully points out that in
postmodernism, consumerism occupies a newly prominent place for
oppositional intellectuals — are caught in the fact that Gramsci plays
almost no role in Jameson's work. Effectively, Jameson, we understand,
misses an opportunity to trace the problems of agency and culture that
a Gramscian approach to the negotiations of consent and resistance
would provide any analysis of the contemporary. Cumulatively, such expressed reservations — and others much more overt — add up to a general indictment of the current state of leftist critique, especially of what is
called "cultural studies," for its lack of rigorous consciousness about its
own position in relation to the contemporary. To put the matter differently, cultural studies, even when certain of its exponents evoke, catego-
rize, and so reify Gramscian notions (who now is not tired of the endless
invocations of hegemony and the like?), is un-Gramscian: it does not
attempt to place itself in the map of the contemporary. Without so doing,
it cannot understand its relations — its resistances and complicities. At
best, it can, as it always seems to do, "concede" that it too is part of commodity culture. Landy's project is to get beyond such market-induced
limitations, such reified criticisms. As a result, most forms of leftist critique appear of value only once their value has been specified by virtue
of a thinking that has the effort at such valuation as its task. More specifically, work flying under the colors of cultural studies appears as just the
means by which the present age imposes nonreflection upon intellec-

tuals in their task of making manifest whatever it is that capital needs to know, about whatever it is that capital needs us to speak.

Landy's book is historical, but not historicist. In this sense, it follows Gramsci. Even though it joins in the project of mapping the present, it recognizes that totalization, which cannot be accomplished, should not, in any event, be its aim. *Film, Politics, and Gramsci* presents us with a set of problems too interesting to be accidental. Landy tells us, for example, that, among her predecessors, Althusser and Negri both return to Marx. Like Foucault, in other words, she tells us that these thinkers are *répétiteurs*, that their authority derives from their place in the project of making Marx "an initiator of discursive practice." Foucault gave us his thinking on this issue in the 1960s, no doubt precisely because, in the immediate postwar crisis, represented not only by Althusser's returns but also by those of Sartre and Lacan (returns to Freud and Hegel as well as Marx), repetition required a new theory that could place it within the power effects of discourse. Althusser, Sartre, Lacan, and others returned to the great originals of their tradition on the condition of those originals' incompletion. Deficit produces surplus: the impulse, as we see especially in Sartre, was to systematic completion where in the original there were lacunae. Foucault elucidates this structure in the age of Algeria and Vietnam. Rather than repeating the earlier Kierkegaardian or Heideggerean theories of repetition as difference, Foucault gives us return as reiterative superfluity, or endless difference that makes no difference. This is a severe notion. It can be read as saying such a thing as "Lacan's reprise of Hegel/Freud is self-authorizing only on the basis of prior inadequacy, and its own accomplishments, specific to its own time, have no value outside its place within such a structure of return." One is tempted to make such a final statement, which does, however, pose an interesting question in some ways older in form than Foucault's. If Foucault seems to postmodernize the matter of repetition by turning it from action to discourse, then perhaps we can follow Landy in another direction and move away from the merely linguistic to another level, that of thought as agency. For what else can it mean when we say that we should learn to think like Gramsci?

Film, Politics, and Gramsci is a book about and an example of intellectual agency. To think like Gramsci is, in a sense, a prescription for action, for self-representation, for legitimacy, and for responsibility. It offers directions for critical identity and, in so doing, raises a peculiar question: can one think like another? Antonio Negri shows us that Spinoza is part of

Gramsci's tradition, but, with the exception of Deleuze, we hear no one today suggesting we should think like Spinoza. And rightly so, for it is not clear that, if we take Spinoza seriously, thinking like him or like Gramsci is a possibility.

One can make historicist or perspectival objections to this kind of repetition. One could object that to think like Gramsci now would be to persist in a degree of literate culture residual to our own imagistic culture; it would mean that a repetition of thinking like Gramsci would be out of place. Of course, this is not what Landy or other sophisticated Gramscians mean. They recognize the situational differences between then and now, or, as in the case of the Subaltern Studies collective, between Europe and India. These differences can be adjusted. Landy cites Gramsci on the significance of postprint media as a way of showing his developing sense of the new political importance he attaches to culture and to the layering of resistance and consent that pleasure and other forces bring about in the production and consumption of film and other mass media. Yet Gramsci himself wonders if a historicized displacement or repetition — such as thinking like Gramsci — does not raise questions more interesting than this perspectival complex.

Gramsci scholars often debate his attitude toward voluntarism, his deterministic sense, and his dialectical rigor to assess his political vision. Landy's work is not, in itself, a theoretical contribution to this debate, but it does offer an opportunity to consider Gramsci's importance to a time when these questions do seem vital.

Gramsci is above all a thinker about his own time, and thus to think like Gramsci means to think of one's own time. This notion is complex and must be treated nonreductively. It is not clear that "one's own time" is the singular; on the contrary, we can see that Gramsci's time was multiple. Not only are residues of past social and economic formations present in his time, but emergent energies and formations, some dying, some flourishing, some unrecognized, combine to produce a map so multidirectional that it presents the reader with no sense of direction, of totality. This is not to say that the present time might not be singular, but that singularity is complex and composite. Landy's own examination of the forces that form British film, of science fiction's conceptions of science, of current Italian film, and so on, delineates some of the complexity of a time. Reading each of these as "symptoms," to borrow an Althusserean term, could result in an analysis that presumes to find an underlying order or totality; yet, the map drawn by these readings and the correlations that emerge among the sites on that map do not assure, in themselves, the existence of an underlying order. But how can the intellectual

work without the assurance of that order, without at least the sciencelike
expectation that order, that something akin to "the laws of nature," can
and will reveal itself?

In one sense, this is Gramsci's challenge to our own thinking. Not
only are our times complex in their singularity, but their singularity
might consist precisely in the absence of a grand reality that can take the
form of a complete analysis or even, à la Fredric Jameson, of an "additive" totality. Gramsci himself confronted this around the classic question of the "interregnum." In prison, facing the undeniable fact of his
movement's political defeat, Gramsci thinks the need to think differently, to think anew in response to a singular present his own prior
thought had not the categories to theorize or to understand. What is
most interesting in this, of course, is Gramsci's willingness to admit the
necessity to discard the mechanics of thought that made up grand systems of theory and analysis — precisely because crisis made evident
their nonrelation to their singular present.

Yet, and this too must be thought, the condition for discarding the old
is precisely the relation to this singularity. It is, if you will, a relation of
nonrelationality, or, more mundanely, a relation of defeat, of irrelevance,
and despair. Gramsci's courage consists in his thinking through the categories to the lesson they teach: their own misfit, their own belatedness,
that is, their own fit with another present other than the new. Then, what
is this new? Surely, it has as one of its chief components the presence of
the old as a residue; it can be thought, and actions can follow from that
thought. In the pragmatic world of politics, their misfit appears: they
lead to defeat and failure. But how and where did they go wrong? As
Landy's reading of the Taviani films makes clear, failure is not a matter
of failure in thought as such. In other words, Gramsci's new thinking is
not an attempt at a correction of a previous mistake; it is not a filling in
of lacunae in an earlier discourse. Rather, it is just a recognition of the
relation of nonrelation. Put vulgarly, it is a recognition that the old discourses and categories, having solidified in their own utility, no longer
work; they have no grasp on reality; they are not current with the fast-
moving forms of societal production.

It might seem idealistic to think of Gramsci this way, but I think that
Gramscian critics from Said to Landy have let us see that Gramsci knows
thought to be inseparable from the formations that drive production,
conceived not simply as the latest mode of economic mobilization but
as the materiality that compels the emergence of new societies and civi-
lizations. Lest this seem too Spinozist, one should recall that when
Gramsci thinks this issue of the interregnum, of the moment when

thought experiences its own belatedness and struggles to bring about its own rebirth, at just this moment Gramsci insists that a new culture, a new society must be brought into being. In its fragmentary form, the force of Gramsci's thought needs to be reassembled. In his thinking, the fact that there are intellectual and ideological crises promoting cynicism and depression must be read as history's demanding a new thinking, but, given Gramsci's profoundly material sense of culture and of thought, of the work of intellectuals, this thinking needs and must be part of a larger societal remaking: "in other words, the possibility and necessity of creating a new culture itself."[1]

The note from which this quotation comes is remarkable. Written in 1930, it portends something of our own time and gives something like a general lesson to intellectuals about the need for new thinking and the potential role it must play in forming new cultures. Curiously, Gramsci's reading of the crisis of fascism, in which, as he indicates, none of the old ideologies works, in which, as a result, force replaces consent and even the working class has no patience with its old discourses and ideological positions, represents his own effort to name his notebooks as an element of new thinking made necessary not merely by political defeat but by the recurrent problem thought faces in keeping itself adjacent to material transformations brought about by an economic system and by foundational transformations to and within the system itself. Indeed, as his notes on Americanism and Fordism indicate, and as Landy's writings about common sense make eminently clear, Gramsci knows that systems may be displaced: international, efficient capital—as represented by the film industry—displaces not only the aristocratic parasitism of the ancient regime but the nationalist models of mass production. Such transformations require that the relations between intellectual work and the most powerful, rationalized, and emergent societal system of any time be fully worked out as such; it means that modes of thought stand defined substantially by their relation to the formations to which they adhere, and which they reveal, critique, and hope to displace. What is significant about this apparent mere historicism is that Gramsci's insight is not restricted, as we might say, to the content of intellectual representation. It addresses the very fact of intellectual production in its own contemporaneity, daring to think such matters as, for example, the value of philosophy in relation to a formation for which "value" itself is a defining category of societal and cultural organization; or, to take a more literary example, daring to think the notion of literary history as itself so related to nationalizing societies (one thinks of Gramsci's comments on de Sanctis as well as on Dante's *Inferno*) that it can only persist in a relation of non-

xvi relationality to the international markets of such emergent facts as the culture industries, their markets, and their capital needs and structures.

It is rare to find a single set of remarks as concentrated in reflection on intellectual work as is this note by Gramsci. Landy's all-important reflections on common sense derive, it seems to me, from the very essence of this reflection. Gramsci is not merely posing questions aimed to reveal the contradictions or unreflected aspects of given positions; he is not, at this point, engaged merely in critique. Rather, like Landy, or like Edward Said, whose own reflections on Gramsci's notion of emergent culture have been very influential, in this note Gramsci is drawing attention to the inseparable connections between the very work of producing cultures and societies and the task of thought. Put specifically, this involves abandoning what was once known about the evolution of capitalism — to old thinking, fascism appears to be a regression from the path to socialism — and, beginning only with the knowledge of what one must abandon, setting out to speak about, to theorize, to represent the new culture emergent as the material universe produces the new society. To critique common sense, if this is taken simply as misunderstanding or misfit between what is thought and what is, is mere negation, a version of the relation of nonrelationality. In an interregnum, Gramsci warns, if intellectuals do not attend to the danger of this relation, then others will "make other arrangements" — a fact that, in his case, furthered the tasks of fascist society.

If we take Landy seriously in her insistence that we must not be Gramscian but think like Gramsci, then we must risk, among other things, abandoning what we think he helps us to know. The hypertrophy of such Gramscian notions as "hegemony," "domination," "subaltern," and so forth, requires not only an effort of scholarship to recover their singular meanings within their contemporary contexts, but, more than this historicism, requires understanding their nonrelation to this present. It is not the case, as it were, that each "present" has thought that is "proper" or "appropriate" to it; rather, thinking must always move, and, if it can, in tandem with the material forces evolving societies. To put it another way, thinking always does go forward; but it need not happen in the uniquely reflective and theoretical manner that intellectuals can provide. In an age of international capital formations and markets, thinking — reflected or not — will occur in the operators of and producers within those markets and formations. These intellectuals — film directors and producers, for example — accompany the movement of society. Gramsci's thinking about organic and traditional intellectuals, dependent as it is upon statist notions of class formation and the

Hegelian dialectic, nonetheless grounds a thinking in which we must
recognize that capital needs its intellectuals not only to operate but to
theorize its systems. Gramsci, of course, would have it that a version of
the traditional intellectual — which he called the organic intellectuals of
the working class — would help form and direct resistance to capital. But
deep in his thinking is the possibility that, despite the desire for socialism, without the class struggle intellectuals will be left only with the
position of being organic to capital, to marginalized groups (who may or
may not form a bloc; such nonclass thinking does not seem possible in
Gramsci) or fragmented opponents of a system that they can describe.

Putting aside, as it were, for the moment, the different politics of these
possible positions for the intellectual, we can see that each and every one
demands of the intellectual the triple task of understanding the relation
between inherited thought and the present; mapping the present; and
joining in the task of building the new culture by developing the thought
that will theorize it and, perhaps at best, direct its formation. To think
like Gramsci is, as Marcia Landy's essays inspire us to understand, a
risky business of putting aside what is known to measure what is as
much by the inadequacies of the devices that have helped us to know as
by what they have taught us about the present world from which they
came.

Throughout these reflections is the unspoken assumption that this
time of ours is an interregnum. We have many people testifying to grand
changes that put our thinking into doubt: the collapse of the Berlin wall,
the decline of the United States, the threats to national sovereignty by
the market and superstates, the misfit between cold-war practice and the
new world order, and so on and so forth. At the same time, we have
many people, especially academic students of culture, perhaps acknowledging these facts (although many seem to have forgotten them), but
nonetheless going on with business as usual. Or, we have unreflective
opportunists, who, having realized that older intellectual formations,
such as the study of literature, have lost some of their legitimacy, at least
within the schools and universities, seize the occasion to install other
models, such as composition or cultural studies (often in combination
with such things as "international business"), that can be advanced in
harmony with market and national impulses to produce a more literate
work force and a more advanced consumer on a world scale. Among
other matters at stake in these processes are academic intellectuals'
desires to find a place for themselves in a system that often seems not to
require or legitimate the skills and knowledge in which they were (often
recently) trained. Hence, I think, the current high market capital of cul-

tural studies (reflecting on ethnic, racial, and geographical difference for the market) and composition, preparing (so it is believed) "critical" consumers and workers for the information society.

Landy's courage lies in avoiding these easy paths. Rather than take up an easy populist position on matters of "resistance" and "identity," she opens up all accepted matters to radical questioning. To think "Gramsci beyond Gramsci," to displace a figure who is both a fetish of radical chic and a conduit for serious reflection on modern societies and their intellectual characteristics, forces Landy's readers into a relation with their own presents. Many of those are the past and appear as such; we can politely, after Raymond Williams, call them "residual." Some are "progressive," formed in media studies and oppositional criticism, and even these find themselves prodded to accept the task of mapping the present and seeking to guide it to formation by theorizing it. Overall, Landy, thinking like Gramsci, accepts the task of directing the emergent. How hard if not impossible this is without the support of older notions about class, the proletariat, the state, and so on, she makes evident from her opening gambit: how to think about getting to socialism when everyone tells us we can't get there from here.

To think about these things as Gramsci thought about them while dying in prison means trying to discover just what sense words like "socialism" can have. Whatever its utopian elements, it must be retheorized as the best hope for what is possible within the leading forces of the newly emergent. I put this matter in Spinozist terms because Spinoza identified the best that could be hoped as the perfection of the best that any moment of history would allow. In Spinoza's world, it is sinful to hinder the evolution of this perfection. Somehow, some have stupidly read in this notion a legitimation of violence, even of extermination. It is, rather, a call to think and to direct. Everyone acknowledges that Gramsci's notions of "directing" or "direction" or even of "leadership" are noncoercive. He believes, like Spinoza, in reason and consent. The task of the intellectual is to lead and achieve consent so what can be emerges; not contributing to this task is sin.

Some worry that without the Party Gramscian notions of leadership are literally merely academic. Such worry is misplaced. What Landy's text shows us is the essential role that thinking plays in the human choices that take place in the interregnum, as new culture emerges. If we read carefully in the essays that make up the argument of this book, what we see is a mapping of the processes by which an order of culture emerges. Clearly, as this order develops—and we can call it postmodern if we choose—it has the residual characteristics of capital's earlier print-based formations, but more important, as it works through its contradictions, it **xix** represents its own development in its presentation of crises and struggles. In the spirit of Landy's fine essay on science fiction, originally co-authored with Stanley Shostak, we might say that Gramscian thinking in the age of the global market gives us not merely dialectical analysis of class conflict, but the impulse to theorize the relation between the entropic decay of older systems and the self-organizing development of order of the new. Landy's book will be read as a book about cultural emergence, important because it does not bog itself down within the study of empirical detail assumed historistically to result in order; rather, it theorizes the fact that the self-organization of societies is there, as it were, even before and inherent within any of the factors traditionally assigned causative and foundational power in Marxist or liberal modes of analysis. That is to say, while, like Gramsci, Landy certainly takes seriously the importance of the economic, while she studies in detail both the nature of value in postmodernism and the fact of value's centrality to our culture—from money to ethics—she does not rely on economistic or psychologistic explanations for what is. One can say that Landy helps us understand that such matters as debates over Gramsci's putative economism or productivism are moot; what matters is adapting his thinking so that we no longer construct it along lines that require our hypothesizing sufficient or necessary causes. Landy's work, we might say, comes not only after Gramsci, but after poststructuralism's critique of the grand narrative. We are always aware that without a narrative that prioritizes what deconstruction once called a "center," we must attend instead to the differend, to the inequality of power that, as Lyotard helps us understand, persists in all social relations. Landy develops this line from Negri's rereading of Gramsci and, although she takes seriously his critique of Gramsci, she essentially displaces it by revealing that it depends on a modern theorizing of Gramsci that is reductivist.

We can see this most effectively in Landy's recasting of Gramsci's thinking about the Southern Question in her essay on the Tavianis. That essay is too lucid to require detailed rereading, but one should stress that we find in it a considerable and important dimension of the present age. The essay is extremely clear and convincing evidence that the national stands mediated if not displaced by more important relations between the global and the local. Gramsci is not, I think, often enough read with an eye on his understanding of the international or transnational market and capital formations. His comments on the film industry alone are evidence that he had noticed the important postnational structures emerging out of Americanism—which is identical neither to Fordism nor to xx the United States. Landy's essay, by taking seriously the issue of language, of dialect, in relation to the transnational medium of film, allegorizes the reality that critical intellectuals need to deal with, namely, the problematic relation of the local to the global as an effect of the market. For it is the global market and its flows that create something akin to the cosmopolitanism that contextualizes the dialect as an archive of historical memory, contradiction, and, indeed, human possibility. Moreover, the same market puts pressure on these local forms of life, language, and memory, forcing their contradictions to emerge and, as we see in such places as Bosnia, creating problems that seem to be old but in fact are quite new.

This returns us to the topic we have never left, namely, Landy's scholarly and theoretical commitment to the proper task of the intellectual. Unlike Fredric Jameson, who has only recently abandoned the utopian thought of the seventies and eighties, Landy's work, although cognizant of the realm of desire and concerned with the problems of subject formation, is hardheadedly realistic. She theorizes the world as it is, putting the fact of utopian desire in its historical and societal place, giving accounts for its existence, analyzing its contradictions, and finally leaving it on the landscape where she found it. Hers is not theoretical advocacy of a position; hers is thinking through, a process that does not come to rest in repeatable categories that, no matter how useful or putatively oppositional, become commodified objects of academic and journalistic circulation. This means that her work is anticapitalist in its very practice and anti-Hegelian in its theory as well. Despite the Marxism, Landy's is not a statist enterprise. The intellectual, after Gramsci, without the myth of the proletarian subject à la Lukacs or of the party à la Althusser, is something of an anarchist. This must be the effect of taking seriously Gramsci's idea that we are in an interregnum. As entropy contests with self-organization, as the nature of agency remains unclear, as the mechanisms reordering the world emerge, the intellectual must speak of and to all this, and without the certainty of fixed positions in thought or service.

Landy's reading of Negri's revisions of Gramsci articulates best the ethos and politics of the moment. Negri, we recall, within his own anarchist moment, can hope to replace the Gramscian party as subject as well as the bourgeois subject by the larger subject of community, no longer defined by the restrictions of the workplace. The communal subject is the remaining articulation of the desire for socialism. Its troubles appear in the contradictions between local and global, between dialect and the market. That is to say, Landy's readings of the Tavianis and others prob-

lematize even this residual socialist desire expressed in Negri's recapitulation of Gramsci. Negri was not thinking like Gramsci, but thinking
beyond Marx. The difference from Landy is sharp; it is a difference of
history.

Landy's reading of Negri rightly insists that, like Gramsci, he aims "to
bring history to bear on an assessment of the possibilities for social
change in ways that do not reproduce past authoritarian structures."
Needless to say, Landy has a similar goal, but, as I have been trying to
make clear, hers is not a history of the past, but of the present. And that
present is not Negri's. Landy admits as much when she tells us toward
the end of her book that Negri's work, if read in the proper way, can take
us beyond current clichés of dominant thought—left and right. Negri
can be read—Landy so reads him—as a prism to help the thinking like
Gramsci sustain itself in our present. As such, Negri is a name for a project admirably carried out by this book: clearing away the detritus of
what Landy powerfully calls "the new 'folklore' of cultural politics."
Negri is critique and desire: elements on the current map, important to
note, with a function very worth theorizing.

All this gives us a model of intellectual work that Landy herself does
not name. The title of the final chapter, "Gramsci beyond Gramsci,"
makes the point nicely. With its echo—perhaps unconscious—not only
of Negri but of C. L. R. James's *Beyond the Boundary*, it tells us several
things: Gramsci's spatial thinking, which, as Said notes, is mostly
national and regional, no longer exists within such "boundaries." Dialect
in relation to a global market for capital and consumption allegorizes the
futility of thinking in those terms. But to think like Gramsci beyond him,
beyond his name, is not only to leave behind the new folklore of cultural
politics and so Gramsci's entombed cadaver, but to carry him beyond
the cipher that entombs him in the pyramid of professionalism and academic iteration. It is to be open to influence, to be Gramsci but in our
time, not his. It is also to name the intolerable boundary opportunity of
historical awareness: to repeat without killing, to carry the past to the
struggle against authoritarianism, but without being smothered by historicist cavils. On this, we recall Nietzsche's *Use and Abuse of History for
Life* as well as Marx's *Eighteenth Brumaire*. Finally, there is one more point
to this title that catches the kind of intellectual Landy's work instanti-
ates: "beyond" seems to mean "within" as well. We cross "beyond" and
we come back to where we were; this is the nature of transgression *within* the limit. In this case, the limit has many dimensions and directions
within its narrow confines. It is to be beyond and so within the history of
cultural critique; to be beyond and so within the stories of the nation; to

be against but within the market; to be formed by, speaking to, that market; to oppose the commodity while producing one; to devastate cultural politics while practicing it. It is to exceed what the law has established and demands, but almost always on the terms it establishes. As Foucault taught us, the limit is something that cannot be left behind.

Landy's work, like Gramsci's and that of some others, exists within the painful space of that limit. It proceeds by meticulous examination of that space, by clear and lucid reporting of what's found—reporting good and bad news alike. It refuses to let the "folklore" choke it off. Most important, it is not restricted to thought about categories academic professionals have decided are important. To put it more forthrightly, Landy's work gains its legitimacy from its struggle beyond the limit. It eschews populist positions and accepts instead the obligations of rigor. It belongs worthily in the traditions to which it opens itself as it moves beyond: Gramsci, Negri, Benjamin, and so on. This book will give its readers much to do if they hope to move in its light, to belong to its tradition.

Preface

The massive repudiation of Marxism in the last decades by prophets of both Left and Right has made the task of creating socialism even more gargantuan. Never has socialism seemed so remote and yet never has it seemed so imperative. At this time of neoconservative hegemony, it seems appropriate to invoke the name of Antonio Gramsci, neither because he was a victim of Fascism (which he was) nor because he is a venerated figure in the development of Marxism (which he is), but because in his writings he offered both an analysis of the totally administered society and tentative suggestions for how to struggle against it in the face of seemingly overwhelming obstacles, including those generated by the Left. Gramsci does not offer his readers a precise set of prescriptions for social transformation but a diagnosis of and tentative guidelines for addressing the problematic relationship of the state to civil society, and for rethinking questions of cultural and political change, specifically as they involve an analysis of the notion of hegemony. To judge by the number of articles and books that invoke his works, for better or worse, Gramsci's writing has become important to the rethinking of culture and politics that has taken place through critical theory everywhere in the world, and my book is geared to assessing Gramsci's writings in relation to current cultural/political analyses and identifying those elements in his writings that are still viable for a socialist critique.

I am mindful of the problems of transposing Gramsci's work into a contemporary context without taking into account historical changes that have occurred since he wrote. Stuart Hall cautions his readers to be wary of an uncritical appropriation of Gramsci's work. "I do not claim that in any simple way," he writes, "Gramsci 'has the answers' or 'holds the key' to our present troubles. I do believe that we must 'think' our problems in a gramscian way—which is different."[1] In British cultural studies much effort has been expended, particularly by the Centre for Popular Culture in Birmingham, in an attempt to develop a "Gramscian way" of theorizing cultural work. In late capitalist society, confronting the notion of culture as political, and the notion of capitalism itself as confounding relations between economics and politics, entails a rethinking of the term "political" in the context of the critical work that has been done since the 1960s on gender, sexuality, national identity, globality, and the role of intellectuals. Such a study of culture is not a mirror of immediate social, economic, and political relations but involves a painstaking reassessment of the ways in which social knowledge is created and disseminated along lines charted by contemporary figures such as Stuart Hall, Gayatri Spivak, Immanuel Wallerstein, and Etienne Balibar, among others, and my work engages with these reassessments. I have sought to make bridges between Marxist and poststructuralist concerns. Gramsci has remained a crucial barometer in a quest to understand configurations of subalternity.

I offer this book itself as a critique of traditional thought on history, science, the human sciences, and the role of culture. The discussion addresses poststructuralist positions and theories of postmodernism in the political terms first raised by Gramsci, in his identification of the political, economic, and cultural dimensions of Fordism, and now problematized by the "post-Fordist" concerns raised by Antonio Negri and other critics. The introduction to the work, chapter 1, surveys the terrain and the key issues that are at stake in current cultural analysis. Chapter 2, "The Gramscian Politics of Culture," is an overview of Gramsci's writings on hegemony, history, the state and civil society, intellectuals, common sense as folklore, and popular and mass culture. Chapter 3, "Socialism and/or Democracy: Politics, Culture, and the State," elaborates on these issues through the writings of recent critics on Gramsci. Chapter 4, "Cultural Politics and Common Sense," expands on the importance of Gramsci's conception of common sense as an alternative to prevailing ideology critiques. Chapter 5, *They Were Sisters:* Common Sense, World War II, and the Woman's Film," tests the efficacy of a commonsense reading in relation to a British film melodrama produced during World War II. Chapter 6, "Looking Backward: Versions of History and Common Sense in Recent British Cinema," explores how common-sense representations of history and national identity are tied to issues of gender and sexuality. "Language, Folklore, and Politics in the Films of the Taviani Brothers" (chapter 7) looks at the ways in which Gramsci's writ-

ings on language, common sense, and intellectuals provide an understanding of the politics of representation in contemporary Italian cinema. "Postmodernism as Folklore in Contemporary Science Fiction Cinema" (chapter 8) examines common-sense representations of science and
technology in Hollywood cinema and the efficacy of various discourses
of postmodernity. The concluding chapter, " 'Gramsci beyond Gramsci'
and the Writings of Antonio Negri," interrogates where and how Gramsci's writings on culture and politics can be usefully reconciled with current political writings on post-Fordism.

The work has not been done in isolation, and my expression of gratitude to people who have helped me in the writing of this book is an
expression of courtesy but even more of indebtedness. In particular, I
want to thank Paul Bové for his suggestion that I undertake this project,
for his challenging comments on portions of the text, and for his continuing commitment to intellectual work. In a similar vein, I am extremely
appreciative of the encouragement of Joseph A. Buttigieg, who, from my
earliest essays on Gramsci, urged me to expand on my work. His own
monumental work on Gramsci has been invaluable. In my recent experiences in teaching I have been extremely fortunate to have as my guides a
group of students—Amy Villarejo, Madhava Prasad, Matthew Tinkcom,
Barbara White, Sally Meckling, and Joy Fuqua, to name a few. The courses
we shared were predicated on the need to rethink traditional forms of
political discourses, to reexamine Marxism in the light of the serious
questions that have been raised by poststructuralism concerning the role
of the intellectual in the period of late capitalism, and to seek new strategies and tactics that can constitute effective forms of political subversion
against prevailing institutional interests.

I am grateful to Lucy Fischer and Dana Polan, friends and colleagues,
who have been constant readers of and critical commentators on my
work. My special thanks to Biodun Iginla for his confidence in the project and to Ann Klefstad for her excellent editorial work. I owe thanks to
Kristin Herbert for her very helpful suggestions for stylistic revision,
and I am extremely appreciative of David F. Ruccio's critical comments
on an earlier version of chapter 7 when it appeared in *Rethinking Marxism* as "Postmodern Folklore in Science Fiction Film," co-authored with
Stanley Shostak. I owe a special debt of gratitude to Stan, not merely for
his permission to include this essay and for his careful reading of the
entire book, but, above all, for his friendship.

Acknowledgments

Sections of this book were previously published as articles, and I want to acknowledge the permission of editors and publishers to reproduce selections: *boundary 2* for "Culture and Politics in the Writings of Antonio Gramsci," from vol. 14, no. 3 (Spring 1986): 49–71, and "Socialism and Democracy: Gramsci and/or Bobbio/Review Essay," vol. 17, no. 3 (Fall 1990): 154–89; *Rethinking Marxism* for "Postmodernism as Folklore in Contemporary Science Fiction Cinema," vol. 6, no. 2 (Summer 1993): 25–46, and "Socialist Education Today: Pessimism or Optimism of the Intellect?" vol. 4, no. 3 (Fall 1991): 9–24; *Critical Studies* for "Cultural Studies and Common Sense," vol. 3, no. 1 (Fall 1991): 105–34; *Film Criticism* for "Looking Backward: Thatcherism and the British Historical Film," vol. 15, no. 1 (Fall 1990): 17–38; *Post Script* for "*They Were Sisters*: The British Woman's Film," vol. 10, no. 2 (Winter 1991): 14–25; *Annali d'Italianistica* for "Neorealism, Politics, and Language in the Films of the Tavianis," vol. 6 (1988): 236–51; and *boundary 2* for " 'Gramsci beyond Gramsci' and the Writings of Antonio Negri," from vol. 21, no. 2 (Spring 1994): 63–97.

Chapter 1

Gramsci, "Knowledge Claims and Knowing Subjects"

In her *Simians, Cyborgs, and Women*, Donna Haraway writes, "My problem and 'our' problem is how to have simultaneously an account of radical historical contingency for all knowledge claims and knowing subjects, [and] a critical practice for recognizing our own 'semiotic technologies' for making meanings.... We need the power of modern critical theories of how meanings and bodies get made, not in order to deny meaning and bodies, but in order to live in meanings and bodies that have a chance for a future."[1] Haraway's comments remind us that theorizing in these last decades of the twentieth century has been concerned with the question of knowledge production, the ways in which we know what we know and how we act on that knowledge. In a parallel concern for a critical rethinking of received knowledge, Gayatri Spivak writes,

> At a time when a rage for order defeminates the academies from every side, ... I am interested in the theory-practice of pedagogic practice-theory that would allow us constructively to question privileged explanations even as explanations are generated.... What I look for ... is a confrontational teaching of the humanities that would question the students' received disciplinary ideology (model of legitimate cultural explanations) even as it pushed into indefiniteness the most powerful ideology of the teaching of the humanities: the unquestioned explicating power of the theorizing mind and class, the need for intelligibility and the rule of law.[2]

It is not accidental that these challenges to received knowledge arise out of the oppositional contexts of feminist and postcolonial theories, and that they are dependent on work that has arisen from work in structuralism and poststructuralism.

2   My study of Gramsci's writings makes the claim that this Italian Marxist who died before the end of World War II has not only prefigured the concern with these same issues but that, in some very important ways, he contributes much-needed insights and correctives to current cultural and political work. A brief survey of some current exemplary positions from poststructuralist writing should indicate how Gramsci's concerns anticipated them. My object, however, is not to make Gramsci a prescient precursor of the critical scene; this is not an influence study. I wish to address the efficacy of Gramsci's insights into the dynamic nature of capitalist formations, into the contradictory positions that constitute subalternity, and into the importance of arriving at a sense of the multivalent relations between economic, cultural, and political phenomena.[3]

The agenda of critical theory, especially that of poststructuralist writing over the past few decades, has been to address the ways in which language, subjectivity, sexuality, textuality, and modernity are interconnected and crucial to understanding the persistence of certain modes of thought and behavior. Lacanian psychoanalysis, which has introduced the hitherto marginalized issue of the formation of gendered and sexual subjects into an examination of the nature of the formation of the subjects, has been particularly fruitful for certain feminists and gay intellectuals in their quest for understanding change and resistances to change. Lacanian theory has complicated the issue of ideology in particular, moving it away from notions of false consciousness. For example, the Althusserian focus on ideology has allowed for a more complex entry into the difficult question of the persistence of dominant ideological practices, requisite for a rethinking of Marxism, and for exploring connections among economics, politics, and culture, reconfiguring traditional notions of base and superstructure, and even calling into question distinctions between ideology and science. Like Gramsci, Althusser insisted on the need to disarticulate prevailing and totalizing sociological notions concerning base and superstructure; even more like Gramsci were the ways in which he saw that folklore was not merely a closed and univalent expression of subjection but also an expression of opposition, if not of resistance. Likewise, Althusser's examination of the role of the state and civil society in the formation of consensus was certainly central to Gramsci's thinking about politics. In his theorizing about hegemony, however, Gramsci offers more flexible, less monolithic, and less stratified insights into how the relation of state and civil society produces forms of consensus and coercion.

The work of Michel Foucault, while critical of traditional Marxism, has offered, in its genealogies of power and its interrogation of classical notions of institutional hierarchies and of victimage, complicated—and at times problematic—theories concerning the relationship between subalternity and social institutions. Not only does his work recall Gramsci's discussions of the ways power is dispersed throughout the culture rather than operating pyramidally from the top, but his ideas of power also involve a rethinking of the nature and role of the state in the present historical conjuncture.[4] Gramsci, especially in his comments in the *Notebooks* on Americanism and Fordism, is aware of the intimate link between modernity and changing attitudes toward sexuality, and while Gramsci's concern is nowhere so pronounced as Foucault's, it is indicative of his attempts to link capital and culture in less monolithic terms than many Marxists of his generation.

Derrida's critique of logocentrism, particularly of the tendency to maintain and hierarchize strict divisions between center and margins, oppressor and oppressed, has called in question the persistence of modes of totalizing thought that have characterized western speech and writing, inflecting the way we are beginning to think about history, agency, thought, and action. Gramsci too was concerned for the ways that language study was central to any understanding of the solidification of meaning and the creation and maintenance of hierarchies. Gramsci's exploration of language, his complication of the nature of representation through his conception of the sedimented and multifarious nature of common sense, is a critical examination of the notion that grand narratives are naturally and inevitably constructed.

Thus poststructuralist work has invited a radical critique of the power of the state, of specific civil institutions, the positions of gendered and sexual subjects, racial and ethnic groups, and the legitimacy of juridical, medical, and academic discourses. Further, in its exploration of and challenge to prevailing notions of representation as constitutive of the real, poststructuralist work has sought to undermine the social imaginary, while not offering prescriptions for or affirmations of revolutionary struggle and transformation. In these times of militant invocation of traditional representations of nation, patriotism, family, religion, and individualism, poststructuralist theories invite a reexamination of the ways in which these narratives have been constructed, what has been left out, and the designs and interests of the narrator. Spivak writes: "To an extent I think the poststructuralist project would look at history not as a series of brute facts but as narratives generated in one way or another. Derrida has a statement where he says that deconstruction is the deconstitution of the founding concepts of the Western historical narrative."[5]

4   In his distinctions between organic and traditional intellectuals, in his explorations of the ways in which knowledge is produced and received, and particularly in his notion of the pastiche quality of many narratives in their common-sense claims to truth, Gramsci's work can be said broadly to share Derrida's and Spivak's concern for "deconstituting" the bases and claims of prevailing narratives.

Gramsci and Mass Culture

Specifically, Gramsci's preoccupation with the nature and impact of cultural production places him alongside other contemporary critics who have in the last decades stressed the importance of understanding canonical, popular, and mass cultural texts, including the role of media. Analysis of media as practiced by such diverse critics as Raymond Williams and Paul Virilio stresses the central and contradictory role played by media in social representation. Along lines charted by Gramsci, mass media work has made it clear that one cannot discuss questions of ideology, subject positions, and value production without interrogating the nature of representation itself as imbricated, in complex and contradictory terms, in the "culture industry."[6] Gramsci's critical concerns are more aligned with than antithetical to those of postmodern intellectuals. As exemplified in his preprison and prison writings, his intellectual and political concerns with popular culture in his critiques of novels, theater, films, and beauty contests, and his preoccupation with the nature of language itself, reveal a broad engagement with cultural texts and a sense of their importance. Gramsci's intense preoccupation with intellectuals and power, his anxiety about the relationship between politics and culture, were not unique to him but were shared by intellectuals of his era—Fascists and Marxists. In particular, along with the Frankfurt school, he acknowledged the importance of the burgeoning culture industry as a problem of modern capitalism. And, like Adorno, he was aware of the affirming aspects of mass culture that were characteristic of Fascism.

   Despite his fears about modern culture, Gramsci was, however, less peremptory and dismissive than Adorno and in some ways closer to Walter Benjamin, who characteristically recognized the importance of addressing mass culture as affirming but also as oppositional, not as an issue subsidiary to economic transformation but as a central facet of modern life that needs to be addressed if change is possible at all. Benjamin's and Gramsci's work is more than merely anticipatory in its concern with the political economy of the sign: it is also instructive for

its emphasis on the need to differentiate texts, audiences, and modes of   5
production and reception. In recent decades, the writings of such theorists as Jean-François Lyotard and Jean Baudrillard have pointed to the
necessity of rethinking the ways in which we perpetuate cultural value.
These conceptions of modernism and postmodernism have challenged
us to reexamine issues of production and consumption. But such critical
work also veers toward monolithic assessments of contemporary culture. Are we doomed to be consumers, trapped in the science-fiction
world of technologically transmitted images? In fact, what do we mean
by consumerism and the role of the consumer?

In the debates concerning the nature of the postmodern, Fredric
Jameson offers one critical response to this question:

> One's sense, in the present conjuncture, sometimes called the onset of
> postmodernity or late capitalism, is that our urgent task will be tirelessly to
> denounce the economic forms that have come for the moment to remain
> supreme and unchallenged.... [T]hat those doctrines of reification and
> commodification which played a secondary role in the traditional classical
> Marxian heritage are now likely to come into their own and become the
> dominant instruments of analysis and struggle. In other words, a cultural
> politics, a politics of daily life, which emerged in earlier decades but as
> something of an adjunct and a poor relative, a supplement to "politics" itself,
> must now — at least in the First World — be the primary space of struggle.[7]

Gramsci's writings are important as a counter to these dire and pessimistic evaluations of the "postmodern condition." The figure of Gramsci,
however, is negligible in Jameson's work, even though it is precisely the
rethinking of economics, historicizing, the changing contours of modernity, and the "politics of daily life" that Jameson invokes that characterizes Gramsci's work, which has been a strong influence on British cultural studies, with its focus on mass and popular culture. A Gramscian
analysis would seem to offer a more flexible, multivalent analysis of
cultural formations than some of the monolithic pronouncements of
many postmodernist discourses.

"The Gramscian Way"

In the struggle to find more adequate cultural and political forms of
analysis, Stuart Hall has cautioned us that the Left is problematic insofar
as it continues to hold on to traditional analyses of power and domination in its romanticizing of the subaltern and its Eurocentrism, as well as
its participation in reformist politics; its denial, contrary to Gramsci, that
it can speak for and liberate the subaltern groups without their active

6 understanding and participation is also a source of problems. In the refusal to acknowledge changing historical conditions for the realization of socialism and to develop strategies more suited to present conditions, the Left's position as a voice for change is foundering. Working with traditional models of social class, work, and economism, the Left is in danger of losing any political efficacy because, according to Hall,

> basically, that model has committed us over the years to an analysis which no longer has at its center an accurate description of contemporary social, economic, and cultural realities. Second, it has attached itself to a definition of how change occurs in society which in no way accurately reflects the actual social composition of the class forces and social movements necessary to produce it or the democratic realities of our society. Third, it is no longer able to politicize and develop the majority experiences and dispositions of the popular forces which the left must enlist. Fourth, it is wedded to an automatic conception of class, whereby the economic conditions can be transposed directly on to the political stage. Marx's formidable distinction between a class "in itself" and one which has developed sufficient political, cultural, and strategic unity to become an active force in history — "for itself" — is wholly foreign to it, though "Marxism" as a sort of magic invocation is constantly on its lips.[8]

With the exception of Hall's fourth point, which is more directly applicable to the British context than that of the United States, Hall's comments can fruitfully be applied to American radical politics, if not to other sectors of Western Europe. Either naiveté or willful neglect about the pervasive and innovative strategies of late capitalism in mobilizing popular consent in the face of political and economic crises has characterized the legacy of the 1960s. A naiveté about popular movements, a lack of any sense of how power works or knowledge of the impetus toward "reformism," is linked to counterstrategies of containment. As Gramsci wrote, "No social formation disappears as long as the productive forces which have developed within it still find room for further forward movement.... [A] society does not set itself tasks for whose solution the necessary conditions have not already been incubated."[9]

The late 1970s and the growing emphasis on the ideology of excellence and merit in tandem with economic retrenchment revealed that there was little space in which to maneuver for this "forward movement of the productive forces," and that there had been no incubation for "necessary solutions." Since that time, the question of what constitutes a political practice has become incredibly more complicated as neoconser-

vatives have adopted the strategies of protest made familiar by opposi-   7
tional groups, complicating further the imperative question of what
political practices are effective for socialism and necessitating a reconfiguring of resistance strategies. Hence Gramsci's explorations of the complexity of subaltern thought and behavior deserve elaboration in the
context of notions of postmodernity, education, and social transformation. His statement that all people are intellectuals, even though not all
function in professional terms as such has more cogency now than ever,
despite his writing at an earlier moment of western industrialism and
modernization, during a period he termed Fordism. His notion that,
even under Taylorized modes of production, workers are not bereft of a
conception of the world invites a different set of speculations about the
nature of the subaltern in the context of mass culture. His conception of
common sense does not make totalizing assumptions about subalternity
but allows for an understanding and recognition of the existence of
antagonism, though not necessarily of active and overt resistance.

Gramsci's writings are concerned with culture and politics under
Fordism. Antonio Negri wants to mark a rupture between Fordism and
late capitalism through positing a change between what he calls the
"mass worker" and the "socialized worker."[10] His postmodern socialized worker is theorized on the basis of the subsumption of contemporary civil society into the political, and also on the general availability of
knowledge formerly denied to the mass worker. If Gramsci's work written in prison under the Fascist regime was in large part an attempt to
account for the rehegemonization of the bourgeoisie, Negri's work is
also an attempt to account for the "innovativeness" of capitalism. Both
writers understand that work toward socialism can be retarded or
advanced through Marxist theory and through an understanding of the
crisis nature of capitalism and the means used to either suppress or capitalize on crisis.

A major difference between Gramsci's position and that of Negri
resides, as Negri himself admits, in the phrase employed by the Third
International and institutionalized in Bolshevism—"pessimism of the
intellect/optimism of the will." The reversal of this dictum for Negri
implies a refusal to settle for voluntarism, for a blind belief "against the
dictates of reason," ending often in reformism. Eclecticism or pluralism
assumes the possibility of "negotiating" difference without the hard
work of distinguishing between workable and unworkable alliances,
without acknowledging historically incompatible positions, and, above
all, by assuming that working to broaden opportunities within existing
institutions is sufficient to guarantee change.

8   In this sense, Gramsci's notions of hegemony have often been read (like his *Notebooks* generally) in totalizing ways against the background of traditional interpretations and practices. The most blatant misreading of his work comes from attempts to interpret his conception of "bloc" in abstract terms as general and merely additive, confusing the popular with populism, to which it becomes erroneously linked. The substitution of "coalition" for "bloc" and "populism" for "popular" when applying Gramsci's ideas to contemporary cultural analysis misrecognizes an element important in Gramsci: identification of existing antagonisms and noncompatibility of specific social groups as a preliminary step to building toward new hegemonic formations, a prerequisite of social transformation. Gramsci has variously been transformed into a Crocean, a Hegelian, a humanist, a Eurocommunist, if not an anti-Marxist. If Gramsci's Marxism was critical of Bolshevism, spontaneism, and vulgar materialism, his work nonetheless remains within a Marxist orientation, attentive to the need to understand culture and social institutions from a historical materialist position.

In discussing relations between civil society and the state, the nature of hegemony and counterhegemony, and the wars of siege and maneuver, Gramsci's work raises questions and examines possible directions for resistance. Neither his historical analysis nor his conception of materialism fits the mold of a master narrative of the realization of class conflict or of scientific socialism. In the recent reappropriation of Gramsci, what gets emphasized in totalizing fashion are his notes on hegemony, on culture, on intellectuals, and on education, shorn of their historical specificity and separated from his struggles to create a notion of a party that is not elitist, bureaucratic, or authoritarian, but is an effective instrument in the creation of socialism. Gramsci's elaboration on the wars of siege and maneuver is not merely classificatory and descriptive but is intimately linked to a specific and local analysis of existing antagonisms and ways of exploiting them in the interests of new and more efficacious alliances.

The centrality of Gramsci's concept of hegemony springs from certain basic assumptions that he makes in his writings concerning the need to understand the importance of identifying preconditions for organization (the party), an identification of the relationships between politics and economics, and a corresponding recognition of civil life as the terrain of struggle, an ongoing concern to understand, not prescribe, the nature of subalternity. Moreover, a politics of civil life, of the everyday, cannot remain at the level of either abstract sociology or uncritical ethnography but requires theoretical elaboration along with concrete analysis. While

Gramsci's writings on culture and politics are attributable to a specific set of historical convergences, his theories are open to translation into contemporary problems: the changing nature of work, the nature of the consumer society, the always-menacing nature of the nuclear state, and the changing nature of knowledge/power.

Thus rethinking Gramsci in Hall's terms requires, as Gramsci himself continually suggests, the need to historicize the notion that "if yesterday the subaltern element was a thing, today it is no longer a thing but an historical person, a protagonist."[11] What are the historical dimensions of the present that transform the subaltern from thing to "person"? Linking Gramsci's writings on education to his notes on the different investment of traditional as opposed to organic intellectuals in relation to change can provide a means to this transformation in knowledge. Gramsci's notions of intellectuals, of common sense, and of history need to be grafted onto a more specific analysis of the nature of contemporary value production and of existing antagonisms; recent concepts of subjectivity derived from the more radical expressions of postmodernity advanced by such thinkers as Gilles Deleuze, Félix Guattari, and Antonio Negri can suggest such directions.[12] Much as Negri returns to his Marx (as Althusser had done earlier and for different ends) to read texts not as continuous, unified articulations but as disjointed, so too Gramsci's work requires a rereading in a much less unified and totalizing vein—not only because his writings as prison notes are fragmentary and tentative,[13] but because his arguments are, like all positions, subject to historical interrogation, challenge, and revision.

Negri's analysis of contemporary society, rather than displacing Gramsci's, offers a way of extending Gramsci's abiding concerns with the transformations wrought by mass society, the crucial role of civil society in retarding or enhancing change, and their implications for producing new forms of political practice and, in particular, for aligning knowledge with existing class antagonisms. The implications of a materialist analysis along the lines of Gramsci's augmented by Negri are far-reaching, extending beyond the notion of institutionalizing programs of media study. A postmodern cultural analysis challenges socialist critics and educators to come up with new strategies and tactics capable finally of confronting these changed and changing expressions of knowledge and power. If cultural analysis is to be more than another form of intellectual consumerism, it has to be situated within the larger concerns posed by Marxists and poststructuralists (e.g., Gilles Deleuze and Antonio Negri). In particular, it will have to address the construction of subjectivities—national, racial, gendered, and sexual—as involving the

10 production of value in late capitalist and postcolonial contexts. Such critical work benefits from a Gramscian perspective. Gramsci's work conveys the complex imperative to face the resilience of capitalism and to acknowledge the importance of cultural politics both in creating new forms of hegemony and in challenging existing hegemonic formations.

Nowhere has Gramsci been so misread as in the notion of hegemony: his notion does not signify either a simple set of oppositions between dominant and subaltern nor a fusion between the two but a complex relationship (not prescribed but negotiated) among various subaltern groups. In the current struggle to assess the existence of and potential for counterhegemonic formations, Gramsci's consistent emphasis on understanding the fragmentary and fragmenting nature of consent provides a starting point for examining the complex ways in which capitalist culture is shaped and perpetuated. Capitalism, and especially late capitalism, is mobilized in the name of pleasure, profit, and survival, rather than through pure coercion, but capitalism is not static. Its culture is constantly undergoing transformations, though not necessarily toward freedom and equality. Gramsci understood this dynamic aspect of capitalist societies in cultural, political, and social terms, as attested to by his *Notebooks*. He was keenly aware of the communications revolution, a major force in global capital and cultural transformation. He states: "The art of printing ... revolutionized the entire cultural world ... allowing an unprecedented extension of educational activity.... Even today, spoken communication is a means of ideological diffusion which has a rapidity, a field of action, and an emotional simultaneity far greater than written communication (theatre, cinema, and radio, with its loudspeakers in public squares, beat all forms of written communication, including books, magazines, newspapers and newspapers posted on walls)—but superficially, not in depth."[14] This note, which is embedded in writing on the need to overhaul traditional rhetorical and oratorical forms in the schools and universities, acknowledges the power of these new modes of dissemination. Gramsci is critical of their "superficiality," but he is aware of their power and of the need to understand their role within the culture.

Gramsci's wide-ranging concern with intellectuals and education suggests a close and critical scrutiny of the role of media as an increasingly important source for the production and dissemination of knowledge and the role of the critic in the selection and transmission of methodologies for understanding the nature of these texts. Much of the "reading" of film and television texts has served disciplinary ends, overshadowing or mystifying the political implications of the works. While

the study of media has found its way into school and college curricula,   **11**
the study of film and television often takes the direction of formalism
and aestheticism, to the detriment of developing accounts of textual
reception, questions of production, alternative media, alternative readings of media, and their relation to questions of imperialism and power.
Too often, film and television studies reproduce single-text readings that
stay within the bounds of a given culture and do not address the ways in
which media are part of a global network that constantly and often arbi-
trarily constructs conceptions of the local and international, the center
and margin. Moreover, the traditional academic notion often assumes
hierarchical notions of literacy and fixed positions in that hierarchy.

Since, in Gramscian terms, a certain degree of literacy already exists
through the accessibility of mass media — though in the form of common sense rather than of "good sense" — considerations of media require strategies that are better able to identify the multifarious ways in
which these texts are not only sites of pleasure but of antagonism, the
ways in which they depend on a wide array of spectators and specta-
torial strategies and draw on a wide array of cultural lore. Examinations
of media need to be cautious of economism and ideologism in accounting for the complex ways in which texts are neither simply dystopian
nor utopian, national-popular nor univocally international, but are, like
common sense, comprised of numerous sediments that appear to fuse
the local and national, national and international, private and public,
and past and present into the "universalism" described by Immanuel
Wallerstein.[15] The challenge is to disarticulate these different layers, to
expose where their seeming contiguities are ill-assorted and, at the same
time, to identify where they mask "good sense," namely, philosophical
or critical understanding of prevailing conditions.

The critical role of technology is central to the study of media, as it is,
more broadly, to an understanding of contemporary culture. Common-
sense assessments of technology waver between a science-fiction dread
or a technocratic, uncritical, and even celebratory adoption of invention.
Stanley Aronowitz and Henry Giroux warn, "We are in for a heavy dose
of the new technicization of the curriculum."[16] Technocrats have moved
into the teaching of writing. In English departments, there are now
counterparts to the social science functionaries. At one extreme, computer methodologies have come to play a dominant role in the teaching
of composition and are in part responsible for producing a new literature concerning the history, aims, and subjects of literacy and for stan-
dardizing elements of the composition curriculum. While the reawaken-
ing of political concerns relating to language, literature, and literacy can

12 be traced to the 1960s, an examination of the routes these concerns have taken reveals yet another instance in which antagonisms arising from social inequities have been channeled and contained through a number of different factors, among which are the following: academic "deregulation" and tightening of state funds; the adoption of the sciences' emphasis on grantsmanship; the marketing of computer hardware; the hegemony of the conservatives and the routing of the Left; the need to appease different political constituencies; and the reintroduction of requirements into the curriculum in the interests of skills and competencies rather than of developing and enhancing cultural analysis in relation to developed and developing technologies.

In his examination of popular literature, Gramsci's purpose "in mapping popular taste" was, according to David Forgacs and Geoffrey Nowell-Smith, "not to produce a static descriptive picture but rather to explore the relations between dominant and subaltern cultural forms in dynamic terms as they act upon each other historically."[17] Gramsci's insistence on the multilayered nature of popular articulations as developed in his conceptions of folklore and common sense is effective in combating monolithic interpretations of social texts and their reception.

Common Sense and Folklore

His conception of common sense as a key to popular thought is related to the processes of deconstruction, with their emphasis on multiplicity and the transgressive but not necessarily progressive nature of social discourses. In relation to the reading of popular novels and film, Gramsci's notes on common sense have been most useful in British cultural studies in breaking down resistances to examining popular culture and in developing ways to discuss texts.

According to Gramsci,

> Every social class has its own "common sense" and "good sense," which are basically the most widespread conception of life and man. Every philosophical current leaves a sedimentation of "common sense": this is the document of its historical reality. Common sense is not something rigid and stationary, but is in continuous transformation, becoming enriched with scientific notions and philosophical opinions that have entered into common circulation. "Common sense" is the folklore of philosophy and always stands midway between folklore proper (folklore as it is normally understood), and the philosophy, science, and economics of the scientists. Common sense creates the folklore of the future, a relatively rigidified phase of popular knowledge in a given time and place.[18]

These comments on common sense are important because they indicate   **13**
that Gramsci was not working toward a monolithic sense of cultural artifacts, but saw cultural texts, as he saw individuals and groups, as het-
erogenously formed. He also recognized the importance of grappling
with cultural texts for elaborating new forms of organization based on
an understanding of both resistances and, in certain instances, emergent
positions.

In talking about the constitution of the human subject, Gramsci describes how, contrary to common-sense notions of the unity of human
knowledge, most conceptions of the world are "disjointed and episodic." He further describes the individual as belonging "simultaneously to
a multiplicity of mass human groups." Common sense would seem to be
the term to describe this multiplicity. Hence Gramsci's conception of
common sense suggests that, in order to understand the ways in which
individuals operate within cultural constraints and possibilities, socialist
analysis must explore, identify, and criticize, not prescribe, the various
elements that constitute reigning "conceptions of the world," paying
specific attention to what has been displaced or elided, what appears as
residual and as emergent, as oppositional and as alternative, in order to
work toward more critical political formulations. The emphasis on heterogeneity would seem to align itself with current practices in the teaching of reading and writing that valorize heterogeneity over unity. Multiplicity and heterogeneity have in fact, however, become code terms for
eclecticism and personal agency, and are indicative of the existence of
the very common sense Gramsci indicates is in need of critique. This
common sense is akin to what Spivak has termed "pop psych" or "baby-
sitting," the transformation of complex relationships into a form of personal encounter that erases the complexity of determinations involved in
the construction of the "personal." In Gramsci's terms, political/cultural
analysis involves an understanding of the uses of cultural antagonisms
and contradictions rather than their pacification through confessional
narratives.

A reading of mass cultural texts in terms of their correspondence to
common sense would entail a probing of the ways in which aphorisms,
clichés, proverbs, and prophecy signify not as interpretive ends but as
invitations to explore the ways in which they may replace, displace, and
contradict prevailing forms of knowledge. Moreover, as Raymond
Williams has suggested, residual and emergent forms, past and present
discourses, coexist in ways that enable a deeper understanding of structures of consent. Therefore, rather than marking ignorance, complete
ideological interpellation, or self-destructive and willful disregard of

14 contemporary exigencies, what is important about a common-sense analysis is that it offers, as in the work of Raymond Williams, "a response to the antinomies of bourgeois ideology and social structure.... Social content does not exist 'outside' the structure of literature [and film] but 'inside.'"[19] An examination of common sense can provide this necessary conjunction of intrinsic and extrinsic.

In his acknowledgment of the sedimented and disjointed nature of experience as expressed in cultural production, Gramsci's position would seem to diverge from those formalist strategies of classifying, differentiating categories, and measuring communication against some abstract norm. Gramsci, while an advocate of a classical education, recognized the importance of locating cultural forms within a specific culture and within specific political structures: the struggle for "good sense" is a matter "of a struggle of political 'hegemonies,' and of opposing directions, first in the ethical field and then in that of politics proper."[20] Thus Gramsci's views on the relationship between common sense and good sense are based on the notion that the subaltern is neither bereft of awareness of nor passive in the face of social conditions. Moreover, Gramsci regards subaltern life as marked by antagonisms inherent to capitalism that can be documented, seized, and made revolutionary, though they are too often channeled into reformism.

The problem for Gramsci is to understand and work with these antagonisms. Gramscian "good sense" begins with an awareness of the need to account historically for the continuing success of traditional political positions, (but not in strict linear terms), to show the ways in which they are articulated in experiential terms so as to offer plausible explanations for events, in terms of melodramatic narratives of suffering, justice, and vindication. Folklore, in the form of melodramatic excess, validates one's sense of suffering while making that suffering appear beyond one's control. Common sense becomes a metaphor for mapping the palimpsest of gender, race, sexuality, and class, all of which have been universalized, naturalized, and mystified through the fusion of archaic and contemporary positions that need to be disarticulated. In this process, it is imperative to distinguish the "conjunctural" from the "organic," since a major problematic of much political thinking involves the misrecognition of strategy and tactics. "This leads," Gramsci says, "to presenting causes as immediately operative which in fact only operate indirectly, or to asserting that the immediate causes are the only effective ones. In the first case there is an excess of 'economism,' or doctrinaire pedantry; in the second, an excess of 'ideologism.'"[21]

In the case of "economism," the danger lies in developing reductive and linear analyses of events that in no way produce the questioning of cause-and-effect relations necessary to rethinking positions nor allow for addressing questions of civil society and the state, the interrelationship between economics and politics, the formation of the subaltern subject, and the multiplicity of determinations. In the case of "an excess of ideologism," Gramsci seems to be wary of "an exaggeration of the voluntarist and individual element," the placing of too great a burden on a form of historical analysis that does not take into account the "disposition of social forces" that would include economic determinations. Such distinctions are to be read in relation to social texts from the past but also in relation to the present and future, and are crucial elements in the consideration of practices aimed at developing criteria and methodologies for an understanding of cultural phenomena.

Thus Gramscian common sense can occupy a place in Haraway's plea for a reconsideration of how "meanings get made," insofar as common-sense analysis is concerned with the convoluted ways in which consensus is formed, not necessarily in the interests of the future, or for understanding and then producing "knowing subjects." Parallel to contemporary ideology and discourse study, Gramsci's writings on common sense provide critical insight into how knowledge about social life is formed, maintained, and altered to suit changing times. His writings emphasize the importance of gaining a proper understanding of the contradictoriness of existing conceptions of knowledge and their implication in the politics of everyday life. Rather than comprising a unified set of ideas, social and political knowledge is multifarious, incoherent, more akin to what Gramsci identified as folklore. Not only does common sense serve to perpetuate existing social practices; it also contains the potential for constructing different conceptions of society and of subjectivity. Critical analysis of knowledge in terms of common sense necessitates a reexamination of the nature and efficacy of the concept of ideology as false consciousness, as in opposition to science and truth, and as monolithic. An analysis of common sense also demands a reexamination of the categories public and private as they have been traditionally demarcated in order to expose the ways they are interconnected.

The Gramscian conception of folklore and common sense and its relation to hegemony has implications for rethinking the nature and meaning of subalternity, a repositioning of it away from melodramatic notions of oppressor and oppressed and toward a more complex understanding of how subalternity is implicated in existing social and cultural formations through mechanisms of coercion and (more relevant to cultural study) mechanisms of consent. Gramsci's description of the "culture of

16 consent" — the interdependence of groups in power and the subaltern — is necessary for an understanding of the creation of hegemony and, therefore, for understanding resistances to change as well as identifying collusion with and opposition to existing institutions. The importance Gramsci accorded to culture as a means for evaluating possibilities and strategies for change has been translated, not unproblematically, by contemporary students of cultural studies into such issues as multiculturalism, postmodernism, pedagogy, and sexual and gender concerns. Therefore, more than ever, evolving studies of culture need to be evaluated for their tendency to drop materialist analysis, especially those that see Marxism as having little explanatory and socially transformative power.[22] Common sense reigns, often unrecognized or valorized as critical wisdom, and eradicates the possibility of alternatives, presenting as natural, inevitable, and intelligible the present state of affairs.

Attempts at the political containment of antagonism have taken to adopting the popularized language of new intellectual formations that address feminism, decolonization, and new subject formations. Expressed in both the university and the mass media as a liberal concern with the "culturally disenfranchised," the form of this address is dependent on modes of self-reflection and eclecticism that obscure the constituencies and the very differences that such programs claim to address, bereft as they are of any sense of history or critical analysis. The concern with literacy, for example, has revivified English departments, producing more courses and more students (owing to requirements) and larger graduate programs as a consequence. Programs have, in fact, become quite standardized, more "professional," and even orthodox in their strategies for reading and writing. Insofar as they have produced discontent, they have functioned to further call into question neoliberal social projects. Insofar as they have succeeded in the profession of literacy, they have reinforced the ideology of competence and enhanced the containment of necessary antagonism. One aspect of a Gramscian analysis would be to understand the contradictory positions of this movement, to see what interests it serves, to expose its co-optation of the language of change, to identify what residual elements it reinforces and what emerging discourses it seeks to circumvent. Initially, cultural studies arose as a way of addressing issues of representativeness and representation with the help of more adequate methodologies and with an awareness that disciplinary boundaries among the natural and human sciences are instrumental in creating and maintaining "regimes of truth."

At this time, when critics of the postmodern have described dramatic global transformations in contemporary society and have attributed

these changes to the technological expansion of late capital, it is impera- **17**
tive to see how division between the natural sciences, social sciences,
and humanities has served to maintain a folklore concerning technology. Divisions in branches of knowledge and disciplinary formations
obstruct any efficacious understanding of continuities and changes. New
folklores are being constructed specifically in relation to technologies
of gender, sexuality, race, ethnicity, and social class. The new folklores
operate in the vein of Gramscian common sense and require a Gramscian commonsense analysis to understand the competing interests of
postmodern narratives. The breaking down of discursive barriers has
been viewed by some as a prerequisite for the production of new knowl-
edges that are more congenial to requisite cultural forms of modernity
than traditional disciplinary formations. Here too it is possible to instru-
mentalize the process, to restrict the move to break down boundaries to
formalist methodology, to the exclusion of questioning of social and
political interests, positions, and powers. In practice, cultural studies
has become a way to maintain disciplinarity rather than a means for
interrogating 1) the genealogy of "disciplines," the conditions for their
appearance; 2) the epistemes to which disciplines gave rise; 3) disciplines' present position within the changing conceptions of information,
science, and technology; 4) the relation of disciplines to existing modes
of production; and 5) the availability of more adequate modes of accounting for social formations and transformation. If, for example, cultural reformulations address nonwestern cultures but fail to address the
ever-shifting discourses of exploitation and commodification, the economic and political dimensions of global relations between "centers and
margins,"[23] implications for the female and male workers in the world
market, historical formations and deformations, the interested positions
of commentators, and the persistence of the ethnographic investigation
in the forms of the "post-colonial subject" and of "postcoloniality," then
knowledge will continue to serve the very ethnographic interests that a
socialist critique would challenge.[24]

Chapter 2

The Gramscian Politics
of Culture

$\mathbf{A}$ssessments of Gramsci's work have often been lopsided. His critics focus either on what they consider the formal politics derived from his work or, conversely, on the modernity of his comments on culture. Moreover, according to Joseph A. Buttigieg, disproportionate critical emphasis is placed on Gramsci's political, as opposed to his cultural, theory.[1] More often than not, Gramsci has been appropriated and valued or criticized for his adherence to or deviance from classical Marxist theory and his conceptions of practice more than for his contributions to an understanding of the crucial role of culture in producing and reproducing the social and economic relations of production. He has been treated as a cult figure, a venerated if misunderstood Marxist patriarch, and as a martyr. The dominance of French and German critical theory has also overshadowed the importance of Gramsci's work. The most striking exception is the work of writers such as Raymond Williams and Stuart Hall and others associated with British cultural studies, who examine Gramsci seriously as a theorist of culture generally and of Fascist culture in particular.

The preprison writings and the *Quaderni* offer valuable discussions of the ways in which culture and politics interact and are mutually dependent, though not synonymous. Moreover, Gramsci's writings are timely for challenging the discourses of culture and politics as totally ideological and totally coercive and for challenging the idea of the power of the state apparatuses as the major force in creating consensus.[2] Gramsci's writings stress the commonplace, everyday aspects of social life that exist even under Fascism, and the ways that life is made to appear "normal," not spectacular and epic, through the operations of language, literature, and even media.[3] But his concern with dissecting the complex nature of hegemony and counterhegemony in relation both to consensus and to the historical formation of ruling and subaltern groups is, of course, intimately tied to a view of Fascism not as aberration but as an extension of already existing and contradictory social processes. For critics of modernity as well as of traditional Marxism, Gramsci's contribution lies in the various ways he probes relationships between politics and cultural production as expressed in historical writing, Marxist philosophy, canonical and popular literature, theater, journalism, cinema, and even beauty contests.

For an understanding of Gramsci's work, it is helpful to place him within Italian culture and, more specifically, within the culture of the Mezzogiorno,[4] if only to understand the ways in which his work is rooted in an examination of the concrete material practices of a particular historical context. The "Southern Question" was and is a fundamental fact of Italian political and cultural life. Gramsci's place of birth, Sardinia, the most underdeveloped and exploited area of the Mezzogiorno (portrayed more recently in the Tavianis' *Padre Padrone*), exemplified all of the ills of regionalism: it was characterized historically by the domination of foreign powers, a highly class-stratified feudal culture, dire poverty, exploitation of peasants at the hands of landlords, repressive taxation, and political manipulation of the region by internal and national governments. Gramsci's emphasis on the interrelatedness of politics and culture derives, in large measure, from this Sardinian heritage, where economic and political differences and inequities are expressed in multifarious ways through language, folklore, family relations, religion, and even dietary practices.[5] His analyses of the interrelationships between the state and civil society grew, in part, from a recognition of the ways in which the organization of social life in the South was due not only to overt political domination of the South but to the specific, and often contradictory, survival strategies developed by subaltern classes in those regions for coping with their social, political, and economic conditions.

Gramsci's concern with the nature and role of consent, the character of civil institutions, and the role of ideology as contributing to the perpetuation of powerlessness occupies an important place in his allusions to Italian regional social existence. His emphasis on the "*quistione della lingua*," arising from his experiences of the oppressed condition of the Sardinians, is similar to the emphasis of the third-world intellectual on the importance of language as a fundamental aspect of cultural, class,

20 and racial oppression and of potential liberation.[6] For Gramsci, the study of language was a study of everyday life and was not an abstract issue but one deeply rooted in the social and economic conditions of subaltern life. Since language is a fundamental element in the legitimation of existing social institutions that are crucial to creating the perceptions, behavior, and attitudes of ruling and subaltern groups, Gramsci saw the study of language as a political act aimed at significantly altering attitude and behavior.[7] Language becomes for him a means not of speaking for the subaltern but of asking crucial questions about the nature of subalternity and of challenging reductionist class analysis.

Gramsci's personal and political life was intimately tied to the rise of Fascism, and he personally experienced the ways in which Fascism co-opted and perverted the issues for which he and others on the Left had struggled. In particular, the intersecting struggles between feudal and liberal institutions, the drive toward "modernization," the awareness of the problems of regionalism, the starkness of class struggle, and the conflict over the containment or advancement of workers and peasants are associated with the defeat of the Left and the rise of Fascism. Gramsci addressed all of these problems in his writings. His critical analysis of Fascism is not merely an interesting historical insight into Gramsci's theoretical and practical stance; it offers still useful and critically powerful strategies for identifying and understanding a protean political and social threat that continues to loom in new guises.

The reader of the *Quaderni*, constrained by limited knowledge of Italian history and language, by problematic translations, by Gramsci's own style, and by his adoption of indirect discourse to deal with dangerous political issues, can underestimate the power of the notebooks for a dissection of the dynamics of Fascism as a central feature of modern life and of mass culture. A major imperative to anyone of Gramsci's generation and politics, as to the contemporary social critic, is the need to identify and understand the specific dynamics of Fascist politics and culture, since Fascism can be produced in a number of guises. Growing as it does from economism, the denial of class conflict and difference, and a valorization of patriarchy, familialism, sexism, racism, and biologism, the ideology of Fascism often merges with "traditional" social structures and institutions as an intensification of already existing ideologies and practices. As long as these institutions remain in place, the possibility of radical change is threatened and impeded by repetition.[8] The Gramscian analysis of consensus probes most particularly the familiar aspects of Fascism in civil society.

Gramsci's writings address questions fundamental to social life in the twentieth century, questions central today to the majority of critics attempting to address the culture of the twentieth century: What is the power of the state? Is modern culture basically coercive, allowing no space for resistance? Do all aspects of modern social life reinforce the sense of powerlessness of the masses? Although for critics like Theodor Adorno[9] the answers may, for the most part, be affirmative, for Gramsci the answers are more open-ended. Gramsci does not deny the coercive aspects of power, but because he is constantly aware of the oppressed as well as the oppressor, he is driven to name and analyze specific strategies that bind subaltern groups to their rulers as well as serve to produce opposition. Consistently Gramsci's mode of analysis probes the extremely practical and political question, "How do power relations change and how do subaltern groups gain power and become hegemonic?" Yet Gramsci does not romanticize the subaltern. His views on subordinate groups (*gruppi sociali subalterni*) are based on a practical assessment of the terms of their subordination and their ability to seize power. One can see why Gramsci's nuanced analysis of the subaltern condition would appeal to postcolonial critics.[10] According to him, the struggle of the oppressed is disorganized and erratic (*disgregata ed episodica*), constantly subject to the pressures of ruling groups.[11]

A tendency toward unity in the face of common political and cultural obstacles, Gramsci believes, does exist, and characterizes the strivings of subaltern groups, though this unity is continually fractured by the dominant forces. He sees the movement toward change as connected to an understanding of power, and as proceeding unevenly. He traces this movement, this uneven and incomplete development, in his historical notes and in his writings on Machiavelli in the *Quaderni* (*Noterelle sul Machiavelli*). Gramsci's notes in "The New Prince" are neither reductively biographical nor historical. He makes use of Machiavelli as an exemplary figure who combined historical understanding and astute political analysis in an effort to understand power, since everything in Gramsci is brought back to questions of politics and power. Like Lenin, Gramsci endorsed the idea of different levels of understanding and capacities, but Gramsci was critical of Marxism for its lack of a theory of political power: "The initial question to pose and to resolve," he writes in his notes on Machiavelli, "is the question of politics as an autonomous science." ("La quistione iniziale da porre e da risolvere in una trattazione

22 sul Machiavelli è la quistione della politica come scienza autonoma.")[12]
Following Machiavelli, Gramsci's writings articulate the necessity of
conscious study, analysis, planning, and timeliness in the gaining of
power.

Through Machiavelli also, Gramsci probed the relations between gov-
ernor and governed, and the importance of myth and folklore as strategies for containing or mobilizing resistance to ruling groups (*dirigente*).
As we shall see, common sense and/as folklore was particularly important to Gramsci, who from his earliest political writings was perceptive
about the role of ideological apparatuses in society. He was especially
committed to the need to create a national/popular culture as a basis
for gaining adherents to counterhegemonic practices. In his desire for a
national/popular culture, his politics and cultural theory merge. In this
respect, he was not unique. For Italians of his generation of diverse political persuasions, the task of creating a unified nation was unfinished and
was a prerequisite for political and social action. What he envisaged as
the "national popular" is much more complex today in relation to the
nation form — to questions of nationalism, ethnicity, and their relation to
the construction of "opposing cultural and political forms" — but his work
struggles with these problems and can be read in ways that are less univalent than the work of many of his contemporaries.

Machiavelli was also admired by Mussolini, and *il duce* compared
himself and was compared to the Renaissance figure by his admirers. (In
Guido Brignone's historical film *Lorenzino dei Medici,* an allegory made
during the Fascist period, the hero, an incarnation of Mussolini, is patterned after Machiavelli, and the writings of Machiavelli are prominently displayed during a crucial sequence.) In using Machiavelli, therefore, Gramsci was also speaking through a figure who was not at all
alien to the prevailing power structure. Machiavelli serves as an image
of Italian unity, touching deep chords relating to myths of the Renaissance and the Risorgimento, myths shared by many Italians of differing
political views and conducive to different and conflicting notions of the
nation. Although speaking to the issue of authority, Gramsci's idea of
the prince departs radically from the concept of Caesarism prevalent
during the Fascist era. As a matter of fact, Caesarism seems, among
other things, an oblique critique of Fascism. Gramsci's notion of the
"new prince" is not the individual hero as in Fascism but the political
party, the group, whose aim is the founding of a new state. Although
Gramsci's conception of the party can easily be misread,[13] in his writings
on the party, he is at pains to develop important distinctions between the
traditional party and the new prince, the new political collectivity. The

traditional party is constituted from the elite men of culture and provides leadership from above of a cultural and general nature, whereas
the other party, the masses, has no other political function within this
context than a generic loyalty (*La sua lealà*).[14]

The new prince, the party, must therefore develop its own cultural
and political view of the state and of civil power. Since his conception of
seizing and maintaining power is not utopian, Gramsci sees necessary
points of affinity between earlier forms of acquiring power and the present need for the subaltern groups to use existing institutions to acquire
power. For Gramsci, the party, composed of friends, kindred groups,
and even opponents and enemies, is the means for educating and "training" the new prince in forms of activism. Moreover, Gramsci does not
conceive of these individuals as coming together with a homogeneous
set of interests and alignments, but as representing a convergence of different groups and different objectives that require critical examination.
Gramsci does not exclusively identify the party with a given social class.
Alignments can occur across class lines, as they did under Fascism.[15] The
petty bourgeoisie can and does identify at certain points with the bourgeoisie, at other points with the workers. Unlike the populist character
of Fascism, which is a form of neutralizing social antagonisms, Gramsci's notion of populism (if it can be properly named populism) confronts the need to identify and to understand antagonisms. Gramsci is
not arguing for a loose form of coalition that "leaves the economic structure intact and merely reforms its local practices."[16] His notion of hegemony is more complex than the uses to which it has been put in recent
cultural studies. It addresses the importance of theory and analysis but
also the need for contestation and activism.

For a party to exist, it must contain the following characteristics: a
mass element, a cohesive element, and an intermediate element—the
intellectuals, traditional or organic. A nodal point in Gramsci's political
thought, in fact a significant point of intersection between politics and
culture, if a distinction can be made between the two, is Gramsci's examination of the role of intellectuals in relation to the legitimation of existing forms of power or the creation of alternate forms of power. In the
case of ruling groups, traditional intellectuals provide the intermediate
element. The subaltern groups must develop their own intellectuals in
the formation of their own power base. One of Gramsci's major contributions to an understanding of political change is his emphasis on a
significant role for intellectuals in the legitimation of power or the
creation of new relations of power. For Gramsci, the study of intellectuals and their production is synonymous with the study of political

24   power.[17] Gramsci's conceptions of domination (*dominio*) and hegemony (*egemonia*) are central to his analysis of power relations. Conditions of domination, those normally associated with the repressive function of the state, are coercive, involving police powers and the formal and public aspects of governmental power. Hegemony refers to the exercise of indirect power as exemplified in such civil institutions as schools, the legal profession, trade unions, the church, and so on. The Gramscian concept of domination resembles Althusser's conception of repressive state apparatuses, whereas the Gramscian notion of hegemony appears similar to Althusser's notion of the ideological state apparatuses. The similarities, however, are superficial. Gramsci's conception of the relationship between the state and existing institutions is less abstract and more dynamic and interactive than Althusser's.

Gramsci's dialectical analysis proceeds from the assumption that everything in life is in constant motion, that everything is interrelated rather than rigidly schematic and systemic. In his analysis of institutions, the church, schools, corporations, trade unions, and forms of "entertainment," social structures are conceived of as sources of lived social relations as well as sources of constant conflict, though the tensions may not be directed toward the transformation of social conditions but toward the legitimation of prevailing conditions. While Gramsci describes the human actor as constrained by economic and political conditions, he also attempts to establish that the dominant structures are not monolithic. His position invites a rethinking of the position of the masses under Fascism and in political action generally.

Following his molecular analysis, an understanding of the adherence of subaltern groups to prevailing social conditions must be sought in both the base and the superstructure, in economic and ideological practices, and particularly in the role that institutional practices play in the shaping of consent on the part of individuals and groups. His analysis of social conditions was directed not only toward describing and analyzing but also toward producing changes in existing power relations. His emphasis on the need to produce a thoroughgoing alteration of social structures led him to develop his own conceptions of revolutionary and evolutionary transformations of society. Thinking perhaps of failures on the left as Mussolini rose to power, and thinking too of the Fascist strategies for gaining consensus, Gramsci insisted that "no society poses tasks for itself for which necessary and sufficient conditions for a solution do not already exist or are already in the process of appearing and developing." ("Nessuna società si pone dei compiti per la cui soluzione non esis-

tano già le condizioni necessaria e sufficienti o esse non siano almeno in
via di apparizione e di sviluppo.")[18]

Whether discussing theory or practice, Gramsci insisted on the importance of historicizing. As Walter Adamson suggests, "Gramsci's starting point was the concrete subject situated in a particular historical environment. This formulation implied a complex interaction of 'subjective' or 'objective' historical factors.... Thus, while Gramsci always set out from objective conditions in analyzing revolutionary movements, he also placed little emphasis on objective conditions as sources of proletarian action."[19] Recognizing that subjects are created through the material conditions within a specific society and that these material conditions were not expressed merely in economic terms but in psychosocial terms as well, Gramsci had little confidence in the uncritical seizure of power, which could only reproduce traditional relations. He was not a fatalist, however. His dialectical analysis of phenomena led him to reemphasize Marx's notion of uneven development. He saw social change as proceeding unevenly because of the conditions of direct and indirect coercion inherent in the dominant forms. Gramsci's theorizing of residual and emergent structures, conceptions stressed by Raymond Williams in his Gramscian *Marxism and Literature,* is an extension of his dialectical thinking.[20] New meanings and new attitudes are in the process of being created alongside the old: change is constantly in the state of becoming just as dominant and traditional practices are constantly exerting their power. As a consequence of Gramsci's dialectical conception of power, his concept of ideology is less unified and totalistic than is the case, for example, in Georg Lukács's writings. Furthermore, Gramsci's dialectical view complicates ideas of revolutionary struggle by adding subjective factors. Ideology is not simply false consciousness that alters when social conditions alter.

The dominant practices in a culture refer to the whole cultural process, not only to social institutions but to the various institutional representations of individuals and groups. Intellectuals must identify the elements of the mosaic rather than imposing a fixed and static explanation for the ways power is exercised. The "ruling class" is more than the producers of wealth and power; it reproduces itself through the institutions, and through the attitudes and behavior of individuals and social groups. Consent gained through seduction and co-optation as well as through coercion is responsible for reproducing social relations, as contemporary analysis of Italian Fascist institutions reveals. Because of the pervasiveness and the subtleties of the operations of power, Gramsci held that no enduring structural change and no organization is possible without political education. The ends of education were to cultivate critical attitudes, proper strategies, and a sense of timing, and Gramsci discriminates between long-standing as opposed to immediate formations and crises. He designates those social conditions as "organic" (*i movimenti organici*) that are ongoing and permanent and those that are occasional and accidental as "conjunctural" (*i movimenti di congiuntura*).[21] From military theory, Gramsci borrows the concept of "strategic conjuncture" to signify the opportune assessment, the proper merging, of the subjective and objective conditions for change.

Correspondingly, the character of social groups becomes far more complicated than in simple reflection theories, and the idea of social change becomes more difficult. A thoroughgoing notion of social change in Gramsci is heavily dependent on the idea of the accountability and greater potential of the masses in maintaining the status quo or in altering social conditions. It seems clear that Gramsci's emphasis on the need for organic intellectuals stems from his awareness that subaltern groups are particularly repressed by not having self-conscious forms to articulate the nature of their oppression. This is not to say that they have no understanding of their condition, but that a critical awareness, a knowledge of their situation and of the ways in which they are trapped in certain forms, is desirable and necessary for change to take place. By placing importance on the power of intellectuals and of ideas, he wished to demonstrate that social change depends on deconstructing and demystifying interpersonal relations, social roles, and all institutional practices, which have been naturalized and considered inevitable.

The challenge of identifying the complex aspects of conformity to social practices led Gramsci to probe the ways in which reasonableness appears in ideas and behavior appears as "the way things are." His own experiences in Southern Italy had taught him that peasants and workers are not mindless automatons, that, in spite of the mythology of primitivism, subalterns have an understanding of their world. Gramsci adopted a position that was not really understood until the articulation of national liberation struggles in the post-World War II era.[22] His conception of the subaltern involves a destruction of the classical schematization of the division of labor in which the ruling class and especially the intellectuals represent spirituality and the life of the mind, while the workers are merely a physical labor force, bodies acted upon by their masters. By asserting that all individuals are intellectuals and explaining what he meant by intellectuals, Gramsci challenged traditional conceptions of intellectual work. He stated that "all men are intellectuals, but

not all men have the function of intellectuals in society." ("Tutti gli uomini sono intellettuali ... ma non tutti gli uomini hanno nella società la fun-
zione di intellettuali.")²³

Language and Folklore

This specific conception of the world, this "philosophy," is contained in
language, and for Gramsci language is not a mere matter of grammar in
the old philological sense. Embedded in language is a totality of concepts and meanings, not always self-conscious, that enable people to
perform and survive in society. He was not, however, inclined toward an
ahistorical view of language. His notion of the specific concepts contained in language points to a particular as well as a general notion of
the operations of language. Thus his conception of folklore accords better with his notion of language practices than does the concept of ideology, which carries the stigma of false consciousness as well as of a monolithic notion of interpellation with its psychoanalytic reductionism.

Interested as he was in struggling to articulate a way of identifying
the presence and nature of folklore in the everyday experience of subaltern groups, he found it necessary to confront the most immediate forms
of self-identification and articulation characteristic of this folklore,
which Gramsci also identified as "common sense."²⁴ Cultural forms are
not, in Gramsci's terms, biological, nor are they emanations of a "world
spirit." Culture is the creation of individuals and groups in history and
is, above all, grounded in the uses of language. Language is for him a
"collective noun," and does not presuppose a single thing in either time
or space. It is culture and philosophy. It is a multiplicity of facts, more or
less organically coherent and coordinated. When Gramsci speaks of the
language question he is not, as is the structuralist, talking solely about
general "structures" but also about language usage that must be contextualized, differentiated across regional, class, and gender lines. On a
general level, his notion of *linguaggio* enables him to explore the collective representations embedded in language, the idea that everyone is a
philosopher because she or he interacts through language with the social
world. Linguistic interaction is predicated on a network of values, attitudes, and specific codes dependent on particular historical phenomena
and personal idiosyncrasies. Hence, an understanding of language
requires a knowledge of these idiosyncrasies as well as an understanding of the historical character of regional, national, and gender differences that have created obstacles to political change. Gramsci's distinctions between the general and specific dimensions of language are

28 consistent with his attempt to move away from a static and abstract systemic form of analysis.

Gramsci's conception of language is divided between normative and "spontaneous" or "immanent" linguistic practices. The normative linguistic practices relate to traditional practices. The sources of conformism and of innovation are identified by Gramsci as radiating from the schools, the church, elite and popular writers, theater and film, radio, popular songs, public assemblies, and local dialects. In his words, "the process of formation, diffusion, and of development of a unitary national language occurs across a complex of molecular processes." ("Il processo di formazione, di diffusione e di sviluppo di una lingua nazionale unitaria avviene attraverso tutto un complesso di processi molecolari.")[25] Hence one must be aware of these many lines traversing and feeding into language in order to effect any change. Gramsci's interest in language as a political/cultural activity is not merely descriptive or theoretical; it has practical implications for understanding existing forms of the popular, as exploited in mass culture as well as in attempts to create a popular culture. At the time he wrote, he advanced the now-debatable idea that the creation of a national unitary language can be an instrument for advancing the interests and the identity of subaltern groups.

The language question is intimately related to Gramsci's conception of "folklore," or what we might call provincialism, another idea that can be traced to his Southern background and also to his preoccupation with understanding the nature of consensus under Fascism. Alberto Maria Cirese describes Gramsci's notion of folklore in the following way: "Gramsci is raising research into folklore from the level of pure scholarship to that of science or knowledge, as well as promoting folklore itself from being a curiosity to being a *conception of the world*. And he takes the further step of locating it socially and culturally, 'in the framework of a nation and its culture': *characteristic of the subaltern classes* on the one hand, and *in opposition to official conceptions* on the other."[26] Folklore is another way of describing how language is a pastiche of a number of conceptions — religion, morality, beliefs, opinions, specific ways of seeing the world, of narrating events, and of action. His notion of folklore encompasses a variety of his intellectual/political concerns: his distinction between traditional and organic practices, between rural and urban life, his concern with education, and his consciousness of the power of ideology. Moreover, his consistent method of identifying the converging explanations led him to his particular conception of the importance of folklore, the embodiment of a common-sense orientation toward the 29 world. He defines "common sense" (*senso comune*) as containing fragmentary ideas, a collage of opinions and beliefs that fails to be not only coherent but also critical. Gramsci is not contemptuous of common sense. He does not seem to have the traditional intellectual's contempt or condescension for such a practice. His Sardinian background, his study of linguistics, his interest in literature, and his broad concerns for social and political change enabled him to understand the role of folklore and common sense in the lives of the subaltern classes and to seek methods for overcoming the passivity and noncritical relationship to the world produced through ideology.

Folklore is not completely mindless nor is it completely negative. It could be said that it is the way that subaltern groups learn to rationalize and survive under conditions of hardship. Folklore is not self-conscious and critical, however, and without self-consciousness and criticism change is difficult if not impossible. Gramsci's revolutionary objective, therefore, was to raise the consciousness of subaltern groups and to provide them with a more critical and coherent conception of the world. Criticism would involve a recognition that, while the prevailing conceptions of the world appear useful, they are in fact inadequate. A critical attitude would expose the ways in which folklore, though it appears to be based on nature, is a human construction and, though appearing unhistorical, it is profoundly related to historical factors. The issue of consent can be seen to have a basis in a fear of deviance and potential ostracism, the convenience of conformity, and the habituation of loyalty in maintaining traditional associations. Through a greater awareness of history and hence of alternatives, the individual can move from the supra-historical into history.

Gramsci did not conceive of history as an automatic movement toward progress and perfectibility, or as providing a blueprint for the future. His interest in history and his emphasis on the necessity of historicizing knowledge to challenge folkloristic attitudes was based on a flexible view of history. In Adamson's terms, for Gramsci "the active construction of history necessarily entails filtering it through present political needs; any effort to avoid this confrontation will only reduce history to the 'external' and 'mechanical.' "[27] Thus Gramsci might suggest that immanentist and totalistic views of history are themselves forms of folklore that must be demystified. Contemporary intellectual practice has raised the same issue in relation to prevailing attitudes toward the role of intellectuals as social critics, namely, the necessity of

30   intellectuals to demystify totalistic and undialectical conceptions of politics and culture that are filtered through unitary and linear notions of history as progress.

The most significant contribution of Gramsci to contemporary critical thinking in the arena of cultural study lies in his provocative notes on the nature of mass and popular culture in tandem with his notion of common sense and folklore. He came closer than any member of the Frankfurt school to proposing a dynamic view of the operations and importance of mass culture not only as an agent of consent but also as an important factor in the encouragement of counterhegemonic practices. But Gramsci was not naive. He understood the profundity and pervasiveness of folkloristic, common-sense thinking among the masses. The biggest obstacle to change is attributable to what he calls "contradictory consensus." In his terms, "the active man of the masses works practically, but has no clear theoretical consciousness of his work that also knows the world in order to transform it. His theoretical consciousness is thus historically in contrast with his work": "L'uomo attivo di massa opera praticamente, ma non ha una chiara coscienza teorica di questo suo operare che pure è un conoscere il mondo in quanto lo trasforma. La sua coscienza teorica anzi può essere storicamente in contrasto col suo operare."[28]

Intellectuals and Culture

Gramsci's emphasis on the creation of organic intellectuals is aimed at addressing stark disjunctions between theory and practice. Gramsci might be talking about the creation of an elite cadre of individuals that can provide the select leadership in the struggle for revolutionary change, but this is misleading. He does not envision a select group of leaders who will direct the passive masses, though he does acknowledge the gap between critically aware intellectuals and the masses who, because of their subordinate position, have inhabited forms of contradictory consciousness. He sees the reality and necessity of those intellectuals who are progressive and have critical consciousness working with the workers and peasants in order to extend the numbers and scope of organic intellectuals and to break the hold of traditional forms of thought. These intellectuals would identify with or be from the subaltern classes. In Gramsci's conception, organic intellectuals must have a critical consciousness of the world, a desire to question and to change existing conditions, and a sense of collectivity with others in working to restructure society. Their task is to enhance and reinforce emergent elements. The factory councils in Turin, for example, were part of an effort **31** to realize new forms of learning and social alignments. Not mere study groups, the councils were also designed to augment the worker's power to make decisions and acquire greater autonomy.

In prison, Gramsci elaborated further on his notions of intellectuals and education. Aware that traditional intellectuals are created by institutions and not by divine fiat, Gramsci sought to identify those forces that shaped them and to draw the most useful lessons from tradition in the creation of organic intellectuals. For example, the tendency of traditional regional intellectuals was toward scholasticism, and they tended to disdain science and technology, though urban intellectuals were more likely to veer toward careerism. The traditional intellectual serves directly or indirectly to legitimize the power of the prevailing institutions. Each new class that has developed has created its organic intellectuals, those who serve as carriers of new ideas and are the legitimizers of its power. Gramsci recognized that the working class had to create its own organic intellectuals who must fuse practical and scholastic activity, philosophy and technology.

Society is conceived of by Gramsci as a vast arena for political education. He espoused the notion of a national/popular culture as a way of creating consensus among different regional groupings. The desire to create a national and popular culture was characteristic of the twenties and of Fascism in particular. For that matter, Mussolini and his son Vittorio along with certain members of the Fascist *gerarchia* also expressed their belief in the necessity of a national culture and conceived of the media as useful toward those ends. Gramsci's idea of a popular culture is neither static nor nostalgic. He understood the power of literature, newspapers, film, and radio in the creation of consensus, but he was interested in a democratic notion of culture. He was no doubt aware that Lenin had discussed literature and especially film as part of the vanguard of revolutionary change, and was possibly aware of how Walter Benjamin had examined the role of newspapers and film in revolutionary and counterrevolutionary terms.

Gramsci's emphasis on the importance of intellectuals and on the demystification of culture seems to speak directly to Fascist practices. Popular culture under Fascism was not conceived of in terms of class conflict, class consciousness, and of empowering subaltern groups, but in terms of the most general sense of "the people." Fascism placed great emphasis on the creation of the "new man." Mussolini was not totally alienated from intellectual life and forms of education. Through the efforts of Giovanni Gentile, educational reform was placed in the fore-

32 ground of Fascistization. There was, however, an anti-intellectual aspect to Fascism.[29] Though Fascist ideology emphasized the importance of history and national unity, its representations of history were, unlike Gramsci's, basically allegorical, melodramatic, and (in Nietzsche's sense) antiquarian.[30]

Gramsci's philosophy also differed from and critically addressed Fascist practices in his conception of the importance of criticism and of the development of organic intellectuals who were properly enlightened on the problematic role of traditional institutions: the church, the family, working-class organizations. In his consistent acknowledgment of different group interests and his recognition of the division of power between dominant and subaltern groups, he saw the necessity of interclass alignments in the attainment of hegemony. He criticized the transformist tendencies that were historically the case in Italy since the Risorgimento and the forms of populism that suppressed any kind of popular interpellations tied to the notion of class conflict.[31] This transformist discourse was certainly evident in the literature and films of the era. Historical narratives were especially popular, for example, and texts of the period that feature workers usually strive to "resolve" their conflicts through psychological means by assimilating the workers into the national cause in the case of heroic films and into the security of family in the case of comedies and melodramas.

Since Gramsci insisted on the interrelationship between culture and politics, he explored all aspects of cultural production in an effort to identify obstacles to the creation of a new hegemony. His discussion of the classic dichotomy between content and form leads him to the conclusion that content is often more in tune with the people, whereas form often takes on a Parnassian quality. Differentiating those authors who write for the people from those who write for a select audience, he echoes classic Left literary notions of the period. Yet, as David Forgacs has indicated, Gramsci's ideas on national/popular culture are not programmatic. Since Gramsci conceived of new cultural/political creations, it is a mistake to imagine "that a national/popular culture will resemble any hitherto existing cultural style."[32] In examining the politics of literary production, Gramsci is critical of Italian literature. He explores the proposition that Italian literature is romantic and that romanticism can be associated with democratic sentiments. Gramsci, noting that romanticism is linked to the French Revolution, concludes that the so-called Italian romanticism is not indigenous.

Woven throughout his discussions of numerous literary and theatrical works is his emphasis on genre and the relationship between genre and

national consciousness. He comments on the Italian penchant for melodrama, but he also indicates that this genre is derived from Europe and
is not expressive of indigenous needs and developments in the creation
of a popular consciousness that would speak for the subaltern class.[33]
But Gramsci's comments on literature are not normative. He is not establishing criteria of good and bad, correct and incorrect, so much as trying
to develop ways of identifying connections between literature and society, different types of writing, and different audiences for the works. It
also seems that his examination of certain literary forms, especially mass
and popular forms such as melodrama, is closely tied to his interest in
the workings of common sense and folklore (both of which I shall examine more closely later, in the chapters on cinema).

He traces melodrama, a genre and style he identifies with "democratic" attitudes, to France in particular. The democratic sentiments associated with the French novel are, for Gramsci, alien to the historical conditions in Italy in the nineteenth and twentieth centuries. The persistence
of foreign models is, to him, revealing about Italian writers and their
penchant for European forms, their resistance to indigenous modes of
narration and hence to national/popular modes of narration. Gramsci
identifies an Italian form and content in melodrama derived from funeral
oratory in the countryside, from the urban popular theater, from the
operas of Verdi, and even from the silent cinema. While Gramsci's criterion for a popular literature depends on the degree to which a work
addresses the needs of the excluded class, his notions of literature are not
narrow and programmatic. In examining Manzoni's Catholic sentiments, Gramsci asserts that *I promessi sposi* was not exemplary of nation-
al/popular literature despite its national and historical setting and its
peasant characters. Gramsci identifies a strain of irony in Manzoni's
treatment of the people. According to Gramsci, Manzoni is more concerned with the interior life of the upper-class characters, such as Fra
Cristoforo, l'Innominato, and even Don Rodrigo, than he is with his
peasant characters Lucia, Agnese, and Renzo. For Manzoni, the church
lies between the people and God, unlike Tolstoy, who makes the people
the "voice of God." Manzoni endows the church with this power. Thus,
according to Gramsci, Manzoni's concern with peasant life is more apparent than real.

In general, Gramsci characterizes the representation of the peasant in
Italian literature as "folkloristic." Gramsci does not tend to romanticize
such literature merely because it presents peasant society. Peasants are
presented as picturesque, romantic, and often as the font of comedy,
characteristics of the representation of subaltern classes. He does not

34 advocate the creation of a popular literature for its own sake any more than he advocates a formal concern with *"verismo."* His point is rather to indicate the absence of a national/popular culture in Italy. He also attempts to account for that absence. He is less interested in prescriptions and more interested in raising analytic questions, such as: "Is there an indigenous Italian cultural discourse? What is the importance of locating and creating such a discourse?" Recognizing that cultural production is integrally linked to political and economic considerations, Gramsci insists that a critical understanding of questions of form and content must be sought in Italian cultural history. His comments on the novel, on melodrama, on individual writers such as Manzoni and also Pirandello, constitute his own effort to test the existence of national/popular elements in Italian culture and, by tracing these forms of writing, he verifies that the form and content of much of Italian literature runs counter to the creation of a popular culture, though not necessarily of a mass culture.

Gramsci was interested in all forms of cultural production—modernist art and literature, detective novels, Gothic romances, novels of intrigue, science fiction, and cinema—and his discussions of various forms were interrogative rather than prescriptive. His primary objective in investigating forms of cultural production is to situate the organic intellectual in a critical practice in relation to all forms of social activities. His readings of literature and cinema are, therefore, an investigation of various aspects of cultural expression as signs and symptoms of Italian life and politics. Just as he insists that intellectuals are not "disinterested," even those traditional intellectuals who see themselves as removed from the direct operations of social power, so too he insists that the artist is not "disinterested" but rooted in historical reality. For Gramsci, the notion of disinterestedness is a major strategy on the part of the elite to maintain their own hegemony and, therefore, whether they acknowledge it or not, the hegemony of those groups in society to which they are related. Gramsci's comments on artistic production and critical analysis represent his way of demystifying the notion that the writer is the bearer of transcendental truths and of showing the necessity of recognizing the writer's politics.

The separation of cultural production from culture is in Gramsci's terms a political act that can be identified as such. He also finds such a divorce to be elitist in the sense that in this way intellectuals, the producers of culture, can maintain a safe distance from practical activity and hence from the majority of the people. Moreover, they can perpetuate the illusion that they are not political. The artist, like her/his

creations, exists in history and artistic representation needs to be trans-   **35**
lated into historical terms, which raises the question of the role of the
critic. In this context, Paul Bové asks,

> If culture is a question of language, as Gramsci suggests, and if hegemony
> and so politics is a question of culture diffused in and by language, then
> what shall we say is the role of the critic? We can begin to answer this
> question by insisting that critical activity is more than "self-reflexivity," as
> many liberals would like to believe. It should always be the dialectical
> reconsideration of concepts and methods based on the problems posed to
> criticism by the cultural environment.[34]

While Gramsci links cultural production to the study of history and
philosophy, he does not suggest that texts themselves, their content or
their form, are direct agents of social change. Just as he does not read the
text to elevate individual authors or individual texts but rather to see
them as part of a larger context of experience and struggle, so he does
not see the text's polemic as its primary source for reinforcement or
transformation of attitudes. Unlike Lukács, Gramsci examines texts not
for the purposes of introducing a preexisting totalistic vision of society
and culture, but for the purpose of interrogating the works to destroy
myths of artistic creation and of formal and textual autonomy. Gramsci
is constantly attentive to historical analysis. Knowledge of past and present forms of production is essential to any charting and understanding
of the uneven development of culture and its relation to technology and
capital formations. In the spirit of his insistence on the importance of
common sense, an analysis of cultural production must articulate both
the persistence of dominant forms from the past and the presence of new
elements, which can either be considered as further aspects of traditional
hegemony or can be identified as counterhegemonic emergent forms.
Furthermore, literary study is not merely descriptive or taxonomic but
provides the basis of a practice for both education and action.

Sexual Politics

In Gramsci's molecular analysis of language, literature, cinema, history,
the church, and ruling and subordinate groups, he is aware of the role of
sexual politics as a powerful force in producing the existing social relations of production. He asserts that "the most important ethical-civil
question tied to the sexual question is that of the formation of a new
female personality: until women shall not only have reached a real independence equal to men but also have a way of conceiving of themselves
and their role in sexual relations, the sexual question shall remain rich in

36   morbidity and will necessitate caution in every legislative innovation." ("La quistione etico-civile più importante legata alla quistione sessuale è quella della formazione di un nuova personalità femminile: finché la donna non avrà raggiunto non solo una reale indipendenza di fronte all'uomo, ma anche un nuovo modo di concepire se stessa e la sua parte nei rapporti sessuale, la quistione sessuale rimarrà ricca di caratteri morbosi e occorrerà esser cauti in ogni innovazione legislativa.")[35] Gramsci describes the ways that rural women are treated as brood mares and as objects of sexual sport, and how urban women suffer the additional psychological strain imposed by a system of social hypocrisy that demands, on the one hand, a rigorous puritanism and familial bondage on the part of the woman, and on the other, libertinism on the part of the man. Gramsci is most conscious of the social, political, and economic implications of this state of affairs that constitutes for him "a form of totalitarian social hypocrisy." ("Si forma in questo caso quella che si può chiamare una situazione di ipocrisia sociale totalitaria.")[36]

In the case of the wives of industrialists, Gramsci comments on the tendency for these women to become mental "prostitutes." Through the media and such spectacles as beauty contests, their images gain currency, a situation he saw as deriving from the United States and having tremendous implications for Europe and for all classes of women. Gramsci anticipates not only the question of how women are positioned in verbal language but also in cultural images. His comments on the important phenomenon of the Italian diva, as exemplified in such actresses of the teens as Lyda Borelli and Francesca Bertini, indicate his awareness that the diva phenomenon is closely tied to the culture's conceptions of sexual relations. He notes: "The sexual element has found in the theater its modern possibility of contact with the public. And it has raped the intelligence." ("L'elemento 'sesso' ha trovato nel palcoscenico la sua moderna possibilità di contatto col pubblico. E ha rapinato le intelligenze.")[37] Gramsci's concern with the position of women is related to his reiterated preoccupation with the suppression of women: that they, like peasants and workers, like members of the subaltern groups, are relegated to a marginal position within the culture and are represented in images of bestiality. The link between women and mass culture also seems not to have escaped his notice. He is particularly perceptive in his recognition of the role of theater and film in positioning women as images and objects of exchange in sexual politics. His discussion of women's position in the culture and in cultural representation is consistent with his general treatment of cultural/political phenomena.

The ideology of Fascism rested heavily on notions of generational and
sexual difference, on biologism, in its emphasis on the importance of the
family, and on the myth of the "new man," who embodies the virtues of
efficiency, loyalty, and service to the state. The woman was seen as the
guardian of the family, the nurturer of the man, and the breeder and nurturer of children. Gramsci's comments on sexual difference as an ideological construction in need of demystification are aimed at combating
conditions that go beyond Fascism and touch the very basis of organized
social relations. Even in his discussions of various forms of artistic representation, he identifies the ways in which these attitudes are present in
literature, theater, and the silent cinema.

Lexical Politics

Gramsci's criticism moves back and forth between historical, economic,
sociological, psychological, and linguistic phenomena in his effort to
identify the ways criticism can become a political practice if it disen-
gages itself from traditional academic intellectual practices that refuse to
confront the political dimensions of art and scholarship. In particular,
Gramsci does battle with an important aspect of academic institutional
practice: the ways academic disciplines and the professions legitimate
themselves and their hegemony through forms of language, special ter-
minologies, which set them apart from other social practices. The effect
of professional language is to protect intellectual practices from vulgar-
ization and to seal them off from access by subaltern groups. He was
well aware that the traditional intellectual in his "disinterestedness" saw
such lexicons as preserving cultural standards of production and as reinforcing the image of the authority of the intellectual in matters of artistic
and scientific judgment. The practice of traditional intellectuals is condescension toward forms of popular cultural production. "Low" or mass
culture is viewed as escapist and diversionary, lacking in moral qualities
and seriousness of purpose; "high" culture is uncorrupted by the "mar-
ketplace," and any signs of a connection to economics and politics must
be erased. The bias against mass or popular culture further reinforces the
separation between the "ignorant masses" and the educated elite. While
Gramsci was not an advocate of mass culture, his work reveals that
political and cultural analysis must incorporate a broad awareness of
cultural production. Gramsci's total critical work is addressed to breaking down any conceptions that obscure the politics of literature and
literary study.

38   By examining forms of artistic representation, Gramsci was attempting to explore old and new expressive forms within the culture, particularly as these forms were revealing of the potential for change, but in this
enterprise he did not merely elevate the notion of newness or originality.
As a matter of fact, in his discussion of *neolalismo,* he looks at the creation of new language forms with suspicion, seeing in neologism a
potentially pathological condition.[38] He considered this aspect of language, because of its arbitrary character, to be indicative of a condition
of cultural crisis diametrically opposed to his notion of language as an
expression of emergent hegemony. In discussing the character of neologism, he is also discussing the character of education, and the politics of
such studies. He would have seen any Babel (to use his own image) of
critical discourses as threatening to the development of a national/pop-
ular culture and hence to the rise of counterhegemony on the part of the
dispossessed. Gramsci did not dogmatically oppose the idea of newness,
however, any more than he was critical of modernism for its own sake.
His criterion for efficacy was based on the question of political unity and
the struggle to transform power relations. Those manifestations of entrenched power in institutional practices were bound to be seen by him
as a problematic sign. *Neolalismo* is a sign of cultural change, if not crisis,
and it is characteristic that Gramsci should frequently identify social
problems in terms of language symptoms. He was aware, however, of
neologism as a problem endemic to modernity, capitalism, and the speed
of change, and their potentially disunifying dimensions.

His comments about neologism may relate to another aspect of his
address of cultural change, language, mass media, and avenues of political dissemination: his experience with and interest in the political role of
journalism. His discussion of journalism, like his discussions of popular
literature and its political implications, stresses journalism's pedagogical
and political role. Journalistic writing should adopt a militant position in
the struggle against illiteracy. The implications of this position are further pursued in Gramsci's discussion of the types of journals and journalistic content under the category of "dilettantism" and "discipline."[39]
By dilettantism, Gramsci means the reproduction of certain attitudes
that reinforce bad traditions in the culture and are the consequence of
the absence of any critical position. This type of journalism thrives on
certain prejudices and on conventional attitudes and can be seen to fall
into skepticism or snobbish cynicism. The notion of discipline would
entail a degree of homogeneity in order to accomplish political objectives. Always on guard against elitism, dogmatism, and coercive forms
of control, however, Gramsci indicates that his idea of discipline entails a

recognition of differences and therefore of the need to confront them
openly and to try to overcome them in the interests of collective struggle.

Gramsci differentiates existing kinds of journals: 1) journals that specialize in criticism or politics, 2) journals that combine criticism, historical material, and bibliography, and 3) journals like the second type that are linked to a newspaper but have a "weekly" section. The kinds of material one is likely to find in such journals is encyclopedic, ranging among current ideas in the various intellectual practices, short biographies, autobiographies, recent work of a bibliographic nature, reviews of work from other journals and papers, book reviews of the informative type and of a more technical nature, and critical-bibliographic analyses situating the work of various individuals in some cultural milieu.

Gramsci is not talking in idealistic terms of the journal of the future but is using as his models existing journals that may or may not represent militant positions. The point to be drawn from his discussion of journalism, however, is that he does not disdain using existing institutional practices as models. His notion of a journal has the same breadth and scope as his conception of the school. The combating of illiteracy is for him more than the question of reading and writing. He discusses the nature and role of schools of journalism, and his conceptions of a journalistic education represent the same depth and scope he assigns to the journals themselves. He does not see a division between scholarly and technical issues. As part of their educational function, the journals address the latest technical developments, and Gramsci does not envision militant journals as separating cultural issues from technical ones any more than they separate information from political education. Gramsci's conception of the role of journalism cannot be separated from his central project of bringing the work of intellectuals to the masses and hence of extending information and criticism to the people. As a major means of transmitting ideas, the newspaper and the journal are powerful forces in developing a new cultural climate and in raising the issues crucial to social change. In the transmission of information, however, Gramsci does not see any reason for obfuscation, sloppiness, the substitution of polemic for criticism, emotionalism for analysis, or of condescension because of the backwardness of the audience. Nor does he see the necessity of hiding internal conflicts in the name of loyalty or a fragile unity. Since the work of criticism is to demystify ideological commonsense positions based on a fragmentary and unselfconscious perception of the world, journalism becomes for him yet another, and a major, means for overcoming cultural stasis. Journalism is a form of education, a forum for the organic intellectual.

40 *Education and Politics*

Since Gramsci's writing consistently returns to questions of activism, in his exploration of ways to produce organic intellectuals education is central to his work.[40] The concern for education can be traced to his own experiences in the *ginnasio* and university and to his indebtedness to Croce who, though holding a traditional and idealized conception of education and culture, nonetheless was energetic in working for school reform. Moreover, the role of education was a major source of interest, conflict, and contention during the Fascist regime, though energies were directed mainly toward "Fascistizing" the curriculum. Recognizing the importance of education in the battle for consensus, the Fascists sought to create their own conception of the relation of politics and education. In Gramsci's struggle to create a sounder basis for a union between learning and social change—in his continuous stressing of thoroughness, antiauthoritarianism, and heuristics—he was attacking the mechanical, traditional, and authoritarian practices of the Fascist regime. The most significant aspects of his conception of the nature and role of schools involve the curriculum, the relationship of the teacher to the pupil, and the importance of criticism and self-criticism in learning. Gramsci strenuously resists the idea that the school is merely a scholastic institution where "pure" ideas are studied and assimilated in a monastic setting. Recognizing the traditional penchant for creating a distinction between scholarship and the world of industry, science, and technology, Gramsci insisted on the need for the schools to incorporate contemporary advances in all areas of social production.

Both Jesuit and exclusively vocational types of training were unacceptable to him, and his ideas were directed toward breaking down the traditional separation between information and "skills," and the barriers between home and school, which perpetuated a fragmentary sense of the world. The compartmentalized role of the family, like that of the school, would seem to perpetuate the division between knowledge and practice so representative of the way in which social classes and women are subordinated. In his conception of education, the relationship between the teacher and the pupil became as important as the material to be learned. Here again, Gramsci is addressing the tendency on the part of existing social institutions to reproduce power relations legitimated on the basis of age, sex, and social role. Consequently, he argues that the traditional relationship of master and disciple or apprentice, whereby the subordinate takes the place of the master and later assumes a position of dominance, must be eradicated. Such a relationship, he suggests, also reproduces traditional authority relations between rulers and ruled. Favoring more reciprocal relationships, Gramsci suggests that the teacher should be accessible to the student. He is not arguing necessarily for a personal relationship, though he does not negate that possibility.

The pedagogical situation must not be dogmatic, and, therefore, the opportunity to question and explore ideas must be made available both to the student and to the teacher. The teacher as well as the student has imposed on her/him a continuous process of self-criticism, continuous reevaluation of ideas, behavior, and methods, and must be flexible in altering positions whenever necessary. In short, education should become part of the general process of modifying social relations and the social environment. In this context, Gramsci's conception of the war of maneuver and the war of position is particularly appropriate, because it illuminates his flexibility in analyzing and developing strategy according to concrete and specific historical conditions.[41] He addresses contemporary political concerns by recognizing that in advanced industrial societies, the idea of open revolutionary struggle may not be possible, and may even be counterproductive as a mode of planning and organization. This would seem to have been the case with the entrenchment of Fascism. Revolutions of force such as the Soviet revolution were for Gramsci characteristic of more primitive and amorphous conditions of industrialization and social structure. What he calls the war of maneuver is most likely under such conditions. A war of position is more likely in Europe and the United States, and entails a long ideological conflict as a necessary precondition for political victory.

By adopting the notion of a war of position, Gramsci was not abandoning the idea of revolutionary change. He was merely augmenting what was central to his political and cultural theory; namely, that no change will come about without conditions for change existing. These existing conjunctural conditions do not occur spontaneously but must be actively produced—are, in fact, in the process of being produced, and, therefore, are in identification in order to be acted upon. Gramsci thus reinforces his mistrust of spontaneism, of the capacity of the oppressed to throw off their chains and create a new society in cataclysmic fashion without education and organization. While he was aware of this well before the advent of Fascism, Fascism confirmed his sense of the power of the ruling order to maintain its hegemony and his recognition of the Left's failure to understand the necessity of unity, criticism, and constant preparation for change. Understanding of the interrelationship of culture and politics thus becomes the necessary weapon in the slow and

42 uneven struggle for hegemony. The "trenches" are in the heart of political and civil society. Gramsci's awareness that there is no revolutionary practice without a revolutionary theory, that there is no revolution without the necessary organization and apparatus, and that preparedness for revolutionary change entails a massive process that reaches deeply into private organizations and private lives, into everyday reality, certainly seems consonant with theoretical concerns of the last few decades, especially those that stress the importance of mass culture, of sexual politics, and of the importance of subjectivity in an examination of culture.

It remains difficult to assess the significance of Gramsci's notions of political/cultural struggle to the contemporary national and international situation. On the one hand, Gramsci's work is rooted in the exigencies of Fascist Italy and in the particular problems of pre-World War II capitalism/imperialism. On the other hand, his emphasis on the necessity of a war of position, on the role of intellectuals, and on the need to create a national/popular culture seem to speak equally to critical dilemmas and preoccupations of the last decades. The challenge his work offers (but does not solve) is the imperative to examine contemporary ways to expose numerous myths that have been self-defeating in the struggle to change existing institutional practices: the myth of "disinterested" intellectual work and of the powerlessness of such work; the quest for the "perfect" political solution, derived from outside one's own immediate social/cultural/historical situation; the myth of "delivery" from bondage by a strong figure; and the expectation of a collectivity based on sentiment, total consonance in point of view, and loyalty. Gramsci's work validates intellectuals and encourages them to regard themselves as central to the process of articulating and realigning power relations. His emphasis on the importance of regarding cultural production as political practice rooted in historical circumstances is not geared to academic discipline and "professionalism" as it now exists but to illuminating self-defeating and ineffectual social practices and to creating nontotalitarian, nonreductive, and viable alternatives to the dominant structures. The most important contribution of Gramsci's work is its insistence on the dialectical relations between part and whole. As Paul Piccone remarks, "In Gramsci, the logic of the whole, unencumbered by a fatalistic Marxist theory of history, can grasp the particular without reducing it to an extension of that logic and thereby suffocating its uniqueness and specificity." In other words, to understand the importance of Gramsci is to become aware of our own specific cultural/historical situation, so that the potential for change can be assessed and realized.[42]

Chapter 3

Socialism and/or Democracy: Politics, Culture, and the State

The post-1968 years have produced writings that either challenge Marxism as inadequate to the complexities of postindustrial capitalist society or reinterpret and revise basic Marxist theories and practices concerning social change. The presumed failure of 1960s radicalism produced a profound disenchantment with traditional Marxist theories and practices and a corresponding abandonment of direct political confrontation in the face of repression and retrenchment. The political situation of the 1980s was, as the editors of *New Left Review* succinctly describe it, "a much harsher one than anything the Left has known since the 30s." They write that "a new imperialist cycle of Cold War is pushing the nuclear arms race beyond the limits of the earth itself. A global recession is steadily increasing unemployment in the upper side of the capitalist world, and spreading debt and famine in its underside."[1] Despair and pessimism about social change among western intellectuals have become more pronounced in the wake of neoliberalism with its supply-side economics and its back-to-basics view of family, body politics, and nationalisms. Structuralist and poststructuralist theories that have sought to account for the resistance to change through the elaboration of complex philosophic, psychoanalytic, and social theories and indict the totalizing and rationalizing dimensions of western thought — including Marxism — cannot offer a practice to address the massive exploitation characteristic of contemporary capitalist and socialist countries. Such work has unfortunately fueled the New Right's opportunistic alignment with, if not actual co-optation of, theoretical work to demonstrate the failure of socialism and communism.

Yet some segments of the Left have not been idle, nor for that matter have the aims of the sixties been completely abandoned. The notion of a

44   "theoretical practice," initiated in part through the efforts of Louis
Althusser, signaled the need to reexamine the crucial problem of state
power and the collusive relations between the state and civil society as
coercive and ideological instruments of repression. But "Althusser's
Marxism is in the last instance a reductionism, where ideology plays the
crucial role that the theory of mediations plays for Hegelian Marxism."[2]
Marxist theory has turned toward more flexible conceptions of history,
human agency, the state and civil society, and hegemony in an effort to
escape this reductionism. As Chantal Mouffe indicates in her introduction to *Gramsci and Marxist Theory*: "For some years now we have been
witnessing an unprecedented development of interest in the work of
Antonio Gramsci and the influence of his thought is already very extensive in several areas of Marxist inquiry. This phenomenon, which has
developed in the wake of the events of 1968, is certainly linked to a
renewal of interest among intellectuals in the possibilities of revolutionary transformations in the countries of advanced capitalism."[3]

Contemporary Gramsci: Sassoon's Gramsci's Politics

Studies have appeared by such writers as Chantal Mouffe, Christine
Buci-Glucksmann, Maria Antonietta Macciocchi, Leonardo Paggi, Nicola
Badaloni, Norberto Bobbio, Joseph Buttigieg, Paul Piccone, Raymond
Williams, Perry Anderson, and Anne Showstack Sassoon that seek to
demonstrate the viability of Gramsci's notions of culture and politics for
current theoretical work on what Aronowitz terms "the crisis of historical materialism." In particular, Anne Showstack Sassoon's revised edi-
tion of her influential *Gramsci's Politics* (1987) tests Gramsci's theories
for their contemporary applicability. She claims that Gramsci's "use
today ... is in suggesting the lines of a research agenda and furnishing
some key concepts which will help us to analyze contemporary society.
Above all, he helps us to ask the right questions about what is new in
social, political, and economic developments, about the contradictory
effects of the historical process, about the implications and consequences
of specific forms of institutional and social relations in different countries."[4] Sassoon also insists that Gramsci's work offers possibilities for an
understanding of contemporary mass culture, the position of women,
the development of democracy and socialism, "the implications of new
technology and the relationship between vocational and academic education, the nature of the new economic order, such as the New Right and
neo-liberalism, and a wide variety of populist political projects in different parts of the world."[5]

Sassoon reminds us of the difficulties the reader faces in interpreting   **45**
Gramsci's work, problems arising from the immediacy of political journalism or, in the case of his prison writings, the fragmentary nature of
the notes designed for elaboration at a future time and for evasion of the
prison censor. His highly coded language necessitates care in translation
and interpretation often not taken by his translators and commentators.
As Perry Anderson has stated: "The result is a work censored twice over:
its spaces, ellipses, contradictions, disorders, allusions, repetitions, are
the result of this uniquely adverse process of composition.... It is necessary to say this as a warning against all facile and complacent readings
of Gramsci: he is still largely an unknown author to us."[6] In an attempt
to introduce the reader to Gramsci's thought, Sassoon is sensitive to the
need to create a composite picture of the events in Gramsci's life, the historical circumstances under which he labored, his relations to other
Marxist and non-Marxist thinkers, and the potential value of his interventions in contemporary critical discourse. Instead of relying solely on
the *Prison Notebooks*, she returns to Gramsci's early writings and political
activities to examine the evolution of Gramsci's notion of "the party,"
which she claims is neither abstract nor "unrelated to a specific historical
conjuncture or to a theory of the state and politics," but, when examined
closely, must be seen as "a clear break with the tradition of the Italian
socialist movement and by extension a break with the way the Second
International in general viewed the problems of the institutions of the
working-class movement."[7]

In articulating his early notions of revolution in *Ordine Nuovo*, Gramsci
stressed the importance of the proletariat's active role in promoting and
advancing revolutionary struggle. He based his opposition to evolutionary socialism and reformism on his resistance to determinist notions of
historical change as automatic and inevitable. Sassoon underscores
Gramsci's early intellectual debts to Benedetto Croce and Georges Sorel;
they helped him to find a language to challenge the determinism of the
Left.[8] By tracing Gramsci's notions of culture to their roots in Crocean
idealism, she differentiates Gramsci's work from the traditional Marxist
grounding in German philosophy, English political economy, and French
political theory. The Crocean elements in Gramsci's thought, some have
argued, were never fully eradicated, but remained the bases for the
greater emphasis Gramsci placed on cultural hegemony.[9] Although
Gramsci did not at first conjoin his analysis of culture to concrete political practice, he was aware of the need to understand culture as a precondition for assessing appropriate strategies for change. His writings on
the Russian Revolution reinforce his insistence on active participation in

46 revolutionary struggle as opposed to passive acceptance of economic realities as the primary determinants of social forces. In stressing the role of revolutionary consciousness, Gramsci cited the active roles of Lenin and the Bolsheviks and thus challenged the Marxian evolutionary view of the need to move to socialism through a bourgeois phase. In so doing, Gramsci reasserted his abiding thesis that revolution is creative, that it must enlist and transform consciousness.

Not until his work with the factory councils and his founding of the party paper, *Ordine Nuovo,* did Gramsci begin to examine in more concrete terms the question of organization and education. He developed his analysis of the factory councils within the context of postwar Italian realities. Sassoon puts it this way: "The necessity of overcoming the inability of the bourgeoisie to develop the forces of production without increasing State intervention, when the bourgeois State itself was in crisis, was a fundamental factor in Gramsci's discussion. Absolutely crucial to a proper understanding of Gramsci's interest in the factory councils is an understanding of the way in which he characterized the post-war period as revolutionary and of how he analysed the weakness of the bourgeois order."[10] The factory councils thus offered an opportunity to exploit this revolutionary potential by creating a mass movement of workers. The councils could serve as an educational and organizational force in economic and political society, and act as a major means for directing the proletariat toward socialism,.

Besides identifying Gramsci's residual idealism, Sassoon carefully underscores those aspects of his early analysis that are the result of rigorous notions of economism that he was later to modify in his prison writings. Moreover, she also indicates that, like Lenin, Gramsci conceived of the bourgeois state as antithetical to the proletarian state and hence to be superseded. For Gramsci, the "new order" must be based on the creation of a new state, entailing new forms of economic production that are themselves the preconditions for the disappearance of classes and the very concept of class. Hence Gramsci argued for new institutions for the working class distinct from the trade unions he understood as merely the corporatist response to capitalist competition and legality. To redefine and restructure workers' activities and their sense of collective effort, Gramsci felt that education can serve to correct the lack of democracy, the authoritarianism of leaders, and the tendency toward spontaneism. Gramsci did not link these ideas to any conception of party, yet his comments are largely within the aegis of the Socialist party, who he saw as removing the workers from capitalism and directing their collective energies to eliminate the possibilities of uncontrolled action as well as the temptations of reformism. In his preliminary discussions, Gramsci **47** theorized the party as the instrument of revolution but not as the revolution itself, revolution being the province of the masses. What becomes evident in his discussion of revolution and the role of the state is his break with the idea that an abrupt crisis in the state can be the basis of the transformation to socialism and also his realization that the very process of revolution is constructed and shaped in the process of building the new order: "These new organizations and this changed relationship between the mass of the population and the State are characteristics of a new mode of politics and the superseding of the traditional division between State and society."[11]

Gramsci's analysis of the transition to socialism and his conception of mass organization became the basis of his criticism of the Italian Socialist party and his quest for a new type of party that would replace those of bourgeois democracy. In particular, Gramsci based his critique of bourgeois democracy (with which he links socialism) on his view that this form of governing depends on a deleterious division between economics and politics whereby the individual is seen only as a citizen of an intricate legal system. Moreover, "Gramsci's argument," comments Sassoon, "is that the classical separation of the State from society typical of early capitalism and of the classical liberal 'night-watchman State' was in fact being challenged by the increasing intervention by the State in society in the period of monopoly capitalism."[12] Gramsci, aware that the Socialist party and the trade unions had worked out a relationship based on the division between politics and economics, was critical of such a separation. He was also anxious about the party's lack of contact with both the working class and the peasants. The party's neglect of the Southern Question—the economic and cultural conditions of the peoples of Sardinia, Sicily, and other regions of Southern Italy, an abiding issue in Gramsci's analysis of Italian politics and culture—was yet another major source of difference between Gramsci and the Socialists.

In her discussion of Gramsci's work in the early 1920s, Sassoon provides examples of Gramsci's analytical method in the role he played in the founding of the Italian Communist party and in his involvement in the international communist movement. At this time, Gramsci wrote to analyze the organizational and political problems of the new Italian party and its relationship to international communism. He debated with Bordiga "his ideas of centralism, the relationship of the class to the party and of the members of the party to the leadership, the need for discussion and debate, and the role of illegal work."[13] And extending his earlier concerns about the nature of revolution, Gramsci insisted that collec-

48 tive, not individual, will is central to the revolutionary process. He once again attacked deterministic and mechanistic notions of change as antidemocratic, as well as condemning liberal democratic notions of consensus. His discussion of the party provided a vehicle for a large number of his political preoccupations: the shortcomings of social democracy and its policies of reformism, the growing power of Fascism, the defeats of the working-class movement, and the need to rebuild working-class organizations. Sassoon writes,

> What had become much clearer to Gramsci is the precise role of the party *vis à vis* the other organisations of the working class. Whereas in the earlier period he was mainly concerned to establish a new relationship between the various working-class organisations in order to adhere to the changes brought about by the development of monopoly capitalism, in this period in a very difficult situation under the consolidation of the Fascist regime, he attempts to determine more precisely the specificity of the political struggle.[14]

Toward these ends, he explored opposition on all fronts — economic, ideological, and political. Gramsci placed great importance on theoretical struggle, which leads him to articulate a different role for intellectuals and to distinguish between bourgeois and working-class intellectuals. His stress on education as a means toward informed democratic participation extends to his notion of democratic centralism, an expression of the need to balance spontaneity and mass involvement. At pains to distinguish democratic centralism from autocratic centralism and bureaucracy, and to stress the importance of unity, Gramsci emphasized the inevitability of differences while urging the need to arrive at collective decisions after extensive debate. In theorizing the relationship of the party to the notion of class, Gramsci insisted that the two must merge and that in the interests of revolution, an alliance must not only exist between workers and peasants but extend to other anticapitalist groups. In turning to Gramsci's ideas as presented in the *Prison Notebooks,* Sassoon argues:

> Certain themes from his earlier work, among them revolution as a process, the political nature of organisational questions, the changed relationship between economics and politics, the importance of culture and the role of the intellectuals, the argument against a mechanistic interpretation of Marxism, and the novel nature of the socialist State and hence of the revolutionary party, continue to be important in the *Notebooks.* Yet Gramsci develops these themes within a problematic whose object is broadened to include the nature of the dominance of the bourgeoisie, a dominance which Gramsci comes to realise cannot be comprehended unless the very tools of analysis at the

disposition of the working-class movement, of Marxist theory, are developed and the consequences of economism in theory and in political organisation and practice are criticised.[15]

Within this context, Sassoon turns to a discussion of the much-used and much-abused Gramscian concept, "hegemony." She stresses that although it refers to the dominance and direction of a given class, it need not be restricted to one form of class rule. To understand hegemony's workings, one must understand its dualistic character, namely, that it combines domination and direction, coercion and consent, political and civil society. Rather than confining himself to the coercive dimensions of the state, Gramsci introduced a more complex and varied notion of superstructure that allows for areas of differing as well as merging functions. As a characteristic of modern societies, hegemony, by virtue of its need to gain consent, must be understood as not relying solely on one class's interests, but as incorporating all segments of society. Gramsci's notion of the state

> goes beyond a view of the State as an *instrument* of a class. The State is a class State in that it creates conditions under which a certain class can develop fully, but it acts in the name of universal interests within a field of constantly changing equilibrium between the dominant class and subaltern groups. The interests of the subordinate groups must have some concrete and not simply ideological weight; otherwise the interests of the dominant class would be merely economic-corporative.[16]

The concept of hegemony is inextricably tied to Gramsci's notion of the "historical bloc," which offers a theoretical analysis of the relationship between base and superstructure and a particular and specific analysis of a given historical and national moment. Furthermore, Gramsci's analysis of the historical bloc entails an examination of the constituencies joined together in the state: social classes, special interests, and traditional intellectuals.

Since hegemony depends on direction, intellectuals serve as a means of articulating, disseminating, organizing, and legitimating the supposed universal interests of the state. Recognizing the importance of these functions in the organization of hegemony, Gramsci made a distinction between traditional and organic intellectuals, between those serving dominant hegemonic interests and those drawn from the working and peasant classes or identified with the work of subaltern classes seeking to establish a new hegemony. Gramsci distinguished the work and the aims of these latter types of intellectuals, who—unlike philoso-

50 phers, clergy, or aristocracy — involve themselves directly in the world of production in technology, commerce, and economics. Organic intellectuals combine theoretical and practical knowledge in the interest of revolutionary change and serve a legitimation function occupied earlier by traditional intellectuals in the formation of historical blocs. Gramsci's discussion of concrete instances of traditional intellectual functions includes an analysis of the rural South and of the role of Croce in deracinating radical intellectuals, linking them to broader European culture and thereby separating them from the peasants.[17]

In *The Modern Prince*, Gramsci orchestrated his notions of hegemony, the historical bloc, the role of intellectuals, and the creation of a revolutionary society. Gramsci's prince is not an individual leader nor a single group but the party itself, necessarily seen as the consolidation of the collectivity. As such, the party is the agency for creating the new state, a fact that obliges Sassoon to examine the all-important question of whether the party is totalitarian. Her answer is "no." Gramsci's party is not capable of achieving power alone, although the "party of the working class according to Gramsci has the potential to expand enormously so that in the *integral* sense, organised to realise a new hegemony and a new conception of the world, it must unite a whole spectrum of the population having different organisational forms." Moreover:

> this unity must be of a particular quality based on a new concept of democracy and going beyond corporative demands to forge a new collective will. The party in its widest sense *assumes* the existence of diversity. At the same time, in creating the organic intellectuals of the working class, it *changes* the relationship between intellectuals and the masses so that in entering the terrain of pre-existing cultural and political institutions, it cannot simply use them as a bourgeois party or parties would, nor can they serve as "parties" of the working class in a similar way, because the institutions themselves must change if they are to express a new relationship to the mass of the population.[18]

The key terms in this passage are "difference," "diversity," and "change." In Gramsci's vision, the party does not reproduce existing forms of political organization but, in the process of forging alliances, becomes an educational force geared toward altering the division of labor with its characteristic subordination of subaltern groups, the precondition for cultural and political change. The force of Gramsci's position on party organization is to challenge traditional notions of leadership, and especially to challenge existing forms of authoritarianism and bureaucratic stasis.

In her effort to emphasize the relevance of Gramsci's theories for contemporary readers, Sassoon underlines Gramsci's reaction against the autocratic centralism and bureaucracy characteristic of many communist and socialist countries, a situation that does not instill confidence in revolutionary political organization. Sassoon, therefore, stresses Gramsci's historical analysis of party formation as well as his meticulous effort to differentiate his notions of leadership, unity, and discipline from Bolshevik practices. In discussing the vanguard party, she reminds the reader that Gramsci's views of history were dynamic and dependent on the notion that human beings actively assume a role in shaping events as opposed to passively being determined by history and the ironclad laws of economic necessity. Because of his rejection of historical determinism and economism, Gramsci's conception of organic and conjunctural movements was central to his analysis of the strategies and occasions for change. In the case of the former, such movements represent longstanding conditions that may or may not erupt into crisis. The organic is the terrain of continuous struggle on all fronts—economic, political, ideological—in contrast to the conjunctural, which represents immediate, imperative, and oppositional responses. In making such a distinction, Gramsci sought not only to combat economism but to identify strategies and tactics for action that would address concrete issues such as timing, organization, and preparedness. In this fashion, he could identify different sectors of necessary and successful struggle, as well as differentiate short-term from long-term conflicts.

In this context, his discussion of the "war of position" motivates the analysis of organic and conjunctural movements; it especially inspires a proper historical understanding of the possibilities and strategies for action. Moreover, as Sassoon writes, "it is the concept of hegemony which is the basis of Gramsci's attack on economism, and hegemony is the link between this discussion and the notes on strategy, in particular what he metaphorically calls the war of position, or a kind of trench warfare, as opposed to the war of movement, or frontal attack."[19] Commentators customarily regard Gramsci's adoption of these two military maneuvers as referring to different historical moments, and especially to the necessary response to Fascism and to conditions of force that inhibit direct action. In fact, Sassoon shows that the military terms are more complex and interrelated than is usually thought. For example, they can also refer to different strategies in relation to different dimensions of social struggle—economic, political, or ideological. In the constant shifting of the arena of struggle, the strategies change, and it is important for

52 the masses to recognize when to attack, when to dig in, and when to retreat momentarily.

Gramsci's notes on the wars of position and maneuver are conceptually linked to his notes on the passive revolution, notes in which he explores those moments that constitute a retreat and defeat of the masses. As Sassoon states: "in order to take account of the phenomenon whereby a dominant class maintains its power more because of a weakness on the part of the adversary, promoted by the form of politics of the dominant class itself, than because of its positive hegemony, Gramsci develops the concept of passive revolution."[20] She admits, as does Christine Buci-Glucksmann,[21] that this concept is one of the most enigmatically presented in Gramsci's work and yet perhaps the most central to Gramsci's challenge to Marxian notions of economism:

> One of the least explicit of his ideas, it is, we would argue, at the same time one of the most important to enable the revolutionary party to understand its task because it is a further explanation of the margin for political survival which the bourgeoisie enjoys despite political and economic crises, and because it indicates the *novel* nature of the building of a new state by the working class.[22]

Examining the effects of the French Revolution and the Risorgimento, Gramsci develops his notion of "revolution-restoration" whereby the segments of the old dominant classes, through reformism, blunt the challenge to revolutionary change. The case of Italy in the Fascist era is a prime instance of the passive revolution: "Fascism did not simply restore a *status quo,* but it changed the way in which masses of people related to the State, a State which had never enjoyed a mass base."[23] Furthermore, Gramsci's conception of Fascism differs from those conceptions that stress its political and coercive character.

Buci-Glucksmann asks: "Does not fascism as a form of state totalitarianism in fact conceal a new form of reformism linked to state capitalism?"[24] Gramsci's aim is not merely to provide a description of Fascism but to stress the resilience of the dominant powers in maintaining their hegemony. He shows how they exploit the weaknesses of their challengers by reformism and by blocking the "organizational autonomy of the working class,"[25] thus stressing the necessity of not only recognizing these strategies but of adopting the covert means to resist them. "The lesson for the revolutionary party is clear," says Sassoon. "Its analysis must be centered on the specific configuration of class forces confronting it in order to be able to know the nature of the alternative historical bloc which it must build."[26] The party must distinguish between the necessity for a war of position as opposed to the mere assumption that a war of maneuver is inevitable and correct—a lesson that could also be applied to the events of the 1960s, when the New Left had not absorbed the lessons of past history and was confident in its power to overturn existing institutions. Gramsci combats spontaneism, the utopian notion that the state will crumble through its internal contradictions and that a new type of state will automatically arise from the ruins of the old. He insists on the necessity of recognizing the capacity of the dominant forces to regroup and of opposing these forces by building an organization that does not rely on alliances with the bourgeoisie and creates a "concrete programme which engenders widespread consent and a system of alliances under its hegemony."[27]

Thus, in summarizing Gramsci's commentary on the party, the state, and democracy, Sassoon directs the reader to Gramsci's contributions to contemporary Marxian political theory and practice. Never claiming more for Gramsci's prescience than his texts permit, while seeking permissible extrapolations of his concepts, she indicates that Gramsci is no mere sycophant in his interpretation of the Russian Revolution, and that he recognizes the inherent difficulties in the transition to socialism. Gramsci's awareness of the necessity, intricacy, and complexity of building a revolutionary movement does not blind him to obstacles in the development of alternative social, political, and economic structures, such obstacles as authoritarianism, opportunism, utopian notions of collective action, spontaneism, reformism, inadequate understanding of historical precedents, and personal disillusionment. In the *Notebooks*, time and again, Gramsci combats the tendencies to misinterpret the roles of the state and civil society and to underestimate the nature and workings of power.

Addressing the contemporary debate over the possibilities of democracy and socialism, insisting that Gramsci intentionally neither outlines the precise nature of a new state nor specifically discusses the nature of pluralism, Sassoon argues for the democratic and nonauthoritarian nature of his position:

> While a significant limitation in Gramsci's writings on the party is that he leaves little space for the autonomous activities of other parties and non-party organisations in a socialist society, and while it is true that he does not explicitly discuss pluralism, the logic of the fundamental concept of hegemony points to the necessity of a continuing plurality of political and social organisations. At the same time there is nothing which guarantees the

longevity or success of a political force which is no longer able to represent the needs of an historical epoch or whose popular base ceases to give it support.[28]

For those readers who have no acquaintance with Gramsci, Sassoon has provided a clearly and carefully constructed introduction to his major political concepts. For those readers who have sought to stress the cultural dimensions of his work to the detriment of the political, she has offered a critical analysis that reveals the importance in any address of "the Gramscian way" of understanding the nature of active struggle and its imbrication in cultural analysis: Sassoon's emphasis has been on Gramsci's political and cultural analysis as inseparable from his activism rather than constituting a different sphere of analysis. Gramsci's position on hegemony, the role of intellectuals, and the party *is* "cultural." In his writings, discussions of contemporary culture are not restricted to an ideology critique but address the role of the state, civil society, history, and the party, as well as questions of social class. Ideology or common sense is inextricably intertwined with these issues. Thus the arguments in her book intervene in current debates over the relationship between socialism and democracy, and the politics of culture and the culture of politics.

"Which Socialism": Bobbio's Gramsci

If Sassoon's writing struggles to locate Gramsci's thought in the broad context of the numerous political, social, and philosophic antagonisms that he sought to examine, other contemporary writers are more selective in their appropriation of Gramsci. In a vein different from Sassoon's valorization of Gramsci's work and as part of the effort to address possibilities for structural change in capitalist and socialist societies, another literature has developed under the rubric of "rational choice Marxism," which claims some connection to Gramsci if not to classical Marxism. Presented in such journals as *Marxism Today* and *New Left Review,* and appearing in the writings of John Roemer, Richard Norman, Michael Taylor, and Norberto Bobbio, "rational choice Marxism" is an umbrella term that covers many deviations from classical Marxist practice. "Rational choice Marxism" holds that "societies are composed of human individuals who, being endowed with resources of various kinds, attempt to choose rationally between various courses of action."[29] Although fully cognizant of classical Marxism's opposition to social democracy, these writers seek to make accommodations between theories of classic liberalism and aspects of Marxism.

Norberto Bobbio can properly be considered an exemplary selective reader of Gramsci's ideas. An Italian political theorist, Bobbio has lived through the major crises and conflicts of Italian society. He lived through the prehistory of Italian Fascism and through the twenty years of its regime. He experienced the Cold War and the students' and workers' revolts in the late sixties and early seventies. He further experienced the "Historic Compromise" that led to alliances with the Christian Democrats rather than with the Socialist party (PSI). And, ultimately, in the wake of political unrest, he has lived to see the rise to prominence of the Italian Socialist Party (PSI). As a political philosopher at the University of Turin; the author of many books and articles on Italian law, politics, and history; a political activist; the controversial subject of books in Italy critical of his positions; and member of the Italian Senate, Bobbio derives his theories from a lifelong commitment to social transformation and particularly from a recognition of the need to abandon doctrinaire positions and develop theories of the state he finds conspicuously absent in Marxism.

Bobbio's critiques of Marxism and his attempts to align socialism and democracy have been slow in gaining the attention of intellectuals outside of Italy. The translations of *Which Socialism? Marxism, Socialism, and Democracy* and *The Future of Democracy, A Defence of the Rules of the Game* may help to evaluate the strengths of Bobbio's position—a position by no means unique at this conjuncture. Bobbio is conversant with the traditions of Marxism and especially with the recent developments in western Marxism in which Gramsci's writing plays a prominent role. We have seen how important Gramsci's exploration of consensus has become to an analysis of capitalist hegemony. In Gramsci's thought, the critique of state power is inextricable from the transformation of cultural institutions, hence his emphasis on education, intellectuals, and his elaboration the necessary conditions for assuming control. These ideas, often shorn of their historical and practical analysis, intrigue many of his commentators, leading them to separate his cultural theory from his revolutionary Marxism. For example, Bobbio's analysis of Gramsci's notions of the state and civil society derives from his own concerns to legitimize classical liberalism and its affinities to socialism.

In contrast to Gramsci, Bobbio's allegiances have been primarily to the Italian Socialist Party. Perry Anderson identifies the particular nature of Bobbio's intellectual and political commitments in the following way: "Bobbio is a philosopher with a wide formation, who measured himself against the phenomenology of Husserl and Scheler before the war, the existentialism of Heidegger and Jaspers during the war, and the posi-

56   tivism of Carnap and Ayer after the war. His own epistemological pref-
erences have been empirical and scientific—going clean against the
grain of what he dubs the 'Italian ideology,' congenitally speculative and
idealist in bias."[30] While not attributing any originality to Bobbio as a
philosopher or an economist, Anderson credits Bobbio with a deep
knowledge of political philosophy, "backed by a training in constitution-
al law and familiarity with political science."[31]

Though Bobbio echoes Gramsci's (and Lenin's) critique of the negative effects of Left spontaneism, economism, authoritarianism, and the
totalizing effects of the modern state, he does not share Gramsci's arguments about the necessity and feasibility of direct democracy. Rather,
Bobbio's concern about the deleterious erosion of even the most basic
elements of liberal democracy leads him to challenge the Italian Communist party and, more generally, Marxism for its failure to grapple theoretically and practically with the nature of the state. In his collection of
essays, *Which Socialism?*, Bobbio chastises recent Marxist writers for having no conception of the alternative state: "What has been lacking above
all and is still lacking today, if I have understood correctly the argument
put forward by Cerroni (whose points of reference include not only
Marx, but Lenin and Gramsci), is a theory of the socialist state or of
socialist democracy which offers an alternative to the theory, or rather
the theories, of the bourgeois state, bourgeois democracy."[32] Citing Lenin
and Gramsci specifically, Bobbio insists that they focus on the means and
not the ends of seizing power. Bobbio's other major contention with theoretical Marxism is that Marxists treat the new state as transitory, as an
intermediate moment before its withering away altogether, and hence
feel no need to explore it: "Marxist political thinkers have traditionally
been much more preoccupied with the extinction of the state in general
than with the construction of the socialist state, even if they have, in contrast to the anarchists, considered it indispensable. Indispensable, yes,
but not destined to last—a sort of purgatory in which the only relief is
the hope of its imminent termination."[33]

Bobbio's knowledge of the history of Marxism qualifies him to make
certain fundamental criticisms of Marxist theory and practices, though
this knowledge does not save him from misrepresenting aspects of Marxist thought. His commitment to liberalism often positions him in opposition to Marxism. While acknowledging the important contributions of
Marx and Marxism, Bobbio maintains a critical distance from them when
he confronts "Marxolatry," the ways in which certain forms of Marxism
have functioned as a religion with heroes, martyrs, villains, and dogma.
"The force of Marx's genius lies above all in his achievement as a critic

rather than as a system builder," he writes, "but the followers who turned his thought into an 'ism,' thus going against his expressed intentions (it is so trite and banal to have to repeat 'I am not a Marxist,' that it is embarrassing to have to do it again) have had to ignore the critique and to concentrate instead on a system which never really existed."[34] Moreover, he charges that Marxists "have an irresistible tendency to be nothing more than Marxists. They tend to isolate Marx and Marxism from the rest of the world and thus to isolate themselves."[35]

Bobbio's critique, while aimed at his Italian Marxist critics, is more than a self-defense for his own departures from Marxism; it is specifically a desperate appeal to put aside sectarianism and to confront the emergence of new social forces set in motion under late capitalism, forces that have led, on the one hand, toward global economic and political repression and, on the other hand, have led to rising demands for change by feminists, ecologists, and the exploited groups in third-world countries. Cognizant of these conditions, Bobbio undertakes a reconsideration of the relationship between the modern state and civil society in his attempt to locate ways of reversing their autocratic trends. In his essay "Gramsci and Civil Society," he discusses the evolution of concepts of the state, beginning with a discussion of theories represented in the thought of Hobbes, Rousseau, and Kant that conceive of the state as "the supreme and definitive stage in the common and collective life of humanity."[36]

In Hegel, Bobbio locates a break "with this tradition of political thought as well as its culmination."[37] Following Hegel and refining his notions, Bobbio undertakes a reconsideration of the relationship between the modern state and civil society in his attempt to locate ways of reversing their autocratic trends. Marx, in accord with Hegel, conceives the state as no longer "an elimination of the state of nature, but rather as its conservation, prolongation and stabilization. In the state, the reign of force has not been suppressed, but has been perpetuated, with the only difference that the war of all against all has now been replaced by a war of one side against the other (i.e., class struggle, of which the state is the expression and instrument).... The state is no longer presented as the transcendence of civil society but merely as its reflection: as civil society is, so is the state. The state incorporates civil society not in order to transform it into something else, but to keep it as it is."[38] The state is thus perceived as a coercive apparatus, an instrument of class domination, in league with civil society, which regulates it.

Bobbio explores Gramsci's conceptions of civil society specifically for the purposes of appropriating Gramsci as a critic who offers a less

58   monolithic conception of the state, especially one critic who has sought
to escape from the traditional dualism between the state and civil society:

> Antonio Gramsci's theory of the state—I am referring particularly to the
> Gramsci of *The Prison Notebooks*—belongs to this new stage of political
> thought where the state is not an end in itself, but an apparatus, an
> instrument. It does not represent universal interests, but particular ones; it is
> not a separate and sovereign entity set above the underlying society, but is
> conditioned by society and thus subordinated to it. It is not a permanent
> institution, but a transitory one which is bound to disappear with the
> transformation of the underlying society.[39]

And Gramsci's conception of the interrelationship of the state and civil
society differs from that of Marx and Engels, who see them in opposition
to each other. This Marxian antithesis "must ... be related to the fact that
it is one of the forms through which the fundamental antithesis of the
system is expressed, that between base and superstructure."[40] Civil society is thus identified with the political economy as the base, whereas the
state is identified with the superstructure. Gramsci's innovation lies in
his connecting civil society to the superstructural sphere, since civil society is related not only to material forces but also to ideology and culture.
His views on civil society place him in a different rather than a symmetrical relation to Marx, one closer to Hegel. The importance for Bobbio in
making this distinction is to dissociate Gramsci from the traditional
Marxist base and superstructure dichotomy, a strategy not uncommon in
recent Gramscian analysis.[41]

Bobbio stresses that Gramsci's notion of hegemony is important for
introducing and reconfiguring notions of cultural as well as political
leadership because it privileges civil society and hence the element of
consent rather than coercion. Bobbio's appropriation of Gramsci also
becomes a weapon to attack more radical contemporary practices.
Gramsci is Bobbio's weapon to reinforce an attack on Marxolatry,
polemicism, and economism. By situating Gramsci in the Hegelian tradition, Bobbio can claim Gramsci as an exemplar of deviations from Marxism, as perhaps a precursor for his own reflections on the nature of the
state. Not only does Bobbio distinguish Gramsci's departures from
Marx, but he also differentiates Gramsci's conception of hegemony from
that of Lenin:

> Gramsci's hegemony includes ... both the factor of political leadership and
> the factor of cultural leadership.... The hegemonic forces therefore include
> not only the party but also all the other institutions of civil society (in
> Gramsci's meaning of the term) which have some connection with the

elaboration and diffusion of culture. As regards its function, hegemony not only aims at the formation of a collective will capable of creating a new State apparatus and of transforming society, but it also aims at elaborating and propagating a new conception of the world.[42]

Thus, Gramsci provides Bobbio a Marxian position from which to address the Marxian issue of the withering away of the state:

> If we look at civil society as a term of the base-superstructure antithesis, the end of the state is the transcendence of the superstructural stage in which civil society and political society are in reciprocal equilibrium; if we look at civil society as an aspect of the superstructure, the end of the state is the reabsorption of political society in civil society. The apparent ambiguity is due to the real complexity of the historical bloc, as Gramsci conceived it. That is, it is due to the fact that civil society is a constitutive factor of two different processes, which happen interdependently but without fully overlapping: the process which moves from the base to the superstructure, and the one which takes place within the superstructure itself. The new historical bloc will be the one where this ambiguity as well will be resolved by the elimination of dualism in the superstructural sphere. In Gramsci's thought, the end of the state consists precisely in this elimination.[43]

Bobbio's reading of Gramsci is illuminating not only for what it says about Gramsci's thought but for what it indicates about Bobbio's project of rereading Gramsci as a bridge over the apparent schism between the state and civil society. Bobbio's conception of socialism depends on his shedding a materialist analysis of base and superstructure as a prelude to focusing on circumscribed strategies for the reform of democratic institutions. The reinterpretation of Gramsci, the polemic against Marxism, and the invocation of classical liberal theory make up Bobbio's attempt to short-circuit large-scale conceptions of social transformation as well as futile assaults on the power of the state.

Although in *Which Socialism?* Bobbio engages in a debate with Marxism to expose the inadequacy of existing conceptions of socialism and to establish his preference for a dialectical interaction between socialism and democracy, in *The Future of Democracy* Bobbio puts his anti-Marxist polemic aside and focuses primarily on an analysis of the precedents, means, and strategies of liberal democracy in a modest common-sense appeal to alter present political practices. The essays brought together in *The Future of Democracy*, presented on different occasions, cover such topics as representative and direct democracy, the constraints of democracy, liberalism, democracy and invisible power, contracts and contractarianism, and the rule of law. The essays are designed to be "general"

60 and "elementary ... written for the reading public who are interested in politics and not for the specialist. They are essays which once would have been classified as 'popular philosophy.' They are prompted by one central consideration: to bring democracy down to earth, from the realm of ethereal principles to where there are flesh-and-blood interests in conflict." In his configuration of a fit audience, Bobbio appeals to the "popular" and to "common sense" when he writes:

> If I were to imagine the type of adversary whom I would like, not perhaps to convince, but make less suspicious of democracy, it is not those critics who spurn it as the government of the incompetent, i.e., the perennial extreme Right which continually re-emerges in the most varied guises but always harbors the same grudge against the "immortal principles" of 1789. The ones I have in mind are those, who seeing this democracy of ours, always fragile, always vulnerable, corruptible and frequently corrupt, would seek to destroy it in order to render it perfect.... To start a dialogue with the first type of reader is liable to be a waste of time.... To continue on with the second enables us not to lose hope in the power of common sense.[44]

In the above statements, while invoking common sense, Bobbio has departed from the Gramscian critique of it and has uncritically reproduced common-sense discourse. The "power of common sense" is deployed by Bobbio in a familiar way to define and to proscribe meaning. In reducing the definition of democracy to a game of rules and decision-making, Bobbio asserts that what distinguishes democracy from autocracy is its set of rules that "establish *who* is authorised to take collective decisions and which *procedures* are to be applied."[45] Common sense is again in evidence when Bobbio says, in terms that cut across political affiliations, that "those called upon to take decisions, or to elect those who are to take decisions, must be offered real alternatives and be in a position to choose between these alternatives."[46] This decision-making process depends on the exercise of free speech and assembly, rights considered the cornerstone of the liberal state. Without the guarantees of liberalism, democracy is impossible: the former is the precondition for the latter. In Gramsci's work, by contrast, democracy is analyzed within a context of cultural, social, economic, and political constraints, many of which are abandoned by Bobbio in favor of insisting on the need to remain within a discourse of law.

What Bobbio does not address critically in his analysis of the "rules" of liberalism and democracy are the ways in which common sense uses but also abuses history, establishing its own arbitrary genealogies and engaging in univalent causal explanations. By tracing democracy to the

contractarian theories of society that emerged in the seventeenth and
eighteenth centuries and to the development of political economy and
utilitarianism in the nineteenth, Bobbio's common sense leads him to
valorize change through an appeal to origins. The use of common sense
is also evident in Bobbio's recapitulation of the notion that initial conceptions of democracy were designed to protect the rights of the individual and that, increasingly, "groups and not individuals are the protagonists of political life in a democratic society."[47] Again, this common-sense
view reproduces a familiar critique of contemporary political life without providing a materialist analysis of the protagonists and of these
changed conditions.

In his overriding concern to restrict the power of the state and particularly to protect democratic processes from domination by one elite
group, Bobbio has abandoned Gramscian class analysis and the notion
of the party, leaving vague and abstract the nature of social and economic interests as determining factors in the formation of groups. The Gramscian conception of hegemony has been reduced to practical questions of
political representation and the obstacles to achieving the least possible
government. One of the most blatant examples of the violation of democratic principles enumerated by Bobbio is the existence of binding man-
dates where the interests of autonomous groups prevail over impartial
political representation. Acknowledging that representative democracy
does not eliminate elites, Bobbio, following Joseph Schumpeter, suggests
that it is not elites that obstruct democratic participation, but the ways
one elite can impose its will on society: "Joseph Schumpeter struck the
nail on the head when he argued that the defining characteristic of a
democratic regime is not the absence of elites but the presence of several
elites in competition with each other for the votes of the public."[48] The
absence of competition thus constitutes a major blockage to democratic
representation. Pursuing this commonsense appeal to his adversaries,
Bobbio reinterprets the notion of elites as representing interests of citizens "in their many particular roles as members of a religious faith, as
workers, as soldiers, as consumers, as invalids, etc."[49] What concerns
Bobbio is not the verbal guarantee of democratic representation, but the
guarantee of that representation through "the power which underwrites
this guarantee,"[50] a power he does not find presently in evidence. Describing the ways in which democratic power is obstructed, again in the vein
of common sense, Bobbio lists how decisions are conducted at the highest levels of government and business, away from public scrutiny and
therefore away from accountability and public control. As is characteristic of common-sense formulations, there is little to contest in this assess-

62 ment. Gramsci reminds us that common sense contains a core of good sense, but the problem lies deeper, in Bobbio's resistance to theory concerning subaltern groups, to challenging, explicating, and complicating the nature and position of the subaltern.

Among the other "broken promises" of democracy, Bobbio lists the failure to educate the masses properly into an understanding of science and technology, the reinforcing of rules by experts, and the theft of citizens' power to make decisions affecting their lives. The growth of bureaucratic apparatus, even when designed for the welfare of the populace, becomes an obstacle to participation, since such apparatus is administered from above. The seemingly endless and often competing demands on the state strain the democratic process and result "in the so-called 'overloading' of government and the necessity for the political system to make drastic choices. But one choice excludes another, and not making certain choices produces dissatisfaction."[51] The acceleration of demands stands in marked contrast to the ability of the system to address them. The Gramscian concern with education and democratic participation is evident, but what is un-Gramscian is Bobbio's neglect of the self-evidence of his own common-sense critique that is a prelude, not an end, to analyzing to whom and for whom one speaks. In his attempt to resuscitate liberal democracy and in his impatience with Marxism, Bobbio does not explore the context for the choices he poses nor does he examine, beyond vague notions of pluralism, the constituency for whom he speaks.

The formidable catalog of problems he presents as besetting representative democracy does not deflect Bobbio from his belief that liberal democracy is the only form of government that will guarantee citizens' rights. Although he confines his comments to the national problems of democratic rule, omitting the international aspect of the relation of nation-states to each other, he insists that "in no country in the world can the democratic method last without becoming a habit. But can it become a habit without recognition of the bonds of kinship which unite all human beings in a common destiny? This recognition is all the more necessary now that every day we are made more aware of this common destiny. We ought, by the dim light of reason which still lights our path, to act accordingly."[52] Bobbio's language alerts the reader yet again to the common-sense beliefs that animate his work, in the familiar appeal to universalism, common humanity, destiny, and reason.

Although he is concerned for enhancing and augmenting democratic participation, Bobbio does not hold out much hope for direct democracy. His mode of argumentation depends on affective appeals to his audience based on experience and on refining existing distinctions about the nature of representation. To make his case, he must first abolish the traditional distinction between representative and direct democracy by arguing that they are not antithetical, as many think, but related: "Between pure representative and pure direct democracy, there is not the qualitative leap which the advocates of direct democracy believe, as if a watershed separated the two and once you had passed over it the landscape had changed completely.... The problem of transition from one to the other can only be posed in terms of a continuum."[53] Though Bobbio insists on this notion of a continuum, he is actually involved in establishing the conflation of the two. Furthermore, he rejects the possibility of the total citizenry's complete participation in the process of decision-making, except in extremely small societies. The most important consideration for him is not the size of representation, but the degree to which adopted representation is responsive to the needs of the constituents and not to those of special interests.

The revocable nature of elected officials becomes for Bobbio an important touchstone in the merits of representative democracy. In defining his notion of representation, Bobbio asserts that "a representative means a person with two very specific attributes: someone who (a) enjoys the trust of the electorate by virtue of election, and so is responsible to them and cannot be dismissed; and (b) who is not directly answerable to the electorate precisely because he is called upon to safeguard the general interests of civil society and not the particular interests of any one group."[54] Bobbio's realism leads him to dismiss arguments for direct democracy as indicative of naiveté and of misplaced emphasis:

> If one can nowadays talk of the process of democratization, it does not consist, as many people erroneously make out, in the transition from representative democracy to direct democracy, but from what is strictly speaking political democracy to social democracy. In other words, ascending power, which hitherto was almost entirely confined to the macrocosm of politics at the national level (and to some small, minute, politically irrelevant voluntary associations) is spreading to various spheres of civil society, ranging from the school to the factory. I speak of the school and the factory because they epitomize the places where most members of modern society spend the majority of their lives.[55]

This passage exemplifies Bobbio's departures from and his indebtedness to Gramsci. Gramsci and Bobbio voice a similar concern for the empowering of under- and unrepresented social groups as opposed to a shared focus on the upper reaches of political power. Both Bobbio and

64   Gramsci place emphasis on the necessity of ascending as opposed to descending power. But, significantly, Bobbio departs from Gramsci's specific and concrete concerns for assessing and orchestrating cultural, educational, and organizational strategies in favor of an exclusive focus on the pragmatics of political representation.

Seeking indications of the possibility for extending actual representation, Bobbio notes signs of movement in the establishment of school councils in Italy. Moreover, he asserts that the "effects of an excess of politicization can be that the private sphere reasserts itself."[56] His greatest hope lies in shifting the trend of the state toward cannibalizing civil society, and restoring the private sphere, which, he contends, has spaces and centers of power other than the state: "Modern societies are not monocratic but polycratic, something that can easily strand the unsuspecting on the quicksands of pluralism.... We come up against centres of power which exist within the state but are not directly identified with the state. Inevitably it is at this point that the problem of democracy encounters the problem of pluralism, and subsumes it, so to speak."[57] Bobbio asserts that he is aware of the problems inherent in placing a naive faith in pluralism; for pluralism can also indicate a "network of oligarchies."[58] Pluralism can only be effective where there is open dissent and the possibility of free contention by competing interests. The emphasis on pluralism also divides the two thinkers. Bobbio, while he recognizes the problematic nature of pluralism, the capacity of capitalism for the subsumption of difference, holds open the possibility that competition can serve as a corrective to abuses of power by the few. Gramsci's writings are wary of this form of idealism and hence more critical of reductive analyses of social alignments based on the existing order and on reformism.

Bobbio's discussion of rules also becomes a vehicle for him to be critical of existing Left politics. For example, in discussing "alternative politics," he rehearses Althusser's notion of a qualified adherence to the rules in the state's transformation and finds himself uncertain about the rules that should be followed and those that should be abolished. In discussing the New Left, Bobbio charges that it has "failed to outline clearly an alternative system, invoking not so much new forms of association of the working class as a whole, and appealing less for new structures of organization than the disappearance of all organization, for so-called 'spontaneous action,' one of the many myths of the working-class Left."[59] He cites political activism on the part of trade unions, the women's movement, gay rights movements, and leagues for human rights as forms of pressure exerted on the system: "A democratic system recognizes these movements, and within limits which vary from country to country, tolerates them, on the basis of the two fundamental principles of freedom of association and freedom of opinion."[60] He does not see these movements as necessarily transforming the system, but he does see them as safeguarding "rules, players, and a code of conduct."[61] In his taxonomy of the perils to (as well as the potential for) democracy, he cites the "new quietism," a "withdrawal from politics, the renunciation of politics, and the rejection of politics." Along with the notion of *qualunquismo*, the condemnation of politics, with its emphasis on "minding one's own business, this quietism constitutes a response to the excessive politicization of contemporary life ('politics is not everything') and a refusal on the part of many to engage in political activity ('politics is not for everyone')."[62] Like Baudrillard, Bobbio sees such apathy as an indication that social life is not completely subsumed and consumed by politics, a concrete instance of Bobbio's conceptions of civil society allowing him to locate counterhegemonic possibilities. What seems to be missing in Bobbio's analysis is the Gramscian recognition of the interpenetration of the state and civil society, so that these are not discrete entities easily disarticulated.

In treating the question of lack of participation, Bobbio emphasizes that the threat to democracy that is greater than apathy is the existence of invisible government. The metaphor of visibility is central to his argument for democracy: "It has always been regarded as one of the cardinal principles of the democratic system that all the decisions and, generally speaking, the activities of those in power must be known to the sovereign people defined as direct government by the people or government controlled by the people (and how could it be controlled if it was kept secret?)."[63] Reminiscent of Foucault, Bobbio interprets representative government as referring also to representations of power, asserting that "the closer power is physically, the more visible it is."[64] In referring to the visibility of power, Bobbio invokes Enlightenment concepts of publicity: "Whatever sphere it spread to, the metaphor of light and enlightenment (of *Aufklärung and illuminisms*) expresses well the contrast between visible and invisible power."[65] Citing Kant, he insists on the public use of reason and the inextricability of power and morality in this context: an act that cannot be made public is an act that violates the public good. Furthermore, Bobbio connects the visibility of the trappings of autocracy and the occult nature of the exercise of power by saying that such occult power encourages occult opposition. Foucault's discussion of the Panopticon in *Discipline and Punish*, where the prisoners can be seen but the observer is invisible, leads Bobbio to comment that "the

66   prisoner is seen but unseeing, the guard sees and is seen, the people closes the progression by seeing but remaining unseen by anyone but itself and hence, *vis à vis* others, is invisible. The unseen seer is again sovereign."[66] The phenomenon of subterranean or "cryptogovernment" extends into all areas of the State, ranging from economic issues to operations of military and paramilitary forces. Bobbio describes an invisible dictatorship, the cure for which he sees in the demand for publicity, for making the invisible visible. The more Bobbio becomes obsessed with the monolith of the state, the more he moves away from the range of problems he himself has brought forward to dramatize the crisis of postmodernity and the more he has lost sight of other aspects of Gramsci's (and Antonio Negri's) social and political analysis, namely, the need to identify, analyze, and exploit the contradictory nature of existing social, economic, and political antagonisms inherent in late capitalism.

For Bobbio, liberalism becomes a folklore that can be traced in philosophic terms to such classical liberal thinkers as John Stuart Mill as well as to more recent writers on liberalism such as Ralf Dahrendorf and Robert A. Dahl. In contrast to socialism, which has derived its theories from Marx, liberalism for Bobbio "is a movement in the history of ideas which develops via a host of writers quite distinct from each other, such as Locke, Montesquieu, Kant, Adam Smith, Humboldt, Constant, John Stuart Mill, and Tocqueville, just to cite some of the tradition's pantheon of classical thinkers."[67] Bobbio uses his vast acquaintance with these writers to differentiate conceptions of liberalism in an effort to isolate historically obsolete forms from those that can, in his terms, be comfortably conjoined to socialism. For example, Bobbio finds that Mill's liberal state is based on a negative injunction, *neminem laedere* ("harm no one"), a position compatible with laissez-faire ideas. This position is inapplicable to the modern "social-liberal" State, which "is epitomized by the shift from a negative to a positive legal apparatus, from one with a predominantly protective-repressive function to one designed to foster or promote the features of an ideal society."[68] The issue of distributive justice, central to modern societies, raises the all-important question of who decides the distribution and by what criteria. Bobbio distinguishes liberalism as economic theory, with its support of a market economy, from liberalism as political theory, with its emphasis on the minimal state. In identifying the main features of early liberalism, Bobbio argues:

> The dual process of formation of the liberal state can be described on the one hand as the emancipation of religious from political power (the secular state) and on the other as the emancipation of economic power from political

power (the *laissez-faire* state).... The liberal state is one which has consented   **67**
to the loss of its monopoly of ideological power by conceding civil rights,
foremost among which was the right to freedom in religion and political
opinion, and to the loss of its economic power by conceding economic
freedom, and has ended up retaining solely the monopoly of legitimate force,
whose exercise is however limited by its recognition of the rights of man and
by the various legal constraints which historically gave rise to the *Rechtsstaat*
or juridical state.[69]

Bobbio's problem is to correlate various types of freedom—economic, political, and ethical—and at this point Bobbio turns to a critique of
neoliberalism, a major obstacle to a rapprochement between democracy
and socialism through its raising of the specters of totalitarianism and
the welfare state: "The vices which were traditionally attributed to
absolute states—bureaucratization, loss of personal liberties, the waste
of resources, poor economic performance—are now attributed point by
point to governments which have adopted social democratic or labour-
style policies."[70] In fact, for the neoliberals, "capitalism is the lesser evil
because it is the system in which power is most widely dispersed and
each individual has the greatest number of alternatives."[71] Invoking
Vico's cyclical view of history, Bobbio recalls how the liberal state, originally intended to curb the excesses of princely paternalism, is now again
invoked to curb the excesses of the welfare state, the "creation not of an
enlightened despot but of democratic governments."[72] Bobbio does not
agree with the neoliberal position that the welfare state and its "excesses" are the creation of social democracy, and he points to the United
States and to Italy under the Christian Democrats as contradictions of
this position. In contrast to Negri and other writers on postmodernity, he
does not see that the benefits of such service states, states created to meet
needs of the destitute and the illiterate, must be removed; moreover, he
finds neoliberal arguments advanced by such writers as Milton Friedman to be based on a form of economics that is confused politics. "The
political market place," he suggests, "if we want to persist in using this
analogy, has superimposed itself on the economic market place, thus
correcting or corrupting it according to which way you look at it. The
basic question is thus whether it is possible to return to the economic
market place, as the neoliberals insist, without reforming the political
market place, or even abolishing it altogether. If it cannot be abolished,
at least its sphere of activity is to be reduced."[73]

The misplaced economism of neoliberalism threatens Bobbio not solely
because it attacks the welfare state but, more particularly, because it

68 endangers modern democracy. Alarmed by these threats and acknowledging the influence of John Rawls's book *A Theory of Justice*, Bobbio invites members of the "democratic Left" to entertain his idea of "a new social contract." Introducing his discussion of contractarianism, he asserts: "The crux of this debate is to see whether, starting with the same individualist conception of society and using the same institutional structures, we are able to make a counter-proposal to the theory of social contract which neoliberals want to put into operation, one which would include in its conditions a principle of distributive justice and which would hence be compatible with the theoretical and practical tradition of socialism."[74]

Contractual relations in the sphere of economics are an accepted fact, whereas this is not the case in international relations nor in "the relations between power centres which exist within the state, over which the state still formally retains the monopoly of force, but which it cannot exercise effectively, and in fact is extremely wary of exercising."[75] Contractarianism constitutes an alternative to state power for Bobbio, a recognition of "the growing ungovernability of complex societies" and also a recognition that "individuals retain, all independently of each other, a small portion of sovereign power."[76] It is in terms of a new social contract that Bobbio suggests that individuals assert their sovereignty, mandating an equal distribution of wealth. How this may be implemented, Bobbio does not suggest, but he does say: "What no one can doubt is that the solution of this problem is the awesome historical challenge which the Left is called upon to meet in a world which is ravaged by the forces of destruction."[77]

The Future of Democracy ends with the essay "The Rule of Men or the Rule of Law," which ranges from Aristotle and Plato through Hobbes, Rousseau, and Hegel to Gramsci and Max Weber. Bobbio here clearly commits himself to the notion that the rule of law is preferable to the rule of men for many reasons. And, "[T]he law comes to be understood, on the one hand, as the highest expression of the will of the sovereign, whether the prince or the people, and hence represents a break with rule based on custom, and on the other as a general, abstract norm, and as such opposed to *ad hoc* decrees."[78] This abstract norm is more conducive to notions of equality, based as it is on a general norm that "applies not just to an individual but to a class of individuals."[79]

In discussing the difficult question of the relationship between the law and freedom, Bobbio invokes the negative conception of law promulgated by liberal doctrine whereby the individual is free to "pursue his or her own ends without being prevented from doing so, except by

the equal right of others to do the same thing."[80] Positive law for Bobbio   **69**
emanates from the democratic doctrine of the state based on collective
will, the assumption that individual interests are inseparable from the
collectivity. Finally, Bobbio aligns the rule of law with democracy; for
"what is democracy other than a set of rules (the so-called rules of the
game) for the solution of conflicts without bloodshed? And what constitutes good democratic government if not rigorous respect for these
rules? I for one have no doubt about how such questions are to be
answered. And precisely because I have no doubts I can conclude in all
good conscience that democracy is the rule of law *par excellence.*"[81]

Thus it can be seen that Bobbio's arguments are also very much a personal response to his frustration over numerous lost opportunities in
Italian political life. "The present writer," he laments, "belongs to a generation of people who lost their hopes more than thirty years ago, shortly
after the end of the war, and have never recovered them except for occasional moments.... As someone who has been through many years of
frustrated hopes, I have learnt to be resigned to my impotence. I am all
the more resigned because, having lived half my life (the formative
years) under Fascism, I stubbornly persist in my belief, like most of my
contemporaries by the way, that a bad democracy (and Italy's is really
bad) is still preferable to a good dictatorship (as a dictatorship Mussolini's was certainly better than Hitler's)."[82]

As these comments reveal, Bobbio's audience is primarily Italian,
though his observations on the state of current Marxist theorizing, his
descriptions of the failures of democracy and of the "democratic Left,"
his insistence on the need for socialists to abandon technocratic and out-
moded notions of the state's political power, are exportable. Bobbio truly
strives to be responsive to the need for creating a new social base that
will empower new social movements, an issue confronting the Left in all
countries at the present moment. The terms in which he casts his proposals for reinvigorating democracy and achieving socialism often seem traditional, if not conservative, but this rhetoric is deceptive. His socialism
is not a reproduction of the technocratic socialism of Craxi and Mit-
terand. In some very important if general ways, Bobbio has not abandoned aspects of Gramscian theory, though he has modified them drasti-
cally and pragmatically to suit the present political crisis of the 1970s
and 1980s.

Bobbio's willingness to attack certain Marxist shibboleths is not dissimilar from Gramsci's willingness to tackle counterproductive interpretations of Marxism, if not actual lapses in Marx's thought. Bobbio too is
uncompromising in his critique of existing socialist practices. A sense of

70 history characterizes the writings of both Gramsci and Bobbio, along with a philosophic perspective on and a deep commitment to change, particularly under conditions that do not seem favorable to socialism. In a more personal vein, Gramsci and Bobbio both experienced Fascism. Yet their similar experiences instead led to differences in their theories and practices. Gramsci's version of Marxism signaled a different sense of democracy, a different sense of cultural change, and a different sense of ideology than Bobbio's. The differences cannot be attributed merely to different time spans, though one would suppose that Gramsci's ideas would surely have been altered had he experienced the postwar world and the political changes that Bobbio describes. A major difference resides in what Perry Anderson has described as Bobbio's "realism," which "derives from the tradition of Italian elite theorists. Although this tradition started in the saturnine guise of the conservatism of Mosca and Pareto, it moved in the next generation into the hands of moderate democrats—men such as Burzio and Salvemini, from whom Bobbio assimilated it without qualms."[83]

The flaws in Bobbio's discussions of liberalism and democracy are due not merely to his adherence to classical liberal attitudes, his inherent conservatism, and his generational affinities and experiences; they derive from the general inability of the Left to locate strategies for change that would dislodge the entrenched economic and political order. This inability is what Anderson describes as Bobbio's lack "of a special attachment to the market.... Capitalism as a system of production, as distinct from a set of injustices in distribution, is in some ways little more than a mildly referential background for Bobbio—on the whole rejected, but never analysed."[84] Bobbio's discussions of politics and social life are largely divorced from economic issues, not merely because he is not interested in economic issues, but more because he seems to feel that there is greater possibility for transformation in the cultural and political sphere at the present time. Bobbio does, however, indicate that his democratic and socialist concerns are rooted in the question of distributive justice.

Seeking a precedent for his exclusive emphasis on the superstructure, Bobbio turns to Gramsci, but in his discussion of civil life, his insistence on the importance of rules and of moral imperatives, he does not advance any notions of change concerning the question of agency. His commitment to democracy is based on description, authority, personal experience, and a taxonomy of social and political ills, but without Gramsci's corresponding concern for the very issue that Bobbio rejects — the notion of *how* to seize power. In his advocacy of liberal democracy and socialism, he argues against his own very real recognition of their present failures in the East and the West. He argues with eloquence for both; yet he fails to confront, except descriptively, the failure of social democracy. "There can be no doubt of the sincerity of his proposals," comments Anderson. "But how can such a critique be relevant to a political order which cannot even realize its own principles *within* their current limits — and not for any want of subjective will, but under the weight of irresistible objective pressures."[85]

Bobbio's position is, in fact, exemplary. His very contradictions are not uniquely his but are characteristic of current attempts to find alternatives to capitalism in the imperative interests of change. In its failures, his work constitutes a testimony to the resilience of capitalism, and his efforts to align socialism and democracy are a necessary and provocative intervention in current critical theory. Moreover, I would argue that Bobbio's work, when seen in dialogue with Gramsci's theories, can help to bring certain issues into relief. For example, in his own discussion of Gramsci's notions of common sense, José Nun challenges theories of social change that are univocal and transparent, arguing that

> a necessary condition for the search for institutional alternatives is the rethinking of the relations between social theory, political ideology and common sense[;] in giving them a materiality respectful of their relative autonomy, these institutions should facilitate "authentic transitions" which allow for their communication and confrontation.... The creation, or potentiation, of these institutional alternatives of which I speak is one of the greatest tasks of a democratic participation grounded in a logic of differences; but it is not possible to imagine in the abstract since it can acquire meaning only in the interior of a network of relations within a historically determinate society.[86]

The ongoing concern with Gramsci's work, as exemplified in Sassoon's *Gramsci's Politics*, is a testimonial to the imperative to find new alignments and new oppositional political practices that are, in Nun's terms, responsive to the need to locate meanings within "a historically determinate society" and not in the abstract. Furthermore, it is clear that, despite differences in the ways in which critics articulate Gramsci's positions, certain common concerns stand out: the need for exploration of linkages between cultural phenomena and formal politics; the interrogation of the binarism of private and public spheres, the reexamination of the role of the state; the recognition — in varying degrees — of the need to rethink questions of national, gendered, racial, ethnic, and sexual identities; and the imperative to examine notions of global mass culture

72   in relation to new forms of power that can alter existing institutional discourses and alliances. After many years of rollback and retrenchment, reconsolidation of capital, greater global capital accumulation, and more intensive forms of exploitation, critical political rethinking is more urgent than ever. For, as Félix Guattari and Toni Negri have written: "From '68 on, we have witnessed an inversion of the cycle of struggle against colonialism and underdevelopment, and some attempts at internal modernization have appeared on the part of the more dynamic sectors of the capitalist and socialist bourgeoisies. But there is a big difference between these ideological efforts—lip service, basically—and the realities of exploitation and new forms of concrete resistance."[87] Reformulating politics in the context of Gramsci's work may illuminate these "new forms of resistance."

Chapter 4

Cultural Politics and Common Sense

Embedded in Stuart Hall's appeal to "think our problems in a gramscian way" are questions about the status of Marxism at the present time and of Gramsci as an aid in reevaluating the efficacy of Marxist considerations of culture and politics. The "gramscian way" encourages a rethinking of cultural production and its relationship to conflicting positions concerning the status and effects of contemporary capitalism, the nature of "consumerism," the changing nature of social class, the position of critical work concerning gender and sexuality, and the role of critical theory and cultural studies in that process. In recent decades, the "gramscian way" has been subject to a great deal of explication and critical analysis, particularly in terms of what it has to offer as alternative notions of culture, history, power, and the constitution of the political subject in the face of challenges raised by poststructuralism and discourses of the postmodern. Although events subsequent to 1968 have produced the dissemination of critical positions expressing disaffection with prevailing conceptions of social change, including those inherited from Marxism, Gramsci's work has continued to engage students of culture, especially those who seek a détente between Marxism and poststructuralist notions of textuality.

I do not pretend in this chapter to engage with the many timely issues addressed by recent writers on Gramsci. I have a more circumscribed objective: to examine the particular issues that Gramsci raises about common sense and folklore as means for understanding the ways in which culture and politics can interact in more than purely descriptive or formalist fashion. In exploring common sense, I am especially eager to test the ways in which this common sense can be aligned with certain dimensions of poststructuralist thought as well as differentiated from it.

74   *Popular and Mass Culture*

A dominant and longstanding issue in studies of culture has concerned the nature and status of mass culture in the struggle for political and social change. As diagnosed by Andreas Huyssen, many critics theorize the relationship between culture and politics particularly in terms of an opposition between high culture and popular/mass culture with a valorizing of the former as masculine and with a denigration of the latter as feminine.[1] In this debate what has emerged is a picture of crisscrossing antagonisms and contradictions, which foreclose on any possibility of arriving at an appropriate assessment of cultural production. Instead, one is forced to choose between political salvation and damnation. For example, the view derived from the writings of Theodor Adorno on the "culture industry" offers a largely negative assessment of mass culture as affirmative, commodified, and identified with totalizing, if not fascistic, tendencies. Adorno's position persists in contemporary cultural analysis, refined and complicated in the writings of Jean-François Lyotard, for example. Opposing this view has been one that seeks to locate "authentic" cultural expression in popular and mass culture as represented by contemporary studies of popular art forms and cinema in particular. In either case, the analyses and diagnoses have tended to suffer from totalizing utopianism or dystopianism, and from divorcing cultural representation from history as well as from specific social conflicts.

Gramsci's *Notebooks*, in his various notes on common sense and folklore,[2] offer the possibility of extrapolating a more flexible theory and practice for understanding mass culture. Perhaps because Gramsci did not provide any systematic methodology, either in his preprison political and cultural writings or in his *Prison Notebooks*, for evaluating cultural production — the effects of literature, theater, journalism, and occasionally cinema — such comments require a careful extrapolation and synthesis vis à vis his comments on politics. Such effort will be rewarded by a fuller picture of the current applicability of his positions on traditional, popular, and mass culture, since his discussions of history, politics, contemporary culture, education, philosophy, and Marxism are not transposable to contemporary concerns without qualification.

In his treatment of such issues as the nature of hegemony, civil society, intellectuals, national/popular culture, the role of the state, mass society, and industrialism, Gramsci was aware of the urgency of rethinking prevailing notions of cultural politics. In fact, the notion of cultural politics as opposed to isolated studies of cultural products can be traced in part to Gramsci's struggles against Fascist and Marxist totalizing conceptions of politics. For him, culture could not be dissociated from politics nor subsumed under politics; he associated culture and politics by redefining the nature of the political through an understanding of the protean forms of "civil society" in relation to and against notions of the state. His objective seemed to be more analytical and exploratory than prescriptive. He does not begin with the assumption that culture is a reflection of social and economic life; nor does he assume that culture is autonomous. Rather than separating society from culture, his writing seems to be directed toward an investigation of the various forms of cultural expression for what they may reveal about social forms. Thus to think in Gramscian terms requires (as we shall see in the discussion of Antonio Negri's work) an attentiveness to existing social and economic structures precisely to consider, rather than to occlude, the multiple factors involved in understanding the relationship between culture and politics. In Stuart Hall's terms, "Gramsci, without neglecting other spheres of articulation, made himself, *par excellence,* the 'theorist of the political.' He gave us, as few comparable theorists have, an expanded notion of 'politics'—the rhythm, forms, antagonisms, transformations specific and peculiar to it as a region."[3]

Gramsci's writings on power constitute a middle ground between such theorists as Foucault, with his concerns for power, institutional apparatuses, and genealogical analysis, and classical Marxism, with its concerns about agency, rationalism, economic transformation, and sociological analysis. Gramsci's work acknowledges "the fact that men can become conscious of their conditions, organise to struggle against them and in fact transform them—without which no active politics can be conceived, let alone practised—[and] must not be allowed to override the awareness of the fact that, in capitalist relations, men and women are placed and positioned in relations which constitute them as agents."[4] In his concerted emphases on agency, politics, economics, and history, Gramsci's writing remains rooted in familiar and historical Marxist concerns.

The most seductive aspects of his work, which make it easier to accommodate concerns raised by poststructuralism, lie precisely in Gramsci's grappling with common sense and folklore, as structures that are as much determined as determining. His attempt to bring theory and practice into a more dynamic relationship with each other as opposed to prioritizing theoretical work or social practice provides an antidote to the abstract description and analysis that often characterize structuralist and poststructuralist practices. Gramsci's analysis and privileging of cultural issues has stood in a marginal relation to the more economistic

76 and scientistic positions of classical Marxism. Specifically in relation to culture, his work offers an alternative to the reflection theory characteristic of many of his Marxist predecessors, and resists monolithic conceptions of domination. Gramsci would not, I think, have characterized the masses in this fashion:

> This is our destiny: subject to opinion polls, information, publicity, statistics; constantly confronted with the anticipated statistical verification of our behaviour, and absorbed by this permanent refraction of our least movements, we are no longer even alienated, because for that it is necessary for the subject to be divided in itself, confronted with the other, to be contradictory. Now, where there is no other, the scene of the other, like that of politics and of society, has disappeared.[5]

In contrast to Baudrillard's totalistic appraisal of social and cultural phenomena in this postmodern conjuncture, Gramsci, because of his differing and more fragmented conception of subaltern life, offers a more dynamic, if not ultimately more optimistic, assessment of cultural and political phenomena.

Gramsci's attention to the specific components of resistance (the shifting nature of social and political alliances, the composite nature of hegemony, the focus on subaltern groups, and especially the rejection of the autonomous nature of the individual) forces him to examine how determination, agency, and accident or chance converge in multiple and uneven ways in political life and in cultural representation. Although his writings acknowledge the coercive aspects of the modern state apparatus, attention is focused on the interacting elements of civil society and on exploring those where consent is manifest or latent. But even where the Gramscian text allows that consent plays an important role in consensus, the analysis of consent is nuanced. Gramsci does not advocate a simplistic notion of agency that places the individual in a place of uncontested power or of victimage pure and simple. He was only too aware of the resistances of subaltern groups to change, of the power of institutional apparatus to deflect and contain challenges to the status quo, and of the need to study, not assume, the forms of subalternity.

Culture and Hegemony

Gramsci's elaboration on the relevance in the social and political sphere of the war of position in distinction to the war of maneuver, and his linking of these to his conception of hegemony, constitute the specific ways in which he set about challenging notions of spontaneity and determinism. His experiences with political organization under the growth of

Fascism had taught him that any analysis of social change must take into account conjunctural forces that at any given moment impede or advance organization and which necessitate differing tactics and strategies. This led him to study not only his opponents but his allies in an attempt to challenge static notions of class and group formation. Hegemony cannot be regarded as the exclusive province of a unified dominating class or, for that matter, of subaltern groups. Calculated change is impossible without an understanding of existing alliances, their constituent elements, and the contradictory nature of their formations. Hence, to regard Gramsci's writings on culture as a basis for understanding resistance in terms of ideological struggle would undermine the complexity of his view of social and cultural formations. For him, though subjects are produced "in the economics of material practices,"[6] the trick is to complicate an understanding of these practices rather than reduce them to the realm of ideology.

In Gramsci's terms, "it is a question of studying 'in depth' which elements of civil society correspond to the defensive systems in a war of position."[7] His consistent attention to the interacting of "force *and* consent, authority *and* hegemony, violence *and* civiltà" enables him to address direct and indirect forms of civil life and the relationship between domination and subalternity. Though he does not conceive subalternity in isolation from forces of domination, his work is directed toward exposing the ways in which the subaltern is not a *tabula rasa*, a blank page, upon which the structures of society are inscribed. The subaltern is not a melodramatic victim of injustice but an integral element in the overall conditions of domination and of change. In relation to critical analysis, Gramsci is wary of descriptions of cultural and political change that promulgate a "rationalist viewpoint." For example, he writes: "Critics assume that certain phenomena are destroyed as soon as they are 'realistically' explained, as if they were popular superstitions (which anyway are not destroyed either merely by being explained)."[8]

This particular comment is most relevant in the context of academic study, where cultural study is often considered an end in itself, divorced from politics: mere description of cultural phenomena is insufficient cause for change. Because Gramsci placed great emphasis on civil society, and since he saw civil society as a crucial political element in the war of position and in the forging of hegemony, he needed to evolve ways for differentiating areas of conformity as well as of resistance.[9] In order to do this, he took a different route from earlier Marxist critics, one closer to the Frankfurt school and adopted by recent French poststructuralists, in his focus on culture as a determined and determining factor

78 in the creation of consensus.[10] In the final analysis, he veers more toward the "culturalist" forms of political discourse described by Stuart Hall, which seek to bring forms of systemic analysis into a relationship with everyday experience.[11] Gramsci's analysis of culture, however, must not be construed as an unqualified endorsement of popular and mass culture. His writings on literature, theater, and cinema, his conceptions of education and of the role of intellectuals, are bolstered by a respect for erudition.

Gramsci was an adherent of a popular culture that emanates from and is addressed to "the people," what he identified as "national popular," and his work appears to make a distinction between popular and mass culture. Though he was concerned to analyze mass forms, he remained suspicious, as we shall show, of their liberatory potential. Yet in his writings it is obvious that he examined—and did not dismiss—mass culture in an effort to find traces of popular discourse, contradictory though they might be. He was also suspicious of intellectual and cultural work that made grandiose claims to produce social change. Specifically, Gramsci's notion of common sense and good sense is the linchpin in his analysis of existing and future hegemonic formations, which brings together his discussions of politics, economics, and culture. His emphasis on common sense derives from his preoccupation with the realm of everyday experience in contrast to an attention paid exclusively to the public domain. Contrary to prevailing views of common sense that regard it negatively as a practical and hence a restrictive mode of understanding phenomena, Gramsci does not interpret common sense as monolithic, mired in false judgment—a totally inaccurate and constraining conception of the world. For him, common sense is polysemic, formed of various strata from philosophy, religion, institutional practices, and individual experience. In short, common sense is a multifaceted representation of social life under determinate conditions, and in Gramsci's terms cannot be separated from notions of conformity and collectivity or from notions of resistance. "In acquiring one's conception of the world," he writes,

> one always belongs to a particular grouping which is that of all the social elements which share the same mode of thinking and acting. We are all conformists of some conformism or other, always man-in-the-mass or collective man. The question is this: of what historical type is the conformism, the mass humanity to which one belongs? When one's conception of the world is not critical and coherent but disjointed and episodic, one belongs simultaneously to a multiplicity of mass human groups. The personality is strangely composite: it contains Stone Age

elements and principles of a more advanced science, prejudices from all past phases of history at the local level and intuitions of a future philosophy which will be that of a human race united the world over. To criticise one's own conception of the world means therefore to make it a coherent unity and to raise it to the level reached by the most advanced thought in the world. It therefore also means criticism of all previous philosophy, insofar as this has left stratified deposits in popular philosophy.[12]

Common Sense as Popular Philosophy

Though common sense is contrasted to good sense, Gramsci does not set the two up as antithetical. Common sense provides the basis for good sense. To understand their relationship, one must refer to Gramsci's conception of intellectuals and philosophy. In his terms, the traditional dichotomy between worker and intellectual, mental and physical labor, is not viable:

> Although one can speak of intellectuals, one cannot speak of non-intellectuals, because non-intellectuals do not exist.... There is no human activity from which every form of intellectual participation can be excluded: *homo faber* cannot be separated from *homo sapiens*. Each man finally, outside his professional activity, carries on some form of intellectual activity, that is, he is a "philosopher," an artist, a man of taste, he participates in a particular conception of the world, has a conscious line of moral conduct, and therefore contributes to sustain a conception of the world, or to modify it, to bring into being new modes of thought.[13]

In this fashion, Gramsci challenges the traditional division of labor between mind and body, as well as reconceptualizing and complicating the nature of subaltern groups. He also steers away from notions of complete subordination or complete autonomy. For him, subaltern groups are not an indivisible bloc but are characterized by conflicting and contradictory allegiances and alliances that must be understood if change is to take place. Through his notion of the contradictoriness of common sense, he asserts that popular conceptions of the world held by subaltern groups are not simple reproductions of prevailing conditions. The philosophy of common sense is not represented in folklore, popular culture, and mass media as simply false consciousness but as a means of negotiating lived, if distorted and counterproductive, conditions endemic to one's social group. These conditions are inherited from the past, and an examination of common sense exposes disjunctions between "thought and action." The contrast between the two, he states, cannot be but the expression of profounder contrasts of a social historical order. It signifies that the social group in question may indeed have its own conception of the world, even if only embryonic; a conception which manifests itself in action, but occasionally and in flashes — when, that is, the group is acting as an organic totality. But this same group has, for reasons of submission and intellectual subordination, adopted a conception which is not its own but is borrowed from another group; and it affirms this conception verbally and believes itself to be following it, because this is the conception which it follows in "normal times" — that is when its conduct is not independent and autonomous, but submissive and subordinate. Hence the reason why philosophy cannot be divorced from politics.[14]

Here, Gramsci orchestrates two concerns: the need to link an analysis of common sense as philosophy to specific social groups rather than treating dominant social articulations in the abstract; and the need to disarticulate the common-sense representations in an attempt to identify the particular strands of their composition. His emphasis on the notion of borrowing, the assimilation by subaltern groups of certain attitudes from other more dominant social groups, is integral to understanding his conception of "submission and intellectual subordination." What Gramsci suggests is that the philosophy of the subaltern needs to be traced in terms of these borrowings, to locate their sources and their particular deployment, particularly to identify and expose how they produce and maintain consent. This notion of borrowing is particularly relevant to the notion of consent, which is not to be construed as either a mere voluntary assent to the status quo or mere mechanistic assimilation of attitudes. Borrowing must be understood in more complex terms, a subtle system involving survival, exchange of services, and uncritical adherence to tradition on the part of the subaltern expressed through the various representations of the family, work, leisure, gender, and sexuality.

A common-sense exploration of cultural texts then would take into account the ways in which past modes of thinking are derived from popular historical narratives, folklore, religious practices, and familial formations. These traditional elements coexist with modern formations and continue to play roles in making the world appear reasonable and expedient to individuals and groups whose interests might be better served by challenging these structures. In talking about the neophobia of common sense, Gramsci neither valorizes nor rejects the new in language, since he is much more interested in locating where and how change and resistance to change can be identified. Therefore, it is as important to examine the neophobic aspects of common sense — its resistance to new words and new concepts — as markers of resistance to change as it is to

identify the entrance of new elements as possible signs of where emer- **81**
gent elements (to use Raymond Williams's terminology) are expressed.[15]

Just as culture cannot be considered apart from existing social and
political practices, so too common sense cannot be regarded in isolation.
Rather it is connected to the "world of experience and practical activity
and a militant repudiation of the Enlightenment glorification of science."[16] The term "experience" is crucial here, and any attempt to come
to terms with Gramsci's cultural politics must take into account the distinct ways in which his work seeks to redefine and grapple with the
importance of experience in relation to common sense. Experience does
not reside solely in the individual's affective and subjective relation to
the world but, as suggested earlier, must be seen as located in the interplay and hegemony of cultural formations. By stressing the notion of
common sense as a form of philosophy, the "folklore of philosophy,"
Gramsci was granting it a different status than had been accorded to it in
the past.

In his notion of popular understanding and action, Gramsci challenged the rationalist conception of common sense. "The rationalist tradition," comments José Nun, "had defined common sense negatively, as
uncultivated, vulgar thought and in contrast to the real activity of reason
which was given the task of overcoming it."[17] Conversely, Gramsci rejected the glorification of common sense as a mere pragmatic activity,
seeing this view as vulgar and ideologically complicit with conservatism. Steering a path through these extremes that suggest either elitism or unreflective populism, he sought to develop a critique of common
sense that would acknowledge its efficacy as well as its limits. Given his
concern with the experiences of subaltern groups it was necessary to
develop a less totalized sense of language practices: one that would
attempt to approximate the contradictory position of the masses and
identify spaces that permit a theorization of resistance.

"Common sense," then, in his terms is not rational, critical, ideologically coherent, or systematic. It is akin to "poetic logic," as outlined by
Vico, "distinct from—but in no way inferior or subordinate to—'rational logic.'"[18] By contrast, "good sense" or philosophy, according to
Gramsci, involves the effort to

> order in a systematic, coherent and critical fashion one's own intuitions of life
> and the world, and to determine exactly what is to be understood by the
> word "systematic," so that it is not taken in the pedantic and academic sense.
> But this elaboration must be, and can only be, performed in the context of the
> history of philosophy, for it is this history which shows how thought has
> been elaborated over the centuries and what a collective effort has gone into

the creation of our present method of thought which has subsumed and absorbed all this past history, including all its follies and mistakes.[19]

There is no doubt here that Gramsci does not elevate common sense to the same level as good sense or that good sense is preferable to common sense, but he is positing a link between the two, seeing good sense as derived from yet addressing the limitations of common sense. Where Gramsci and contemporary critical theory depart from each other most decisively is not in this concern with deconstructing common sense but in the rationalist cast to Gramsci's notion of good sense. Gramsci's position on good sense is neither simple nor reductive. The relationship between common sense and good sense suggests that the movement toward good sense is provisional and not absolute. Given Gramsci's intertwining of the two, the priority for study must be accorded to common sense, since that is the locus of conflict, conformity, and resistance.

The work of the philosophy of praxis entails attention to the features of common sense in their various expressive forms and a particular focus on isolating those elements that offer verbal clues to the split between practical and theoretical awareness. Like other seeming binaries in Gramsci, one sees that these opposed elements are in fact not distinct but interrelated and interactive. "Critical understanding of self," Gramsci says, takes place therefore "through a struggle of political 'hegemonies' and of opposing directions, first in the ethical field and then in that of politics proper, in order to arrive at the working out at a higher level of one's conception of reality. Consciousness of being part of a particular hegemonic force (that is to say, political consciousness) is the first stage towards a further progressive self-consciousness in which theory and practice will finally be one."[20]

Gramsci's Marxism

In his elaboration of such critical and political consciousness, Gramsci explores, as did Lenin, the importance of the party in the formation of a socialist culture and society, but with different effects. Gramsci's conception of the party is closely linked to his notions of hegemony, the creation of organic intellectuals, and the role of the socialist state. In particular, Gramsci's treatment of the party and of intellectuals is less elitist and hierarchical than Lenin's, more concerned with addressing the issue of developing and integrating intellectuals into every aspect of social life. While I recognize the importance of Gramsci's conceptions of the party for education, organization, and class realignments, I choose to bypass this side of Gramsci and to focus on those elements that speak more directly to new types of knowledge and social organization. In so doing, I run the risk of falsifying the historical Gramsci and particularly of falling into culturalism, but, as Stuart Hall has suggested, "the gramscian way" entails rethinking Gramsci's work in the context of contemporary political and economic conditions and their representations.

Certain aspects of Gramsci's work run parallel in many ways with the work of Marxist structuralism: its emphasis on the importance of ideology, of identifying determinants in the construction of human subjectivity; its concern with language as a social text; its focus on the formative dimension of civil apparatus; and especially its concern to identify the element of consent among subaltern groups. The work of poststructuralism has, I think, been most helpful in reviving the important political and cultural aspects of Gramsci's thought. In its concern with power, its assault on constituted hierarchies, and its exploration and critique of transcendental theories of subjectivity, Gramsci's work has affinities in the broadest terms with the work of such writers as Foucault and Derrida. Like these writers, Gramsci does not reproduce familiar cultural analysis that attempts to unify and totalize contradictory and complicated aspects of culture.

Gramsci's notion of politics comes closer to recent formulations than is characteristic of traditional Marxist thinkers. "Gramsci understands that politics is a much expanded field," writes Stuart Hall. Therefore, Hall concludes that

> especially [in] societies of our kind, the sites on which power is constructed will be enormously varied.... Where Gramsci departs from classical versions of Marxism is that he does not think that politics is an arena which simply *reflects* already unified collective political identities, already constituted forms of struggle.... Politics for him ... is where forces and relations, in the economy, in society, in culture, have to be actively worked on to produce particular forms of power, forms of domination. This is the production of politics — politics as a production.[21]

In this analysis of the "politics of production," the domain of common sense has been most neglected by many critics until recently, rejected perhaps because of its less systematic and "unscientific" nature, or perhaps because of the protean and elusive nature of Gramsci's concept of hegemony. The importance of stressing common sense resides in the ways this concept confounds traditional notions of subalternity, power, agency, melodramatic affect, and of ideology as false consciousness.

Gramsci's contribution to altering classical notions of Marxism — an alteration Bobbio traces to Gramsci's Crocean legacy — is the role that Gramsci assigns to civil society:

> The unique position that civil society occupies in Gramsci's conceptual system causes not one, but two reversals as regards the traditional, scholastic interpretation of the thought of Marx and Engels: the first consists in his according primacy to the superstructure over the base; the second consists in the primacy given, within the superstructure itself, to the ideological factor over the institutional factor.[22]

Moreover, Bobbio argues that within these reversals are other dichotomies — between necessity and freedom and between force and consent. In all these cases, Gramsci attempts to extricate Marxist thought from both cultural and economic determinism. He also seeks to locate a conception of agency that views behavior as the product of determinate and determining conditions while acknowledging areas of potential autonomy.

The National Popular

In his historical analyses of Italian history and in particular his analysis of Fascism, Gramsci might be considered a maverick. He resisted interpreting Fascism as the inevitable outcome of force on the part of the industrial classes. He avoided too a mystical or psychoanalytic account that might portray Fascism as the outcome of modernity and madness. But he also refused to blame the passivity of its victims as evidenced by their failure to produce a needed economic, political, and social revolution. In fact, he recognized that a revolution had indeed occurred, and he attempted to locate the conjunctural elements that produced the particular combination of coercion and consent that seemed to characterize Italian Fascism. In order to do this, he had to steer clear of rigidly economistic interpretations while not ignoring the impact of industrial and capitalist development. He had to also take into account the interactive dimensions between culture and modernization. His rethinking of questions concerning the relation of coercion and consent in the formation of Fascist hegemony had led him, even before his incarceration, to examine specific cultural institutions such as the church, the schools, and business, and the roles that these institutions play in any understanding of hegemony as cultural and political. In the *Notebooks*, especially in "Americanism and Fordism," he tackled changes that had taken and were taking place in European culture, especially convergences between industrialism and sexual politics.

In his explorations on the "national/popular" he was able to identify the multiple social, economic, and cultural conditions that converged in Italian Fascism. In accounting for the disunity of Italian politics, he was also accounting for the failure of the Left to offer an alternative to regional, class, generational, and cultural conflicts. His concept of the national/popular is tied to specific aspects of Italian history from the Renaissance to the Risorgimento. His is not a nationalistic concern. Rather, his emphasis on the national and the popular constitutes an investigation — often comparative with other nation-states, such as France — into the culture to discover why such conditions did not develop in Italy.

His discussion of the national popular is particularly cogent in the context of recent reevaluations concerning nation formation and national identity. But his dispersed comments in the *Notebooks* seem to be more descriptive, analytic, and exploratory than rigidly prescriptive. In his examination of Italian unification as developed during the Risorgimento and pursued under Fascism, he is less concerned to produce a polemic in the interests of establishing the positive dimensions of nationalism than to distinguish existing constructions of national discourses based on a severing of the national from the popular. In particular, he elaborates on the multifaceted aspects of nation formation in relation to the changing roles of the state and civil society under conditions of what he terms "passive revolution." From the case of Italy he derives a model which enables him to describe how it is possible to have a revolution from above. In this form of "passive revolution," a new hegemony is created whereby the class interests of the aspiring bourgeoisie are allied with traditional ruling classes rather than with the people. This form of the nation-state, through consent and coercion and in the name of the nation, is able to thwart popular aspirations and to frustrate revolution from below. Gramsci is also cognizant of the need to provide a complex political and cultural account for the weakness of subaltern groups. His discussion of the impedances to the creation of a national popular hegemony thus serves as a means for him to examine how common sense, folklore, the role of intellectuals, and the forms of cultural production are inextricably fused with economic and class interests — not merely their underpinnings. It is obvious from his notes on literary and popular novels, the theater, cinema, and journalism that what animates those comments is the need to explore (not interpret) cultural representation within the context of specific historic conjunctures and in relation to Ital-

86 ian culture specifically and European culture more generally for what they reveal about the production of consent.[23]

Gramsci does not give us a biographical study of an individual novelist, nor a close textual reading of any specific work. These representations are not for him reflections of existing social conditions but are themselves a social text active in shaping attitudes. For example, in "Father Bresciani's Progeny," he focuses on the "prehistory" of this literary phenomenon, its expression in a number of other Catholic novelists prior to and after Antonio Bresciani (1798—1862). Not interested in judging whether the novels are aesthetically good or bad, not reducing them to being merely politically regressive or progressive, Gramsci situates the writing in an exploration of types of Italian intellectuals. The writers under consideration are examined by Gramsci from the vantage point of their relation to a national-popular literature: their positions in relation to a number of different genres and to a wide range of thematics and stylistics. His brief discussions are exemplary of his preoccupation with identifying common-sense elements. Of his research, he says, it is "into a history of culture and not literary history; or rather it is into literary history as a part or an aspect of a broader history of culture."[24]

It is in this exploration of the "broader history of culture" that Gramsci finds the nature of folklore, and through his discussion of folklore he returns again to a discussion of common sense. As he writes, " 'common sense' is the folklore of philosophy and always stands midway between folklore proper (folklore as it is normally understood) and the philosophy, science, and economics of the scientists. Common sense creates the folklore of the future, a relatively rigidified phase of popular culture in a given time and place."[25] The notion of folklore in Gramsci, like that of common sense, has extended beyond its customary academic sense as a particular form of popular oral representation. Like Gramsci's expanded notion of common sense, folklore is not the property of one class, but it is part of the thinking of all classes and is "the document of its historical reality." It is not necessarily the document of "good sense" but it does seem, in Gramsci's terms, to represent reigning social discourses.

In contrast to academic notions of folklore that entail ethnographic techniques—methods of collecting, selecting, and classifying material—Gramsci's conception insists that

> folklore should instead be studied as "a conception of the world and life" implicit to a large extent in determinate (in time and space) strata of society and in opposition (also for the most part implicit, mechanical, and objective) to "official" conceptions of the world (or in a broader sense, the conceptions

of the cultured parts of historically determinate societies) that have succeeded one another in the historical process. (Hence the strict relationship between folklore and "common sense," which is philosophical folklore).[26]

These statements provide the clearest parallels between folklore and common sense. It is evident that the two work in similar fashion. Both are unsystematic, composite, contradictory, and above all, share the quality of containing "fragments of all the conceptions of the world and of life that have succeeded one another in history."[27] Gramsci's insistence on the historical elements in folklore seems to run counter to studies of folklore as ethnography that focus on the timeless and ahistorical character of narratives and reinforce the tendency to resist change through an uncritical attachment to past experience.

Taking folklore seriously involves rethinking traditional modes of cultural study. For example, in talking about popular music, Gramsci finds that there are different ways of dividing such music: "1) songs composed by and for the people; 2) those composed for the people but not by the people; 3) those written neither by the people nor for the people, but which the people adopt because they conform to their ways of thinking and feeling."[28] Of these categories, borrowed from a contemporary critic, Gramsci selects the third as subsuming the other two. This category is especially useful when talking about mass culture, since so much of what is produced is in fact not for the people but is assimilated by them. Gramsci's concern here is with the dynamic and functional nature of these works, and even more with the ways in which it is possible to disarticulate their traditional, residual, and emergent elements. Rather than regarding them as manipulative, inauthentic, or vulgar, he sees them as presenting "numerous and variously combined cultural stratifications."

In his quest for works that strive toward a national/popular culture, a culture that articulates the "needs, aspirations, and feelings" of the people,[29] Gramsci interrogates groups of texts, from Pirandello's works to adventure novels and serials. His discussions of these works, which run parallel to his comments on folklore and common sense, are fragmentary.[30] According to Forgacs and Nowell Smith, "Gramsci, writing in prison, could only tentatively sketch out in these notes different strata reflecting the intervention of different and discontinuous histories in different and regional areas."[31] In other words, Gramsci did not have a unitary sense of the composition of popular literature: his method of mapping popular taste in this way was not to produce a static picture but rather to explore the relations between dominant and subaltern cultural forms in dynamic terms, as they act upon each other historically. Just as

88 folklore contains the sediments of earlier dominant cultures that have seeped down into subaltern cultures, so Gramsci sees in the popular literature of rural areas residues of earlier dominant literary forms (such as "romances" of chivalry) and scientific conceptions of the world. By a converse process, he sees popular cultural forms being "raised" into the dominant "artistic" literature.[32]

Gramsci's comments on folklore, common sense, and popular literature address issues that have been especially important in the contemporary debate about "high" and "low" culture by such critics as Fredric Jameson, Andreas Huyssens, Tania Modleski, and others, who have sought to expose the traditional disjunctions between canonical and marginalized cultural productions. Gramsci's work suggests a context for such considerations. He too does not see that high and popular culture stand in irrevocable opposition to each other. Rather, high and popular culture are intimately connected in complex ways. Just as popular literature contains elements of earlier and dominant forms, so too popular forms are absorbed into dominant forms. Moreover, in late capitalism, distinctions between dominant and popular forms have become blurred.

In this vein, Fredric Jameson has written that

> we must rethink the opposition high culture / mass culture in such a way that the emphasis on evaluation to which it has traditionally given rise and which—however the binary system of values operates (mass culture is popular and thus more authentic than high culture, high culture is autonomous and therefore utterly incomparable to a degraded mass culture)—tends to function in some timeless realm of absolute aesthetic judgment, is replaced by a genuinely historical and dialectical approach to these phenomena. Such an approach demands that we read high and mass culture as objectively related and dialectically interdependent phenomena, as twin and inseparable forms of the fission of aesthetic production under late capitalism.[33]

Jameson's position seems to extend Gramsci's concern not only to foreground the question of popular or mass culture but to situate it within a historical perspective in order to allow for a more adequate understanding of its regressive as well as its potentially utopian elements. Also, by introducing historical considerations, Jameson invites more complex considerations of the centrality of cultural texts in any political analysis. By historicizing the relations between modernism and mass art, for example, Jameson suggested that new forms of evaluation cannot depend on formalist analysis alone. The practice of "reading against the grain," while seeking to attribute to hitherto marginalized mass works, especially film, an expression of resistance, if not of opposition, seems constrained to working within the formal text and also within limited intertextual relationships, reading the social text as exclusionary in relation to other social formations. Jameson's proposal here seems closer to the Gramscian way of situating texts within more specific and contradictory social and historical considerations.

In the recent study of popular and mass culture in literature, cinema, and, most recently, television, critics have attempted to create an adequate methodology for understanding mass culture's production and reception. In the past, the work of the Russian Formalists, the New Critics in England and America, the Surrealists, the Futurists, the Constructivists, the Frankfurt school, even Fascist and Nazi propaganda, were attempts both positively and negatively to address or exploit the politics of mass society. Until the 1960s, mass cultural study in the universities was largely one of contempt or benign neglect. The post-World War II era in Europe, however, especially among cineastes, was to provide a major impetus to reconsiderations of mass culture. The artists and critics associated with the French New Wave, with their emphasis on the role of the auteur, and their attempts to identify the personal element in mass art as opposed to its impersonal qualities, marked a significant moment in reexamining the nature and impact of forms of mass-cultural representation. If auteur analysis often selected as its object works that had heretofore been considered vulgar and escapist, the method of auteur criticism was largely focused on locating high cultural techniques in the works of mass culture. The auteurist tendency to reread these works in the light of certain modernist considerations, especially estrangement and reflexivity, while downplaying aspects of commercial cinema, was consonant with attempts to create a more flexible and politically responsive form of cinema.

Since that time, due in part to the increasing influence of writers such as Roland Barthes as well as other poststructuralist and feminist critics, the nature and modes of analysis have changed in favor of more intensive analyses of mass culture on its own terms, terms that pay particular attention to questions of sexual difference, genre analysis, modes of production, and questions of reception. In particular, the auteur theory of cinema has undergone several revisions to allow for the recognition of conditions of production beyond the individual stylist, including the roles of specific studios, producers, stars, and writers, and extending to an examination of all the "tie-ins" that are part of the production and consumption of mass texts. The study of genre has also moved away

90   from an exclusive preoccupation with the auteur, and away from the rigid and often ahistorical analysis of structuralism: an analysis using neoformalist explorations of binary structures and static and reductive conceptions of a work's psychic or economic components.

Gramsci's writings on common sense are germane to the attempt to forge new and more responsible readings of cinema and literature. For example, his examination of such writers as Pirandello, Bresciani, Manzoni, and others situates literary works in relation to issues of philosophic, national, and historical import, seeking precisely those qualities that are indicative of the workings of common sense and folklore. What this means specifically is that Gramsci does not judge and reject contradictory aspects of a work nor seek unifying principles. His search for contradictions and also for areas of popular concern does not permit this kind of discussion. To identify common-sense elements does not mean to establish their truth or falsity, since, as he has noted, common sense is "an ambiguous, contradictory, and multiform concept.... To refer to common sense as a confirmation of truth is nonsense."[34] But to refer to common sense as a struggle is not. Moreover, since neophobia is a crucial element in common sense, a sign of resistance to change, it is in need of elaboration. Hence, it is important to identify those places where antipathy to new attitudes expresses itself. Understanding the resistance to change is fundamental to the reading of a work in any attempt to understand the perseverance of traditional attitudes. Thus, Gramsci's valorization of common sense runs parallel with developing criteria that can better illuminate signs of change and resistance to change.

Along these lines, recent studies of mass culture have focused on cultural forms not formerly sanctioned by the literary and artistic tradition—westerns, melodramas, and romances in popular literature and in cinema, radio, television, sports, and fashion. Linked to the study of semiotics, mass cultural scholarship has undertaken the challenge to understand the nature of the "postmodern" condition. And the point of view in the treatment of popular genres has ranged from the purely descriptive and dispassionate to a virulent criticism of the society of spectacle. The major intersection, though, among recent critics of popular and mass culture has been the need to interrogate the realism/illusion opposition in the analysis of representation. The works of Roland Barthes and Michel Foucault, for example, have been influential in undermining the sense of a text as a seamless unity and as a "reflection of reality," or conversely, as a distortion of the real. As a play of more than one voice, as the work of a collective "author" rather than a unique and totally autonomous producer, and therefore as a locus of contradictions, this

form of reading has questioned the designs and interests that texts have 91
on their audiences as well as the ways in which audiences might receive
the text. The predilection for the modernist text and the emphasis on
"dialogic" and polyphonic discourse has been applied to "classic realist"
and popular forms alike, and critics of mass culture have found new
readings possible for texts that had previously been regarded as monolithic and regressive.

The work of Mikhail Bakhtin has also become important in this search
for modes of reading texts in more heterogeneous fashion.[35] Parody, representations of the grotesque body, and images of the world turned
upside down are important in Bakhtin's reading of literature. His linking
of these phenomena to social life and to the ways in which language
reveals the interplay both between the literary and the social and between high and low culture are particularly relevant, as is the way literature marks existing class and social conflicts. Bakhtin's enterprise can be
compared to Gramsci's efforts better to distinguish the polysemic elements that compose common sense. Bakhtin's conception of heteroglos-
sia bears a resemblance to Gramsci's description of common sense (also
dependent on a concern with linguistics) as composite, fragmentary, historically eclectic, and heterogeneous.

In *The Dialogic Imagination,* Bakhtin remarks that

> the centripetal forces of the life of language, embodied in a "unitary
> language," operate in the midst of heteroglossia. At any given moment of its
> evaluation, language is stratified not only into linguistic dialects in the strict
> sense of the word (according to formal, especially phonetic, linguistic
> markers), but also — and for us the essential point — into languages that are
> socio-ideological: languages of social groups, "professional" and "generic"
> languages of generations and so forth.[36]

Gramscian common sense too, as we have noted, can be identified by its
heteroglossic nature, its residues, its competing and contradictory voices.
While Gramscian common sense is aimed at locating the complexity of
popular discourses, however, important differences emerge between his
work and Bakhtin's. These differences may be due in part to the cryptic
and elliptical nature of Gramsci's prison writings and even more, perhaps, to a lack of his working out of relationships between written and
oral texts. Gramsci emphasizes written more than oral language, revealing a tendency to slight the everyday dimension of language. Gramsci's
notions of culture remain dependent on a concept of culture derived
from the traditional socialist thinking that shaped his early cultural-
political formation. For socialists of his generation, "culture" largely

meant the literature and education that the working class were to make their own, wresting it from the hands of the bourgeoisie.

The affirmative political impulse behind this concept of culture conceals serious limitations that Gramsci never entirely overcame. Though his concept of culture became richer and fuller, it retained uncritical residues of its original bias toward the written word as the core of cultural formation in individuals and society.[37] While it is true, as David Forgacs and Geoffrey Nowell-Smith state, that the emerging forms of radio and cinema receive minimal attention in the *Notebooks,* and while it is also true that Gramsci remained suspicious of these mass cultural forms, his discussions of common sense and folklore can be extrapolated and applied to mass cultural production. In contrast to Bakhtin, Gramsci's analysis of literary form maintains a consistent dual perspective toward literary and social history. Most important, in contrast to Bakhtin, Gramsci complicates the notion of the popular, making it less exclusively the province of subaltern groups, in an attempt to differentiate populist from popular conceptions of resistance and counterhegemony, as his analysis of Manzoni's Catholic populism indicates.

Forms of Mass Culture

Though in rudimentary and scattered fashion Gramsci attempts to address the increasing sway of cinema, especially in relation to literature, to the cultural role of the diva, and to the issue of sexual difference, he does not, like Walter Benjamin or Theodor Adorno, accord the media a predominant position in his discussion of popular and mass culture. He shares with more traditional Marxists (and with Benedetto Croce) a predilection for more unified, intellectual, and "elevating" works. At the same time, he indicates in his criticism of literature and in particular in his discussion of Tolstoy's and George Bernard Shaw's criticism of writers in moral terms, that their criticism is "cultural," and that "the conception of the world implicit in their works is narrow and impoverished, not national/popular but that of a closed caste. The study of the beauty of a work is made subordinate to the study of why it is read, 'popular,' 'sought after,' or, in the opposite case, why it does not touch the people or arouse their interest, showing up the lack of unity in the cultural life of the nation."[38] These comments reveal the importance for Gramsci of finding ways to understand better the production and reception of literary texts. The comments also reveal a rejection of aesthetic criteria as the prevailing measure of cultural value. These comments on literature need to be aligned more closely with his notes on common sense in order to invite a reading that opens up the question of cultural exchange value — produced by whom, for whom, and in whose interests. Moreover, in the above passage Gramsci once again acknowledges the existence of popular elements in traditional literature, though they are often present in distorted fashion, just as he recognizes the elements of fantasy that pervade popular literature.

In the context of contemporary theories on gender that acknowledge the importance of pyschosexual analysis, Gramsci's comments on psychology are also in need of elaboration, particularly as they relate to sexual discourses. Gramsci understood that, among the many elements that comprise common sense, new sexual practices were becoming increasingly prominent as indices of social, political, and economic changes. For example, in discussing the "sexual question" in "Americanism and Fordism," he states that

> sexual instincts are those that have undergone the greatest degree of repression from society in the course of its development. Regulation of sexual instincts, because of the contradiction it creates and the perversions attributed to it, seems particularly "unnatural." Hence the frequency of appeals to "nature" in this area. "Psychoanalytical" literature is also a kind of criticism of the regulation of sexual instincts in a form which recalls the Enlightenment, as in its creation of a new myth of the "savage" on a sexual basis (including relations between parents and children).[39]

In this brief allusion to psychoanalysis, Gramsci seems to be referring to several familiar concepts: that an analysis of mass cultural phenomena cannot be considered apart from changing sexual practices, and, even more, in a vein anticipatory of Foucault, that discourses on sexuality are an important element in the regulation, manipulation, and control of civil life. In particular, Gramsci cites the family and reproduction as having an integral bearing on ideology, affecting questions of population and notions of "feminine personality" as well as of "masculinism." He questions the directions that the "regulation" of sexual life have taken, producing new conceptions of "sex as sport" and the woman as "dolly" or "brood mare." In the upper classes, he describes women as being transformed into "luxury mammals." Moreover, "beauty competitions, competitions for new film actresses (recall the 30,000 Italian girls who sent photographs of themselves in bathing costumes to Fox in 1926), the theatre, etc., all of which select the feminine beauty of the world and put it up for auction"[40] are further indications of the transformations and commodifications of social life in terms of creating further divisions and diversions along class and sexual lines. Since, as he states, "The forma-

94 tion of a new feminine personality is the most important question of an ethical and civil order connected with the sexual question,"[41] the problematic of sexuality remains a major one in modern society, producing contradictions among the upper classes as well as for subaltern groups. The implications of Gramsci's comments are that there can be no critical examination of sexuality in isolation from questions of reproduction, leisure, work, the family, cultural institutions, and mass culture with woman as spectacle within it.

In discussing the serial novel, another mass literary form, Gramsci again refers to psychoanalysis. He finds that "the serial novel takes the place of (and at the same time favours) the fantasizing of the common people; it is a real way of day-dreaming. One can refer to what Freud and the psychoanalysts say about day-dreams. In this case, one could say that the day-dreams of the people are dependent on a (social) 'inferiority complex.' This is why they day-dream at length about revenge and about punishing those responsible for the evils they have endured."[42] Gramsci's comments echo the conventional view of popular literature as the narcotic of the people, but if one looks more closely his use of the term "real" in describing daydreaming suggests Louis Althusser's discussion of ideology as a "lived but imaginary" construct. Moreover, in his allusion to Freud's conception of daydreams, Gramsci invokes the sense (along with his references to fantasies of revenge and punishment) that daydreams are not mere escape mechanisms but bear a complex relation to people's needs and aspirations. His discussion of folklore as a mosaic of tradition and various conceptions of life can be expanded to include—along with religion, biological conceptions, ethical injunctions—these "social day-dreams."

In the context of poststructuralist activity, which has insisted on the impersonality of the creator, on the nonseamless nature of texts, and on textuality extending beyond individual texts to social life generally, Gramsci's work on folklore, common sense, and popular literature cannot be dismissed. His various commentaries on individual texts, genres, and literary groups reveal that he was not concerned, even where he discussed individual writers, to treat those writers as examples of individual inspiration and autonomy. He describes their work as the effect of particular conjunctures involving history, the status of language, and the relation of cultural products to certain already existing conceptions of the world that are perceived to be natural and inevitable unless examined carefully to identify their contradictory nature.

Gramsci's brief comments on sexuality also validate his concern for a complex understanding of social forces, but always in the context of a

specific social and historical conjuncture. The point of intersection between Gramsci's cultural concerns and recent psychoanalytic work resides in his recognition that questions of pleasure and desire are essential ingredients in any attempt to understand the interaction between
politics and culture. As Terry Eagleton has suggested, in language reminiscent of Gramsci's, "We live in a society which on the one hand pres-
surizes us into the pursuit of instant gratification and on the other hand
imposes in whole sectors of the population an endless deferral of fulfill-
ment. The spheres of economic, political and cultural life become 'eroti-
cized,' thronged with seductive commodities and flashy images, while
the sexual relationships ... grow diseased and disturbed."[43] Thus it is
incumbent, especially in an age of wide dissemination of media representation and the pleasure that it offers, to be able to understand and not
only denature but also decompose the elements providing clues to the
different and contradictory ways in which texts work on their audiences
to promote the sense of gratification and, at the same time, defer any
gratification.

The need to find better modes of describing and situating the role of
mass culture becomes an imperative one, affecting any understanding of
the role of intellectuals in the academy, of the work of dissenting intellectuals and artists, of the nature of media programming in relation to
notions of "reality," and of the character of consumerism on a national
and global scale. The descriptions of the consumer society that occupy a
central place in the work of Lyotard, Baudrillard, and others are only
inaugural in Gramsci's work, due in large part to the Fordist moment of
capital in which he lived. Gramsci's comments on sexuality as spectacle,
however, suggest that he had an incipient awareness of the emergence of
new forms of exchange and their importance for understanding mass
culture and modernity. Furthermore, like contemporary critics, Gramsci
explores these issues in the context of questions of power, and like Foucault particularly, he does not see power as an overarching monolithic
phenomenon but as a matter of dispersal among different centers, requiring an analysis of various and dispersed discursive formations.

Gramsci's conception of hegemony as formed of various strata in
society, including various subaltern groups, is opposed to traditional
(and common-sense) notions of power as exercised univalently and
coercively by the few controllers of wealth in conjunction with heredi-
tary and newly created aristocracies. Hegemony implies, in James Joll's
terms, that "a political class ... had succeeded in persuading the other
classes of society to accept its own moral, political, and cultural values."[44] Hegemony entails a strong component of persuasion as opposed

to the use of force (although force is never totally ruled out). In creating new structures, hegemony entails the attraction through compromise of groups who can align themselves with subaltern aims. The element of consent then plays a central role in this process, and this is where, in contemporary terms, the study of culture becomes crucial in identifying the ways in which the reigning hegemony has succeeded in persuading subaltern groups of an identity of interests, and also in identifying areas where hegemony is, in fact, fragile and untenable.

In this context, Gramsci's notions of common sense and folklore are especially appropriate for identifying the hybrid and political nature of mass cultural texts as they negotiate issues of family, nation, gender, race, and property, both through consensus and through exposing the contradictory nature of that consensus. The Centre for Contemporary Cultural Studies in Birmingham, England, has been most active in exploring the applicability of Gramsci's work for the study of popular texts. In their study of popular forms of literature, critics at the Centre write that

> initially striking similarities between romances and thrillers we were reading and Gramsci's characterization of common sense ... suggested that the two might fruitfully be brought together. First, popular female romances are characteristically formed from an amalgam of modern and pre-capitalist elements. The simplified characterization, the withdrawal from society on the part of the reader and the romance heroine, the happy ending, the strongly enforced code of conduct are all continuing formal elements of romance as a genre which predates capitalist society. Second, Gramsci points to an analysis of "spontaneous philosophy," language determined by, and carrying the signs of culture, and not just words grammatically devoid of content.... Third, the persistent moralizing of popular fiction suggests a relation to the *content* of common sense—for example, true love never runs smoothly, money can't buy you happiness (but it helps). Last, and more tentatively, there may be a similarity between Gramsci's definition of popular religion as a more systematic fragment of common sense, providing "a unity of faith" between a conception of the world and corresponding norms of conduct, and the work of narrative form in popular fiction.[45]

This extended description of Gramsci's concept of common sense and folklore and its relation to popular literature captures several key elements in his definition of common sense—its stylization; its withdrawal into fantasy and yet its contact with immediate modes of survival; its ethical implications; its selective ties to religion; and its focus on familial, sexual, and economic matters. In its folkloric aspects, common sense retains magical qualities, popular psychology, science, and proverbial lore and wisdom. Though a popular work can be identified by its formal elements, as the quotation above indicates, common sense is a collage in form and content, containing elements of past narrative modes grafted onto more contemporary representations. In short, it is not merely archaic and purely conventional. Its treatment of time is equally contradictory. Ill-assorted beliefs and magical formulas mingle with everyday contingencies. The past is anastomosed onto the present. The proverbial language is double-edged. It seeks to rehearse clichés that serve to create a sense of continuity and control over contingency while at the same time acknowledging the futility of the formulas in the face of basically insoluble dilemmas (despite the ubiquitous happy endings).

The stylized treatment of "character" and of plots often inherited also from folklore clashes with the contemporary representation of agents and events, thus calling attention — as do clichés — to disjunctions between fantasy and everyday experience. The conventional everywhere jostles against the mundane, and raises the question of whether audiences are so mired in folklore that they cannot perceive these disjunctions, thus returning us to the judgment that mass culture is essentially manipulative, and that the audience is in the position of hapless victim. Gramsci's notion of common sense would seem to acknowledge a different conception of audiences, one that sees them being as composite as the texts that they experience. From a Gramscian position, such questions as whether audiences are totally unaware of commercial "tie-ins" and are mere consumers of fashion, popular music, and social values, or whether they are totally cynical about representations, need to be contextualized and seen in terms of more complicated notions of reception.

The dichotomy between total absorption and totalizing forms of opposition would not seem to be consonant with Gramsci's cultural politics. As workers at the Centre for Contemporary Cultural Studies state, "popular culture is not oppositional in any simple way"[46] any more than it is totally affirmative, in the Frankfurt school sense of mass culture as affirmative. What needs to be examined, therefore, is the connection between cultural representations and everyday experience. In other words, "the clichés of everyday life cannot be considered in isolation from everyday utterances." They are "spoken daily as part of the lived experience of women and men within different class structures, different age groups, and different familial positions, and they have a range of connotations depending in part on when and by whom the magic words are uttered."[47]

But the problem still remains of establishing these connections in ways that are not reductive, that do not valorize the notion of individual

98   or group experience as an end in itself. For this reason, the workers at the Centre have insisted that the notion of popular culture cannot merely be regarded as ideology, common sense, or subaltern experience. Rather, popular literature must be seen as occupying a "contested space between highly developed ideologies, common sense, and women's lived experience."[48] It is precisely the sense of what is meant by "contested space" that becomes important. Rather than regarding utterances in a fixed context situated between total affirmation and total negation, the concept of common sense only has efficacy if it can be seen, in Gramsci's context, as an intersection of various conflicting positions.

The notion of contestation suggests that the pastiche of common sense with its various appropriations of bits and pieces from religion, science, proverbs, folklore, magic, and history is potentially dynamic and accessible to analysis. It is clear too that the study of common sense need not be confined to literary texts but can be, and has been, extended to other popular forms—music, cinema, and television. Not only do the different contexts for these articulations, their different modes of reception, their specific audiences, and especially their relations to the minority culture need to be studied, but these media issues need to be related to broader developments within the larger culture and the various groups composing that culture. Most particularly, the practice of isolating texts for study from the contexts in which they are produced and consumed inhibits an understanding of the meaning or possibilities of "contested space." Cultural politics in the Gramscian sense would remain aloof from narrowly construed conceptions of textual study, as it would from the strategy of polarizing political positions around notions of pure liberation and pure domination. This cultural politics would pay attention to locating and analyzing those moments of "good sense" embedded in common-sense discourses as a sounder basis for understanding the limits and possibilities of social transformation.

Chapter 5

They Were Sisters: *Common Sense, World War II, and the Woman's Film*

> "There are millions of families like us.... God's in his heaven, all's right with the world."
>
> *They Were Sisters*

A fundamental feature of mass cultural forms is their dependence on melodrama, and the basis of melodrama is common sense and folklore. Melodrama and common sense are almost synonymous. Though studied as a genre, melodrama has been claimed by critics such as Peter Brooks[1] to be a dominant form of cultural expression, deserving serious analysis. In its excessive affect, Manicheanism, obsession with justice, and fixation on victimage and verbal and physical violence, melodrama addresses every conceivable form of social antagonism. Gay and lesbian critics acknowledge the cultural importance of melodrama in their writigs on sexuality.[2] Feminist critics in recent years have studied popular melodramatic forms for insights into cultural representations of and by women.[3] Feminist theory, particularly that on the woman's film, a subgenre of melodrama, has addressed women's representation within prevailing distinctions between private and public spheres. The private sphere has been theorized as the arena of woman; the public as the arena of man. Unlike action genres — westerns, thrillers, crime films — that focus on the social order and subordinate the domestic sphere, the woman's film (like the family melodrama) is preoccupied with familial conflicts, troubled gender formations, and problematic sexual relationships.

The woman's film has become an important genre in its dramatization of conflicts involving women: mother-daughter, mother-son, and marital relations, and the tension between conformity and rebellion. In

100 particular, critical readings of the woman's film have sought to challenge the ways in which gender and sexual relations are replicated as natural and inevitable. Moreover, analyses of these melodramas suggest that the films are indicative of a crisis in social relations and are telltale indicators of a displacement from the public onto the private sphere. The conflicts presented, particularly as they involve issues of gender identity, are symptomatic of profound tensions in sexuality, tensions inextricably tied to social formations and not merely to psychic formations. The persisting binarism of private and public spheres as reproduced by much cultural analysis reveals how critical discourses function to valorize this distinction rather than to acknowledge the various and dynamic ways the two spheres are linked, and the differing class positions and resultant political agendas involved in maintaining such a distinction. Any binary division between private and public spheres that links the "public" sphere to action and adventure and the private sphere to domesticity as social order tends to efface the ways in which constructions of the family and of gendered and sexual identities are inseparable from discourses involving questions of nation, race, and class. Through its deployment of affective strategies, its uses of familiar folk narratives that produce a sense of familiarity with character and situation, and its dependence on juridical and medical discourses, melodrama relies on every conceivable form of social and political discourse, though often not in direct fashion and, as such, offers evidence to the contradictory nature of the binaries it relies on as well as clues to the complex nature of consent.

A common-sense reading of melodrama offers an opportunity to reassess the workings of mass culture: especially to rethink traditional formulations of gender and sexuality, and of private and public spheres, within the debates concerning representations of women. A Gramscian reading is particularly compatible with questions of genre as a means of describing and analyzing the ways in which subaltern life is represented and circulated throughout the culture. Effectively synthesizing discourses of politics, economics, and production and reproduction from the Gramscian perspective of common sense, the study of mass cultural forms is not simply a matter of exposing dominant discourses but of uncovering how these discourses are composed of heterogeneous elements that strive for a sense of unity and the overwhelming of differences. Mass cultural representations speak not only to constraints on women, how through representation women are fixed within patriarchy, but to the specific and contradictory ways these representations are constituted.

It was through a study of genres that critics began to take seriously the possibility that genre texts were not as vacuous and impervious to social analysis as had previously been claimed. The study of film melodrama has profited from this work. By exploring stylistic excesses as indicative of fundamental disjunctions in narrative structure and style in melodrama, critics such as Laura Mulvey, Thomas Elsaesser, and Geoffrey Nowell-Smith sought to locate signs of psychosocial conflict, indications of "trouble in the text," symptomatic of bourgeois ideology and its discontents.[4] The focus on the family further opened the possibility of more intense focus on women's representation. Yet there is no consensus concerning the ideological impact of these films. For some critics they can be read as "progressive"; for others they represent yet another instance of woman's objectification and commodification. In Gramsci's discussion of sexuality in "Americanism and Fordism," the figure of woman signifies one of the intersecting determinations that compose cultural value and exchange; his observations on the "woman question," however, debated by Gramsci critics who want to align his work with the feminist project, are yet to be elaborated.

Although traditional "woman's work" was earlier dismissed as outside the network of exchange value, an analysis of affective value that questions reproduction, woman's work in the home, familial relations, and woman's sexuality has become central for any understanding of the woman's film. According to Christine Gledhill, the cultural analysis of popular texts "emerges around gender, as concerns critical value, genre (the relation of the woman's film to melodrama) and representation (where melodrama's investment in woman as patriarchal symbol conflicts with the usual space it offers to female protagonists and women's concerns)."[5] The multifaceted nature of melodrama—its ties to bourgeois ideology, its ties to Hollywood and mass culture, its status as a genre or as a world view, its "specializing in heterosexual and family relations, its uses by, for, and against women"[6]—offers a context for the critical questions that this chapter addresses. How is the woman's film exemplary of common-sense forms of representation? What light does common sense shed on how, for whom, and to what ends consensus functions?

In *From Reverence to Rape*, Molly Haskell was one of the first critics to call attention to the critical significance of this genre, especially prominent in the pre-World War II cinema, and to discuss at length its specific

102 cogency for an understanding of representations of woman.[7] She did not invent the term "woman's film." The term was employed by the movie industry and, along with other genre designations, circulated through the culture at large. Haskell's discussions of these woman's films, however, added a new and critical dimension to the term. She used the films to expose the constraints on women's position in society and in the cinema through her identification of the varying types of female figures present in these films and the situations into which they were set. She recognized that in its representation of women—its use of female stars, its foregrounding of female characters, and its thematics—the woman's film stands in a different relation to other Hollywood genres. Haskell saw the films as revealing cultural stereotypes and reproducing certain middle-class biases.

Following Haskell's lead, feminist critics have developed further generic distinctions between the woman's film and the family melodrama for the purposes of delving more fully into how the woman's film, in contrast to the family melodrama, provides an opportunity to identify a female voice or, in a Gramscian sense, the traces of a polysemic common sense, a folkloric discourse relating to women. For example, Linda Williams's study of Vidor's *Stella Dallas* (1937) and Tania Modleski's study of Hitchcock's *Rebecca* (1940) attempt to expose the contradictory elements central to the woman's film.[8] Incorporating textual analysis, psychoanalysis, popular literature, and film, and focusing through the lens of audience identification, these two studies demonstrate how the woman's film, despite its apparent phantasmatic character, has access to everyday female experience. Their attention to issues of female identity, self-representation, choice of love objects, sibling relationships, and mother-child relations as well as to the domestic landscape, fashion, and issues of health and illness attest to the commercial cinema's engagement with woman's quotidian experience in common-sense fashion.

Too often, analyses of cultural texts have served in binary fashion to denigrate everyday experience, privileging instead the extraordinary, the ahistorical, and the exotic. Injecting the notion of common sense into an examination of cultural production introduces historical considerations, and places them in a dialogue with archaic and mythic aspects of experience that might otherwise have been privileged to the detriment of specific historical and social practices. In their concern to identify gender difference in women's representation in literature and cinema, feminist critics have turned to psychoanalysis to expose the ways the female reader/spectator is placed in subjection to patriarchal discourse, and thus the ways in which the culture reproduces itself.

The issue of female spectatorship has been central to feminist film   **103**
theory, and specifically to the work on film melodrama—tied closely to
male Oedipal conflict, to phallocentrism, and to aggressive forms of control through the power of the gaze. This critical work has posited a
monadic and passive position for the female viewer. Though this form of
theorizing has permitted a double analysis—of the subject positioning
of the spectator, and of the various textual strategies through which difference is inscribed in the unconscious—the theory has been based on
conceptions of preformation of the subject, the atemporal dimensions of
subjectivity, and, above all, a scenario that does not admit of resistance
so much as projection, displacement, and a host of symptoms that are
clues to the repression of women's experience. In Jane Gaines's words,
however,

> Recent psychoanalytic theory hypothesizes that all conventional language
> and pictorial representation is male-biased, for reasons rooted in the
> psychology of infantile sexuality. To understand the dominant cinema as
> thoroughly voyeuristic and to identify all sexual representation of women
> within it as phallic substitutes implies a definite political analysis. If even
> everyday viewing is organized along these lines, with patriarchal power
> relations being reproduced in every depiction of a woman on a magazine
> page or billboard, then we are all ideological captives.[9]

Paradoxically, the very attempt to understand the nature of women's
representation and to remove it from the realm of determinism leads to
another form of totalizing that works against the possibility of understanding the complexity, heterogeneity, and dynamic dimensions of
existing discourses. Just as behavior cannot be reduced solely to economic factors, so too it cannot be reduced to psychoanalytic discourse,
itself a form of cultural common sense.

Common Sense in Melodrama

Nothing escapes the operations of common sense and, hence, there is a
need to account for what common sense is and how it works. Given its
incoherent nature and its antirationalist cast, common sense offers a way
of locating the intersection between fantasy and everyday experience.
For example, the excesses characteristic of melodramatic style are often
derided as "escapist" and as remote from any consideration of "real life"
and "history," but they are charged with significance for gender and sexual representation. The language of melodrama as the language of the
disenfranchised appears "unrealistic" from the vantage point of the dom-

104   inant discourse. Because access to language and overt power on the part
of the subaltern is restricted, marginalized, and often reduced to covert
forms of articulation, it has been necessary to look to culturally derided
forms to see if there one can find traces of a subaltern voice. For example, although "domestic space" may constitute an "unreal" landscape
for hostile critics, it offers feminist critics a way of locating cultural information on women and femininity. According to Christine Gledhill and
Gillian Swanson, "Dramatisation of the domestic sphere offers more
space to feminine values, and by insisting on a playing through rather
than evasion of the Oedipal issues for the hero, uses the counter-desires
of women to foster different styles of masculinity, and to temper the
expression of patriarchal authority, redirecting its goals toward more
integrated objectives."[10]

   Tania Modleski and Charlotte Brunsdon have argued that the
woman's film of the 1940s, like the melodramas of the 1950s — and much
like the soap opera with its multiple plot lines and diffused perspectival
positions, its focus on maternal figures, its blatantly contrived and temporary closures — offers complex instances not only of female socialization and sexual repression but of antagonism and resistance to prevailing norms, even though resistance might end in failure. Thus in
common-sense terms the films contain the residue of traditional forms of
experience geared toward personal and group survival strategies, but
they also contain information about the constraints of these accommodations and hence about the potential for change that can be unleashed
through education and critical awareness. Though common sense may
appear to approximate a unified conception of the world, when subjected to critical analysis its contradictory elements become obvious. Not
rational, it is akin to "poetic logic," a mode of experience often denigrated
in opposition to rational thought, and composed of affections, moral
insights, and values. The domain of common sense is "practical action,
guided by interests; and, as a consequence, its chief governing criterion
is pragmatic, relating to everyday interactions and to collective patterns
of thought and action."[11]

   Although melodrama has been traced to theatrical and novelistic
sources, less has been done with its connections to folklore or oral storytelling. The common sense of the woman's film can be seen to depend on
the strategies of folklore in its narrative structures, treatment of character, and use of images. Like folklore, the films provide a very tenuous
sense of history. Time is measured through personal recollection (often
flashback) and typically enacted through rituals (marriage, anniver-
saries, and funerals). Through verbal and visual clichés, the texts depend

on commonly shared knowledge and commonly held assumptions about life. That the very solutions of the posited narrative conflicts in the films are frequently doomed to failure only reinforces the common-sense notion of inevitability and a confirmation of the familiar truism, "Expect the worst." The films rely on proverbial wisdom and forms of magical thinking as defenses against unwanted contingency. In this respect, like popular culture generally, the films utilize strategies akin to storytelling rather than novelizing. For this reason, they embody a question that has been central to feminist theory: Is woman outside language or merely outside male language?

World War II and Gainsborough Films

When read in the context of the language of common sense, it might be possible to see the films as speaking to and for women, even if not authored by them.[12] The Gainsborough melodramas produced in Britain during World War II and immediately after are exemplary of films that sought a female audience. The narratives were meant to directly or indirectly address conflicts germane to women during the war years and immediately thereafter. Pam Cook has argued that "any discussion of the Gainsborough women's pictures in terms of the way they discuss femininity to appeal to a female audience should recognize the historical specificity of this female audience as British and wartime or immediately post-war."[13] Cook cites such contemporary conditions as the wartime need for women's labor, the creation of child-care facilities enabling women to work outside the home, the falling birth rate, and the threats to family unity created by conscription, greater mobility, and the existence of a somewhat more permissive sexual climate that favored fleeting heterosexual relationships.[14]

The films produced during the war were an important factor in articulating and affirming the quasi-populist, potentially "progressive" aspects of war against its more destabilizing dimensions. The films express the necessity of maintaining a sense of the importance of maternal functions and recognize threats to traditional domestic institutions. The dual sense of the films as operating within traditional parameters of class and gender discourse while allowing for changes occasioned by contemporary exigency characterizes a good deal of commercial films during the war.[15] British films of this period present a contradictory treatment of class and gender akin to that presented by Michael Renov in his description of the double bind in which women in the United States during World War II found themselves.[16] After the war, although there was a

106 concerted effort to recuperate women's domestic role, the efforts in that direction did not totally succeed. Pam Cook argues that "the idea of the emancipated 'free' woman, monogamous but active, dedicated to self-help and capable of fighting for what she wanted was important to post-war democratic ideals of a better world for everyone."[17]

The high point of Gainsborough popularity occurred during the war years and for a short time immediately thereafter. The popularity of these films was indicative of social factors specific to the times and of the character of commercial film production. These films, like Hollywood films of the same era, were addressed to a large female audience; hence it is not surprising that they relied on female authors, placed female actors in prominent roles, and chose domestic conflicts as their central preoccupation. The Gainsborough costume cycles were an important cultural intervention in the representation of women and, unlike so much of British film production of both the 1930s and 1950s, constituted an indigenous contribution to the history of cinema. The films probe fundamental patriarchal structures, frequently situating at least one of the female protagonists in a role adversarial to conventional domestic positions.

Often set in an earlier historical context, the films appeared to bear no connection to everyday life. Reviewers of the time described them as "escapist" vehicles. As one critic of the 1940s railed, "By all means let us escape on the wings of the movies to less troubled epochs than the present.... But for the Lord's sake let's evoke it properly.... In short, if the future of the British film industry hangs, as some say, on the success of *The Wicked Lady*, then let us dispense with that future."[18] Not all of the critics found the melodramas inane and unrealistic. Some acknowledged these films to be a sign that the British film had reached maturity; but few were able to locate the ways in which the films touched important facets of British culture.

A penchant for realism coupled with a condescension, if not distaste, for genre films and hence for the popular cinema played a role in the inability on the part of British critics — not of British or even U.S. audiences — to appreciate the Gainsborough films' impact. Even more, the films' address of women's issues and sexual politics may have played a role in the critics' unwillingness to seriously contend with the films. The tendency to denigrate highly stylized forms of representation in the post-World War II era, with its emphasis on neorealism and social problem films, was also responsible for the lack of critical seriousness about the woman's film on the part of critics and reviewers. Few of the comments on the films reveal that there was any attempt to explore the social basis for the widespread popularity of the films. In its attempts to reexamine neglected texts, to probe them for the information they can yield about women's position within cultural representation, feminist film criticism has awakened interest in the social, historical, and psychological importance of these works.

Responding to the trivializing of these films and to the charges of escapism and lack of "realism," Sue Harper finds that "visual style at Gainsborough until the advent of Box in late 1946 ... presented the historical past as a site of sensual pleasure; it was neither regular or linear, nor 'closed.' "[19] Through examining the visual language of the film—the historical settings, the costumes, the intricate hairdos—Harper indicates how the films are able to distance the spectator from history—namely, by using historical artifacts and set decoration in an eclectic fashion.[20] In this way, the films' refusal to create a sense of "actual" historical context serves to accent psychological conflicts and the issue of sexuality, and enables the spectator to appropriate events as contemporary to the viewer.

The decor of the films—their eccentric use of historical detail—is designed to evoke female pleasure and desire. According to Harper, "Contemporary analogies are clearly being drawn in the area of sexual pleasures, and richness of 'decor' is, by implication, supernumerary when compared with the 'richness' of desire."[21] The focus, then, of such films as *The Wicked Lady* and *Madonna of the Seven Moons* is not only on male desire but, as the nuances of style indicate, specifically on female desire. Despite their conventional endings and the narratives' marginalization of threatening female positions, the films expose psychic and social conflicts touching many aspects of women's experience. The presence of women at various stages of the production process may account in large part for the woman-centered concerns of these films. Many were based on novels written by female writers: *The Man in Grey* (1943) and *Caravan* (1946) were derived from Lady Eleanor Smith's popular novels; *They Were Sisters* (1945) was based on a novel by Dorothy Whipple; *Madonna of the Seven Moons* (1944) was based on a novel by Margery Lawrence; and Magdalen King-Hall wrote the novel that inspired *The Wicked Lady* (1946).

The staff at Gainsborough Studios boasted women in decision-making positions. Muriel Box was responsible for selecting scripts to be filmed. She also directed films in the post-World War II period that featured women and women's issues. Of the films she was involved in at Gainsborough, she has said, "During our period at Gainsborough, we made a programme of films, not politically oriented but nevertheless sympathetic, we hoped, to the problems facing people in everyday life and the

108 way we dealt with them."[22] In addition, Betty E. Box was a producer for many of the films, having served her apprenticeship as a documentary filmmaker in the 1930s and later as director of Islington Studios. Although both women are modest about their roles at Gainsborough, there is no doubt that they were influential in shaping the nature of Gainsborough production.

The most popular and commercially profitable Gainsborough films were the costume melodramas. These films are not identified primarily with the director but with the studio, though many of them were made by a handful of competent directors such as Leslie Arliss, Arthur Crabtree, Compton Bennett, and David Macdonald. The Gainsborough style was heavily dependent on set designers who were able to provide the requisite spectacle. The actors were also a significant factor in the films' style and popularity. As Robert Murphy writes, "The success of the films was heavily dependent on the stars Black and Ostrer had managed to build up at Gainsborough: Margaret Lockwood, Phyllis Calvert, James Mason, Stewart Granger, with Jean Kent, Pat Roc, Dulcie Gray as able second stringers."[23]

The popularity of the films was due in large part to successful typecasting. Lockwood, for example, was most often cast as the dark seductress, the déclassé, if not lower-class, female who stops at nothing to gain her goals. Sue Aspinall discusses how "the screen persona of Margaret Lockwood added strength to the case for immoral behavior. Her early film roles had already typecast her as smart, opinionated, and bitchy. In both *The Man in Grey* and *The Wicked Lady*, her energy and determination to get what she wants are central sources of the pleasure offered by these films."[24] In contrast, Phyllis Calvert usually played the role of the repressed upper-class woman, representing marriage and domestic responsibility. The class opposition between the women represents the opposition between different expressions of female desire: the upperclass women were sexually restrained, whereas their lower-class counterparts were associated with sexual and often adulterous passion.

The men were similarly polarized in these films and represented differing class and sexual attitudes. James Mason played the aristocratic male, sexually powerful, bored, unscrupulous, and even violently aggressive; Stewart Granger was cast as the gentlemanly rescuer, gentle, adoring, and compliant to the woman's demands. In short, there was no attempt to individuate or complicate the characters who were familiar in this type of melodramatic narrative. Rather, the films drew on a repertoire of male and female figures who served as codings of individual and collective aspirations. They formed part of the common-sense montage in which everyday survival and desire are superimposed. The stars themselves represented the intersection between the ordinary and the extraordinary, the commonplace and the fantastic, and, as such, contributed to complicating the spectator's responses to the figures represented on the screen.

They Were Sisters

One of the extremely popular Gainsborough woman's films of the 1940s was *They Were Sisters.* The narrative of the film is loosely constructed, initially involving vignettes of the three sisters' courtships and then their departure from the paternal home. The next episodes dramatize their contrasting marital situations, leading to the death of one, the humbling of another, and the successful accommodations to family life of the third. This loose, quasi-soap opera structure allows for the leisurely development of the women's relationships to their father, to their husbands and children, and to each other. This film is exemplary for doing a common-sense reading of a cultural text. The film reveals how a popular text enacts an uncritical but adaptive mode of thinking based on what Gramsci designated as folklore. According to him, "The language of melodrama is folkloric." ("[É] folkloristico il linguaggio melodrammatico.")[25] Folklore, with its reliance on anachronism, provincialism, and excessive affect, is an important basis for common-sense thinking, though not its sole basis. If we recall that common sense (as opposed to good sense) is "disjointed and episodic," a collage of ideas and images, of inherited conceptions from folklore, philosophy, science, and from official history, we can see the film as relying on ill-assorted conjunctions from both the past and the present. Although the film's dependence on common sense is "ambiguous, contradictory, and multiform,"[26] an examination of its strategies reveals that its reliance on common sense is not static but constantly shifting according to changing historical exigencies. In these respects, *They Were Sisters,* although a woman's film produced during World War II, is a broadly representative text, providing a test case for understanding the ways history is constructed in and circulated through popular texts.

Although costume melodramas were among the most popular films at Gainsborough, the studio also produced woman's films set in contemporary contexts. For example, though *They Were Sisters* (1944) abandons the conventional trappings of the historical film genre, especially those of the "biopic," it does not eliminate many of the stylistic and thematic preoccupations of the costume drama—especially its romance and

110 sometimes gothic elements.[27] Nor does *They Were Sisters* attempt to create "authentic" locales. Although situated in a contemporary context—
as indicated generally by the modern dress of the characters, the presence of automobiles, and the allusions to current social practices
concerning law, medicine, psychiatry, and business—the treatment of
conflict, setting, and dialogue is indeterminate.

Most particularly, the style of *They Were Sisters* is consonant with the
costume films along the lines of folkloric representation. Visually and in
terms of narrative construction, the film polarizes character, creates class
oppositions, and juxtaposes different conceptions of sexuality and gender identification. Although the setting evokes an apparently familiar
world, the presentation of the houses, the garden, and the landscape are
as unspecified as are the Restoration and Victorian settings in the costume films. The film makes little attempt to conjure up a specific sense of
place to create the specificity of everyday life in the manner of a "realistic" representation. This cavalier and even anachronistic treatment of
setting fuels, at least in part, the derision for the woman's film. Yet the
vagueness of the mise en scène displaces attention onto character and
affect. This haziness of setting also blurs the lines between rural and
urban life by making the world appear more phantasmatic and by recall-
ing the pastoral world of earlier literature and drama—the world of the
folktale. Exterior landscapes—gardens, streams, the seashore—and the
interiors of houses are sparse; pieces of furniture, paintings, and drapery
are sufficient to convey a sense of the environment. The economy of
detail suffices to divert attention from the mundane and distracting
aspects of domestic life and to focus on the psychosexual conflicts of the
characters. Place functions to highlight the excessive and transgressive
aspects common to many woman's films: rituals of passage from adoles-
cence to maturity; competition and conflict among women; affliction,
sacrifice, and marital conflict; and maternal issues—all in the context of
the significance of the sisters' relationships to each other.

The film's potential contribution to the critical literature on the
woman's film resides in the thematic of sisters, and it is in this thematic
that the film is most dependent on folklore. Though much work has
been done recently on the maternal melodrama, there has been much
less attention paid to female sibling relationships.[28] Along the lines of
folklore and consonant with the binarism of melodrama, the representation of sisters is usually schematic: good sister / bad sister—with the
"bad" sister eliminated from the narrative, as in the case of such films as
the British version of *A Stolen Life* (1938). Similarly, in *They Were Sisters*,
the narrative is, as in folklore and in the fairy tale, highly dependent

on schematization, on a fracturing of character through doubling and tripling, symmetrical and oppositional structuring of characters and events through parallelism and antithesis. Three female characters are pitted against each other and pitted against or matched with three male characters. Each of the models represents different psychic and class characteristics.

As is so often the case in narratives that involve the splitting of attributes among the female characters, the father figure is present, but the mother is banished without explanation and presumed dead. In fact, her existence is scarcely mentioned. The narrative is preoccupied with the sisters' relationship to each other after the father too disappears into the shadowy background when the women acquire husbands. Through the schematizing of the three female protagonists and their husbands, the film establishes the similarities as well as the differences in the characters' relations to patriarchy. As with the polarities of the fairy tale, each couple configures a particular expression of monogamous heterosexual relationships that differentiates it from the others. As the narrative progresses, the sets of couples are evidently hierarchialized, according to traditional values of service and familial and conjugal duty. But, in the fashion of common sense, the film accommodates to the rhetorical changes concerning women and marriage introduced during the war. The fracturing of the characters can also be considered emblematic of a general decentering of character in wartime cinema, and of a more general fracture of female ego and splintering of the world characteristic of women's situation. The folkloric splitting of character is also characteristic of a common-sense investment in comparison and contrast, sameness and difference, ultimately for exclusionary purposes.

Frequently, romances emphasize the conversion of the male figure from a position of cruelty, arrogance, and domination to one of gentleness. In the case of *They Were Sisters*, the strategy of splitting male characters serves a similar function, which Tania Modleski describes: "the phenomenon of the 'splitting of the male' in female literature has been little noted in feminist critical writings.... Feminists (as well as traditional psychoanalysts) have frequently cited the male tendency to divide women into opposing and unreconcilable classes: the 'spiritualized' mother and the whore. But there is also a corresponding tendency in women to divide men into two classes: the omnipotent, domineering, aloof male, and the gentle, but passive and fairly ineffectual male."[29] Taken together, the sets of male and female characters evoke the numerology and symbolism of folklore, signifying unity and conjuring up a magical, supernatural world in which the audience can measure its

112 own desires against everyday experiences. The film's treatment of time also resembles folklore in its indeterminacy. The schematization of the narrative appears, as in the fairy tale and romance, to invite a sense of déjà vu, interrupted from time to time by a reminder of the present.

Considered in the context of folklore and common sense, the woman's film suggests a relationship between woman's language and the oral tale as characterized by Walter Benjamin.[30] In the final analysis, the narratives address practical experiences—illness, familial antagonisms, and conflict with other social institutions—in spite of their highly patterned style. The film language of *They Were Sisters* is formulaic, characterized by a paratactic narration in which all events seem to carry equal importance. The formulaic qualities are not only a form of genre shorthand but are indicative of the existence of a common fund of information, common conflicts, and shared strategies of survival, on which the film relies. As much recent analysis of romances and woman's films suggests, the film takes on a number of narrative burdens relating to women, the family, power, and sexuality. *They Were Sisters* is concerned simultaneously with courtship, separation from the parental home, marital struggle, maternal-child conflict, and sexual desire and repression. What distinguishes it from other woman's films is its treatment of these issues in the context of the sisters' relationships to each other.

The narrative, like the presentation of character and setting, is also fractured, split into two sections. The first part of the film involves the period of courtship and the marriages of the three sisters, through which the different characteristic of each of the sisters emerges; the second part treats the consequences of their choices of husbands. Clearly, their choices are circumscribed: to marry or not marry; to marry out of desire, social necessity, or lack of an alternative; to marry an aggressive and domineering male figure, a shadowy and ambiguous male, or an unthreatening fraternal companion.

Vera (Anne Crawford), the eldest, is the least romantic of the three, the one who seeks to maintain her independence. Inclined toward promiscuity and scornful of marriage and romantic love, she finally marries Brian (Barrie Livesey) although admitting to him that she does not love him. In contrast, Charlotte (Dulcie Gray), the most passionate of the three and the most romantic, is totally devoted to Geoff (James Mason). Completely captivated by his commanding and arbitrary treatment of her, she is deaf to her sisters' entreaties to guard herself against him. Lucy (Phyllis Calvert) occupies a middle position between the sisters. In summary, Charlotte is portrayed as the archetypally afflicted female:

enslaved to feeling and verbally inarticulate; Vera is the archetypal "liberated" woman: devoid of passion (until she meets her male nemesis) and controlling. Lucy is presented as the mean between these extremes.

This schematization is reinforced through the dress codes of the film. Vera is a fashion victim. Her clothing distinguishes her from her sisters and identifies her with modernity, with her flouting of traditional notions of courtship and marriage. In the mirror shots of her, the film underscores her preoccupation with her appearance. Charlotte, the youngest, is clothed in soft and clinging dresses that call attention to her body and identify her with traditional conceptions of femininity. Of the three sisters' costumes, hers are subject to the greatest change. Eventually, she appears in dowdy and nondescript clothes that express her self-devaluation and her retreat into physical symptoms. Both sisters' appearances are indexes to their refusal to mediate social conventions. By contrast, Lucy, the film's pivotal figure, wears plain suits and dresses without much jewelry: clothing that is not calculated like Vera's to be fashionable or like Charlotte's to call attention to her body. Though there are numerous allusions to fashion (including the film's opening, which presents a montage of fashion images from contemporary magazines), the emphasis on dress underlines a number of issues orchestrated in familiar common-sense fashion throughout the narrative: women's place in the home, connections between family and national identity, the conflict between tradition and modernity, the position of women as desiring subjects and desired objects, the ambiguous nature of female identity, and the threat of female sexuality.

The house, a central image in the woman's film (and particularly in Gothic films featuring women in distress) is also an index to the characters' differing positions, the ways they are split, within the narrative. Vera's modern and spacious house is filled with flowers and furniture. The dining room is never shown, nor is any space represented as belonging to her husband, Brian. The shots are primarily of her own bedroom, as if to emphasize her narcissism, her distaste for and physical separation from her husband, and her preoccupation with sexual intrigue. Charlotte's house is old-fashioned, dark, and heavily wainscoted; space in it appears to be controlled by Geoff's presence. The bedroom is never shown; only the living room and study, and a bare, unidentified room, possibly an attic room, where Charlotte sits alone, are evident. The setting emphasizes her alienation from family. In neither house is there a place where the family congregates, in contrast to Lucy's house, where the living room, dining room, and even bedroom become gathering

114 places for William (Murray Hill), Lucy, the visiting sisters and their children. Lucy's house, like her clothing, attests to her maternal role.

Devoted to her father and her sisters, a figure of service, Lucy appears to be the standard-bearer of "natural" and "normal" sexual and familial relations, the one who upholds family values. She is the figure who attempts to keep the sisters together as a family by seeking to protect Charlotte from Geoff's brutality and urging Vera to support her in her defense of Charlotte. According to Pam Cook, "A number of ideals of social health are set up ... among them the ideal family (no more than four children), the ideal mother (active) and father (tolerant), the ideal house (large enough to contain an array of attractive consumer goods and a maid), and the ideal relationship (heterosexual monogamy)." In the contradictory and revealing strategies associated with common sense, the work of the film seems not to legitimate these values but to "seriously undermine their value as social propaganda."[31]

The third sister is the character who most undermines the "social propaganda." Charlotte is a figure of excess. Dulcie Gray as the tormented Charlotte is the least physically attractive of the three. She is the one who changes most physically and psychically during the course of the film. Although in many other films she would be dismissed or ridiculed as a grotesque and pathetic doormat, in this film she assumes an importance far beyond her well-adjusted or defiant and cynical sisters. She is the carrier of otherness, the abject figure who embodies the desires of the others (if not also displaced negative sexual qualities often associated with working-class characters) that cannot be admitted in the film's project of establishing a modest readjustment of female subjection.

An object of Vera's scorn and Lucy's pity, Charlotte marries a man who is contemptuous of her. Vera describes Charlotte as "the kind that likes a man to wipe the floor with her." Her sisters warn her against Geoff, but she is adamant in her attachment to him. Her relationship to him is presented through scenes that portray Vera's or Charlotte's perspectives, Lucy's life as counterpoint, and Geoff's mockery or manipulation of her. Charlotte is the only one of the sisters who gives herself over wholeheartedly to desire, in ways that can only lead to her self-destruction. Her attachment to Geoff is immoderate and obsessive. Although the narrative punishes her excessiveness, it dramatizes her relationship to her body and to her husband most fully, in contrast to Vera and Lucy.

Charlotte is a striking example of the woman whose history is visible on her body for all to witness. Slight, nervous, halting of speech, and constantly ill with headaches and eventually alcoholic addiction, she is, like the heroines of Thorold Dickinson's and George Cukor's *Gaslight* (1939 and 1944 respectively), fused with her tormentor. Her husband describes her as a "sick headache." At first on his own initiative, later by enlisting his eldest daughter, Geoff plays games with Charlotte: separating her from the children by mocking her in their presence, undermining her competence, and roughly rejecting her physically. When she is at the point of leaving, he reverses himself and seduces her into remaining. Charlotte's drinking only becomes an opportunity to deride and isolate her until she retires to an unfurnished room where she stays and drinks until Lucy intervenes.

Charlotte's husband, Geoff, is also a figure of excess. Unlike the other two husbands, he is a social climber. His marriage to Charlotte is portrayed as a vulgar effort on his part to better his situation. He is cruel and sadistic toward her and his younger children as distinct from his eldest, using her when it suits his purposes and then casting her away. He is crass and zealous on behalf of making money, in contrast to the more genteel men that Vera and Lucy married. Neither James Mason's nor Dulcie Gray's portrayal is subtle. They both present distillations in grotesque form of the socially threatening effects of female desire and the ways in which sexual power relationships are structured through denial and aggression. The more Charlotte seeks to achieve intimacy with her husband, the more he abuses, humiliates, and rejects her. He refuses her the comfort of her sisters, and when she seeks to escape his control, he offers the affection he had formerly denied her, only to begin the cycle of abuse again. The excessiveness in portrayal does not permit any normalization of the sadism inherent in Geoff's and Charlotte's relations but underscores the undeniable failure of an ethos of subordination and dominance. Gray's abject character does not admit of unadulterated sympathy on the part of the spectator any more than does Mason's boorish portrayal of Geoff. Their situation, set off as it were in italics, calls attention to the impossibility of accommodation to destructive heterosexual relationships.

Charlotte is the incarnation of middle-class ideals of femininity, the "angel in the house" celebrated in Victorian mythology and in the pre-World War II British cinema. Her father describes her as "so like her mother, dear girl," and, like the absent mother, she represents the survival of archaic forms of female behavior, the residual element in contemporary society. Her final refusal to succumb yet once more to Geoff's humiliating treatment of her leads her to run out of the house (on the anniversary of her wedding) where she is killed by an oncoming auto-

116   mobile. Her death fulfills the narrative necessity of eliminating what she represents and constitutes a narrative judgment about her mode of existence as degraded. The ambiguity of her demise, whether it was the result of an accident or suicide, is consonant with the film's resistance to delving deeply into "explanations" for the characters' behavior.

In terms of the triadic relations of the characters, with the death of Charlotte one mode of excess is eliminated from the text: the channeling of female desire into total subordination to the male and the subsequent drama of annihilation. Of her death, Lucy says, "All that power she had for loving ... wasted." Yet this is not the whole story concerning Charlotte. She is the locus of the film's contradictions concerning female desire. In a sense, Charlotte's hysteria, her physical and psychic symptoms, is a masquerade of femininity in extremis. Through her figure more than those of her sisters, the spectator is made aware of the complexity of women's desire and its distortion under patriarchy. Unlike her two sisters, Charlotte confronts the spectator with the horror of denied desire, a horror that is not mitigated by finding a proper husband, the path taken by Lucy and ultimately by Vera.

The excessiveness of characterization and its elimination from the narrative is consonant with the common-sense operations of the text that finally focus on the immediate, the pragmatic, and the realizable. Having split the characters three ways and having assigned negative valences to the extremes, the film has no choice but to present Charlotte's behavior as destructive and, hence, to eliminate her from the narrative. However, her very elimination signals a trouble in the text, unsettling the balance set up through the initial presentation of three sisters. The film does not employ the more familiar good sister / bad sister dichotomy, which lends itself more easily to the expulsion of the unwanted other. Instead, Charlotte's otherness is never fully acknowledged, and her presence haunts the film in spite of the pragmatic alternative resolutions held out through the remaining sisters.

Through Lucy, in particular, the film offers the alternative of reciprocal family relations, mutual respect between husband and wife, and renunciation of personal desire for the public good. The audience of the time might have recognized Lucy as a composite portrait of the 1940s image of woman presented in that era's literature, journals, and cinema, an image often mobilized in the interests of the family unit and modified in affective terms, to allow more autonomy to the female within the parameters of domestic relations. Lucy's apparently greater autonomy is realized through a comparison with Charlotte. Though Vera is meant to contrast to her two sisters, she is presented in more problematic fashion.

If Charlotte is set up to represent a view of womanhood that is archaic, Vera is presented as a caricature of the "modern" woman: careless of relationships, entering into a loveless marriage with a man whom she holds in slight esteem, and insufficiently concerned with the fate of her family, especially that of her own child and Charlotte. Vera fails to assist Lucy in a plan to divert Geoff so that Lucy can bring a psychoanalyst to see Charlotte. As a model of cultural anxieties concerning the postwar woman who is casual if not promiscuous in her relationships with men, Vera is portrayed as cynical and indifferent until she finally falls in love with a man who asks her "to give up everything" and go to South Africa with him. Her nonchalant request for a divorce from Brian contrasts with Charlotte's desperate and self-destructive attempt to leave Geoff.

If Charlotte's husband is the most commanding and overwhelming of the three male characters, Vera's is the most shadowy and undeveloped character of the three. He is portrayed, like Charlotte, as completely subordinating himself to another in his acceptance of a loveless marriage and in his tolerance not only of Vera's affairs but of her mocking him in front of her lovers. In this sense, Vera's behavior to Brian parallels that of Geoff's to Charlotte without the affect, and Brian is allowed to vanish inconspicuously from the narrative. Vera is "punished" for her offenses against family by being deprived of her daughter, who prefers Lucy's home to hers, but she is morally "recuperated" by falling in love with a man, Terry Crawford (Hugh Sinclair), who disciplines her by forcing her to choose a monogamous life and to abandon the comforts of her home for the hardships of life in South Africa. The figure of Vera is the clearest evidence that wartime representations of women were always, even at their most generous, attached to notions of woman's place in the family.

The portrayals of Lucy and William (Murray Hill) appear to be emblematic of the solid virtues and myths of British middle-class family life. As in so many of her other roles in the costume melodramas, Phyllis Calvert as Lucy is the opposite of the desiring libidinal woman. Her strengths are portrayed as rooted in social and familial concerns. On the surface, her presence can be read as yet another and updated recuperation of the "angel in the house," but a closer look at the character reveals a number of contradictions. For example, although she is the character who is the most nurturing, adopting her sisters' children when their mothers are unable to care for them, Lucy is the one character who has

118 no children, having lost a child earlier in her marriage. Lucy's and William's relationship is portrayed as desexualized, albeit it is companionable, gentle, and tender. They are represented as having limited physical contact, and, for the most part, they are portrayed with other characters rather than as a twosome. Even at night they are with others; for example, with William's assent, Lucy invites her disturbed young niece into their bedroom. William's androgynous character is common to the ideal male protagonist portrayed in romance literature.[32]

In the polarized extremes of *They Were Sisters*, the choice is obviously on the side of the maternal male and on the equalization of domestic power within the home. In effect, Lucy and William are united by their common concern for family, each other, and their house and garden. Lucy is the focal point of the action, however, not William. She initiates the plan to rescue Charlotte. Not only does she bring Charlotte home to nurse her, but in desperation she arranges for the visit of a psychiatrist to assist Charlotte in extricating herself from Geoff's baleful power. The scheme collapses. Vera, who was to have preoccupied Geoff on the pretext of business, fails to meet with him. He returns home to find Lucy and the psychiatrist with Charlotte, and exerting his influence over Charlotte, sees to it that she sends the doctor away.

Unlike some woman's films of the 1940s, such as *The Seventh Veil*, the psychiatrist is not a primary figure "who acts simultaneously as a moral and social guardian."[33] This film presents the psychiatrist as largely ineffectual in confronting Geoff's power over Charlotte. Armed with the righteousness of wronged womanhood, an avenger on behalf of the family, it is Lucy who is able, with the assistance of a written report from the psychiatrist that she reads to a courtroom, to publicly expose Geoff's abuse of his wife and children. Thus the driver of the car, whom Geoff has accused of manslaughter, is exonerated and Lucy is able to assume custody of Charlotte's children. Her testimony, which exposes Geoff, is also the means of freeing Charlotte's daughter, Margaret, from a relationship with her father that has been debilitating for both mother and daughter. Before the audience in the courtroom, Lucy accuses Geoff of killing Charlotte through his cruelty. She describes how he snubbed her before the servants and children until Charlotte finally became the fool that Geoff said she was.

The courtroom scene is a major reflexive moment in the film, both calling attention to cinema as an enactment of private conflict for public scrutiny and undermining the rigid division between public and private spheres. The concern with the law is exemplary of the melodramatic necessity of adjudication and the elimination of sources of antagonism.

Folklore perpetuates the myth of salvation at the same time that it poses serious threats to order. The law is the instrument of that order, wielded in the interests of British justice. The confrontation with law in the film also functions as a strategy for exposing the customary silence that surrounds domestic brutality, a concession once again to emerging concerns brought to public attention during the war. Lucy, who had been bribed by Geoff to keep silent in exchange for her getting Charlotte's child Judith, decides to break silence and openly expose Geoff's actions. Her standing before the judge, the jury, and the spectators and naming names, thereby violating the bonds of secrecy that keep the family intact, precipitate the most radical moment in the film. She strips away the lies, secrets, and silences that confine women to their domestic prisons. The film explodes the myth of the silent woman. In the name of the dead woman, Lucy makes public what women such as Charlotte keep to themselves. The emphasis on publicity is reinforced by the image of a newspaperman on the telephone, reporting the trial.

The ending of the film portrays William and Lucy surrounded by their adopted children in their middle-class, pastoral environment with William describing Lucy as "ordinary," as making the best of things, "muddling through." "It's good to be home," he says and quotes Browning's *Pippa Passes:* "God's in his heaven / All's right with the world." With the sisters eliminated, one dead and one banished to South Africa, and with Geoff contained by the law and Brian exiled to America, the film abandons its schema of tripling and moves into the "ordinary" world. Lucy and William are thus reincarnations of the folklore of family life, which entails images of individuals achieving an integrated sense of themselves in the bosom of the family as well as of the dyadic nature of heterosexual relations, of the couple as the carriers of law and order. The ending is a Gainsborough convention, a convention that accords with the endings of many woman's films and novels. The disruptive figures are eliminated and the external everyday world is reinstated with modification. William's description of Lucy's "muddling through" was a phrase common to this period of upheaval and threats to personal security and family stability. Geoff's cruelties to Charlotte and to his children coupled to his authoritarianism evoke images current at the time of Fascist dictatorial figures. The wartime deemphasis of social class in the interests of national unity is also indirectly addressed in the portrayal of Geoff, whose drive toward power and status is antithetical to any sense of collectivity, community, and egalitarianism. Lucy can be seen as an incarnation of the "nurturing mother [who] became the linchpin in conceptualising national unity" as described by Christine Gledhill and

120 Gillian Swanson, "a mythical centre, expressing family, and hence national, unity."[34]

William's final speech, where he alludes to "millions like us" and to "muddling through," is especially indicative of the film's dependence on common sense. Nothing more adequately describes the nature of common sense than the attempt to valorize practical concerns and the primacy of everyday interests. The film, through Lucy, associates women with the family, nature, and with gardening in particular (a traditional metaphor in English literature representing the maintenance of social order), and, by extension, with qualities of nurture. Lucy's house is described by William as "old" and "calm" like "English history." Moreover, theirs is the only house of the three sisters that has a garden, and she and William are the only couple as much associated with outdoors as they are with the house. The emphasis on the family, property, and the law, especially as centered in Lucy's support of Charlotte and her defeat of Geoff, is further indication of the way in which the film works within the sphere of everyday life while seeking to alter its more repressive aspects. At the same time, it is obvious too that the accommodations to the domestic world portrayed are tenuous.

Like the beginning of the film, which consists of a series of shots from women's fashion magazines, the ending appears to belong to the media world, calling attention to the fictional necessity of closure and seeming resolution but, in the process, announcing itself, like the common sense that it relies on, as a fictional construct. The blatant "happy ending" does not erase the events that have preceded; rather, it calls attention to their irresolvability. The eclecticism and the fusion of traditional and emergent attitudes are indications of the film's adherence to a common-sense position, but it is the presence of ill-assorted and disjunctive positions that provides a dead giveaway of the film's inability to reconcile the contradictions it poses.

In its schematic nature, the film can be understood as approximating women's divided consciousness, especially the conflict between a struggle for self-realization and the exigencies of conformity. Lucy's commonsense victory might suggest that self-realization and conformity are not really in conflict with each other. As is characteristic of common sense, the narrative struggles to overcome the fractured, disjointed, and episodic elements: in Gramsci's terms, the "fragmentary collection of ideas and opinions."[35] The film jumbles together the many conflicts it dramatizes, resolving some conflicts by eliminating characters and other conflicts by rationalizing behavior. Other conflicts are evaded altogether by reiterating clichés concerning women, family life, and the law. Also, characteristic of common sense, the antagonistic elements can never be ignored or suppressed; they are needed to dramatize the conflicts that can only be resolved in the imaginary world of melodrama. Thus the presentation of Charlotte's situation is necessary to the narrative as the prime melodramatic vehicle for Lucy's challenge to and victory over Geoff's destructive treatment of women and children. Although one can see that the film functions to recuperate the position of women within familiar domestic space, it is also obvious that this recuperation is partial. In divided fashion, the film explores modifications in power relationships between men and women; it also exposes constraints through the figure of Charlotte. Though the narration of *They Were Sisters* appears to dismiss history, historical considerations are inscribed in the text: specific events characteristic of British wartime experiences. The film can be read for the ways it might have evoked for its 1940s female spectators such concrete experiences as the adoption of war victims and orphans. Also, the Gainsborough emphasis on women's clothing and hairdos speaks to the drabness of the wartime uniforms worn by many women as well as to the scarcity of consumer commodities.

They Were Sisters also dramatizes concerns common to the literature and films of the time about the shape of postwar society. High among these concerns about the anticipated return of the men from service was the question of woman's place in the home. The film reinvests the nuclear family with power by banishing threats to its stability through Lucy, whose marriage to William grafts values from the past — loyalty to family, tending one's own garden, and, above all, concern for the new generation — to the present need for new accommodations for women within the confines of the domestic sphere. The contrasts between Lucy and her sisters and the contrasts among the men are doubly charged. On the one hand, they serve as a link to immediate historical and social needs as dictated by the culture; on the other, they reveal quite blatantly that the woman is positioned yet again as an instrumentality; they reveal even more the disparity between the magnitude of the conflicts presented and the inadequacy of the attempts at recuperation.

In its portrayal of the other in the figure of Charlotte the film exposes the complicity of juridical, medical, and class discourses in legitimating the position of women as the necessary intermediaries in the folklore underpinning the nation-state. For the critical spectator, the film challenges the normative aspect of common sense. Though seeming to focus primarily on psychic, social, and familial conflicts concerning women and their support of the family, *They Were Sisters*, like popular melodrama generally, draws heavily on national discourses in its appeals to

122   patriotism and service, and in its revelations of the necessary union between the national and the domestic spheres, which is heavily reliant on heterosexual familial discourses. In its exposing to vision the strategies and tactics of common sense, the film vindicates the effort to explore popular culture as a medium of antagonism as well as consensus.

Chapter 6

Looking Backward: Versions of History and Common Sense in Recent British Cinema

History in Film

Historical narratives offer individuals and groups a way to assimilate dominant conceptions of the world and, perhaps, to consent to them; more importantly, what is offered is the opportunity to express an awareness of their conceptual limitations. As a mechanism of consent, common sense offers a means of interpreting the world in terms of everyday shared experiences, attitudes, and beliefs. In order to be effective, common sense must bear traces of a world that contains familiar landmarks. An understanding of melodrama's connections to common sense, folklore, myth, and history begins the development of a critical conception of the social relations expressed through representations of national identity. From the perspective of common sense, personal experience is invoked as a self-evident explanation for failure and loss, and is tied closely to images of national failure or success. Melodramatic films' preoccupation with memory often takes an elegiac form, seeking through recollection to overcome melancholy and to compensate for a sense of loss. I do not mean to deride melodrama and its reliance on common sense as a form of historicizing but to interrogate how and toward what ends the past is recollected. Too often, melodrama has been studied as an escapist form mired in narrowly conceived notions of subjectivity that substitute individual for broadly social concerns, has been read as a retreat from history, and is construed narrowly as either a form of containment or of liberation of radical political impulses rather than as a contradictory component in the making of history. As a no-nonsense account of "experience," common sense and folklore seek to create a sense of things "as they are" by reducing knowledge to clichés and proverbs

124 legitimated by tradition, repetition, and widespread use. Folklore's primary characteristics are aphorism and mnemonics, which tend toward the elimination of complexity.

The films under consideration in this chapter—*Chariots of Fire* (1982), *Gandhi* (1982), *Hope and Glory* (1987), *Plenty* (1985), *Prick Up Your Ears* (1987), *Another Country* (1989), *Scandal* (1989), *Dance with a Stranger* (1985), and *The Naked Civil Servant* (1980)—all reveal a dependence on historical reconstruction, relying on an earlier moment in time not merely for context but as a means of endowing the past with affective value. These texts bear testimony to the protean character of melodrama, how it serves a number of discourses that circulate as cultural value. These discourses are drawn from a variety of sources—psychoanalysis, medicine, and the law, to name a few—and are endemic to melodrama and to its dependence on forms of historicizing. Recollection of past events serves, as in popular notions of psychoanalysis, to reconstruct events in the present by means of uncovering repressed material, bringing what has been hidden to light, and recovering loss. Because melodramas center on repression and transgression represented usually in the guise of traumas and secrets, the psychoanalyst and physician are familiar figures in this genre. They serve as intercessory figures, as mediums through which discourses of nation, sexuality, and gender circulate.

Increasingly studies have begun to address uses of the past, especially how the "national past" has been represented within films and within narratives of film history.[1] Although studies like Pierre Sorlin's *The Film in History: Restaging the Past* and Marc Ferro's *Cinema and History*, along with Siegfried Kracauer's earlier *From Caligari to Hitler*, seek to locate the ways in which an understanding of history is crucial to representations of social life, the focus of historical analysis is often restricted to external, public events. As Gilles Deleuze comments in the conclusion to *Cinema 2*, "What is interesting in Krackauer's [sic] book *From Caligari to Hitler* is that it shows how expressionist cinema reflected the rise of the Hitler automaton in the German soul. But it still took an external viewpoint."[2] Deleuze complicates our understanding of representation in his efforts to release cinema from its sociohistorical chains, its obsession with "real" factual history and its bondage to the binarism of objectivity and subjectivity. In writing about national cinema and history, critics such as Marc Ferro are nowadays more willing to concede that films are history whether or not they address past events or "real people." He writes, "What is our hypothesis?—that film, image or not of reality, document or fiction, true story or pure invention, is History. Our postulate?—that what has not occurred (and even what has occurred)—beliefs, inventions, human imagination—is as much history as History."[3]

From the first actualities, newsreels, and documentaries to feature films, national cinemas have offered various versions of their history in diverse genres: costume dramas, biopics, and historical epics. Benedict Anderson's "imagined communities" and Immanuel Wallerstein's and Etienne Balibar's "ambiguous identities" of race, nation, class, and sex are concepts intrinsic to any understanding of the ways in which the "national past" comes to be represented through the cinema and to pass for "objective" history. Through the familiar techniques of flashback, voice-over narration, the use of photographs, diaries, portraits, newsreels, classical and contemporary music, monuments, and architectural images, the films invoke a sense of the past and of place.

In the silent cinema, feature films reproducing earlier historical eras in the national past were a familiar staple of filmmaking—the Roman Empire in the Italian spectacles of the teens; the American Civil War in *Birth of a Nation;* the 1905 Russian Revolution in *Potemkin;* and the Napoleonic era in Abel Gance's *Napoleon.* The sound cinema of the 1930s and 1940s witnessed the flowering of the biographical film, which explored historical figures such as Catherine the Great, Queen Christina, Disraeli, Zola, Pasteur, Rembrandt, and the younger William Pitt. That the biographical film or the British "heritage film" (as examined by Andrew Higson) continues to be a source of interest is evidenced by such contemporary British films as *Gandhi* and *Chariots of Fire,* produced during the period of Thatcherism, which evoke memories of British pre-World War II cinema.

The biopic, a genre that is very much alive in the era of the media, is only one expression of the cinema's plunder of history.[4] Other films focus on an era, connecting their fictional or actual protagonists to specific and cataclysmic events at a particular moment, a crisis in the nation's history. World War II remains a perennial subject for dramatization in European and Hollywood cinemas as well as in the non-European cinema of such filmmakers as Ousmane Sembène (e.g., *Le Camp de Thiaroye*). Numerous films retrace the history of Italian Fascism in the footsteps of Bernardo Bertolucci's *The Conformist* and *1900,* Lucchino Visconti's *The Damned,* Pier Paolo Pasolini's *Salò,* and Federico Fellini's *Amarcord.* The New German Cinema has produced a spate of films remembering Nazism: Hans-Jürgen Syberberg's *Hitler: Ein Film aus Deutschland* and *Confessions of Winifred Wagner,* Edgar Reitz's *Heimat,* and Rainer Werner Fassbinder's *Lili Marleen.* In such films as *Hope and Glory* and *Plenty,* the

126　British cinema continues to produce versions of that war that resurrect images of national identity and honor.

In their study of World War II representations in British cinema and television, Graham Dawson and Bob West argue in terms reminiscent of Gramscian common sense that "reconstructing the past through popular memories functions to generalise meanings in such a way as to pull together and give a shared form to a multiplicity of individual and particular experiences, and so to *reconstruct* people's sense of their past."[5] The reconstructed past thus plays an essential role in the construction of the national narrative and ultimately produces a "linear equivalence of event and idea, masking contradiction and temporality, and producing a romance-melodrama in which the excesses of the attempt to elide difference become only too apparent and moribund."[6] About such historicizing, Nietzsche writes, "by excess of history life becomes maimed and degenerate, and it is followed by the degeneration of history itself."[7] In his terms, and in those of critics of historical narratives, the overvaluation of memory, the nostalgia for origins, and the fear of death translate to a passion for eternity, affects that support the "excess" of history. Historicism portrays the individual as a "play-actor," doomed to emulation, repetition, and an obsession with endings. The passion and error with which history is endowed are conducive to a sense of melancholy that arises from the notion that "life is an injustice which no future life can set right again"[8] or, conversely, the mistaking of egoism for justice.

In a similar vein, Walter Benjamin warned, "To articulate the past historically does not mean to recognize it 'the way it really was.' ... It means to seize hold of a memory as it flashes up in a moment of danger.... The danger affects both the content of the tradition and its receivers."[9] The notion of seizing memory, of realizing its forms, and of the "danger" entailed in confronting the past creates a space for melodrama. Externally directed discussions of representations of social history are committed to uncovering "the way it really was" rather than searching for the subjective factors that are also crucial for understanding the past and repetition. In the process of reanimating the past, melodrama represents events in terms of an affectively satisfying narrative that can unite past and present in terms of issues relating to nation, gender, ethnicity, family, and sexuality. In her discussion of the "foundational fictions of Latin America," Doris Summer has suggested how "romance and nation building come together in very fruitful ways in Latin America."[10] In constructing the intersecting and contradictory discourses that produce "ambiguous identities," melodrama, as the adhesive of history, signals the attempt to reconcile these ambiguities.

In examining the ways in which history as folklore is deployed in the cinema, in its pretensions to reconstruct or reinterpret the past, different modes of historical treatment become evident. Jean Gili has identified what he terms the "historical film" (*film storico*) and the "costume drama" (*film in costume*).[11] Both of these film types belong to diverse genres such as musicals, melodramas, comedies, and adventure films. These films can be further classified. The first and most common group — basically biopics — treats, in whole or in part, the life of an illustrious personage. These works often present the life of the protagonist in chronological fashion, starting from birth and culminating with the death of the individual. The trajectory from youth to old age reinforces the sense of the naturalness and inevitability of the protagonist's life and actions. This sequence of events serves to present a life in organic and "natural" fashion. Through the spectacle of exemplary figures — monarchs, nobles, religious figures, military heroes, artists, musicians — the spectator is immersed in domestic or public issues that relate to questions of gendered identity, sexuality, and family. In many cases, the films begin in the present, revert through flashback to the past, and finally return to the present.

A second category involves those films that subordinate the private actions of a historical personage to specific political events. These films articulate a process of socialization of the individual into the nation. Historical figures are specifically identified with, even subordinated to, events of national importance such as struggles for imperial expansion, national independence, and revolution. The films that subordinate character to major events depend on constructing history in terms of crisis and situating it in terms of melodrama. The protagonists find themselves immersed in and embattled by decisive events, and it is the monumental nature of these events that determines the character of the individual. Images are filtered through oral and written accounts of the past, of tradition, and of ethical norms. Authorial intention is not the major consideration for understanding how the films encode these issues. Their specific discourses are drawn from folklore and myth. In these films that privilege events over individuals, one is more likely to become involved in questions of nation and "peoplehood." Social institutions are seen as an extension of natural phenomena; nature is often invoked through landscape shots of city and especially country, and through "rites of passage" associated with generation, reproduction, and death.

The costume drama, a third category, links historical events to fictional personages. Although these films do not make a serious effort to treat historical events with any accuracy, they are nonetheless engaged in the

128 process of constructing or rewriting the past. The worlds that they recreate through costume, dialogue, and mise en scène function to shape the social imaginary as much as do the biopics. The linking of history and spectacle in most modes of historical representation is signaled by an emphasis on the iconography of exceptional protagonists through their physiognomy, costume, and gesture. The spectacle is heightened by uses of statuary, architecture, familiar national landmarks, and expansive landscape, and is dependent on the choreography of large groups of people. In many of the films that involve contact between Europeans and non-Europeans, elements of exoticism are very much in evidence. Thus the description and classification of various historical films are not purely formal, but are tied to the the films' discursive positions.

The British films from the last decade that I've selected to discuss in this chapter are exemplary of the contemporary obsession with and recycling of the national past. In their presentations of public and private life, the texts are often resurrected earlier forms of melodrama such as the woman's film, the family melodrama, and the social problem film. The narratives are organized according to Nietzschean categories of monumental, antiquarian, and critical modes of historicizing. The films all reveal a dependence on historical reconstruction, not merely because of their reliance on an earlier moment in time for verisimilitude but for their exploitation of the past as a determinant of the present. The texts testify to the protean character of melodrama and to its dependence on a number of discourses that circulate as cultural value: psychoanalysis, medicine, and the law, to name a few. I have chosen *Chariots of Fire, Gandhi, Hope and Glory, Plenty, Prick Up Your Ears, Scandal, Dance with a Stranger,* and *The Naked Civil Servant* to examine common sense as a critical construct. These films, historical reenactments ranging from the 1920s through the 1970s, offer versions of history as a strategy for recuperating (or resisting) the traditional dichotomy between public and the private spheres that currently underpins prevailing notions of work, identity, and agency.

History and Common Sense

Historical films are never innocent; their practices of reconstituting the past often function as rebuke or consolation for present failures, as prophecy, as nostalgia, or as critique of prevailing conditions. Since the guiding principles in the reenactment of the past are often determined by common-sense versions of history, the commercial cinema depends on common sense in its historical treatments. David Puttnam (the pro-

ducer of the Academy Award-winning *Chariots of Fire* and other British **129**
spectacles) underscores the importance of common sense to filmmaking:

> What I've always tried to apply is commonsense, which is a commodity
> rarely used in reference to the film industry. People get mesmerized by the
> film industry, by the movies themselves, the people they become involved
> with, by the sums of money involved. And the first thing that seems to go
> out the window, tragically, is commonsense.... We apply commonsense
> rigidly to the manufacture of films, the development of them, and the
> marketing of them. And commonsense doesn't stack up elegantly with any
> one's notion of art. Because I believe so sincerely that it's the core of the
> success we've had as a little company I can't allow the illusion of art to creep
> in and start damaging it. Because my principal grounding was in marketing,
> I'm not really interested in something that can't find an audience.[12]

As an important strategy in filmmaking, common sense has not been
accorded the seriousness it deserves, due perhaps to the taint of marketing alluded to by Puttnam, but more because of the taint attached to
mass culture and its audiences.

Common-sense historicizing offers a seemingly unified narrative by
relying on a sense of individual agency and of history as the final ground
of moral and religious judgment. But through a critical lens, common-
sense reconstruction of the past dissolves into a melange of competing
perspectives, a multifaceted, polysemic representation of scenes, actors,
and events. Moreover, common sense, according to Gramsci, is "ambiguous, contradictory, and multiform ... is crudely neophobe and conservative ... [and] to have succeeded in forcing the introduction of a new
truth is a proof that the truth in question has exceptional evidence and
capacity for expansion."[13] Thus, Gramsci offers critical insight into Puttnam's notion of common sense as well as into the power of popular conceptions, and in this instance, of memory. Though common sense and
folklore are resistant to the new, change is indispensable to mass culture
and the regeneration of cultural forms. Folklore, although it appears
unchanging and timeless, is after all a historically situated conception of
the world. It is constantly subject to modification and responsive to discourses of everyday life, science, religion, and magical thinking. The
common-sense mobilization of history as folklore draws on forms of
spirituality, abstract morality, and folk wisdom to render everyday life
comprehensible and rational. Common sense as folklore is a way subaltern groups entertain, if they do not assimilate and assent to, conceptions of the world. For these reasons, an understanding of common
sense, its relations to folklore, myth, and history, is a beginning for

130 developing a critical conception of social relations as represented in cultural formations.

The decade of the 1980s saw the high point of Thatcherism in Britain and Reaganism in America, both of which were associated with supply-side economics, military expansion, global policing, and class and race war. As with Italian Fascism in the twenties and thirties, Thatcherism cannot be seen solely as coercive. The consent of different segments of society was necessary to the transformation of the political economy. Through an assault on the decades of labor policies and on the role of the state in social welfare, its espousal of deregulatory policies, and its support of untrammeled entrepreneurism, Thatcherism sought to transform British culture.[14] In the Gramscian sense, Thatcherism can be (and has been) described as a passive revolution that succeeded in aligning different groups against both liberal and radical proposals for change. The main lines of such an "authoritarian populism" were an extension of the Fascist mode of enacting policies in the name of "the people" while maintaining strong control from above in the very name of the state with which at the same time it is identified as the source of the problem. Above all, the terrain of this war to gain the hearts and minds of the people has been social, economic, and cultural.[15]

In *The Hard Road to Renewal,* Stuart Hall explored the main lines of Thatcherism, paying careful heed to linkages of politics, economics, and culture. Hall was particularly concerned to explore all the ways in which Thatcherism sought the consent of various groups in British society:

> Areas of contestation which may appear, to a more orthodox or conventional reading, to be "marginal" to the main question acquire in the perspective of an analysis of "hegemony," an absolute centrality: questions about moral conduct, about gender and sexuality, about race and ethnicity, about ecological and environmental issues, about cultural and national identity ... these are as central to Thatcherism's hegemonic project as the privatization programme or the assault on local democracy.[16]

Notions of education, abortion, law and order, permissiveness, and "the people" are very much inscribed in this project.

In relation to Gramscian common sense as the basis of a culture of consent, its relations to everyday life, and its neophobic nature, Hall writes,

> To a significant extent, Thatcherism is about the remaking of common sense: its aim is to become the "common sense of the age." Common sense shapes our ordinary, practical, everyday calculation and appears as natural as the air we breathe.... The hope of every ideology is to naturalize itself out of

History into Nature, and thus to become invisible, to operate **131**
unconsciously.... But common sense, however natural it appears , always
has a structure, a set of histories which are traces of the past as well as
intimations of a future philosophy.[17]

Thus the ideological projects of Thatcherism, its appropriations of history, its use of past histories as they relate to the present and to the future, are seductive but also contradictory, and the contradictions become
evident through an analysis of the structures in and histories of the representations.

For many decades, Hollywood has been a reservoir of common-sense
conceptions of the world, appealing to vast audiences and able to export
its versions of the world to all corners of the globe. By contrast, British
cinema, along with other colonized cinemas, has been forced to struggle
against Hollywood and has, as a result, produced two types of films:
films for local audiences that embed British values and films made for
export. In the contemporary situation, British cinema seeks to treat British subjects in the context of a global culture. The vaunted New British
Cinema of the 1970s and 1980s appeared to be thriving but, as in the case
of the New German Cinema, the national audience for these films is in
question. As Geoffrey Nowell-Smith writes,

> cinema in Britain means films to be shown, places to project them, and
> people to see them; at a secondary level it also means a culture of cinema, by
> which I roughly mean a certain level of discussion of the cinema experience
> whether in the media or in ordinary conversation and some sort of
> machinery to support this discussion.... These different aspects — film-
> making and cinema-going, economics and culture — do not in practice exist
> in isolation from each other, but it is worth making the effort to imagine that
> they might, since such a scenario is by no means unreal.[18]

The earlier British cinema was, Nowell-Smith argues, less popular than
Hollywood because it was less democratic:

> When matched against American films of the same period, their British
> counterparts come across all too often as restrictive and stifling, subservient
> to middle-class artistic models and to middle- and upper-class values....
> When the British cinema has attempted to break out of this restricted mold, it
> has tended to produce merely an inverted image, rather than a
> transformation, of traditional values.[19]

Recent British cinema has attracted international attention with such
films as *Gandhi, Chariots of Fire, The Killing Fields, Cry Freedom,* and *Super-*

132   *man,* as well as with such independent productions as *My Beautiful Laun-
drette, Sammy and Rosie Get Laid,* and *Caravaggio.* Despite this recognition,
British commercial cinema continues to be enfeoffed to American capital, and this dependency continues to have an impact on the kinds of
films made and the ways in which these films are received. Despite
international aspirations and capital, what we see in the British films is
an address of familiar themes involving nation, race, gender, and class; a
simultaneous preoccupation with global issues; and a contradictory representation of traditionally British concerns relating to history and tradition. In discussing *Chariots of Fire* and *The Ploughman's Lunch,* films that
draw on British history, Sheila Johnston maintains, "It is scarcely surprising that questions of 'Britishness' should have been so central to
these two films made at an historical moment when notions of national
unity were once again being dusted down and re-mobilised in the interests of political expediency."[20] In linking these films to contemporary
political developments in Britain and to the British tradition of producing historical films and costume dramas in the interests of British myths,
Johnston articulates the hope that subsequent films will continue to
move away from "hoary national mythologies and conventional narrative formats rather than safely choosing to reproduce the mixture as
before."[21]

   That films such as *Gandhi, Chariots of Fire, Hope and Glory,* and *Scandal*
are preoccupied with the past, with British imperialism and British politics, is indicative of the search for capital to maintain a film industry and
of the ongoing desire (on both sides of the ocean, especially during the
Reagan and Bush years) to export British culture as a commodity, a
"brand image," to use Elsaesser's words.[22] Large-scale commodification
is especially illustrative of the Thatcherite agenda, and the engagement
of many commercial and independent films with British history as a
commodity for export is not surprising. But it is surprising that the films
are not homogenous; they are not identical in their politics. For example,
Peter Wollen finds that "Thatcherism succeeded paradoxically in politi-
cizing filmmakers across the political spectrum."[23]

National Identities: The Old and the New

In *Chariots of Fire,* a "monumental" film (in Nietzsche's terms), common
sense is at work in a collage of traditional and new attitudes, cemented
by a heavy dose of the discourses of nation and of religion. Private and
public spheres merge through the portrait of the male community's

involvement in education and sports. The rhetoric of elitism merges with the democratic emphasis on the ability of, and opportunity available to, the meritorious outsider in the upper reaches of British society. Characteristic of common sense, the film is "Janus-faced ... It looks both forward (Abrahams's prophetic announcement that 'the future lies with me') and back (the memory of the 'lost generation', the flower of British youth cut down in World War I, which haunts the film); and it can be both hailed as the vanguard of a 'new' British cinema and, in Puttnam's little trailer, quietly takes its place in the 'Great Tradition' of that cinema's glorious past."[24] In focusing on the identity of the protagonists in their struggle for success, the film merges with the Thatcherite ideology by addressing "the fears, the anxieties, the lost identities, of a people. It invites us to think about politics in images. It is addressed to our collective fantasies, to Britain as an imagined community, to the social imaginary."[25]

Chariots of Fire counts on the common sense of identity—the "natural" desire to "belong." Based on the lives of two recipients of Olympic medals for running—one an English Jew, the other a Scots Presbyterian—*Chariots of Fire* dramatizes the obstacles in their path as they compete with each other and struggle to excel. In portraying differences between the two men, the film develops their relations to family, friends, educational, religious, and athletic mentors, to the British Olympic committee, and to the then Prince of Wales. The narrative foregrounds the outsider's struggle to perform a significant public role and highlights the rewards conferred on him for his success. Familiar images of British power and world leadership are modified by invoking an American version of an aristocracy emanating from "natural" and "spiritual" excellence, despite obstacles of birth and breeding. The sense of the naturalness of British achievement is conveyed through the film's numerous sequences of male bodies in close-up slow motion, accompanied by the now-familiar swelling musical refrain. The close-ups of the men, and especially of the two protagonists, catch them in moments of passionate self-preoccupation. In its evocation of the narrative of traditional public life, the film maintains continuity with past representations of British national identity and power through its images of architecture and landscape—the stately homes and university settings of England and the lushness and greenery of the Scottish hills identified with the singing of familiar hymns. The race becomes a dominant metaphor for the men's struggle to succeed and their winning the means of overcoming their ethnic and religious differences.

134   Religion, an issue closely tied to the common-sense articulations of the neoliberal agenda, is introduced through Abrahams, a Jew, and his competitor, Eric Liddell, a Scots Presbyterian. Abrahams legitimates his quest for success in terms of his father, an immigrant who has attained wealth, who "loves this country" and who made "true Englishmen of his sons." Though he knows that "this England of his is Christian and Anglo-Saxon and so are its corridors of power," he is committed to taking them all on one by one. When reprimanded by the masters of Caius for adopting an unsportsmanlike, professional attitude toward winning, Abrahams responds to them in common-sense terms redolent with 1980s elitism and aggressive individualism: "I believe in the pursuit of excellence and I carry the future with me." The film distinguishes between Abrahams's aggressive and competitive notion of success and Liddell's more self-abnegating and pious rationalizations. Abrahams's objectives are articulated in more worldly terms: vindicating his father as a self-made man and eradicating his own sense of marginality. Religion is an issue for Liddell too, as he is a missionary and a devout Scotsman. Associated with rural Scotland, he says, as he surveys the glen, "I am and will be as long as I live, a Scot." Religion and identity politics merge in the sermon of Eric Liddell's pastor, who describes the Kingdom of God as "not a democracy, but a benign loving dictator[ship]." And Liddell, justifying his obsession with winning races, rationalizes by attributing his quest for excellence to nature and divinity: God made him for a purpose—to serve and to gain pleasure in running. Upon discovering aboard ship en route to France that his race is scheduled for the Sabbath, he threatens to drop. Despite appeals in the name of king and country, he still refuses: "God makes country and king. The Sabbath is His and I intend to keep it that way." Lord Lindsay, another classmate and runner, intervenes and relinquishes his place to Liddell, thereby earning the approbation of the Prince and the British Olympic committee as "a true man of principle, a true athlete."

Class and regional differences are universalized through the film's merging of religion and national honor. The framing in the church of the narrative that eulogizes the death of Abrahams underlines the importance of memory and aligns personal identity to public recognition and to immortality. Through Abrahams and Liddell, the trope of mourning, one of the significant aspects of melodrama's designs on history, becomes evident. The men's actions are offered as a means of compensating for the deaths of many young men in World War I. The welcoming speech to the students at Caius College is accompanied by an image of the lengthy list of World War I dead on a wall plaque. Drawing particularly on mementos of World War I and associations with "a lost generation" and offering a compensation for that loss in the figures of the protagonists, the film's treatment of history consists mainly of images that evoke a moment of past glory in British national life. When the headmaster exhorts the young men to carry on for the dead by saying that since "by tragic necessity their dreams have become yours," his words reverberate with patriotism. The film's celebration of male competitiveness, of the male body, and of the routes to personal initiative and success—professionalism in the case of Abrahams and religious zeal in the case of Liddell—reaches deep into the elements that configure national common sense and connects a past moment in British history with present criteria for success.

The position of women in the film further underscores the film's melodramatic focus on meritocracy and male anxiety. Sybil, an actress and the woman desired and courted by Abrahams, is portrayed as dismayed but powerless to divert Abrahams from his obsession over the loss of a race to Liddell, a loss that leads him to engage a trainer, an outsider and a professional, Sam Masubini, and to immerse himself completely in compensating for his deficiencies. Sybil recedes into the background, only to reemerge when she greets the victor at the train station on his return. Liddell's sister, fearing that it will distract him from his Christian work, actively opposes her brother's running, though she becomes a proud spectator at his victory. The other female figure, Montague's mother, to whom his voice-over narration is addressed as he recounts the events leading to the Olympic victory, is never seen, although the importance of family is implied through these relationships. The "natural" nuclear family is augmented and transformed by the sense of national community among the runners and by the bonding between Abrahams and his surrogate father, Masubini, who tells him after his victory, "We've had it today, you and I. We got it for keeps."

The style of the film, monumental and nostalgic, focuses on nature, the lake, the glen, the strand, and, above all, on the choreographed male bodies filmed in close-up, in slow motion, and with diffusion filters. The specific time of the events recedes, and they become (as in Riefenstahl's *Olympia*) transhistorical and timeless and, therefore, as relevant for the present as for the past. We become conscious that the film works in terms of what Higson refers to as a "modern past"[26]—another clue to the presence of common sense. While the film romanticizes the world of Cambridge and the rural splendors of Scotland, it also creates a space for

136   the "modern" values of individualism and personal initiative. In Gramscian common-sense terms, the past and present merge into a pastiche of
tradition and entrepreneurism.

Gandhi *as Monumental History*

Unlike *Chariots of Fire,* whose thin allegory seeks to sell its images of
reconstructed Britishness, Richard Attenborough's *Gandhi* is after seemingly bigger ethical and moral game in the historical uses of its biographical subject. The film is tied to the national past in more ambiguous fashion than *Chariots of Fire.* In its use of spectacle, *Gandhi* evokes
memories of the empire film despite its focus on a moment in British history when the empire began to disintegrate. Is this film an oblique critique of contemporary British politics, a remythologizing of the imperial
past, or a valorization of British national honor, greatness, fair play, and
generosity?

As a biopic and one of the most successful historical films of the
1980s, the film presents events largely through the determining position
of the protagonist. *Gandhi* offers monumental history as "mythical fiction."[27] According to its producer-director, the film took twenty years to
realize, another dimension of its attempt to self-consciously present itself
in monumental terms.[28] *Gandhi* was funded by Goldcrest Film, part of a
conglomerate "controlled by Lord Condray, reputedly the second richest
man in Britain," and by Columbia Pictures.[29] The film opens with a
proverbial apologia: "No man's life can be encompassed in one telling.
There is no way to give each year its allotted weight, to include each
event, each person who helped to shape a lifetime. What can be done is
to be faithful to the spirit of the record and try to find one's way to the
heart of the man." These sentences suggest that there is a definitive record to which the film has privileged access and that there is a way to
recover the "way it was." Melodramatic designs on history are evident
in the reference to finding the "way to the heart of the man."

The film relies on flashback to reconstruct events that mark the excep-
tionality of Gandhi (Ben Kingsley), beginning with his death and, after a
lengthy flashback, returning to that fatal moment. This film too becomes
an elegy, enacting through mourning the loss of a great man. In the vein
of the biographical film that alternates between an emphasis on public
life and on the "keyhole" view of history, *Gandhi* portrays the gradual
but eventually complete assimilation of the protagonist into a national
narrative. In the chronology of events that "shape a lifetime," the film
selects the following: Gandhi's rise to prominence in South Africa, his

mobilization of local Indian sentiment, his treatment at the hands of the
authorities, his subsequent incarceration, and the growing impact of his
idea of passive resistance. As he tells an audience, "There is no cause for
which we are prepared to kill.... Through our pain, we will make them
see injustice.... They may torture my body, break my bones, even kill
me, but they cannot have my obedience."

Religion dominates the film's portrayal of Gandhi's nationalist politics. The narrative moves in the direction of spiritualizing secular
events. This hagiographic chronicle interprets the events of Gandhi's life
through an implied parallel with Christ by stressing elements of personal
renunciation, asceticism, exhortation, conversion of the masses, prophecy, martyrdom, and transfiguration. In his conversations with Western-
ers, Gandhi concedes to the comparison between his beliefs and Christian teachings. Again, Gandhi's ties to the West are reinforced and the
Indian sources of his beliefs and actions are rendered invisible. In the
words of Margaret Bourke-White (Candice Bergen), "He offered the
world a way out of madness, but he does not see it nor does the world."
The film ends with images of the scattering of Gandhi's ashes on the
Ganges, while the sound track recapitulates his sayings, including the
prophetic one, "There have been tyrants and murderers, and for a time
they have seemed invincible, but in the end they always fail. Always."
Serving to elevate Gandhi to martyrdom and sainthood and dramatizing
the power of spirituality in the interests of reform, not revolution, the
film's preoccupation with Gandhi's nonviolent philosophy is a major
source of the melodrama. Resistance to British rule is made to appear a
creation of the British-educated Indian elite who breathed life into the
subaltern classes. The film does make reference to Indian politicians,
including Jawaharlal Nehru, Mohammed Ali Jinnah, and Sardar Patel,
who are involved in the struggle for independence, but equal, if not
more, time is given to European admirers and supporters of Gandhi: the
clergyman Charlie Andrews (Ian Charleson); Mirabehn (Geraldine James),
the British woman who dedicates her life to Gandhi; the Americans
Walker (Martin Sheen), the newspaperman, and Bourke-White.

The melodrama is heightened by spectacle through the film's exploitation of the vastness of space and of sheer numbers. Spectacle is further enhanced by the fact that such prominent British actors as John
Gielgud, John Mills, John Clements, Trevor Howard, and Michael Hor-
dern make cameo appearances as historical personages. For many years
of British cinema history, these stars have been associated with biographical films, films of empire, and patriotic films. Their presence provides further testimony to the film's drawing on different "sheets of the

138   past" derived from both the history of film and history on film. They have been instrumental in creating, reinforcing, and circulating British national folklore throughout the world.

Challenging traditional historians of Gandhi and of Indian independence, Shahid Amin identifies ways in which the Gandhi legend in India was politically constituted. Amin focuses on a visit of Gandhi to the district of Gorakhpur in 1921 as a basis for examining how "the Mahatma as an idea was thought out and reworked in popular imagination in the subsequent months," in terms of "peasant perceptions of Gandhi" at that time.[30] His essay is instructive for the ways in which it challenges the dominant western ways of uncritically isolating Gandhi as the monumental hero. The view promulgated in the west, as in the film, takes no account of the ways in which the deification of Gandhi served differing political interests, was managed by certain political elites, and may have been ambiguously received and transmitted by Indian peasants. The film conveys images of childlike, passive, and adoring masses. Gandhi's speeches are selected for their congruence with western images of spirituality. How they were received and interpreted is omitted, thus leaving the impression that the meanings of his words and actions are transparent to the spectator. The film's treatment of the colonial other, despite its interest in a nonwestern protagonist, perpetuates the familiar discourse of the colonizer who purports to have adhered to an "objective" account of his subject when in fact the Indian figures have been objectified and transformed into symbols of a people and of "powerful ideas." The scenes are often shot from Olympian heights or from an excessively familiar tight close-up; both techniques create a sense of the exotic and the sublime familiar in both ethnographic filmmaking and photography of women.

The success of the film, its garnering of numerous awards including the U.S. Academy Award for Best Picture, suggests that *Gandhi* struck responsive chords in its audiences and among the moguls responsible for filmmaking. The film does not seem to echo the militant language of Thatcherism's crusade in the name of British honor and glory (or of Reagan's crusade, for that matter); instead, it offers a critique of imperialism in the name of national liberation and of nonviolent resistance to imperialist domination. The film's presentation of the disciplining of extreme elements such as General Dyer offers a truism: the eventual decency of the British in according India its independence. Accompanying this truism is another cliché: that nonviolence and spirituality were the major factors in resolving India's and England's imperial problems. In more subtle fashion than *Chariots of Fire*, the film's use of history looks to

traditional views that uncritically and affectively affirm the ultimate   **139**
sporting behavior of the British ruling class. Thus common sense once
again dictates that reform, not revolution, is the way to guarantee the
rights of subaltern groups in the 1990s, when religious and national differences from the west are equated with terrorism. In short, the film presents nonviolence as a strategy that can efface existing economic, social,
race, and class differences and needs. The positions that the film es-
pouses can be affirmed by even those most adamantly opposed to social
change.

"National Fictions": World War II

World War II is a favorite source of contemporary British historical
reconstruction that works with and against folklore and clichéd images
from that period. The repeated return to the war in the cinema of the
1980s and 1990s can be attributed to a number of factors beyond mere
nostalgia: the conservative invocation of the past as justification for present policy, the resurgence of national questions in the era of rampant
internationalism, the impending sense of the "end of the century," the
preoccupation with, if not fear of, the return of Fascism. Television's recycling of images of the war in its endless quest for visual material also
helps to keep this period before the public.

In 1984, the British Film Institute published *National Fictions,* a collection of essays by different writers that explores the representations of
World War II in the British cinema of that time and in later film and television production. In the context of the Malvinas/Falklands crisis and of
Thatcher's deployment of a rhetoric reminiscent of World War II, the authors sought to examine the persistence of certain conceptions of British
national identity. Geoff Hurd wrote that "the Falklands/Malvinas crisis
reworked the ideologically powerful myths of the British nation in its
'Finest Hour,' this time on behalf of the right-wing authoritarian populism of the Thatcher government."[31] Among the myths explored in the
collection are Britain's reputation as a tightly knit community, the meaning of Britishness, the creation of a "Home Front," the importance of
family, the "women's war," and the notion of a familiar world become
strange. The notion of "unity in the face of crisis from without" is central
to the myth of national identity and offers a continual resource in new
formulations of that period in British history.

Hope and Glory is a prime instance of a shift from monumental representations of that era used to create a simulacrum of everyday life.
Eschewing grand narratives of heroism and self-sacrifice, the film fo-

140 cuses on the drama of survival through the perspective of a boy ignorant of the larger issues to which he is spectator. The melodrama enacts a series of familial conflicts in which the boy is involved or of which he is an observer. Unlike the biopic's monumentality, this film seeks to sift through popular memory and, by implication, to judge monumental conceptions of the past by substituting for them more banal, everyday versions of history, in the vein of Nietzsche's description of antiquarianism with its excessive attachment to the past.

By focusing on a time of crisis, the early years of the war, the film develops its major common-sense position: moments of crisis such as war unify the nation by reducing the antagonism of different and opposing regional, ethnic, generational, and class groupings. The film plays with history. Its inclusion of newsreels and of radio broadcasts featuring Chamberlain and, more prominently, the voice of Churchill, and its shifting from black-and-white to color call attention to the contrast between wartime media and its own reconstruction of events. The common-sense belief in a division between public and private spheres is reinforced through the film's assumption of indifference on the part of the public to propaganda and through its invocation of domestic family melodrama as a substitute. The common person as hero is evoked, albeit in ways different from such wartime films as *This Happy Breed, In Which We Serve,* and *The Demi-Paradise.* In *Hope and Glory,* unheroic aspects of everyday life in war are highlighted along with the heroic. *Hope and Glory* focuses on the experiences of one family, involving the parents, three children (two girls and a boy), grandparents, and close friends. The family is presented from the perspective of Billy, who, like other young children, is awakening to the existence of marital conflict, sexuality, gender difference, and male identity. The gaze of the young protagonist problematizes official forms of historicizing, substituting a naive perspective qualified by the voice-over narration, spoken in the present, by Bill, now a grown man.

A primary conflict in the film concerns the oldest daughter, Dawn, who has an affair with a Canadian soldier and becomes pregnant. In spite of the mother's initial attempts to keep the two apart and her anger over the pregnancy, the couple is married, and Dawn gives birth to the child at home. By contrast, the loveless prewar marriages in the film are presented as compromises with the world. The various scenes that dramatize separations, losses, and reunions are conveyed in melodramatic terms, as if to suggest that life was lived with heightened intensity. After a bombing, when the group gathers around a piano, one character, Molly, comments that they never sang so much before the war. For all generations but especially for youth, the sense of life wrested from death, of the differences between the present and the past, is attributed to the exceptional circumstances of the war.

In its representations of women and of sexuality, counter to such 1940 films as *The Gentle Sex, 2000 Women,* even *Millions Like Us,* in which women are presented as moving into society, taking a place in the public sphere, contributing to the war effort, *Hope and Glory* positions women as maternal figures and as sexually promiscuous.[32] Grace, like her mother, is presented as a figure of discipline, nurture, and continuity who holds the family together. By contrast, Molly, who maintains that she needs a man and is dissatisfied with her conjugal sexual life, leaves her husband to run off with a Polish pilot. Grace's daughter Dawn is obsessively fixated on her Canadian soldier and cannot be restrained in her desperation to meet him and have sex with him. Finally, Grace retorts (in response to Dawn's plea that "I want him so much") by saying, "Go, if you want to. What does it matter? We'll all be dead tomorrow." The younger children are presented as being precociously initiated into sexuality as they witness couples having sexual relations in the rubble and also as they peep through a keyhole to see their sister make love with her Canadian. In the reunion of Grace and her sisters at her grandfather's home, the women are portrayed as experiencing a sense of solidarity with one another through family identity.

The effects of the war are treated in common-sense fashion as indication of the emotional rewards of adversity: "Times of crisis bring out the best in everybody." Rather than lamenting the hardships experienced by women at the time—the shortages of food and clothing, the general drabness of life—the film offers the excitement of "making do." As Grace says, "It's patriotic to be poor." A scene of the women at a second-hand clothing store focuses less on their struggles and more on the perspective of the young boy who wanders around amid a bevy of women in slips, underpants, and bras. Grace's loss of her ration books in the fire that destroys the family house is compensated for by the "miracle of the fishes," when Billy and his younger sister go fishing and a bomb falls in the water, causing hundreds of fish to come to the surface. The film draws to a close with the "miracle" of another benevolent bomb. The reluctant Billy is led back to school by his grandfather only to discover that the school has been bombed. They find the children wildly celebrating. A boy shouts, "Thank you, Adolf!" In the car with his grandfather on their way back to the river, we hear Billy as an adult in voice-over reflecting, "In all my life, nothing quite matched the perfect joy of that moment. My school lay in ruins and the river beckoned with the

142 promise of stolen days. Oh, what a lovely war!" The image of the river
and the reflections cast on it serves as the flow of time and the importance of memory in creating connections between past and present. The
creation of an alternative folklore based on a sense of experience and the
immediacy of community seems consonant with contemporary disaffec-
tions with public life and the concomitant retreat into familial and personal relations. The last shots of the film recall the endings of *Chariots of
Fire* and *Gandhi*, both of which also end with images of the river.

Hope and Glory could be said to converge with the common-sense
practices of Thatcherism in its melodramatic invocation of crisis, its emphasis on the resourcefulness of "the people" and their perseverance in
the face of adversity, a perseverance that has its rewards in the heightened sense of life and the sense of belonging to a family and, by extension, to a small community that is more tangible than the conception of
nationhood. Though the common-sense orientation of the film, unlike
Gandhi, is linked not to discourses of religion but to family and personal
gratification, it still draws on a reservoir of homespun wisdom to present its version of history and a more currently acceptable, because more
personal, notion of national belonging.

The Past as Plenitude: Plenty

Images of World War II serve to reproach the present as a critique of contemporary social life. The 1985 film *Plenty* selectively resurrects World
War II by focusing on a disaffected female protagonist. Beginning with
events during World War II, *Plenty* dramatizes the adventures of an En-
glishwoman involved in the Resistance in France. She returns to England
after the war and experiences disillusionment in the post-war era as
she struggles to find a place in society as career woman and wife. The
film evokes memories of the woman's film produced in the war years.
Through the star image of Meryl Streep, her identity as an American and
her association with roles that highlight current representations of wom-
en's disaffection, the narrative juxtaposes past and present. The protagonist, Susan (Streep), is first seen during wartime as a British courier
working behind enemy lines. Tracing her life through several decades in
which she seeks to accommodate to peacetime and to England's "plenty,"
the film draws parallels between the degeneration of her postwar private life and that of the public arena. Scenes of the coronation of Eliza-
beth II and the Suez crisis are intercut with Susan's affairs, friendships,
and marriage.

Susan poses her attachment to the past in melodramatic terms:

"Those of us who went through this kind of war, I think, have something in common, a kind of impatience. Back in England, the people who stayed behind can seem a little silly. They haven't suffered." The distance between past and present is also measured in the words of John Gielgud, who plays a disillusioned civil servant. He says of the Suez incident, "The government lied to me. They are not in good faith.... When the British are the cowboys, then, in truth, I fear for the future of the globe." Discontent with the present, dramatized in terms of public and private life, is juxtaposed by flashbacks to the fleeting wartime romantic encounter between Susan and a British wireless operator. Her desire for adventure, passion, transformations in British manners and morals as promised during the war, become a reproach to the competitiveness, materialism, conventionality, and continuity with the past attributed to contemporary existence.

In the narrative ending, Susan returns to France in what seems like a flashback, since it repeats images from earlier in the film. The initial encounter with her wartime lover is reenacted but, it turns out, this time she is with a different lover and the terms are more sordid. The man confesses to Susan that he had hoped for "some edge" to life after the war, some "feeling that their death was worthwhile," but he hasn't done well. "I gave in always.... I work for a corporate bureaucracy as well." The film ends with a flashback to the French countryside and to a young Susan articulating her hope that the British "will grow up, change, and improve our world." This notion of the past as a reservoir of fullness, danger, and crisis and as an impetus toward change seems to reenact Nietzsche's notion of suffering from the "malady of history." The melodrama plays on nostalgia, on excessive attachment to a romantic moment in the past, and on the inevitability of betrayal. Although critical of contemporary public and private spheres, the melodrama remains mired in a nostalgia for national honor, romance, imperial integrity, and loyalty to the values of the past as exemplified by the war years.

Confounding the National Narrative: Prick Up Your Ears

Heterosexuality, not social class, is the primary vehicle for developing social disaffection in many of the melodramas that rely on monumentality or antiquarianism. In their reverence for the past and their commitment to folklore, the films provide no overt dramatizations of alternate conceptions of gender and sexuality. However, in several other, more socially critical, films of the 1980s, melodrama is enacted through same-sex relations. In a version of Nietzschean critical history, Stephen

144   Frears's *Prick Up Your Ears* offers a sardonic and violent sense of the 1950s and 1960s by producing direct and transgressive images of homosocial relations capable of being extrapolated to "the sexually repressive and puritanical eighties."[33] Through flashback, this unconventional biopic poses the enigma of the murder of Joe Orton (Gary Oldman) by Ken Halliwell (Alfred Molina) through dramatizing the evolution of their relations up through the trajectory of Orton's rise to success and Halliwell's deterioration. Before its retreat to the past, the film presents a grotesque darkly lit vignette shot of the murderer and of an eye looking through a keyhole. Flashback is linked to Orton's agent, Peggy Ramsay (Vanessa Redgrave), who secretes Orton's diary under her coat and takes it with her from the murder scene. The order of narrated events is not rigidly chronological. This darkly satirical drama is centered on the relationship between the two men. Of the various elements involved in the film's journey from Orton's death in 1967 to the 1950s and early 1960s, the most important element involves the reversal in relations that takes place between Joe and Ken. Joe's working-class origins and his lack of education serve initially as a source of contact between the two. At first, Joe is dependent on Ken, who nurtures him, but then Ken's increasing reliance on Joe and on their relationship to the exclusion of others begins to produce friction as Joe becomes successful.

The narrative created by Peggy for Orton's biographer, John Lahr (Wallace Shawn), is a parody of a domestic melodrama in which Ken assumes the position of a disaffected and neglected wife: the rising fame of Joe and the sinking self-esteem of Ken place Ken in a position similar to the female protagonist of the woman's film. Ken becomes the incarnation of the destructive and possessive maternal figure, though Peggy inserts herself into the domestic melodrama. "Ken was his first wife," says Peggy. "What does that make you, the second wife?" Lahr asks. "Better than that," she snaps, "the widow." Thus, as narrator and as character, the figure of Peggy Ramsay provides the elements that enable a reading of the events in the film in terms of a critique of the folklore of melodrama and especially of the woman's film. The film's drawing on past events and placing them in the context of melodramatic domestic conflicts creates a familiar space from which to assimilate the drama of same-sex relations. These strategies serve also to highlight the uneasy relation between visualized events and their narration. Through the figures of Orton's agent and his biographer as the possessors of his narrative in the form of his diary, the melodrama becomes complicated. The history of the men and of the times is mediated through the interests of the narrators, obviously differing from those of their gay subjects.

The framing of the film by the murder and the inclusion of scenes of gay life in London and Morocco disrupt the familiar domestic narrative and destabilize the reliability of the narration. The common-sense explanations for the violent relationship between the two men, which are rooted in the familiar heterosexual narrative of morbid domesticity, are complicated by these scenes, which cannot be easily assimilated into a conventional narrative, and which serve to unsettle common-sense conceptions of gender, sexuality, and family.

"Another Country"

In more direct and polemical fashion, *Another Country* uses melodrama to undertake a critique of traditional Left politics and gay issues on the terrain of the power politics of the public school system, the breeding ground for England's ruling class. *Another Country* reveals a kinship with the nostalgic genre of the school film, exemplified by such texts as *Tom Brown's School Days*. The school films seek, in their various ways, to dramatize the connections between the public school system and entrenched notions of class, privilege, male relationships, and male same-sex desire. The school film genre has the status of a national folktale, and the film's use of the genre's conventions to different ends helps to unsettle and question the traditional values embedded in the national folklore.

The enigma of the melodrama is introduced through a female interviewer, but it is the narration of Guy Bennett (alias Guy Burgess) that poses the problem of memory. The film begins in 1983; then, through flashback and the reiterative image of water, it returns to the 1930s. The narrative traces a series of episodes that portray male relationships in the British public school of the 1930s. The interviewer's objective is to find the answer to the enigma of why someone "of his background ... despised it?" Guy enigmatically describes himself as the "last of the happy few" and as wanting his words "reserved for posterity." Rather than focus on the question of class, he answers the interviewer's question by introducing politics into the context of same-sex relations, into the politics of desire. The love affair between Guy and James Harcourt animates the film's polemics by bringing to crisis the connections among public schooling, colonialism, military discipline, sexual desire, the production of the British ruling class, and the question of defection from that upper-class privileged world.

The era is conveyed, as in *Chariots of Fire*, through images of the school that conjure up the solidity and continuity of British social and cultural life, but with far different effect. The darkly lit interiors, the tight

146   framing of the characters, the absence of musical accompaniment, the disjunction between monumental images, and the disruptive nature of personal relations among the men may evoke nostalgia for another time but they also highlight contradictory notions of politics.[34]

The character of Judd injects Marxist notions of class struggle and inequity often marginalized or caricatured in narratives from and about the 1930s. Bennett too is more than a benighted or victimized defector to the Soviet Union, as historically portrayed by the common-sense versions of the cold war media of the 1950s. Bennett's decision to protect his lover rather than to gratify his desire for political power is the mainspring of the melodrama and the means for rewriting the history of the 1930s, and introduces the limitations of traditional conceptions of politics, including Marxist politics. As Bennett says to Judd, "You still believe that some are better than others because of the way they make love." Bennett reminds him of how gay men are named "pansy," "nancy," "fairy," "fruit," and "brown noses." In the final analysis, "commies" and "queers" are linked as outsiders. But both Judd and Bennett flee desire, trapped in the disjunction between politics and sexuality. Their melodramas become the means of undermining official history and traditional ways of representing national and cultural expectations concerning men in public life, the subsumption of the private into the public, the displacement of desire onto service.

Public school decorum and continuity are threatened by Bennett's and Judd's refusal, in their differing ways, to play by the rules. The film introduces a folklore of gay men, producing a narrative of how they are constituted, particularly playing with the traditional conflict between desire and duty. In Bennett's pained recollections of his father's death during sexual intercourse, in his encounter with his mother prior to her remarriage to a stodgy military man, in the pivotal scenes dramatizing Bennett's relationship to James, and in Bennett's encounters with Judd, the film struggles to complicate questions of identity, loyalty, and betrayal. Guy's loyalty to his lover evokes the male melodramas of the 1930s involving romance, heroism, and loyalty, but in unexpected fashion. The issue of Guy's betrayal—generated out of the interviewer's prurient curiosity about disloyalty to one's class and nation—complicates the conventional melodramatic conventions, since the romance between the two men is not equivalent to heterosexual romance, as Bennett (and the film) seek to explain. The film calls conventional notions of loyalty into question in relation to sexual and political forms of desire by dramatizing the disjunction between the two. In some ways, judging by the predictable titles at the end that record the fates of the protagonists, the film works within the same elegiac mode as *Chariots of Fire*; but in memorializing Bennett's defection and Judd's death in Spain in 1937, *Another Country* questions and does not valorize public service. As Slavoj Zizek describes the film in the context of his Lacanian analysis, the crux of narrative desire lies in the self-deception or self-betrayal of the characters, whose "real terror is the unbearable pressure of enjoyment," and "another country—Communism"— ... an escape into the transcendence of belief.[35]

Women and the Law: Dance with a Stranger

Melodramatic representations of the 1950s tend to highlight sexual transgressions of various sorts, using them to introduce problematic relations between public and private spheres. *Dance with a Stranger* reconstructs disturbing images of British social life in the 1950s through the transgressive behavior of a female protagonist, Ruth Ellis (Miranda Richardson), the last woman to be executed by the state. *Dance with a Stranger* evokes earlier genres in its affinities with the 1950s "social problem film," a form that eclectically brings melodrama, sociological analysis, and crime detection to bear on a specifically designated social infraction. The 1950s are memorialized through the protagonist's encounters with men, which dramatize violent class and sexual relations and culminate in her execution. In contrast to the formulaic "private life" film and to the costume drama featuring an aristocratic, wealthy, or famous figure and capitalizing on spectacle, on fascination with star image, and on endowing the narrative with "freedom to move its way through narrative codes,"[36] this film exploits the notoriety of a particular individual, a "glorified brothel keeper," whose story reveals "the limits of what a society will recognize of itself."[37]

The melodrama draws on a social folklore derived from 1950s films concerned with transgressions of female offenders[38] such as *The Weak and the Wicked* and *Yield to the Night*. *Dance with a Stranger* follows a familiar narrative trajectory that works within a chronological schema to trace the disintegrating, violent, and unpredictable relationships between two men of the upper middle class and a working-class woman (a class relation similar to the one in *Prick Up Your Ears*) that led Ruth Ellis to commit murder. The film relies on familiar representations of class difference and heterosexual conflict. Claustrophobia and repetition characterize the encounters between Ruth and the men in her life. Repeated

148 and violent sexual encounters dramatize her entrapment, escalating in intensity until, after repeated rejections by her lover, David Blakely, she kills him.

The drab atmosphere of the 1950s is evoked through the use of black-and-white period footage, the portrayal of the club where Ellis worked, her dreary lodgings, and her clothing. Her bleached-blonde hairdo and heavy makeup in the vein of sensational blonde stars of the period such as Diana Dors can be read as contributing factors to Ellis's crime, and may signal a collusion of social history with modern media. Her fate becomes a metonymy for the times, emblematizing violence and sexual intrigue with women as the source of social disruption. The film offers as explanation of Ellis's violence a commonsense pastiche drawn from the union of law and psychiatry[39] and embellished with different melodramatic conventions: economic necessity, divorce, maternal neglect, sexual obsession, promiscuity, betrayal, and male aggression. Her relationships with the two men — exploiting one for money while withholding sex, and succumbing to physically brutal sex with the other — present her as a woman unable to assume control over herself.

Everything in the narrative — the comments of the other hostesses, the verbal judgments of the two men and of Blakely's friends, the Findlaters — builds a case for the inevitability of her demise. Her inability to assume responsibility for her child becomes an indictment of her, as do the titles at the end tracing the subsequent fates of the men in her life — the suicide of her son and the emigration to Australia of Cussen. The terse reference to her execution and the letter of explanation in which she informs David Blakely's stepmother that she "should feel content that his death has been repaid" underscore, in Gramscian terms, her (and the narrative's) entrapment in common sense. A number of familiar explanations are advanced for her erratic behavior: her failure as wife and mother, her lack of sexual control, her lower-class status, her abuse at the hands of Blakely. However, the fact that she is presented sympathetically as victim and aggressor complicates the melodrama as it complicates prevailing myths and norms of femininity, sexuality, and familial responsibility.

Melodrama, Tabloids, and Power: Scandal

The portrait of the 1950s in British films of the 1980s is drawn as a past tainted by sexually transgressive scandals. *Scandal* addresses another and not-so-heroic moment in British history — the fall of the Conservative party in 1963. Based on Christine Keeler's book, *Scandal* portrays her rise to prominence, her relationship to Stephen Ward, the man who introduced her to upper-class society, her later betrayal of him, the sensational revelations in the press about her relationship to John Profumo and other prominent figures in the British government, the courtroom drama that ensued, and the suicide of Ward. Like many historical films treating the recent past, this film utilizes newsreels and television reports from the period. The film offers no spiritual leader, no sportsman running for the glory of England; in fact, there is no single protagonist and certainly no central figure who is exemplary. The film presents a trajectory of events tracing the career of Christine Keeler (Joanne Whalley) and her mentor, Stephen Ward (John Hurt), and their roles in producing the sex scandals that ultimately forced the resignation of John Profumo and, later, Prime Minister Harold Macmillan. The film's treatment of the past evokes many more images of British public life in the late 1950s and 1960s than *Dance with a Stranger*. The opening shots reproduce actual newsreel footage from the times and include images of then Prime Minister Macmillan and U.S. President Dwight D. Eisenhower, accompanied by a Frank Sinatra song. A news report announces Profumo's involvement in a sex scandal, thus placing the Christine Keeler story within this larger context of tabloid sensationalism.

Through flashback the narrative returns to 1959 and to Ward, ogling women on a London street. The film's preoccupation with sexuality intensifies in the numerous scenes of the clubs that Keeler and Ward frequent: she as a dancer and his companion, he as voyeur and erstwhile pimp. He articulates his rationale for befriending Keeler with such statements as "When I see beauty like yours.... I long to liberate it." Ward's relation to Christine can be variously understood as paternal or perhaps as maternal, as commercially exploitative and as voyeuristic. He is less interested in physical sex with men or women than in gratifying his desire to look. The film takes its title seriously, entertaining a variety of sexual practices. ("If I fail to please, beat me," reads a sign on one of the seminude men at a club.) Bodily images, especially images of the female body, to a lesser degree of the male body, are abundant. The film lingers on the minutiae of women's toilettes. At one point, during a dinner party, a huge ice statue of a penis sits in the middle of a table. Scenes of private parties that portray nude women and couples in various sexual postures and Ward as a Peeping Tom reinforce the film's preoccupation with voyeurism.

Ward uses Christine to implicate a Soviet official in a sexual liaison, but the juiciest element in the scandal involving the Conservative party is reserved for Keeler's relationship to Profumo. Like *Dance with a*

150 *Stranger, Scandal* makes connections between sexual exploitation and upper-class corruption. Sexuality is portrayed as cause and effect in this critical history of British national life. The upper classes gratify their desires at the expense of working-class women and men. The working-class women and men, such as Christine, seek to gratify their desire at the expense of marginalized blacks. The common bond among the characters is their commodified and aggressive sexual relations. The linking of sexuality with marginalized groups — subaltern women and blacks — provides, in common-sense fashion, a critique of British social relations and a legitimation of the linkage between subalternity and sexual promiscuity. The film's treatment of sexuality is the linchpin in the exposure of the film's contradictory attitudes toward politics, cultural representation, and sexuality.

The film stresses various ways of looking and links scandal to media and entertainment. Repeated television shots of political corruption and scandal punctuate the film. At her trial, Mandy Rice-Davies reduces the courtroom to a nightclub and her testimony to a comedy act that makes the spectators laugh. In response to the statement that one of her clients has denied having intercourse with her, she replies smartly, "He would, wouldn't he." The courtroom "audience" guffaws. The film foregrounds crowds at the beginning and end of the film (shots that reproduce the black-and-white newsreels of the time) ogling Mandy and later Christine emerging from the courtroom after the sensational trial.

The titles at the end suggest that not much has substantially changed in the moral and political landscape of England from the 1950s to the present. The titles state that Ward was "found guilty in his absence of living off the immoral earnings of prostitution. He died without regaining consciousness. Memorial services were held on August 10, 1963. Nobody came." Keeler's sentences for perjury, her time served in prison, and her residence in an obscure housing project are noted. Mandy Rice-Davies is described as having become "a cabaret singer [with] a string of nightclubs abroad. Married for the third time, she now resides in London and Florida." Finally, John Profumo is said to have left politics and dedicated his life to charity: "In 1975, the Queen awarded him one of England's highest honors, Commander of the British Empire."

Why have these 1950s events been resurrected in the 80s? Is it a veiled exposé of contemporary practices? Is it a critique of Thatcherism? Is the film's examination of this earlier scandal consonant with the neoconservative emphasis on law and order, decency, and a return to traditional values? In the film's emphasis on sexual exploitation, it both encourages and disavows any complicity in profiting from the notoriety of the scandal. The focus on prostitution, promiscuity, the female body, and the selling of entertainment seems more in keeping with the 1980s than the era it reenacts. Moreover, the treatment of these issues in the context of a scandal situates the film in a frame of reference that is confined to the lives of the rich and famous and depicts women and blacks in familiar ideological terms as willing victims and as contributors to the larger moral degeneracy; but, wittingly or unwittingly, the film exposes the inevitable presence of sexism and racism within the national narrative. The representation of blacks in the film recalls an earlier treatment of race in Basil Dearden's 1959 *Sapphire,* and like that film, *Scandal* portrays blacks as sexually potent, physically aggressive, and linked to the under-world of dope peddlers and pleasure seekers.

The linking of sexuality to politics is reinforced through the film's emphasis on looking: private acts are exposed in court and to the media. In this way, the film orchestrates several issues: the exposure of class antagonisms, the disjunction between media representations of public officials and their private practices, the role of sexuality as commerce through the complicity of the upper classes, and the contradictory role of the media in exposing scandal while profiting from it. Because of news-paper tabloids and television (as well as the film itself), it is no longer possible to maintain the hiddenness of private actions. The use of television newsreels and photography and the shifts from color into black-and-white underscore this preoccupation with recording.

The use of history in the film, rounded out by the melodramatic ex-ploration of the characters exposed to the public eye, relies on an exist-ing folklore of public life not dissimilar from theatrical representations of backstage life. Public officials are treated like actors and, like actors, live in the public glare, no longer protected from exposure. In particular, the film's highlighting of sexuality not only enhances the melodrama by reducing the glamorous aura surrounding the rich and famous, but, from a common-sense perspective, also reveals in clichéd fashion that "from top to bottom everyone is corrupt." The film therefore identifies existing antagonisms—class, racial, and sexual—and serves to under-mine confidence in public life even as this exposure opens a space for reconfiguring different relations between the private and the public. The uses of melodrama thus resurrect familiar fears about contemporary social and cultural life with its political corruption, racial conflict, politi-cizing of sexuality, and the contradictory role of the state in relation to sexual practices, but these fears mask real antagonisms that cannot be

152   resolved. In the Gramscian way of taking common sense more seriously, it can be seen that the film's common sense is not completely wrong. The problem is, as Gramsci has suggested, to find an analysis that does not remain mired within that common sense but that can be used for different social and cultural ends.

History as Masquerade: The Naked Civil Servant

The predominant mode for recreating the past has often involved a rather straightforward adoption of melodramatic conventions drawn from earlier periods and from existing melodramatic subgenres. The films are largely dependent on familial, sexual, and gender conflicts involving questions of loss, relations between public and private life, and ambivalent attitudes toward the past, as well as toward remembering and forgetting. Like *Prick Up Your Ears*, *The Naked Civil Servant* (1980) is no exception; it differs only in how it enunciates questions of "illusion" and the "real," by exploring different formulations of such issues as self-constitution, identity, subjectivity, and power. In employing the autobiography of Quentin Crisp—one of the "stately homos of England"—from his childhood to the 1970s, the film undermines the traditional voyeurism and exoticism of such filmmaking by inviting the spectator to confront events that are usually omitted, elided, or muted. A number of devices are introduced to bring conventional representation into crisis. These devices include an episodic structure introduced by a witty voice-over narration that intrudes on the flow of events.

The film begins in the present with the actual Quentin Crisp and then retreats to the 1920s with John Hurt as Crisp only to move forward again through succeeding decades and to return to the present time (though without returning to Crisp). Titles and captions are used, as if this were a silent film, along with an arch and stylized form of acting. Typical melodramatic incidents involving familial conflict, verbally aggressive and violent relations among and between straight and gay men, medical and juridical encounters with physicians and the law, are treated in parodic fashion. Clichéd language and behavior are held up to ridicule. The film draws on every conceivable dimension of folklore concerning gay and heterosexual culture, using subtitles, witticisms, clichés that cancel each other, and images that violate conventional expectations of behavior and dress. Scenes with family are presented so as to play on familiar conceptions of the formation of the gay man—dressing in women's clothes, maintaining close relations with maternal figures, harboring hostility toward paternal figures. These stereotypes are not presented with heightened affect as in the family melodrama but in arch, stylized fashion. The film calls attention to these scenes as filtered memory. The viewer is constantly reminded of the retrospective nature of the events.

An important technique in the film for invoking common sense and folklore only to undermine it is the deployment of theatricality and self-dramatization. For example, after a scene that portrays physical violence among gay and straight men, Quentin comments: "I seem to have hit on a home truth. Some roughs are really queer and some queers are really rough." This use of aphorism extends to the way the film visually undermines the high seriousness that accompanies common sense by blurring the melodramatic line between victims and aggressors, between gays and straights. Moreover, the quotation calls attention to the act of naming and its dual role as both producer of identity and mode of survival. Quentin does not refuse the naming that comes not from him but from others, but his language and gestures reveal the constraints of language. In response to a psychiatrist's comment, "male and female created he them," Quentin quips, "Male and female he created me."

A familiar and potentially intense melodramatic scene, the encounter of the criminal offender and the law, produces not disavowal but acquiescence. Accused by the police of soliciting on the street, Quentin names himself "a sexual pervert.... I am a self-evident, self-professed effeminate homosexual.... How could I hope to solicit anybody in broad daylight in a crowded London street looking as I do? ... My appearance sets me apart from the rest of humanity." His comment on his acquittal is, "Well, I flatter myself that London has not seen a performance like that since Sybil Thorndike's *Saint Joan.*" The emphasis on his theatricality and masquerade and on self-conscious excessiveness calls attention to and undermines the ways melodrama is often used to valorize the past so as to create affective responses to marginality. The film uses Crisp's history to reproduce familiar conflicts concerning the individual and social transgression; at the same time, it challenges notions of victimage and memory by its invocation of and then refusal to inhabit the excessiveness of affect required of melodrama. In all the episodes, the folklore involving gay life is reproduced but then called into question through Crisp's insistence on fictionalizing and on refusing to naturalize and to identify the "essential" nature of homosocial relations. The film becomes an encyclopedic commentary on, if not parody of, melodramatic representation in the uses of flashback, voice-over narration, photographs, and titles, and in the ways it caricatures figures in melodrama — parental

154   figures, physicians, representatives of the law, and romantic attachments. Through parody the film uses common sense against itself.

Epilogue

Despite differences in technique and in point of view, the films discussed above share characteristics that provide insight into contemporary problems of politics and representation, and illuminate how common sense motors their narratives and their images and sounds. Whether distanced through parody or affectively excessive, the texts expose the inevitable bonding of history *as* folklore and melodrama. Whether monumental, antiquarian, or critical, the films address people and events in the context of a national narrative, drawing frequently on the national past and its folklore to make a case for or against the status quo, for or against the past as opposed to the present, for or against tradition and continuity, and for or against official history or popular memory. To a greater or lesser degree, negatively or affirmatively, the films acknowledge the importance of media as a source of contemporary knowledge, particularly as a new archive of the national past (including national tabloids) and the figures and events associated with them. The films' dependence on cliché, proverbial wisdom, nostalgia, and parable is particularly evident in the ways that the narratives construct their protagonists largely in terms of the affective value associated with religious, national, or familial rituals, with figures from the past, or with images of transgressive sexuality often linked to violence. At times, the films appear to affirm the status quo, but more frequently in their affect and in their uses of historical situations, they confound—whatever their motives—conventional generic and affective expectations. Thus, while the films reveal that common sense plays a crucial role in forging identities and alliances, they reveal the dependence of common sense on the past. If there was any doubt as to the existence of collusion rather than antipathy between history and melodrama, these films provide ample testimony to such collusion. If there was any doubt that melodrama is a powerful instrument in producing consent, these films also provide testimony to the contrary.

Chapter 7

Language, Folklore, and Politics in the Films of the Taviani Brothers

Gramsci's writings are especially illuminating for an understanding of the role that language (*la questione della lingua*) and folklore play in the formation of conceptions of nation and state. For Gramsci, language was synonymous with culture and politics, and was hence an arena to be carefully explored in any attempt to understand hegemony and counterhegemony. The creation of a national popular culture is closely intertwined with the uses and abuses of history; with the role of intellectuals, ethnicity, and social class; and especially with the relationship between hegemony and common sense and folklore—a central feature in Gramsci's critique of existing and possible forms of political alignment. Hegemony, according to Gramsci, is "common sense 'instrumentalized,' so that a minority can, without resort to violence, dominate a majority *by imposing upon it* a common sense."[1] Thus we are reminded that formations of national cultures and identities are inextricable from the consensus character of common sense. In Gramsci's writings on Italian history, in his exploration of the construction of the national/popular, in his attempts to distinguish between organic and traditional intellectuals, in his analysis of the nature and role of intellectuals in society, and in his notes on education, he grappled with and sought to chart the different ways in which nation-states are constructed—not naturally or divinely ordained.

His comments on the character of the political obstacles in the formation of a united Italy are important as a case study for his explorations of the concept of hegemony. What one learns from his comments on Italian history is that the bourgeoisie succeeded in gaining control during the Risorgimento, a very fragile control, through compromises effected with the traditional ruling classes. This "passive revolution," a

156 "revolution without revolution," was effected with the passive consent of subaltern groups. Gramsci examines a number of factors that contributed to this situation: the "paternalistic" as well as Jesuitical character of moderate intellectuals in their relations to the peasants and their servile attitudes to the ruling classes, the subordination of other intellectuals to the moderates, the conflict between rural and urban groups in North and South and within the South itself rather than the creation of alliances between town and country, and the prevalence of political uncertainty manifested in a wavering "between despotism and constitutionalism.[2]

Gramsci's emphasis on the creation of a popular national hegemony is a central feature of his attempt to build a theory of social change in behalf of the people. This concept, which has been subject to much debate, is not akin to traditional notions of nationhood. Gramsci does not advocate a notion of the nation as a natural "ethnic base ... possessing of itself an identity of origins, culture, and interests which transcends individuals and social conditions."[3] In his comments on the Mezzogiorno, Gramsci reveals that he was aware of the negative ways in which racism and language were central features in the construction of Italian national identity and obstacles in efforts toward radical social and cultural change. His notion of national popular hegemony is linked to his discussions of popular culture and popular culture is, in turn, inextricable from his comments on common sense and folklore. The identification of the character and importance of common sense and folklore is a medium for understanding the affective power of race, class, gender, and ethnicity, the basis of their exchange value as the currency of consent and force.

In addition, a national popular culture in his terms is unthinkable without the creation of intellectuals, organic intellectuals who are aligned with the people in contrast to traditional intellectuals who are oblivious to and removed from popular concerns. One of the tasks of intellectuals, in their organizational and directive work, is to elaborate new forms of philosophy and critical understanding, and to help encourage the formation of new intellectuals. Presumably, these intellectuals are receptive to and committed to an analysis of existing popular phenomena — folklore, folk customs, proverbs, proverbial wisdom, magic, popular science, popular song, dietary practices, and popular psychology — which are not to be considered as signs of false consciousness or of a superstructure divorced from concrete social conditions but as material signs of an affective investment in the past. This common sense impedes change, though change might be in the best interests of individuals and groups.

Thus, critical understanding or "good sense" entails an understanding of how conceptions of peoples in terms of nations, ethnicities, and gender and sexuality are circulated and how they are instrumental in producing consent.

Cinema has played a prominent role in the representation of "national communities" by reinforcing, elaborating, complicating—according to changing circumstances—representation of "the people." Cinema is hence an important resource for probing the ways in which the uses of history contribute to the circulation of folklores concerning national identity. Historically, the Italian cinema has, along with other national cinemas, addressed representations of nation, folklore, and cultural identity in various genres and styles. In early silent epics, in such early sound films as Blasetti's *1860*, and in other historical films of the Fascist era, the celebration of the historical precedents for the creation of the Italian state and for its unification were represented in epic fashion. During the late 1930s and early 1940s, the Italian cinema dramatized familiar and problematic cultural, regional, and class differences between North and South by focusing on various regions in celebratory populist fashion. In the post-World War II years, these differences were to be addressed in more critical fashion. In particular, the memory and effects of the war and the Resistance were central to national concerns for postwar intellectuals. For example, the work of Pier Paolo Pasolini, a poet and filmmaker influenced by Gramsci's writings, was "deeply affected by the Resistance," as was the work of "an entire generation."[4] The memory of Fascism continues to haunt contemporary Italian cinema, as represented by such films as *Open Doors* (1990) and *Three Brothers* (1981).

Interrogating History

The films of the Taviani brothers dramatize all of these particular concerns from the vantage points of historical perspectives and from contemporary views. Moreover, whether directly influenced by Gramsci or not, the films of the Tavianis, along with the films of Pasolini, appear germane to issues raised by Gramsci concerning national history and culture. Through the medium of the feature film, the Tavianis' texts address the nature of organic and traditional intellectuals, especially the roles they play in political struggle. The Tavianis' exploration of the nature of subalternity touches on familiar conflicts in Italian society, centering particularly on questions of regionalism and the problematic history of North/South divisions. With respect to their films' reenactments of the past, the Tavianis' work can be said to explore, not monumentalize,

158 historic images and issues relating to contested positions over popular memory. Whether selecting for representation the recent past and political struggles during the 1960s, as in *I sovversivi;* the more remote internecine conflicts during World War II, in *La notte di San Lorenzo;* or the nineteenth-century struggles for unification, as in *Allonsonfan;* their treatment of history is predominantly interrogative, analytical, and ironic, not melodramatic and nostalgic. In the process, in all of their films and in their own roles as filmmakers the Tavianis explore the role of film along with other forms of cultural expression. They are consistent in portraying the struggle for cultural self-expression and engagement on the parts of both their upper-class and their peasant protagonists in ways that reveal an indebtedness to Gramscian conceptions of common sense.

The concern with language in the Tavianis' films is not confined to linguistic structural questions but entails an engagement with questions of national identity, regionalism, familialism, emigration and diaspora, social class, and sexuality. In short, language represents for them as for Gramsci a confrontation with fundamental and critical aspects of cultural representation, an issue that has been important to many Italian filmmakers since World War II.[5] The films of Paolo and Vittorio Taviani are political in terms of Gramsci's expanded sense of cultural politics, where emphasis on a social and political change involves a rethinking of the composition and history of subaltern groups and the discourses about them. The Tavianis seek to awaken the spectator to imperatives for change; they are not polemicists; they have no program. Rather, they use their cinema to experiment, to raise questions about Italian history, about the role of intellectuals, about the workings of common sense, and about film culture itself, especially through exploring the politics of film. More specifically, they investigate the form of filmmaking designated as "neorealist."

The uses and abuses of history are a central concern in the Tavianis' films and this concern bears a close relation to Gramscian historical analysis. In his discussion of "historico-political analysis," Gramsci found that

> a common error consists ... in an inability to find the correct relation between what is organic and what is conjunctural. This leads to presenting causes as immediately operative which in fact operate only indirectly, or to asserting that the immediate causes are the only effective ones. In the first case there is an excess of "economism," or doctrinaire pedantry; in the second, an excess of "ideologism." In the first case there is an overestimation of mechanical causes, in the second an exaggeration of the voluntarist and individual element.[6]

The Tavianis, in seeking to develop their film language, are looking to avoid the extremes of "economism," of reducing character and event to "mechanical causes" and to determinism; at the same time, they seek also to avoid the reductions of "ideologism," which would emphasize individual volition, uniqueness, and freedom from cultural restraints.

Though the Tavianis' films are recognizable in an international idiom, they can best be understood within the context of Italian cinema, from the post-World War II era to the present. Italian films of this epoch have certainly addressed political issues, perhaps in more sustained, direct, and intense fashion than in other European cinemas. But, as the Tavianis are aware, the audiences for their films today are different from earlier audiences, especially the audiences of the immediate post-World War II era. They find that "there's a certain amount of cynicism setting in among the Italian populace. It's a great crisis, one involving the questioning of values, many hopes that were never realized, myths that have fallen forever, a very difficult economic situation, a time of flux."[7] Recognizing the need to address this new audience, the Tavianis made their films an arena of research for social transformation, at a time when commitment to political alternatives was waning. Their explorations have a precedent in the history of contemporary European cinema. Many of the filmmakers of the French New Wave turned to the auteurist aspects of Hollywood, singling out such filmmakers as Alfred Hitchcock, Sam Fuller, and Nicholas Ray, to establish the possibility of creating a personal style in the midst of the "studio system." In particular, as critics they explored ways of deconstructing the nature of the classic narrative and the spectator's role within that system in an attempt to call attention to the cinema and to the ideological nature of cinematic expression. Their experience in documentary films, as well as the impact of neorealism, allowed them to work eclectically and self-consciously with narrative, gestural language, imagery, and sound.

The Italian filmmakers were more preoccupied with the legacy of neorealism, especially with questions of national identity, and with the need to confront its possibilities and limitations. In the films of the Tavianis, a recognition of the relationship to neorealism is indispensable for understanding the forms of Italian political cinema. Of their relationship to that film movement, they have said, "When we started our first film we realized that neorealism was degenerating. It had become an expression of petty bourgeois, heavily naturalistic stories. So, when we embarked on our career in the cinema, we wanted to depart from neorealism, to make it react to something new and something old.... In this sense, we felt that we were burying a beloved father. Although this 'father' is dead

160 and buried, he remains a strong influence in our memory."[8] This "strong influence" can be seen in the Tavianis' choices of subjects for their films: Italian history, especially the history of Fascism, peasant life, regionalism, continuing conflicts between urban and rural existence, generational conflicts, and familialism.

Although sympathetic toward the attempts of neorealism to produce a cinema that was sensitive to history; more auteurist in its mode of address; more conscious of the issues of social class, if not of gender; and more concerned to bring a sense of "reality" to the screen, the Tavianis were also aware of the pitfalls of a realist aesthetic as articulated by its practitioners and critics, especially Cesare Zavattini and André Bazin. The ideology of neorealism, its common-sense orientation (in Gramscian language, if not in consistent practice) with its emphasis on the poor and dispossessed, its special pleading in behalf of materialism (albeit it was not Marxist for the most part) and humanism, posed problems as they began to explore the possibilities for a political cinema.

Increasingly, the Tavianis experimented with style by veering more toward examinations of the bourgeoisie rather than focusing exclusively on workers and peasants, and by moving away from the strictures of documentary forms of filmmaking and from the unexamined adherence to melodrama and sentiment. However, the Tavianis' departure from neorealism was, like that of Jean-Luc Godard, more of an adjustment than a rupture. While maintaining the neorealist sense of context and upholding the importance of location shooting, the Tavianis diverge most from the neorealists in their treatment of narrative and in their use of a film language that is closely tied to modernist practice. Their preoccupation with language as an instrument of oppression and as a potential vehicle of change is their particular means for providing an implicit critique of neorealism and for addressing issues that are endemic to Italian culture and society. The Tavianis have acknowledged the importance of *Paisan* in shaping their sense of World War II. Roberto Rossellini's film and other neorealist films, as Millicent Marcus suggests, provided "a way of rethinking the entire event and of beginning to give it meaning for the future."[9]

Neorealism is for the Tavianis, as it was for Italian filmmakers moving out of the 1940s, an attempt to break from the cinema of genres, spectacle, and melodrama, the cinema produced during the Fascist years as well as in the studio system of pre–World War II Hollywood. By utilizing semi- or nonprofessional actors, by shooting on location, and by focusing on workers and peasants, the neorealists struggled to create a film language that was new and spontaneous in its approach to the cinematic image and consequently to the world. The neorealists wished to escape the bondage of narratives that they felt were a misrepresentation of everyday life. In the cinema of genres, the neorealists claimed, the spectator is concerned with the conventions and codes that are negotiated between spectator and text. The filmmakers sought to create a different environment for the spectator through minimizing the effects of spectacle, providing direct access to the images by means of long take photography and minimal editing, and through middle distance shots that could enable the viewer to assimilate the character's specific relationship to the environment.

The quality of the interactions between the characters in neorealism was of far greater importance than the plot, and the style of acting, in particular, marks a break from more stylized melodramatic treatments characteristic of the cinema of the Ventennio. Moreover, many of the films made a studied, though not always successful, attempt to avoid the binary structures of melodrama and its formal excesses. The language was deflated along the lines described by Gilles Deleuze, writing of Roberto Rossellini's work: "Rossellini's pedagogy, or rather his 'didactic,' does not consist in reporting discourses and showing things, but in revealing the simple structure of speech, the speech-act, and the everyday manufacture of objects, small or large works."[10]

The filmmakers associated with neorealism sought to create a sense of the immediacy and specificity of interactions. Contrary to uncritical assessments of neorealism, the representation of reality was not unmediated. The physical appearances of the actors, their physiognomies, their bodily movements, the language they speak, the images of their world, and the musical scores were constructed to realize for the viewer the poetic aspects of everyday life. This strategy was also adopted as a way of mitigating the usual condescending or pathetic portraits of working-class life. The treatment of history was also crucial to neorealism. Reacting against the grandiose spectacles of earlier Italian cinema such as *Scipione l'Africano* (1937),[11] the neorealists sought to avoid the "epic" representations of monumental history with their glorification of the past. The selection of events was thus geared to immediate social realities confronting postwar Italy. Though their cinema can be considered political, the neorealists sought to redefine politics as well as history. In reaction to the public sphere of politics and spectacle characteristic of the Fascist regime, the postwar filmmakers identified politics in more personal terms. They also rejected the style associated with Soviet cinema of the 1920s or the Italian newsreels of the 1930s.

The neorealists recognized that cinema was not an arena of polemic

162 but an imaginative medium in which they could experiment with cinematic language. As Peter Bondanella states, "the cinema neorealists turned to the pressing problems of the time—the war, the Resistance and the Partisan struggle, unemployment, poverty, social injustice, and the like—but there was never a programmatic approach to these questions or any preconceived method of rendering them on celluloid. And the phenomenon was clearly unlike other avant-garde movements in the sense that it never adhered to a governing manifesto or ever felt one was even necessary."[12] Despite differing strategies, the neorealists shared certain basic attitudes. According to Millicent Marcus, "neorealism is first and foremost a moral statement, *'una nuova poesia morale'* whose purpose was to promote a true objectivity—one that would force viewers to abandon the limitations of a strictly personal perspective and embrace the reality of the 'others,' be they persons or things, with all the ethical responsibility that such a vision entails."[13] These are the aspects of neorealism that align its ideology with the 1940s and with traditional humanism, in the emphasis on ethics and on general assumptions about human nature; and its faith in the potential access to "truth."

In the 1950s, a period of change for Italian culture, aspects of neorealism were abandoned for experimentation with more personal explorations as exemplified in the work of such auteurs as Fellini. For others, including the Tavianis, neorealism was more of a political challenge calling for new forms of contestation. In general, the cinema of the late 1950s and 1960s never totally departed from neorealism but salvaged certain elements, altered others, and eliminated still others.

In the 1960s, with the rise of political activism and with Italy's move toward the left, filmmaking became more overtly political in Italy as it did throughout Europe. This political cinema sought a cinematic language that was conscious of the role of social institutions and of the role of cinema itself as an institution, as an instrument of conformity, and as an agent of political change. In that exploration, neorealism was acknowledged as a problematic precursor. The modernist political cinema, exemplified in the work of such filmmakers as Antonioni and Godard, placed greater emphasis on the spectator and on strategies for making the spectator aware of the cinematic experience. Modernist techniques such as distanciation, self-reflexivity, and the creation of ruptures between image and sound were strategies adopted to call attention to the nature of cinematic language as constructed rather than given. According to the Tavianis, the language of neorealism to a large extent inhibited these forms of intervention.

Concerning the limitations of neorealism as an effective medium for communicating with contemporary audiences, the Tavianis have said:

> In postwar Italy, during the neorealist period, the feeling was that good and evil were very distinct things which could clearly be distinguished from each other. As the years passed, good and evil became more difficult to distinguish from one another; they seemed to blend.... Those who came out of the neorealist movement found themselves constrained to *find* new instruments, new tools to express themselves. And that's how the cinema of the Sixties came about.[14]

Unwilling to abandon the social concerns of neorealism, but equally unwilling to perpetuate the notion of access to a seemingly unmediated reality, the Tavianis have continued to experiment with various modernist techniques in order to disrupt what they interpret as the spectator's easy assimilation of the filmic events in classic cinema.

The presence of melodrama in neorealist representation has not been given the attention it deserves. The challenge to neorealism, I believe, derives from the same critical impetus that led the neorealists to challenge the cinema of genres, with its common-sense and folkloric dimensions. When the Tavianis refer to the clear-cut division between good and evil that seems so often to characterize many neorealist films, they are referring to the issue of melodrama with its affective excessiveness, its clearly drawn demarcation between victim and oppressor, its fixed conceptions of subaltern identities, and its tendency to totalize questions of social justice. As recent research on melodrama has made clear, melodrama is not just another genre or film style; it is a worldview, and an integral dimension of many representations of history.[15] By narrating the trials and tribulations of its protagonists, melodrama seeks to account for human misery in ethical terms; based as it is on humanist privileging of the individual over the collective, melodrama produces a history of oppression from which the victim must be saved or to which he or she succumbs. In the Tavianis' work, increasingly the telltale signs of melodrama recede as the films come to develop Gramscian strategies for identifying how common sense, not individual idiosyncrasies, reproduces a familiar image of social relations. For them, culture must be examined not in terms of individual effort but in relation to the structures and strictures that individual groups inherit, inhabit, and either legitimate or seek to resist.

Un uomo da bruciare (1962), the Tavianis' first feature film, exemplifies how their films maintain certain ties with neorealism while also struggling with melodramatic elements, and especially with suspicion of politics and the role of collectivities. The protagonist of the film is a political activist, but the film explores subjective as well as objective obstacles in his political conflicts. The choice of the trade union leader as a protagonist, the focus on workers, the explorations of workers' lives, and the use of documentary footage are reminiscent of neorealist concerns and techniques. The film addresses the issue of leadership, specifically the relationship of the leader to the group; in the sense of Gramsci's preoccupation with this question in his notes on "The Modern Prince," the leader "cannot be a real person, a concrete individual. It can only be an organism, a complex element of society in which a collective will, which has already been recognized and has to some extent asserted itself in action, begins to take concrete form."[16] Salvatore becomes the narrative vehicle to explore the failure of traditional political activism. In Gramscian terms, the film exposes ultraradicalism, the lack of collectivity in the name of collectivity, the chasm between the subaltern and those leaders who would assume that they know better than the subaltern what is to be done — motifs that will recur in various guises in so many of the Tavianis' films. Moreover, Gramsci's emphasis on the need to understand the relation between organic and conjunctural conditions — to assess the possibilities of action in relation to the "relations of force" that exist — is relevant to this film as well as to other Taviani films. The protagonist of the film is, in Bondanella's terms, "bent on exercising power at the head of the peasants even if they reject him and find his leadership dangerous."[17]

This film calls attention to the filmic discourse in ways that neorealism often effaces. In R. W. Witcombe's terms, the style of the film is theatrical, if not operatic, so that the protagonist becomes an object of investigation rather than merely a center of emotional involvement.[18] The operatic/theatrical element so often associated with Italian culture, with historical representations of the early silent cinema, and with the cinema of the 1930s is once again introduced but in ironic fashion. The theatrical treatment of the protagonist and the dramatic use of long shots and tracking shots constitute major departures from neorealism, create an alienation effect, and provide a critique of the protagonist by undermining the accompanying melodrama. This process of detachment and involvement becomes paradigmatic of the ways in which the filmmakers invite a general response to the film. Of the oscillation between these two poles the Tavianis have said, "Alienation and detachment we go along with. But we're also Neapolitans, which means we're all for a totally expressive, expansive viscerality which is not Brechtian."[19] In

many ways, these comments are reminiscent of Fassbinder's modifica- **165**
tion of the Brechtian *Verfremdungseffekt:* "I like to make my audiences
think and feel."

The filmmakers also experiment with narrative positions, choosing to
explore various characters' viewpoints rather than focusing rigidly on
one or two of them. By so doing, they undermine simplistic readings of
motivation and minimize the autonomy and omnipotence of character. If
melodrama tends toward bifurcation by isolating ethical positions, the
type of films that the Tavianis produce tends toward blurring clear-cut
distinctions and away from consolidating character and positionality.
Their films explore positionality rather than motivation.

I sovversivi (1964) traces the lives of four different characters: Erman-
no, a philosophy student who decides to become a photographer; Giulia,
the wife of a Communist official who explores lesbianism; Ettore, an
exiled Venezuelan activist, who decides to rejoin the political struggle at
home; and Lodovico, a filmmaker, who abandons a film on Leonardo da
Vinci to make political films. The film traces the various ways in which
personal and political change are interrelated and are threatening to the
individuals as well as to their families and friends. By dispersing the
narrative interest among several characters rather than following the
usual tendency to focus on a single protagonist, the film dramatizes the
Tavianis' concern with examining, not prescribing, collectivity. The shifting perspective contrasts with the selective neorealist focus on the representative individual and on normative ethical considerations. In the pro-
liferation of the various characters and in the movement away from the
binarism of melodrama, one sees the emergence of a style that conveys
irony and complexity. Also, the film contains actual footage of Togliatti's
funeral, which serves as a reference point for the characters' struggles
and as a self-reflexive reference to photography and filmmaking. Along
with its concern to trace the transformations of its several characters, the
film probes the question of the relationship between politics and representation. Through the four protagonists, the film seeks, in content and
in style, to invent new political possibilities for intellectuals that do not
resemble traditional political rhetoric and practices. This Gramscian
focus on intellectuals and culture is representative of much radical
thinking of the 1960s. Through the focus on intellectuals, the film
explores the politics of party, conflicts between traditional political allegiances and organization, and the need for rethinking personal relationships. Gender and sexuality here, as in other Taviani films, are obliquely
treated.

Questions of national identity are central to their work, juxtaposed

166 often with the problems of regionalism. The film's problematic is conveyed through the uses of landscape, dialect, choreographed movement of the actors, and disjunctions between sound and image. *Sotto il segno dello scorpione* (1968), a film that the Tavianis consider their most experimental, concerns a group of revolutionaries who leave one volcanic island and land on another. On the second island, the inhabitants live a ritualized, hierarchical, and traditional existence. In their attempts to convince the inhabitants to leave this island, they resort to rape and killing. The film's focus on myths of social groups engages with questions of folklore and ethnography along with questions of origin, biological determinism, and ritualized behavior. The film explores the issue of leadership in relation to revolutionary goals by tracing the failure of the revolutionaries back to their unexamined and misguided efforts to institute corrective decisions by force.

The thematic of failed leadership appears in other Taviani films. The style of *Sotto il segno dello scorpione* provides a deeper understanding of that failure. The film plays with the reduction of verbal language as the voices are frequently drowned out in cacophony, in music, and in the sounds of nature. The emphasis on sound and silence has many ramifications in their films. It signifies the nonverbal, habituated, and nonreflective nature of the characters' behaviors. The Tavianis' unconventional uses of dialogue, music, and silence provide new perspectives on character and theme. Paolo Taviani has said that "in our film ... the question of language is a vital element and it is a constant provocation for the public."[20] The Tavianis' involvement with language calls to mind Pasolini's concerns with language and hegemony, as does their engagement with Gramscian questions of the nature of subalternity and common sense. Silence and cacophony together come to signify the failure of language, the triumph of force, and the loss of meaningful community. Silence represents the unknown dimensions of the relations of force, the muteness of the subaltern, and the absence of any cohesive bonds.

The treatment of landscape in this film—also reminiscent of Pasolini's films—is central to the visual language of the film and the thematics. The Tavianis have said, "We want to present people in all their complexity and so it is necessary to place them in the larger context of their relationship to nature."[21] The barren volcanic landscape becomes the correlative for the eruption of violence among the men on the island. The stark landscape aligns to the stark living conditions. Moreover, the emphasis on ritualized chanting and dancing and the volcanic eruption of violence at the end undermine any sense of nature or human relationships as simple and benign. Although the film concerns itself with the ethical implications of the struggle among the Scorpionids and the islanders, which is suggestive of neorealist concerns, the treatment of the conflict, especially the emphasis on the failure of discourse, provides a critical commentary on the ambiguity of prevailing representations of community, particularly those involving regional groups or family. The dramatization of regional and familial concerns suggests that the film seeks to undermine common-sense conceptions of social behavior, particularly those involving altruism.

In films made in the last years of Fascism such as *I bambini ci guardano*, and in early neorealist films such as *Roma, Open City, Shoe Shine,* or *Bicycle Thief* the struggle for community, which tends to become melodramatic, is portrayed through representative individuals (often children) and the more intimate family group. The Tavianis' more detached form of filmmaking probes the complexity of human social groups by emphasizing, without judgment, the existence of aggressivity and the fallibility of leadership. Their film offers no "solution" but it does explore an issue central to Gramsci's writing, namely, the problem of creating hegemony, and also touches, in allegorical fashion, on the various obstacles — springing from power, economics, sexuality, and gender — that stand in the way of creating collective action.

Experimenting with Language and Folklore

The Tavianis' next two films, *San Michele aveva un gallo* (1971) and *Allonsonfan* (1973), are also concerned with the betrayal of and by revolutionary leaders. The films investigate the role of leadership and commitment by focusing on the relationship between traditional intellectuals and subaltern groups. In the case of *San Michele aveva un gallo*, the protagonist is portrayed as out of touch with the peasantry. Bereft of a language with which to communicate, unable to find an outlet for his zeal, the protagonist regresses into the past and finally commits suicide. In the case of *Allonsonfan*, a historical film set in the post-Napoleonic era, the protagonist, Fulvio Imbriani (Marcello Mastroianni) is a disillusioned revolutionary who retreats into the past. After being freed from prison, he returns to his family and resolves to obliterate his prior life, only to be reminded of it by the return of his former mistress. Fulvio betrays his son, his mistress, and his former colleagues and is finally destroyed. This film probes the nature of that betrayal and subversion more deeply than did the Tavianis' previous films. The film orchestrates questions of Italian history with an emphasis on the difficulties of creating organic intellectuals in contrast to the creation of traditional intellectuals. Fulvio

168 occupies a role similar to that of Togliatti in *I sovversivi:* a figure belonging to the past. The revolutionaries belong to the future, but, as the Tavianis have said, "too far into the future ... and, in the middle, we have Allonsonfan [the character] and utopia. Utopia is the only winning element in the film and it is that which punishes Fulvio, and that which gives Allonsonfan strength to go back into his dream."[22]

This film too is highly stylized in its presentation of character and mise en scène. Tony Mitchell describes how " 'exaggeration' involved in a vision of revolutionary Utopia is built into the presentational structure of *Allonsonfan;* self-reflexive theatricality abounds in the film's half-operatic, half-Brechtian format, along with more popular commercial overtones."[23] Verbal language in this film takes the form of misprision and is the prime vehicle of betrayal. Other and more positive uses of language are suggested in the music and in the peasants' dance, and the question of language — that of the characters as well as that of the form of the film itself — is again accorded prominence. This preoccupation with different aspects of language allows the Tavianis to challenge the socially directed preoccupations of the neorealists, to enable a representation of their protagonists as figures of contradiction and the events themselves as bordering on illusion. The film's portrayal of the silent watchfulness of the servants and of the other peasants along with its uses of song and of religious ritual are contrasted to the portraits of pretentious and self-deceiving upper-class family relationships. The treatment of the revolutionaries too violates conventional heroic or antiheroic treatments and offers instead a composite, multidimensional treatment of political figures and of Italian history that invites comparisons of those times with present political problems.

In the vein of a Gramscian analysis of Italian history, the film poses the question of a radical Jacobinism in conflict with more moderate positions, and in this struggle a number of issues are orchestrated: the conflicts between North and South, between peasants and aristocracy, between clergy and laity, and consequently between different cultural interests and forms. Gramsci, in his notes on Italian history, describes the complex problems dramatized in *Allonsonfan:*

> The Italian bourgeoisie was incapable of uniting the people around itself, and this was the cause of its defeats and the interruptions in its development. In the Risorgimento too, the same narrow egotism prevented a rapid and vigorous revolution like the French one. This is one of the most important problems, one of the most fertile causes of serious difficulties in writing the history of the subaltern social groups and hence the (past) history *tout court* of the Italian States.[24]

In this allegory, Fulvio, the bourgeois, is a reincarnation of the untrustworthy revolutionary; the traditional intellectual, tired of privation, who finds himself unable to abandon his class privilege, and who abandons collective goals for personal ends. The Jacobins, by contrast, are presented as nonanalytic, adhering to unexamined notions of party and loyalty and unwilling to assess the efficacy of certain acts.

The Taviani film that appears most to adhere to Gramscian issues and analyses concerning Italian history is *Padre padrone*. The film orchestrates a number of concerns, especially the question of language as intimately and specifically tied to cultural and political differences relating to the longstanding North/South question. The film explores common-sense strategies of survival through the legitimation as well as resistance to regionalism and familialism.

Organic Intellectuals

Padre padrone appeared in 1977. Made for television, the film received international attention and acclaim, and, among the Tavianis' productions, the film is exemplary for the ways in which it adopts a neorealist style at the same time that it radically and ironically modifies it. Though the film begins in the present, it retreats through flashback to the past to trace significant episodes dramatizing the childhood, growth to manhood, and the education that transforms the protagonist from a verbally inarticulate shepherd to a highly articulate professor of linguistics and to an author. It adopts flashback, voice-over commentary, dream sequences, and sound-image montage, as well as other strategies. The film interweaves fact and fiction in its incorporation of the actual Gavino Ledda with the fictional Gavino. The presence at the outset of the film of Ledda, author of the book *Padre padrone,* not only complicates the relationship between fact and fiction but also raises issues of education, modernization, and the role of the organic intellectual (including the "authors" of the film) as necessary but contradictory elements in the transformation of the peasant.

Padre padrone is set in Gramsci's Sardinia, one of Italy's poorest regions, and the Sardinian landscape is integrally identified with the struggles of the peasants to survive. Like the Gavino of the film, Antonio Gramsci grew up in this environment and was later to use his experiences as a basis for developing his ideas on the role of the Mezzogiorno in the transformation of Italian culture and society. Of Gramsci's connections to Sardinia, James Joll states: "Gramsci's roots in Sardinia were deep, not only because of his earlier experience of the poverty and social

injustice in the island, but because he had come to respect the indigenous folk culture of a backward community. He was fascinated by the
Sardinian dialect, by its traditional poems and stories, and by its linguistic origins."[25] However, this fascination was not one of nostalgia or exoticism for Gramsci: "Despite his deep affinity with Sardinia, Gramsci
never romanticized it. From Sardinia he acquired an attitude of realistic
assessment of the enormous difficulties impeding radical change.... Sardinia taught Gramsci how long the past was and how deeply entrenched
were the habits of heart in the way of revolutionary social change."[26] The
experiences narrated by Ledda in his book and transformed onto film by
the Tavianis reveal a similar fascination with the Sardinian world and
the ways in which this world is representative of an important but
neglected aspect of Italian political and cultural life. In unsentimental
fashion, the film is determined to examine the impedance to and possibilities for change in this rural part of Italy.

The film does not take the usual condescending view of peasant life.
By situating the perspective on events in the eyes and ears of the young
Gavino and of the film's narrator, the grown and educated Gavino, *Padre
Padrone* undermines an omniscient narration. By mixing the young and
the mature Gavinos, the fictional character and the actual individual, to
complicate perspective, the film works to defamiliarize traditional associations with peasant life, a technique that makes it possible to experience the narrative in less clichéd and melodramatic terms.

The peasants are portrayed as intelligent, struggling human beings
confronting their harsh environment, armed with a knowledge of their
world necessary for physical survival and continuance. This is not say
that they have a critical awareness of the terms of their existence or of
the potential for change, but rather that common sense — the complex
melange of information based on knowledge they have acquired about
their environment, respect and fear of the past, adherence to traditional
practices, superstitions, and family loyalties — is mobilized as a mode of
protection. Unlike the neorealist texts, *Padre padrone* does not utilize an
affective language toward the ends of forcing a sentimental or melodramatic alignment with one character to the exclusion of empathy for the
other. As Robert Kolker says of *Padre padrone*, "No one mood is permitted to wear itself out, and no one opportunity is missed to manipulate
the viewer's perspective and the tone of particular events, and to comment upon them in the imagery or on the sound track in a manner that is
not quite psychological, sociological, or directly political, yet manages to
combine these three modes of inquiry.... We are engaged and yet asked

to keep our distance, and we learn with some force of an exotic and appalling way of life through a film that is somewhat exotic in mixture of styles and levels of discourse."[27] Kolker's reference to exoticism is crucial in relation to the Tavianis' representation of peasant life. Conventional treatments of peasants are usually characterized by voyeurism. The spectator is invited to gaze at an unfamiliar and exotic world that remains alien and fascinating in its remoteness.

The style of the Tavianis' film, and specifically the variation of perspectives, not only make the spectator aware of irreconcilable differences but often frustrate any attempt to make sense of and to bridge differences. By using the grown-up Ledda as the narrator, the film closes some, but not all, of the distance between the familiar and the alien. But the most striking way in which *Padre padrone* makes the experiences of peasant life accessible is through the film's concern with education, an issue that is central to Gramsci's focus on the nature of the subaltern and the problematics of social change. The Tavianis have said that Gavino's father and the hills of Sardinia "represent a brutally paternalistic conditioning process in Gavino's school of hard knocks."[28] The key terms in their statement are "conditioning" and "school of hard knocks." In this film, the life of the peasant is seen as a form of education, though a form of education far different from the life of the city and from traditional notions of education. In the scenes with the father, the boy is taught, though harshly, what he needs to know to survive and be productive in this environment. This perspective further breaks down the alienating aspects of rural existence. Peasant life is thus not mindless but represents a certain traditional form of learning that must be challenged in order for change to take place. In this respect, the film does not idealize nature and agrarian life, but sets it up as a mode of life that is contrasted to the urban life and to the exigencies of modernity from which even remote areas like this cannot escape. The knowledge of the subaltern that served well for survival in one context is now, through the portrait of Ledda and his conflict with his father, subject to interrogation.

Gramsci's assertion that "all men are intellectuals ... but not all men have in society the function of intellectuals. There is no human activity from which every form of intellectual participation can be excluded,"[29] is applicable to the ways the film treats knowledge. In the film, when Gavino is wrenched out of the classroom by his father, a contrast is made between the kind of knowledge represented by his father and that of the school, which sets up a sustained contrast throughout the film between the father's shrewd and obsessive commitment to the position of

172 a pastoral padrone and Gavino's increasing consciousness of the modern world. His father's behavior, however, is not arbitrary. In terms of common sense, his actions are based on his traditional belief that formal education is not necessary and might perhaps be detrimental to the life of the shepherd. The boy is removed from verbal language and books and transported to a world of sounds in nature.

The father's world is a traditional world in which survival depends on generational continuity, submission to paternal dictates, and a mistrust of professional and traditional intellectual pursuits. This traditional culture is not bereft of a view of the world, and it does not imply that the peasants are lacking in a philosophic sense of the world. Rather, the question is posed whether traditional common-sense positions are not most conducive to an understanding of psychosocial conditions and thus presumably of alternative forms of behavior and action. Through strict discipline, the father initiates Gavino into the environment, and teaches him the skills necessary for becoming a shepherd. The young child receives his education in isolation from his mother, from other children, and at times even from his father. This separation from human contact makes him acutely conscious of the sights and sounds of nature. He mitigates his loneliness and is initiated into sex through observing the animals as well as observing other young shepherds buggering the sheep. It is clear that, through him, the film wishes to dramatize his desire for pleasure and the constraints of his education. Gavino is introduced to music, for example, through two itinerants who sell him an accordion, which he tries to play and then destroys in frustration when he cannot produce the sounds of music. These episodes dramatize that Gavino does not merely submit to his conditions and that he is aware of the harshness of the world that has been imposed on him.

Generally, Gavino is seen as humorous, and is portrayed as seeing the humor and irony of his situation. Some scenes are brutal. Kolker comments on the particularly harsh thrashing that the father gives the boy: "The camera frames the two in a perfect image of a *pieta* and the father's singing is joined by other voices on the sound track as the camera drifts away from the two figures to the countryside. The viewer is permitted to experience revulsion at the beating, relief at the father's show of concern."[30] The act is thus not seen as an act of sadism but as inherent to this type of existence in which the father is doomed to repeat blindly his own history. The double vision of the film apparent in the contrast between Gavino and his father, music and language, language and silence, isolation and community, is always present and indicative of a conflict over folklore and history, common sense and good sense. Gavino's rebelliousness is also not unique but is characteristic of the other young men from his part of the country and characteristic too of the changes affecting Italian rural life, and Sardinia in particular. The army, where he rediscovers the power of language, intervenes to alter what might have been a repetition of his father's life. The language he acquires is verbal, technological, and artistic. He learns to speak and to read, as well as to construct a radio by reading directions. Through these painful experiences he becomes detached from his class and, through acquiring new language and skills, is placed in the position of having to come to terms with a number of differences, especially those involving social class and regionalism. His decision to go to the university provokes a confrontation with his father in which Gavino is the winner, but the victory is in no way clear-cut, as it would be in a film that celebrates upward mobility.

Though Gavino has fought against the constraints of this world—against familialism, and against the harsh patriarchal society represented by his father—he does not totally sever his ties to it. His decision to return to Sardinia signifies his sense of belonging and his commitment to his culture, but also his ambivalence about his identity. As Witcombe states, "In Sardinia, his sense of rootedness serves him as a kind of scourge, by which he can muster a sense of dynamism and mission."[31] Gavino becomes a representative of what Gramsci termed the "organic intellectual" through his acquisition of education and his (and the film's) emphasis on the importance of language as a means of controlling one's world, as opposed to being subordinated to it. Organic intellectuals are, like Gavino, a creation of modern rather than traditional societies. They occupy an organizational position in relation to their class. Through his experiences of the world beyond his rural environment and through his subsequent education, Gavino is not only able to understand and articulate his situation; he is also in the position to transform his earlier environment instead of becoming a spokesman for the professional class to which he now belongs.

Language becomes a means of escape not only for him, as he learns through his initial contact with words and later with writing, but also for others in his village. For Gramsci, too, language enables individuals and groups to make sense of their world and, hence, to transform it. The absence of language signifies imprisonment, a form of chaos in which the entire community (but particularly the young) are contained by the triple structures of patriarchy, class, and generation. Thus, language is

174   associated with a form of education that enables individuals to develop new ways of understanding and altering their world. The film closes but does not resolve the conflicts. The now educated Gavino is both alienated from yet very much a part of this world to which he returns. His state seems to represent the position that the problems of modernity and of economic and social transformation are not eradicated but constitute themselves in new forms.

Fascism and Folklore

In *La notte di San Lorenzo*, the Tavianis turn toward the north of Italy, though not away from the rural environment, as they address a subject that has been only indirectly alluded to in their work — Fascism and World War II. Told in retrospect through the eyes of a young girl, the film has personal meaning for the filmmakers. The town of San Martino is the fictional name for their hometown of San Miniato, and the Tavianis had earlier made a documentary on the town of San Miniato and the events of 1944. The 1982 narrative dramatizes the last phases of World War II as the Nazis intimidate and persecute the inhabitants of the town. Gathered in the cathedral, the citizens agonize over whether to go or to remain. Under the leadership of a peasant, one group decides to leave and find the Americans; the other group votes to remain. The film follows the group that sets out on the road. Like *Padre padrone*, the use of a child's perspective serves the purpose of providing a disingenuously naive way of narrating events and therefore of circumventing associations with the history of Fascism that are heavily laden with ideological meanings and closely tied to folklore and common sense.

As Millicent Marcus has written, "Vulnerable as they are to the caprice of personal reminiscence and to the emendation of communal testimony, the events conjured up in the film lose their status as historical fact and take their place among the items of folklore that make up the collective consciousness of San Martino."[32] The emphasis on folklore in the film is exemplified in the blending of religious imagery with Virgilian images from the *Aeneid*, and in the magical incantations recited by the child. The fusion of religion, myth, and folklore is not merely a matter of stylistics but is the Tavianis' way of characterizing folklore as an essential element of ideology, as in *Padre padrone*. Indeed, the fusion of these elements is intimately related to Gramsci's conception of "folklore" or what he might call provincialism. Through the film's treatment of past and present and through its exploration of characters from different parts of the country as well as from Europe and America, language becomes a locus for a number of intersecting conceptions—a mixture of religious beliefs, moral precepts, social prejudices, and proverbial sayings, as well as specific ways of narrating events and of acting. The film explores the multiple ways in which the characters—young and old, Fascist and anti-Fascist, peasant and upper class, inhabit a world of fragmentary and inherited ideas. The characters exchange knowledge, present their opinions and beliefs, under the illusion that they possess a coherent worldview, although their ways of acting are instead not at all coherent and are certainly not critical.

The conflicts between those who stay in the church and those who leave, between the Fascists and the anti-Fascists, are indicative of divisions in a community that, through contiguity and history, should acknowledge solidarity; these divisions, however, are deadly. The film also illustrates the possibility of canceling difference, as in the case of the romantic, though temporary, union of the elderly Galvano and Concetta, who endured years of separation based on perceived class differences only in order to come together on this night.

The film's structure, like that of so many Taviani films, is not dependent on a single protagonist but is dispersed among several characters. In this way, the film undermines identification with the plight of isolated individuals and focuses attention on the composition and struggles of individuals as members of a community. The spectator's expectation of the unified text is further undermined, as in *Padre padrone*, by the evident distinctions in narration between the voice of the child and the voice-over of the adult. The disjunction between image and sound makes the viewer conscious of different time frames: the moment represented and the moment of reflection. Sound is used as counterpoint; for example, it functions to exonerate the young Cecilia from ultimate responsibility for her words. The Tavianis' emphasis on the sound track as well as on language indicates at least in part their insistence on the audience's hearing as well as seeing. In this way, the Tavianis review the sense of language in all of its aspects, including the ways in which physical movement, as in the scenes that depict choreographed battles or the group's journeys on the road, also enhances an understanding of the multiple character positions and points of view.

The union of pagan and Christian elements in *La notte di San Lorenzo* points to the ritualistic aspects of peasant life, which are part of its common-sense orientation. The role of religion is important as we see by the several scenes that take place in the church. Religion and common sense

176   merge, as they do in Gramsci's analysis. To give but one instance of the combined incoherent elements that compose common sense and its reliance on religion: Catholicism is, for Gramsci,

> in reality a multiplicity of distinct and often contradictory religions: there is one Catholicism for the peasants, one for the *petit-bourgeois* and town workers, one for women, and one for intellectuals which is itself variegated and disconnected. But common sense is influenced not only by the crudest and least elaborated forms of these sundry Catholicisms as they exist today. Previous religions have also had an influence and remain components of this common sense to this day.[33]

This residual element of other forms of thought, rituals, and practices is also portrayed in *La notte di San Lorenzo* and constitutes yet another dimension of the Tavianis' examination of cultural practices. Their concern with folklore also serves as an instrument for their exploration of the nature of collectivity.

In its dependence on narrative, especially that taken from folklore, common sense is dependent on (as Gramsci has reminded us) residual elements from the past, and an important aspect of the style of *La notte di San Lorenzo* is the film's address of different forms of storytelling. Storytelling, rather than the events themselves as narrated, self-consciously constitutes the central preoccupation of this film as well as *Padre padrone*, and serves a number of different and conflicting functions within the films and possibly for the spectator. As with Cecilia's and Gavino's narration, the act of telling, like the act of creating a film, is itself a collective act, not the product of one individual in isolation from others. Folklore embodied in storytelling is the Tavianis' medium for exploring questions and problems concerning group identification and the precariousness of community relations. For the Tavianis the sense of community is never static and is constantly beset by resistances to change and by differences that often cannot be acknowledged except through conflict and force. In *Padre padrone*, the Tavianis distinguish between the inarticulate Gavino and the professor of linguistics that he has become. In *La notte di San Lorenzo*, they distinguish between the child, Cecilia, and the woman that she has become. In both films, they contrast past and present life in rural communities to dramatize changes that have taken place.

The filmmakers use the notion of storytelling as a metaphor in their search to understand the ways in which communities are constituted; how they produce leaders, followers, and social conflicts; and also how the potential for new alignments arises. For example, the contrast between the images from the *Aeneid* and those of contemporary warfare operates multivalently to distinguish modes of storytelling, to associate history with folklore, and also to distinguish between past and present. In his essay "The Storyteller," Walter Benjamin associates the tale with an older form of narration, one that "counsels," is not easily consumable, and attempts to forge a vital link between storyteller and audience.[34] The language of the tale is not exclusively the language of the individual author but of individual voices within a collectivity. In their exploration of storytelling, the Tavianis juxtapose the traditional tale against contemporary forms of narration; by so doing, they opt for a dialogue between tale and modern story as a part of a necessary process for dramatizing both the limitations and potential of traditional storytelling.

Complicating Narratives and History

In *Kaos* (1984), which is a portmanteau film containing four different though thematically related narratives based on Pirandello tales, the Tavianis continue and complicate their preoccupation with language and cultural identity. As with their use of Ledda in *Padre padrone*, the use of Pirandello constitutes an acknowledgment of cultural affinity between literature and film and a shared sense of cultural analysis, particularly in the treatment of folklore and modernity. Links between the Tavianis' uses of these two authors are made evident in the exploration of various language practices: language as a vehicle for common sense, for survival, and for subversion. In contrast to the strategies of neorealism, in *Kaos* as in other films, the Tavianis sever the easy fit between language and narrative. They call attention to dissociations between words and meaning, gesture and verbal language, sight and sound. The presence and voice of the fictional Pirandello as well as his printed words in *Kaos,* and the adoption of literary narratives as the basis for the film text, signal that the film acknowledges the existence of bourgeois forms of writing and places them in dialogue with the speech of the peasants and filmmakers. The film thus creates dialogues between literature and film,[35] speaking and writing, and language and silence. In *Kaos,* language is also intertwined with the "Southern Question" and reinforced both by the choice of the works of a writer from the South, Pirandello, whose works address that region and by his fictional persona in the film.

The film opens with a Pirandello quotation, the words superimposed on images of a landscape: "I am the son of chaos, not allegorically but in actuality, because I was born in our country near a dense wood, denominated in dialectal form by the inhabitants of Girgenti, *Cavusu,* a corruption in dialect of the ancient Greek word, *Kaos.*" With these words, the choice of Pirandello's novellas as a basis for the stories, and the epilogue employing the figure of Pirandello returning to Sicily, the film presents a contrast between the act of writing and that of speaking: not necessarily a set of alternatives. The film is not a formal exercise and essay in cinematic representation for its own sake but a way of further examining how language structures behavior within the narrative and in the interaction between film and the audience. By dramatizing the destructive role as well as the survival values of ritual and custom, the film examines forms of adherence, subversion, and escape through language.

Kaos is marked at crucial points by the absence of speech, though not of music or natural sounds. Like *Padre padrone*, the film is filled with silences and characterized by economical dialogue. The viewer is made aware of numerous strategies that call attention to the absence or sparseness of verbal communication. The drowning out of words by music, the overlay of words on words, and the distortion of speech by erasing the verbal sound track all act as distancing devices and create a disruption in the normal expectation of the flow of dialogue. This form of silence calls attention to speech as constituted rather than as natural and inevitable, and to the importance of physical gesture in communication that is often overlooked when sound and image are synchronized. In *Kaos*, the disjunction between image and sound is also apparent in the use of a voice-over narration. The films experiment with the voices themselves, employing different time frames, separating the moment represented from the voice-over commentary, and using unconventional voices such as those of children, peasants, and women in opposition to the traditional voice of a male narrator.

As in other Taviani films, in *Kaos* landscape plays a central role. It situates events specifically within the Sicilian context and calls attention to the uniqueness of the terrain and to the struggles of the inhabitants to survive in that barren, mountainous milieu. The aerial shots of the terrain also provide a detached perspective on the narrative and on the characters involved. The audience is invited, literally, to take a bird's-eye view of the landscape (through the image and hence the perspective of the soaring bird with which each episode begins). The folkloric element is earlier underlined in the men's placing a bell on the bird of ill omen. By presenting the characters within the larger context of their relationship to nature and by allowing the audience to view the characters with a degree of detachment that permits critical involvement with the issues rather than invoking a sentimental bonding with the characters, the Tavianis seek once again to complicate their narratives. This unconventional treatment is particularly important, considering the ways in which peasant life has been traditionally represented in the Italian cinema as buffoonish, exotic, or melodramatically victimized. The Tavianis dignify their characters by calling attention to the difference between them and the audience rather than by assuming an easy comprehension. Much as in the ethnographic film, the audience is asked to contemplate another culture, the culture of Sicily; but unlike in conventional ethnography, the existence of difference is not a subject of fascination. Differences in appearance, language, behavior, and values are everywhere evident and are not mitigated.

The sense of entering another world is highlighted and reinforced by the camera's insistence on panoramic vision through the bird's-eye perspective but also through the film's emphasis on speech and writing, a dimension in the ethnographic film often suppressed in the presentation of third-world cultures in the first world. The dominant culture's presentation of the subaltern culture tends toward aestheticizing the subjects and hence silencing them. As in so many Taviani films, silence is crucial as a signifier of a number of conflicting cultural issues. In some of the tales, silence is related to secrecy. In others, it marks the limits of class, gender, and ethnic discourses. In all the tales, it is related to the question of power, of who speaks for whom. Both verbally and visually, the focus on the issue of language and silence is central to *Kaos* as it positions the audience in an active, though separate, relationship to the figures and events represented. The audience is not allowed to forget for a moment that it is confronting a different world, one that has its own complex rules and strategies for survival.

Distinctions between writing and speech figure prominently in the film's individual tales, as they do in "third cinema." In the first story, "L'Altro figlio" (The other son), the mother seeks to communicate with her emigrant sons by dictating a letter to a village woman who is also unable to write and instead makes scratches on a piece of paper. The fraud is exposed by a doctor, who, exercising his power over the written word in response to her request to write the letter, extorts her life story from her. At the end of the tale, unaffected by her own narration, the mother reiterates the same letter she had initially dictated to her illiterate amanuensis (also a woman). The link between women and language surfaces as an issue of disenfranchisement and reinforces the notion that women are outside language and hence outside culture. The mother is trapped in her lack of access to writing, and trapped therefore in a history of oppression that is traced back to the Risorgimento as well as to a

180 personal history of rape and familial disintegration. The mother has remained in Sicily while her sons have left for America, and the emigrants that she examines as she seeks to find a bearer for her "letter" are indifferent to her desire to create a bond between Italy and America, between customs at home and new practices abroad. A man whose son is emigrating tells her flatly that he wants to hear nothing from his departing son, but the mother cannot relinquish her attachment to the absent sons nor her hatred for the son who remains behind to remind her of her past sufferings—the brutal death of her husband, her rape at the hands of his murderers, the loss of her favored sons to America, and her inability to communicate with them due to her illiteracy. Ironically, the rehearsal of her past does not liberate her but reinforces her unwillingness to relinquish her nostalgia and her resentment. Through the mother, the episode introduces the folkloric elements of melodrama—stylized splitting of character types, anguished and affective encounters, the valorization of gesture over verbal language in the familiar narrative of revenge and retribution. The treatment of the other characters, however, the musical overlay, the counterpoint of the emigrating groups, and the presence of the doctor, offer different positions, though not necessarily corrective of hers. What is evident is that her common sense is not invalidated, not treated unempathetically, but exposed to examination.

In "Mal di luna" (Moon sickness), the second of the four tales in *Kaos*, the mother is a pivotal figure. Similarly, the tale plays with common sense and folklore. The happiness of a newly married couple, Batà and Sidora is threatened by the husband's madness on nights when the moon is full. The madness is traced to his infancy and is closely linked to his mother, who left him exposed at night to the moon when forced to work during a harvest. After Sidora abandons Batà in terror, having witnessed his "moon madness," and returns home to her mother, Batà comes to town. In the town square, he confesses both his regret at not having told his wife of his infirmity and laments her failing to understand his condition. The confession enables Batà to articulate his suffering; it does not endear him to Sidora, whose preference for another man, Saro, has also been a factor in her lack of empathy for the distraught Batà. The mother craftily arranges for a common-sense resolution to her daughter's dilemma. She arranges to visit her daughter on the night of the moon madness accompanied by her daughter's lover, Saro. The lover is expected to distract the daughter but, upon hearing the cries of the husband, refuses to betray him. The tables are again turned on women,

as the wife is thwarted in her desire for sexual gratification by Saro's
empathy for the howling man outside.

The relationship between husband and wife is characterized by his reluctance to tell her of his condition initially and by her ignorance, which grows from fear. Secrets play a key role, as do notions of superstition and of confession, but in contrast to melodrama the secrets are not condemned or forced into the light of day. Instead, the way secrets are handled in this tale serves not to judge the characters or the existence of secrecy but to introduce through folklore the possibility of different modes of knowledge. This many-layered tale is exemplary of the Tavianis' predilection for folklore, but as with Pirandello it dissects the folkloric elements through ironic juxtapositions and reversals. In style and content, the episode confronts the language of folklore and fantasy with that of everyday survival. The Tavianis' use of folklore does not suppress or complicate links between the moon and notions of sexuality — the eerie uses of light, the intense close-ups of the moon and of the characters' faces, and the emphasis on bodily movement and gesture. Verbal language is practically negligible in this tale, underscoring the core of wisdom in the common sense of folklore. Folklore is not derogated, but is subjected to intellectual and critical analysis and shown to contain wisdom, if in terms different from (but not necessarily in opposition to) psychoanalytic discourse.

The third Pirandellian tale in *Kaos*, "La Giara" (The jar), introduces yet another aspect of common sense that treats individual property and collectivity. The conflict is between Don Lollo, the owner of the local olive fields, a tyrannical employer of the town's inhabitants and workers, and an artisan, Zi' Dima Licasi, who repairs a broken vessel that Don Lollo has bought for his unusually large olive crop. Zi' Dima Licasi inadvertently seals himself in the container while repairing it. More concerned with his property rather than with the plight of the poor man sealed in the jar, Don Lollo seeks the advice of a lawyer to find a way to inculpate the victim. The villagers become the audience for a verbal combat between Don Lollo and Zi' Dima over property and personal rights. Zi' Dima's refusal to be intimidated by the landowner becomes the occasion for the workers to express themselves collectively and in opposition to the will of Don Lollo. Little dialogue passes between master and workers except for the issuing of orders and of chastisement on Don Lollo's part. There is also limited dialogue between Don Lollo and his mistress Sara, who, like Ruth in the Old Testament, sleeps at the feet of her master, but who, in joining the peas-

182   ant's rebellion, it turns out, is not naive about Don Lollo's cruelty and exploitativeness.

The dialogue between the lawyer and Don Lollo reveals how the language of law is like a container, designed to imprison the workers within prevailing notions of property and authority. The story ends on the note of carnival as the workers celebrate Zi' Dima's outsmarting Don Lollo, who is separated from the people as they dance and sing outside the town walls. Language thus becomes more than therapy; it is also a means of subversion. Also, the substance of the tale, like the style of the episode, in its repetition of images and gestures, stark character contrasts, and minimal verbal exchange, draws, like the other tales, on folklore. Folklore emerges as a dynamic form of expression that dramatizes (in Gramscian terms) the multilayered social conflicts in a way that reveals how characters are trapped in their milieu and at the same time explores the possible ways available to the subaltern to undermine constraints.

The final story of the film, "Requiem," dramatizes the power of common sense as folklore to generate overt resistance. The conflict is between peasants, who claim rights of common usage and therefore ownership of their land, and a landowner who refuses to relinquish his titular claims. Under the stern dictates of the village patriarch, the peasants plan to bury their leader, an old man, on the land and not in the village burial plot. In this way, they plan to assert a claim to a burial place, but the baron calls in the police to frustrate them. The baron is outsmarted by the wily old man, the founder of the community, who pretends to be dead and ready for burial. If the man is buried on the land, the baron, by custom, forfeits his claim. The people's remonstrances, the words of their priest, their articulations of outrage about the violation of custom and of their needs, and the resistance to authority as expressed by the old man juxtapose the language of law, authority, and property against the language of custom, use, and communal rights. Afraid to violate the rituals and superstitions associated with the dead, the police flee, leaving the peasants victorious over the baron, underscoring the wiliness of the peasants.

The epilogue of the film, *Colloquio con la madre*, also derived from Pirandello's work, portrays the return of the writer to his childhood home. Brought by the coachman (the model for Saro in "Mal di Luna") to the empty house, Pirandello fantasizes the appearance of his mother. He asks her to recount an event that had always eluded him in his fiction, involving a trip to the island of Gozzo in 1848 when the family was exiled to Malta. Through flashback, the film portrays that incident as the mother describes her awakening desires as a woman. Gavriel Moses has suggested that the mother's narrative exposes the "implicit drama of female separation and individuation."[36] Specifically in this last episode, language serves the function of exploring, even blurring, boundaries between past and present, child and parent, youth and age, and male and female.

The recreation of the past through the mother's narration highlights the importance of memory and storytelling in relation to history and personal identity in the present. Like an elegiac poem, this episode probes the relationship between loss and creativity; the dead mother's image is recreated, incorporated, and relinquished. Like the process of mourning, the telling recovers the lost object through memory, and as with mourning, the purpose of the telling is to be able to let go. Pirandello is a surrogate for the two filmmakers who through their film have also returned to the past. Like Pirandello, they seek knowledge about their history.

Kaos orchestrates the multiple Gramscian concerns that animate all of the Tavianis' films. The films' preoccupation with the "language question" can be seen as multilayered and hybrid: a focus on an allegorical treatment that invites the spectator to think in multidimensional ways about language and representation. The concern with storytelling encompasses considerations of national, class, family, and regional identity; traditional and modern forms of narrativizing; and especially the positions of artist and intellectual in relation to the politics of cultural representation. The numerous concerns that animate the films are reminiscent of Gramsci's commitment to rethink the role of intellectuals, the nature of education, and the complex nature of subaltern life, as well as his need to rethink common sense and folklore in the context of the clash between tradition and modernity. In their treatment of subaltern groups particularly, the films reject a melodramatic treatment of the subaltern as unproblematically knowable and knowing, dependent and victimized. Concomitantly, the style is interrogative and tentative rather than assertive, fragmented rather than seamless and unified. Such style suggests that narratives are constituted in the context of different and competing interests and explanations rather than being given and deterministic.

The films insist on taking common sense and folklore seriously as contradictory resources for understanding the tendency toward nostalgia, conformity, and repetition in social relations. The films also dramatize how common sense can be understood as a means toward survival,

184 one that contains overt and covert expressions of opposition. In their emphasis on peasant life and on the rural environment, the films maintain a neorealist concern; but the filmmakers have gone beyond neorealism to probe the possibilities and limits of storytelling in relation to official forms of historicizing. The Tavianis' concern with storytelling is indicative of the ways in which the filmmakers construct their films as testing grounds to explore the changing political and social climate.

Chapter 8

Postmodernism as Folklore in Contemporary Science Fiction Cinema

Far from languishing in the "ghettos" of mass culture, science fiction has "moved uptown" to academic journals and book-length studies.[1] Much recent critical work has served as catalyst for rethinking the nature of representation in the context of what has been termed the "postmodern" by such writers as Jean Baudrillard, Jean-François Lyotard, Paul Virilio, and Fredric Jameson.[2] In particular, feminist theorists such as Sandra Harding and Donna Haraway have called for the critical examination of existing notions of science as a necessity, and as an alternative and not an obstacle to prevailing conceptions of sexual difference and the body politic.[3] In these reconsiderations of modernity, the science fiction film has come of age; it has become a focal point for speculation on the supercession of modernism, changing conceptions of history, the disappearance of the human subject, and the appearance of what has been described as the postmodern biotechnical body. The presence of the ubiquitous figure of Frankenstein, his permutation from physicist to biologist, and his gradual disappearance into the "intelligence network" (and corporate structures) would seem to validate the increasingly popular, though problematic, "narrative" of postmodernity.

The discussion of science fiction in this chapter examines how certain contemporary filmic productions of the genre have circulated a discourse, or more properly a folklore, of postmodernity in relation to science. This folklore addresses questions of control, selection, change, and scientific management through technology. In common-sense fashion, representations of biology and medicine converge with other issues relating to the effects of industrialization, urban life, epidemiology, and sanitation. The urban landscape and especially the subterranean aspects of the city—the sewers and the gutters—have become in science fiction the spawning sites of the monstrous, of disease, and of mutations. These representations are a further indication of the discursive relations between biology and politics and their positioning in a discourse of postmodernity that creates a pastiche of urban life, architecture, technology, and media. A basic distinguishing feature of the discourse of postmodernism is its investment in the "narrative" of the hyperreal:

> No more mirror of being and appearances, of the real and its concept; no more imaginary coextensivity: rather, genetic miniaturization is the dimension of simulation. The real is produced from miniaturized units, from matrices, memory banks and command models—and with these it can be reproduced an indefinite number of times. It no longer has to be rational, since it is no longer measured against some ideal or negative instance.[4]

In the "postmodernism condition," we see the dematerialization of the scientist along with the historian (though the filmmaker may assume the place of missing scientist and historian). There is no doubt that considerations of science and technology are central to formulations of postmodernism. Increasingly, science fiction films entertain as their central concern questions of simulation. Whether simulations be in the form of doubling, through replicating human life synthetically, or whether they are the product of information technology, the simulacrum has been identified as a major characteristic of postmodernism in the many analyses of recent science fiction cinema. Furthermore, an analysis of these films suggests that there is some consonance between popular representations of science and the various ways in which the discourses of academic and professional science present themselves. Such films as *Re-Animator* (1985), *Frankenstein Unbound* (1990), *Creator* (1985), *They Live* (1988), and *Overdrawn at the Memory Bank* (1983) offer a range of articulations concerning science: physics, chemistry, and medicine in league or in contention with biology; biology in contention with or conjoined to new information technologies; science linked to politics and power; popular as opposed to elite science; and the affiliations of research with changing corporate structures.

The various figurations of the scientist—the lone researcher, his absorption into the corporate structure, and his disappearance as an isolated figure of power—have produced different conceptions of the body, of gender and sexual identity, and of technology in relation to the information sciences, the role of research, and, most prominently, the relationship of research to existing corporate structures. Fusing and confusing past and present history through various representations, endowing technology with theological properties, fusing the public and the private spheres in melodramatic fashion, and also maintaining a familiar and longstanding binary conflict between technology as hero and as villain, perhaps contemporary science fiction films as collages of these various attitudes are not evidence of something called the postmodern condition so much as they are its folklore.

Does the Gramscian conception of common sense and its relationship to folklore posit an alternative to the scientific narratives of postmodernism? Does folklore, with its fragments derived from "the Stone Age to the present," pose a challenge to the "pastiche effect" identified with postmodernism and offer a countervailing argument to monolithic assessments of contemporary culture and society? Specifically, what effect would a Gramscian stance on cultural production have for an understanding of the fictions of science in contemporary science fiction film production? Would a reading of these texts in Gramscian terms complicate the ways in which critics address the role of cultural production under late capitalism? Would a common-sense reading shed light on the ways in which postmodernism is itself a recycling of the familiar linear dystopian or utopian narrative?

Science and Common Sense

In the *Prison Notebooks*, Gramsci writes, "Philosophy and modern science are constantly contributing new elements to 'modern folklore' in that certain opinions and scientific notions, removed from their context and more or less distorted, constantly fall within the popular domain and are 'inserted' into the mosaic of tradition."[5] His notion of folklore bears examination for the possible light it sheds on the role that scientific culture plays in the perpetuation of social and political structures as well as in their transformation, and in particular for the ways science becomes part of the common sense of modernity. "Folklore," he writes, "can be understood only as a reflection of the conditions of cultural life of the people, although certain conceptions specific to folklore remain even after these conditions have been (or seem to be) modified or have given way to bizarre combinations."[6] Folklore is not only persistent but protean; it is capable of assuming a number of forms and drawing on all forms of knowledge, past and present.

Gramsci's comments on folklore encourage the reconfiguration of scientific knowledge as belonging not merely to the domain of the traditional intellectual or to a sphere apart from conventional considerations of art but to every aspect of cultural expression.[7] The terms "folklore" or

188 "common sense" suggest that representations of science are accessible (even if in distorted form) to the popular imagination. The consideration of science fiction as common sense or folklore provides an entry into the various ways in which science is intertwined with rather than dissociated from other cultural considerations. Familiar representations of space travel and of imagined worlds, the staples of science fiction narratives, are pretexts for exploring questions of history, biology, and medicine. The narratives offer differing conceptions of scientific research in relation to reproductive technologies, gerontology, epidemiology, cybernetics, robotics, pharmacology, and psychoanalysis. Folklore as common sense is linked to everyday, commonplace notions of physical life — birth, growth, illness, and death, as well as conceptions of the "normal" and the "monstrous." Not mere false consciousness or ideology in opposition to science, common sense is raw material for understanding coercion and consensus in relation to the production of knowledge.[8]

In a contemporary examination of scientific folklore, Paul Feyerabend asserts:

> Every piece of knowledge contains valuable ingredients side by side with ideas that prevent the discovery of new things. Such ideas are not simply errors. They are necessary for research.... scientists often just don't know what they are talking about.... Most of the time they depend, they have to depend (because of specialization) on *gossip* and *rumours*. ... At this point the similarity between "modern" science and the Middle Ages becomes rather striking.[9]

Concerned with the state of knowledge in relation to change and resistance to the new, Althusser too, in his discussion of spontaneous science, refers to the scientist's implication in philosophical idealism and to the fact that the scientist is critically unaware of this complicity — in much the same ways that philosophy uncritically exploits science. The spontaneous philosophy of scientists is "contradictory and contains both an 'intra-scientific' element and an 'extra-scientific' element — the one originating in their practice, the other imported from outside."[10] For Gramsci, science does not stand in opposition to truth. It partakes of the same problematics as other forms of historical and political analysis. In this vein, he writes, "the element of causality used by the natural sciences to explain human history is in fact quite an arbitrary assumption, if not actually a return to old ideological assumptions."[11] These views of science are consonant with Gramsci's notion of folklore as contradictory — uncritical, if not negative, toward change. Viewed through the lens of common sense, the fictions of science can be regarded as complicated

responses to innovation: they tend in some instances to ward off what is 189
new; in others to mediate between tradition and the new; and in still
others to replace the conventional with the new.

Science fiction is not a linear but a multidimensional genre, requiring
a multidimensional analysis, and my intention is not to offer a taxonomy
of science fiction subgenres. For the purposes of this argument, I will
take the "Frankenstein paradigm"—the various representations of
Frankenstein in the cinema—and analyze its permutations in some
recent science fiction films. Consonant with folklore, the Frankenstein
narrative has come to signify not one but varying and contradictory conceptions of science inherited from the past and altered to suit contemporary audiences. I will explore various representations of the scientist as
physicist, physician, biologist, or technologist; of science as magical,
"real," or discursive; of scientific creations as magical, natural, or simulated; and of the monster as imaginary, human, or alien. Given the protean nature of folklore, the Frankenstein paradigm, offering crucial
insights into contemporary cultural production, is ripe for "postmodern" exploitation.

Physician/Physicist to Biologist

The abiding concern with the physician and with medicine in science fiction encodes the changing relationships between doctor and patient and
establishes the role of research as an integral and threatening element in
those relations. The earliest renditions of the relationship seem to be connected with the physician and the physicist. These figures are legacies of
eighteenth-century science and dramatize notions of regularity, abstraction, and predictability that are associated particularly with electricity
and chemistry and that have profound implications for the biological
sciences. In relation to questions of biology and medicine,

> it might be said that up to the end of the eighteenth century, medicine related
> much more to health than to normality; it did not begin by analyzing a
> "regular" functioning of the organism and go on to seek where it had
> deviated, what it was disturbed by, and how it could be brought back into
> normal working order; it referred rather to qualities of vigour, suppleness,
> and fluidity, which were lost in illness and which it was the task of medicine
> to restore.[12]

What Foucault seeks is a connection between social and medical/tech-
nological "discourses" in relation to conceptions of the body. With the
introduction of new ways of reading symptoms—through the auspices

190 of the clinic, the hospitals, physicians and researchers — the body became the site of a new drama of supervision and power. This drama is enacted in various permutations of Mary Shelley's narrative. The Frankenstein narrative came to be constituted as a horror story. The folkloric elements — the schizophrenic scientist, his grotesque creations, and his threat to traditional and stable forms of community life — converge with Foucault's and Georges Canguilhem's explorations of the links between science and social power.

The emergence of the physician/physicist heralds new discourses of the biological sciences involving the dematerialization of life, a process that subtends biopolitics. Of this dramatic change in the study of the life sciences, Georges Canguilhem writes, "consider a crystal of DNA today. It exists not as an artifact but as a 'superreal,' nonnatural object, the product of considerable technical and theoretical labor. It is the latest in a long series of new scientific objects invented since the end of the nineteenth century ... Life is now studied as far as possible as though it were nonlife, as devoid as possible of its traditional attributes."[13] Canguilhem's description aligns with narrative representations of the physician/physicist who is involved in reducing and transferring energy from nonliving sources to living organisms. In terms of the common-sense representations of this figure, s/he (but usually he) is portrayed as aloof, antihumanistic, sadistic, and obsessive, and concerned with power over nature. The objects on which he experiments are dead humans and animals, as he seeks to recreate life through energetics. In the case of animal experimentation, he does not seek the "secret of life" so much as he works to produce new forms of life. In his obsession to study life, he is remote from organic and holistic conceptions of organisms. He does not treat life as an entity to be preserved and understood in terms of its functioning but as an entity to be broken down, dematerialized, and controlled.

The fans of the pre–World War II Hollywood cinema would have been familiar with this version of the scientist, if not from Mary Shelley's novel then from its numerous adaptations to film, largely in terms of the mad scientist.[14] In these early sound films, the mad scientist can be identified by the fact that he does his work in isolation, usually in a place removed from other community institutions — a ruined castle, the basement of an old building, an old mill. His creative efforts are usually supported by a lone assistant, and his mode of work seems to be more artisanal than industrial. Like an artist, the Frankenstein figure of the scientist plays with the creation of new life forms — miniaturized, human or animal — in such films as *Dr. Cyclops* (1940) and *The Island of*

Lost Souls (1931) both based on H. G. Wells's *The Island of Dr. Moreau.* The   **191**
clichéd elements, earmarks of common sense, identify the physician/
physicist as a threatening authority figure. If not a member of the upper
class, he is a respected member of the community, though ultimately
malevolent. But he leads a double life. As physician, he is a preserver of
life; as physicist, he is detached from life, unrestrained in his appetite to
explore and uncover new knowledge about life and death. If the traditional physician synthesizes, the physician/physicist analyzes. The scientist's creations incorporate both roles, and these roles seem to be at
odds with each other. This duality is nowhere more evident than in
James Whale's *Frankenstein* (1931) and in the various versions of *Dr.
Jekyll and Mr. Hyde* (1920, 1932, 1941). The physician/physicist's creations are presented as a menace to the integrity of the human body and
to stable notions of life and death. As such, these figures are disruptive
of social institutions.

The preoccupation of the physician/physicist exemplified in the
Frankenstein narrative, from Shelley's novel to film versions from 1931
to the present, was with specific organs of the dead reorganized and
revivified to produce a new human being. In many variants of the films,
the emphases on the corpse, on the mismatching of the organs, and on
the nature of the monstrosity created are linked to the conflict between
the "physician" and his newly formed "patient" who is at first supine
and totally dependent on his creator. For a number of reasons in the various retellings — the insertion of a criminal brain, the physician's dehumanizing treatment, the carelessness of an assistant, or a criminality
identified with deviance — the creature turns against not only the physician and his family but society at large.

The isolation of the physician/physicist as the other specifically
embodied in his creature seems to point in two directions. The physi-
cian/physicist is presented as being threatened, driven to the point of
madness by his differences from others, produced by his unrelenting
search for knowledge. The physician/physicist is also threatened by the
hostility of the community endangered by the disastrous effects of his
research.

The Frankenstein figure popularizes a view of science that "would
not have been possible without the physical sciences leading the way.
Because physicists and chemists had 'dematerialized' matter, biologists
were able to explain life by 'devitalizing' it. What man since time
immemorial had sought to perceive in and about organisms as they
existed in nature, scientists now studied under laboratory conditions."[15]
In the case of Frankenstein and his variants, the role of electrical energy

192 is the key to creating new life. In its earliest expressions, the dehuman-
ization of life and the desubjectification of the individual are by-prod-
ucts of the creation of human beings by artificial means; in this case, the
means is technology derived from harnessing electrical energy. The role
of electricity encodes a popular fear of science; more particularly, however, it provides a visual analogue—for example, the electrical rods—
an emblem of the scientist's objectives: power and control over his subjects. The fearful image of the scientist and his laboratory in popular
representation may also be enhanced by the adoption of electricity for
purposes of capital punishment in the late nineteenth century. In the
many-layered pastiche of common sense and folklore, the images of
electricity also come to be associated with history and myth, and particularly with archaic forms of magic. But, characteristic of common sense,
the present is also accounted for: the physician/physicist's manipulation
of electrical energy as represented by his laboratory and his one assistant
presents a view of "modern" science as the work of individual entrepre-
neurs and of these figures in conflict with the community.

Many post-World War II representations, though still concerned with
physics and with altering life forms, tend to popularize a notion of science for the masses as exemplified through the intervention of public
institutions. More often than not, the scientist is presented as linked to
the government and to the army, particularly to military intelligence. In
such films as *The Thing* (1951), *The Blob* (1958), *The Fly* (1958), and *Inva-
sion of the Body Snatchers* (1956), the portraits of the scientist seem to be
depersonalized, if not anti-intellectual, and often abandon the model of
the inspired but mad genius exemplified by prewar versions of Dr.
Frankenstein. The films increasingly dramatize the tension between the
positive aspects of the sciences and their negative consequences, as seen
in new drugs, new surgical techniques, new technologies of surveillance,
new weapons, and, above all, in the symbiotic relationship between scientists and the government, the product of which is the power to colo-
nize the world and even the universe.

This postwar cinema expanded its images of science and the scientist,
which contributed to a widespread sense in the cultures of the United
States and Britain that science, which had played a prominent role in the
winning of the war, was more closely linked to various aspects of everyday life than had previously been envisioned.[16] Shorn of its magical elements, science, both social and natural, helped to contribute to the sense
that all aspects of life—family malaise, sexual impotence, prostitution,
disease, and deformity—could be controlled and altered.[17] Psychic issues,

most often prominent in the earlier horror film, could now be subject to examination from a scientific rather than supernatural perspective.

The science fiction of the cold war era is filled with mutants, nuclear threats, and environmental imbalances as well as with ambiguous figurations of scientists who are often in conflict with each other and who seem to be more impotent than malevolent in the face of external threats. Several texts exemplify ways in which cinema converged with broad cultural concerns about science gone wrong. For example, in *Seven Days to Noon* (1950), the physicist as a post-World War II Dr. Frankenstein occupies a contradictory position. In having once created monstrous atomic weapons, he must now eliminate them, and he sets about obtaining his goal by threatening the community with annihilation if it does not cooperate. This British film exemplifies the ways in which science fiction folklore relies on melodramatic effects to express profound cultural anxieties. The literary allusions to the poetry of John Milton, the references to the Bible and to religion, and the reminders of World War II mingle with images of science and technology to create in this film the tension between tradition and modernity that is central to science fiction.

Paul Virilio, in *War and Cinema*, has described how technology from World War II to the present, particularly the development of surveillance devices, has contributed to a logistics of perception that "allow[s] everything to be seen and known, at every moment and in every place."[18] This logistics of perception extends to medicine and psychiatry, as these fields too seek to make everything knowable concerning the human body and brain. To judge by postwar science fiction films, Virilio's linking of cinema and the military is not restricted to critical discourse but embedded in popular and threatening representations of science and its links to the state. These images accompany new views of the scientist subordinated to a technology that has exceeded his knowledge and control.

Dr. Frankenstein does not disappear. Still viable in the 1980s and 1990s, the Dr. Frankenstein figure is complicated by increasingly self-consciously parodic treatments of science and the scientist. *Re-Animator* (1985) is preoccupied with the Frankensteinian notion of creating life from death but not by reassembling various organs. The film portrays a young scientist, Herbert West (Jeffrey Combs), working on a serum that when injected into human and other animal corpses reanimates them. For the purpose of experimenting, West kills his victims before he revives them; however, the serum alters their personalities, making them

194 aggressive and violent. West's counterpart is Dr. Hill (David Gale), an anatomy professor at Miskatonic Medical School and an entrepreneurial scientist who, on the basis of his successful grantsmanship, manipulates the dean of the medical school. A major trajectory of the narrative involves different methods for exploiting science and experimentation. Science is identified with grants, prestige, and power. The struggle for power is dramatized in interactions between Hill and his students. The older established scientist seeks to humiliate and exploit his students by expropriating their work. As he says to West, "We are both scientists. Let's get to the point. I want your discovery."

West seems to inherit earlier views of the pure scientist who will stop at nothing to enlarge science in his quest to develop the antidote to death but, unlike that earlier figure, he is not presented as having any altruistic objectives. Hill is equally unscrupulous. The dean is a bureaucrat who becomes the victim of both scientists, first of West who injects the dean, dead of a stroke, with the serum that reanimates him and later of Hill who performs a lobotomy on the dean to restrain his aggressiveness. Distinct from the other scientists, Cain (Bruce Abbott) expresses an ethical relationship to science. His romantic relationship with Meaghan (Barbara Crampton), the daughter of the dean, reinforces his humane concerns; but he becomes the victim of West, the dean, and Hill, and loses everything, including Meaghan. The duel among the scientists culminates in an orgy of destruction and violence. The reanimation of the corpses ultimately includes Meaghan, who is given the serum by Cain in his effort to save her. She screams as the screen goes black in the final scene, leaving the audience "in the dark" about the proliferating effects of the serum.

The common-sense elements are to be found in the ways the film orchestrates personal relationships in terms of science as a battleground for control of the mind and the body. The representation of science we see in this film is, in the vein of folklore, "many-sided—not only because it includes different and juxtaposed elements, but also because it is stratified, from the crude to the less crude—if, indeed, one should not speak of a confused agglomerate of fragments of all the conceptions of the world and life that have succeeded one another in history."[19] In this vein, the film juxtaposes a number of conflicts involving death, immortality, the family, sexuality, and archaic and modern conceptions of science. Re-Animator betrays an anxiety about questions of identity, the subsumption of the private into the public realm, the linking of scientific knowledge to corporate institutions, and the death of humanist conceptions of science.

In the scientists' various quests to gain power over death, sexuality is transformed into violence. Even the humanist scientist, Cain, becomes implicated in the process. Rather than science signifying human evolution into more sentient and intelligent life forms, it comes to signify a form of devolution evident both in the extreme and bizarre image of the animated severed head and in the reanimation of the corpses. Like *The Crazies* (1976), the film becomes a parody of science fiction: overloading and stretching its images to the limit in the service of explicating the bizarre nature of the fictions of science. More cogently, the motif of science gone wrong, unlike the immediate postwar films in which the finger could be pointed at the institutional misappropriations of science by the government or the military (e.g., *War of the Worlds,* 1953) now suggests, in apocalyptic terms, an irreversible and ubiquitous course of death and destruction. The "living dead" have multiplied and signify the inability to control the devastating effects of science. The physician/physicist as a corporate figure has also proliferated; he has been integrated into the social fabric.

A further complication of these representations of science and the scientist and of the conventional generic landscape is Roger Corman's *Frankenstein Unbound* (based loosely on the Brian Aldiss novel of the same name).[20] The film juxtaposes two scientists — Dr. Frankenstein (Raul Julia) and Dr. Buchanan (John Hurt), a contemporary scientist — who meet as a consequence of a "time slip" brought about in the film by weapons testing. In novel and film, the scientist-time traveler becomes a historian — of science and of science fiction. Mary Shelley (Bridget Fonda) appears and plays a part in the fiction. The character of Mary Shelley (Elsa Lanchester) also appeared in Universal's *The Bride of Frankenstein* (1935), directed by James Whale, which employs the author to introduce the fiction. In the Corman film, Shelley's role is more complicated. It provides a historical dimension to the film by enabling comparisons between the two scientists in the elaboration of the destructive course of science.

The Corman film spends minimal time in the laboratory, developing a pathetic relationship between Frankenstein and his monster. Rather, the relationship is one of unmitigated antagonism. The "unbinding" involves the free roaming of the marginal figure of Frankenstein's creation instead of his destruction. Any sense of the utopianism of science, its ability to alter biological life for the betterment of humanity, is put in question. The tendency of science to "go wrong" is conspicuous but is an understatement of the role of contemporary science, since *Frankenstein Unbound* reinforces the impossibility of inhibiting the ecological and cul-

196 tural changes that have been set in motion. The "unbinding" signifies that control by the individual is no longer an imaginable goal. The destructiveness of the monster in his contemporary incarnation is unabated, thus intensifying the contemporary sense of lack of agency in the face of modern technology.

Biology becomes a contested zone in these representations of the scientist, as in *The Boys from Brazil* (1978). The focus is particularly on the medical researcher who clones his subjects. He too is not a lone researcher but an institutional representative like the modern scientist in *Frankenstein Unbound.* He uses his position and his patients in the interests of private profit, personal pleasure, fame, status, social conformity, or political objectives. In the case of *Dead Ringers* (1988), he is an obstetrician/gynecologist whose aesthetic interest in experimenting on the female body is basically legitimated by his colleagues and linked to his own curiosity about the limits of experiencing and inflicting pain. The physician's fascination with antique gynecological instruments is also linked to sadomasochism.

Not all the films portray the victims' powerlessness against the physician/biologist and his technological instruments. The conventional targets of violence — women, youth, the dispossessed — are not merely the passive recipients of the sadistic and power-hungry behavior of the researcher but are instrumental in controlling the threats. In such films as *Alien* (1979), *Aliens* (1986), and *Aliens III* (1990), the women and young people are less naive and are often the agents of uncovering scientific malfeasance, exploitation, and mystification. The scientists may be presented as diabolical, indifferent, sadistic, or muddleheaded, but the force of the narrative resides in the struggle against these authority figures. Significantly, the embattled parties are linked to other institutional figures in the school, the laboratory, the spaceship-cum-laboratory, and especially the family. In films such as *Outland* (1981) the physician is seen as a facilitator, enabling the protagonist to fight the corporation and to survive.

Despite certain changes that dramatize the containment of the biologist, the folkloric elements in the films retain contradictions concerning the body, especially the female body, and issues of reproduction. Reading these films from the vantage point of contemporary feminist concerns, I find, in the films' treatments of female sexuality and gender positioning, recurring images and situations: "the archaic mother," monstrous and proliferating female genitalia, grotesque birthing images, numerous and deformed offspring, usurpation of the reproductive process by the male scientist, and the subjection of the spectator to the spectacle of female engulfment in images of otherness.[21] This preoccupation with reproduction and female sexuality suggests that the biological role of reproduction continues to be a terrain fraught with gender conflict. Biopolitics has assumed increased prominence in the rise of contemporary concern with women's control over their bodies and with the contest over artificial means of controlling birth and the creation of new forms of reproduction.

The hierarchialization of different forms of life in relation to issues of mortality, disease, heredity, intelligence, and evolution has been central not only to science but to conceptions of the individual organism and of social groupings as they inflect human behavior; thought on connections between human behavior and that of other animals has also been affected. In the controversies in recent decades surrounding ethology and sociobiology, scientific concerns with primate behavior have revealed themselves to be a "union between the political and physiological."[22] With respect to the popularization of genetic engineering and its commercialization, the increasing practices of transplantation, and the study of dominance behaviors, stress, aggression, and hormones, we are told that "with the advance of civilization, this biology has become a problem. It is now often maladaptive because of our accelerating technological progress. Our bodies, with the old genetic transmission, have not kept pace with the new language-produced cultural transmission of technology."[23] Donna Haraway's observations have gained circulation among feminist critics, inviting a reexamination of representations of biology as a challenge to atavisms of science, inflecting cultural attitudes concerning sex, gender, and reproduction, though one might ask if Haraway's faith in technology resurrects the folklore of science as salvation (or damnation) familiar to viewers of science fiction films and to writers on postmodernism. With the increasing emphasis on cybernetics, however, the issue of body politics and gender has, for some feminists, veered in an affirmative direction by addressing the possibilities of undermining biological determinism and humanist discourses of the body, agency, and subjectivity.

The preoccupation with reproduction in such films as *Creator* (1985) is intricately tied to economic and political issues and dramatizes familiar tensions in recent science fiction between humanism and antihumanism, modernism and postmodernism, and individualism and corporate capitalism. The many films that dramatize reproduction in relation to the female figure adopt psychoanalytic readings that explore the monstrous female as a threat and testify to the cultural hysteria over female sexuality and reproduction. These psychoanalytic readings need to be aug-

198   mented by a recognition of the role that the biological sciences have played in the ideological, political, and economic landscape of the 1970s and 1980s. The fact that many of the scientists/technicians/inventors are biologists or physicians would seem to argue that, in addition to the representations of the Oedipal scenario, the primal scene, and the threat of female sexuality, one must explore such images within a larger context of a struggle for social dominance in which biotechnology is implicated.

Entertaining the problematics of the so-called postmodern text and its concern with the threats of technology, *Creator* can be read as a response to the threatening world of *Re-Animator*, as well as an exploration of a possible return to humanism. Starring Peter O'Toole and Mariel Hemingway, *Creator* explores familiar motifs and tropes of the duplication of life, though without the melodrama and horror of many science fiction films. As in *Frankenstein Unbound* and *Re-Animator*, there are not one but several scientists. The old-style scientist, Wolper, played by Peter O'Toole, is a holistic biochemist who is after "the big picture." The new-style scientist, Sid Kuhlenbeck (David Ogden Stiers), is a surgeon, committed not only to high technology and grantsmanship but to the desirability of reducing everything to its most elemental biochemical form. The core of the narrative centers on Wolper, who has cultured the cells from his dead wife, Lucy, for twelve years and plans to implant a nucleus from one of Lucy's cells into an egg from another woman, Meli (Hemingway), in order to produce another Lucy, that is, a clone of Lucy.

In a parallel plot line, Wolper's student, Boris (Vincent Spano), defies Kuhlenbeck's urgings to terminate the life support system of his lover, Barbara, when she falls into a coma. Encouraged by Wolper, Boris saves Barbara not by medical means but by psychic means, talking to her until she regains consciousness. In this instance, the film creates an opposition between holistic and reductionist science and raises questions about the power and objectivity of the scientist as well as about the limitations of technology. The biologist is identified with female reproduction in the cases of both the older and the younger scientist; whereas the reductionist—their common enemy, Kuhlenbeck—appears to be the technological villain lacking regard for women and reproduction. The film's preoccupation with reproduction serves as a reminder of the homology of biological reproduction, social reproduction, and the reproduction of commodities: the female body serves as the prime vehicle and instrument for such explorations. The film's oppositions—natural versus artificial production, machines and technology versus "human" reproduction—are constructed on the essential edifice of "woman's" control over bodily and psychic functions and thus reinvoke nature but on behalf of "saving" women.

Rather than confounding boundaries, *Creator* insists on invoking oppositions between male and female, the physical body and machines, nature and culture, and bodies as given and bodies as artificially created. In resolving these oppositions, the film opts to assign reproduction to an individual woman, and to a natural process. In this way, the film naturalizes cultural events through traditional and common-sense biological discourses of reproduction. Through the characters of Wolper, Boris, Meli, and Barbara, the film produces a science fiction romance in which biological reproduction, individuality, identity, and the scientist as creator are in crisis. But alongside Barbara's restoration to life, the Nobelist Wolper wins a grant, is rescued from academic oblivion, and starts a new family with Meli, naturalizing and reaffirming the continuity of heterosexuality and the nuclear family. Even if science cannot be saved, the scientist can be—through the triumph of common sense in the realignment of family, reproduction, economic success, and, above all, the accommodation of these institutions to science.

Disembodiment and Incorporation of the Scientist

François Truffaut's *Fahrenheit 451* (1967), George Lucas's *THX 1138* (1971), and the 1984 version of *1984* provide futuristic images of society given over to technology and images of social engineering in which populations are controlled by the state, particularly by the police and the military with the aid of intricate apparatuses of surveillance and elaborate technologies of punishment. The notion of the alien invader has been extended to include simulated humans (occasionally as scientists) in the form of replicants, cyborgs, androids, and robots (e.g., *Android* [1982], *Blade Runner* [1982], *Alien* [1979], *Aliens* [1986], and *Alien III* [1992]). If Frankenstein has receded into the background, his creation has not, and, like his earlier monster, the new artifact is treated with ambivalence. He or she is most often presented as an object of limited existence, possibly threatening to human life, to be controlled (e.g., *The Terminator*, 1984). By contrast, *Blade Runner* reverses the Manichean and melodramatic struggle between good and evil in which humanity must struggle against the malevolent or pathetic ravages of the monsters by situating these creatures alongside the heroic humans and against the dehumanizing effects of corporate power embodied in scientific institutions.

The artificially constructed creations can be superior to humans; this

200 accentuates and reaffirms the traditional antinomy between humans and their productions. In this respect, the new corporate technology that disavows its creations is the successor to Dr. Frankenstein. In such films, wherever the scientist is represented, he is an organization man, a bureaucrat rather than a tormented genius. For example, the Tyrell Corporation in *Blade Runner* and the corporate structure in the *Alien* series, with its robotic scientist, present the image of the contemporary scientist as a member of or a creation of industry. Through their emphasis on simulation, doubling, or replication, the films challenge familiar ways of knowing the world; they then herald the disappearance of any notion of the "real" and announce the "postmodern condition," the world of the "hyperreal," a mediated world produced by technology and information systems.[24] In the case of *Blade Runner,* the process of replication raises the threatening possibility of irrevocable alienation from any familiar notion of the real, that humans are themselves nothing but replications and perhaps inferior to the copies that they have created.[25] This preoccupation with replication functions as a sign of cultural malaise in the face of recent technological research concerning gender, race, and sexual identity. *They Live* forcefully and even polemically addresses this dilemma from a largely dystopian position. In the case of *Blade Runner,* the superiority of the replicant to the humans dramatizes what critics have described through an analysis of the fictions of science as a "discursive crisis ... when categories previously taken for granted become subject to dispute."[26]

The late 1970s and the 1980s saw the return of a group of aliens who are not the creation of human scientists and whose knowledge is often superior to human knowledge. Their appearance is attributed to a number of factors, including ecological imbalance and space travel or penetration of unexplored territories on Earth in the present, the past, or in some future time. Although aliens from outer space frequented the screen in the immediate postwar era, in such films as *The Day the Earth Stood Still* (1951) and *The Thing* (1961), these new aliens in *Close Encounters of the Third Kind* (1977), *The Abyss* (1989), *E.T.* (1982), and *Millennium* (1989) are part of a different milieu. The new aliens are not necessarily threatening, especially not to those who are "in tune" with them; they are not the products of an inspired or mad scientist; the aliens are usually not hostile and threatening objects of investigation to scientists but may even be benevolent, as in *E.T.* and *The Abyss*. The aliens are not overly anthropomorphized but may appear as harmless plants or toys. The scientists are not creators, nor are they presented as responsible for the existence of the aliens, but as agents of the corporate state structures, hired either to examine, to explain, or to contain the effects of alien intrusion. Of course, the alternative image of the "other" is not without representation. The alien may attempt penetration (e.g., *They Live* [1988]) or threaten human life (e.g., *Predator* [1987]). But these representations only provide new versions of the Frankenstein paradigm.

Although critics have read the 1950s films as social allegories relating to the cold war, the fear of communism, and anxieties about atomic testing and nuclear fallout, films such as *Close Encounters of the Third Kind* and *E.T.* have been read as responses to anxieties concerning advanced technology, the colonization of space, and psychic threats to the integrity of the family and to individual and national identity. These later films have been seen as reassuring and have been linked to the resurgence of religion; but they also present a different picture of the scientist as engineer, as intermediary, and as translator from life as we know it (i.e., folklore) to alien life as created by some intelligence beyond folklore ("machinic lore").

The preoccupation with electronic media and the role of technology in these texts is seen as first threatening and then amenable to management. The exaltation of media is nowhere greater than in *Close Encounters of the Third Kind*. We see the scientist as aesthetician (in the person of French director François Truffaut), serving as an intermediary in the process of translating alien communication to his audience. And through hi-tech animation, the filmmaker complements the scientist both as a recorder of this transformation and as a signifier of the triumph of media and information systems over other forms of scientific production.

The various representatives of the scientific establishment provide problematic links between government, military, aliens, and the community. The notion prevalent in 1950s science fiction and in such recent films as *The Fly* (1986) or *Altered States* (1980) of science gone wrong and of the obsessed scientist as an individual entrepreneur is not evident. Specific scientists are presented not as malevolent, indifferent, or impatient but as interested in working with the government, the military, and industry to uncover the secrets of the aliens and to communicate with them if not to overcome them. The decoding of the music of the spaceship, the worshipful scenes in which the various profilmic audiences are invited to gaze in *Close Encounters* at the visual and auditory event, introduce the celebratory dimensions of technology — the technology of the spaceship and scientific research as well as the technology of cinema.

The most important variant in these recent dramatizations of science and technology in science fiction involves the motif of media as totalizing, as explored in such films as *Total Recall, Overdrawn at the Memory*

202 *Bank, Videodrome* (1983), and *They Live.* The dominant motif of media, the technology of visualization, is portrayed as a major force in a utopian or dystopian landscape. Although spectacle through special effects is a central aspect of science fiction, from the inexpensive films of the 1950s to opulent productions such as *Star Wars* (1977) and *Robocop* (1987), and although the notion of surveillance has taken many forms in science fiction, recent science fiction films are explicit in their concern with the hegemonic aspects of visual technology as well as with their challenge to the traditional bifurcation between the real and the illusory. Whether as science fiction epics, with their expensive technological magic, from *2001: A Space Odyssey* (1968) to *Close Encounters,* or as criticism of media manipulation, as in *They Live* and *Overdrawn at the Memory Bank,* such films are versions of the metamorphosis of the traditional Frankensteinian scientist.

Science fiction film's preoccupation with media technology produces new narratives, and characters new to science fiction make their appearance. In a dystopian version of media technology and social engineering, we find evangelists who use science and technology to make links with a worldwide, if not galaxywide, communication control system. Threads of electronic media, religion, and science are knotted together. Evangelism on a mass scale is portrayed as a profitable and powerful force that works to produce conformity as well as new forms of resistance to conformity, as in *Repo Man* (1984). And in the case of the Carpenter film, *They Live,* evangelism provides a focal point of resistance against a totalizing vision of the mass media. Gone are the images of the laboratory, the figures of the isolated scientist and his single assistant, the notion of inspiration and creativity, and the quest for "pure science."

The melodramatic scenario of the constricted interaction between the scientist and his usually female victim has broadened to include larger social groupings: on the one side, the institutional representatives of science and technology, and on the other, oppressed social groups, often the poor and homeless, the objects of exploitation and control. Carpenter's *They Live* dramatizes electronic media specifically in relation to questions of social management. This film is concerned with programming, with the corporate control of media and its consumerist orientation. Although there is no schism here between mind and body, the film focuses on the specialization of sight and on the transformation of the world through visual electronic devices in the service of capitalism. And, as in *Videodrome,* media are regarded as a "virus." The spectator is presented with images of urban decay, garbage, homelessness, racism, and police brutality. Earth is one big ghetto. The homeless are harassed and hounded, and their advocates are destroyed. The "first" world now looks like the "third" world. Political opposition is carefully monitored electronically and eliminated.

The film is presented from the vantage point of a white unemployed man who comes to the city to seek work. In the process of experiencing, at first skeptically, the attempts on the part of homeless and unemployed individuals and those working in their behalf at rebelling against big business and its intermediaries, the protagonist learns that the major weapon in the arsenal of the corporate structure of capitalism, along with surveillance and military power, is media in the form of subliminal persuasion reminiscent of Vance Packard's "hidden persuaders." By means of special eyeglasses (distributed by a revolutionary group) that counteract the visible signs of commerce, the protagonist discovers that insidious messages are embedded in advertisements promoting social conformity (i.e., folklore). The messages order the consumers to be monogamous and reproductive, to be obedient and submissive, and above all to consume. The seductiveness of the advertisements on the billboards is stripped away, and the revealed messages are exposed as having a basis in the common-sense rhetoric of religion, morality, law, family, and state. If advertising attempts to substitute a brand name for a particular commodity and hence to efface its concreteness as an object of exchange, by reducing the blandishments of advertising to stark messages concerning reproduction and consumption the film works to mimic (but for different ends) the common-sense nature of the media messages—their dependence on brevity, sloganeering, reduction, and abstraction. Also, by exposing the commands on the billboards—"reproduce," "submit," "obey," and "consume"—the film itself falls into another familiar form of common sense associated with a prevailing tendency in media criticism: namely, the tendency to simplify and reduce the complexities of exchange value to mere coercion.

They Live does not account for the unleashing of monstrous figures from outer space or explain the creation of the glasses and other devices to fight the media by the revolutionary opposition. Nor does the film even explore the nature of the aliens, their arrival, and their larger motives for colonizing Earth. The aliens are not immediately recognizable as alien. Their monstrosity is only exposed through the revolutionaries' glasses. The aliens intermingle with the humans as middle-class consumers on the streets, in the supermarkets, and in the beauty parlors. The image of the consumer as an alien functions to defamiliarize and estrange the spectator from the benign images of the consumer as conveyed in media advertising. It is the familiar that is alien. Instead of the

204 futuristic metropolis, the landscape is familiar city streets and suburbs. As in *Repo Man,* the landscape is not only contemporary but also disquieting. Although vision in the film serves as an instrument to perpetuate violence on the part of financial powers in league with the state, seeing also becomes the means by which the world is to be transformed, the means through which the forces of opposition seek to transform society on behalf of the poor, the unemployed, and the victims of racial discrimination. In monolithic and melodramatic fashion, the film critically addresses the commodity fetishism of late capitalism as described by Wolfgang Fritz Haug in his *Critique of Commodity Aesthetics.* He writes in a vein reminiscent of the Frankfurt critics: "The aestheticization [of commodities,] not only of politics ... lies ... at the very heart of bourgeois society. Also intrinsic to it is the need on the one hand to constantly legitimize the ruling class, while creating the needs of the subjects on the other, both of which can find only the illusory satisfaction of (amongst other things aesthetic images) inside and through the capitalistic system."[27]

The film's linking of science, technology, economics, and social class does not include the consummation of a heterosexual romance, which is undercut as the woman, Holly, turns out to be an agent for Cable 54, the channel source of the alien signal that operates and programs spectators. The extended scenes developing at first antagonistic but later affectionate ties between the protagonist and his black friend ("Ain't love grand," quips Frank as the two men seek safety in a hotel room) suggest, however, that their verbal and physical bonding is an alternative to the duplicities of heterosexuality. The growing relationship between the two men is doomed, and the black helper is eliminated from the narrative, killed by Holly. In short, the film maintains strict oppositions between haves and have-nots, control and resistance to control, males and females. The world is fascistic and only revolutionary struggle seems adequate to attack the alien medium. There is no longer any sense of private life; everything is subsumed in the public arena that the film struggles to explore and to resist. Like so much recent science fiction, *They Live* acknowledges a mediated world, but it resists the celebration of the postmodern by viewing media and advertising as instruments of exploitation that only reappropriation by the people can mitigate. The film regards contemporary society as in a perpetual state of war (the war against the poor is conducted with the aid of helicopters and military weapons). Unlike conventional science fiction melodrama, which often demonizes science and technology, the film focuses on consumerism and capital as the primary targets. In this sense, *They Live* acknowledges the need to rethink the "modern folklore" of science and technology, and hence certain narratives of postmodernism. By acknowledging the role of media in modern society and conjoining science — in information technologies, in economics, and in contemporary culture — within the context of late capital, the film complicates notions of control and resistance.

A film with a less antagonistic perspective toward media is *Overdrawn at the Memory Bank*. Starring Raul Julia, *Overdrawn* is a low-budget production designed for television and for commercial distribution as a film. Computer, cinema, and video technology assume a central position, as in *Videodrome*. Set in the confines of Novicorp, a world governed by computer programs, the film explores the threats to the traditional unity of mind and body as a consequence of living in a totally controlled environment. Aram Fingal (Raul Julia) is sent to "Nirvana Village" for rehabilitation after committing the offense of breaking into Novicorp's programs and watching a film, *Casablanca* (1942). He is ordered to be "doppled." Doppling, as described by his "computech," Appollonia (Linda Griffiths), consists of drawing the subject's identity into an "identicube" that is then implanted in another animal, which permits the subject to experience herself or himself as that animal. Ideally, the identicube is retracted at the end of the doppling and the identity returned to the person's body. Fingal is assigned to a baboon for 48 hours, but complications develop when the baboon is attacked by an elephant. Moreover, a mischievous schoolboy has switched Fingal's identity tag, and Fingal's body is misplaced. When his identity must be returned to his body, it cannot be located, and the operator of the doppling machine must load Fingal's identity into Novicorp's mainframe computer to store him temporarily. In the computer, Fingal creates a simulated reality "out of his own memories and fantasies" until he can be returned to his own body.

The chairman of Novicorp, Dr. Frankenstein's new incarnation, is an entrepreneur and computer scientist who threatens to "terminate" Fingal. But Appollonia convinces the chairman that stocks in the corporation will plummet if she fails to retrieve Fingal from the computer. Meanwhile, in his simulated world and through characters Fingal has fantasized from *Casablanca*, Fingal is animated to overthrow the chairman and destroy Novicorp's sterile world system. In Fingal's simulated "reality," he plays out a version of the Warner Brothers film, visible to Appollonia through the monitor and to the chairman through a spy's mediation. When Fingal learns that his body has been "lost" and decides that "We are nothing but a byte in a giant computer," he begins to resist the efforts to return him to his body, announcing, "I'm not going to go on being a zombie. I'm going to punch my own buttons." Fingal suc-

206 ceeds in tapping into the main computer, which causes all kinds of problems for the chairman: from changes in the weather to the redistribution of the stocks of the corporation to the workers. Fingal, however, is not out of the woods. At the moment he is about to disappear into the electronic world, Appollonia risks her life to retrieve him. The final shot of the film shows the workers at their monitors watching the opening credits of *Casablanca*.

Overdrawn at the Memory Bank, like *Total Recall* (1990) and even *The Fly* (1986) and *The Fly II* (1988), presents a notion of the human body and identity based on fabrication rather than on organic reproduction. Novicorp "sells dreams" electronically and programs its subjects. But resistance to this programming is exemplified by Fingal's and Appollonia's struggles to subvert the system through manipulation of the technology on behalf of themselves and the other workers. Through the recognition of the power of electronic media, complete submission to this fabricated world is resisted. Cinema, specifically the film *Casablanca*, functions as a way out of the conventional opposition between reality and illusion. In *Overdrawn*, the representation of cinema serves to reinforce the power of media and to set the relationship to media technology. Cinematic pleasure offers the means to subvert the computerized world of media: *Casablanca* becomes a text that is available through video in ways that are different from common-sense notions of media spectatorship as passive. The film becomes a text to be altered by the spectator, which calls attention to the film and to its status as a simulated object, a strategy common to modernism and incorporated into descriptions of postmodernism.

Overdrawn does not unilaterally reinforce a negative image of contemporary culture but raises the possibility of its utopian dimensions. The film's technical effects—its use of computers, video, and digitalized images—become a metacommentary on postmodernity and pose both its dire scenarios of control and its liberatory potential. *Overdrawn* is far removed from the science fiction scenario of the lone anguished scientist, as well as from that of the scientist as visionary. Though the chairman of the corporation is a computer scientist, he is first and foremost a capitalist committed to economic profit and power. Unlike the representations of the physician/physicist and the physician/biologist, which embody the malignant and benign aspects of scientific genius, the technological world of *Overdrawn* is closer to the *Alien* series, *They Live,* and *Blade Runner* (1982) in which the corporate world has replaced the scientist. The defeat of the chairman is the defeat of the Dr. Frankenstein myth. *Overdrawn* does not ultimately make technology the villain but impugns the various ways in which technology is implicated in corporate forms of power and hence entangled with the questions of profitability and value. Although *Overdrawn* conforms to notions of postmodernity, its pastiche qualities, its situating itself in the realm of the hyperreal, and its dramatization of identity as fluid in its romance elements, the film still maintains the conventional heterosexual narrative. The romance, however, is itself implicated in the simulated world that has been produced by the film; it is then, like all other events in the film, subject to renegotiation.

In comparison to such films as *Re-Animator* and *Frankenstein Unbound*, *Overdrawn at the Memory Bank* draws on a different set of discourses. Although these films struggle with anxiety over the status of technology, technology's links to corporate structures, and the effect of technology on the populace, *Overdrawn* bears a similarity to academic discourses that entertain the celebratory dimensions of postmodernism and that conceive of mass culture as liberating. In more pessimistic terms, through his examination of the power of information systems in relation to mass communication, Umberto Eco writes:

> As a rule, politicians, educators, communication scientists believe that to control the power of the media you must control two communicating moments of the chain: the Source and the Channel. In this way they believe that you can control the message ... but I begin to fear that it produces skimpy results for anyone hoping to restore to human beings a certain freedom in the face of the total phenomenon of Communication.[28]

Eco posits the need for a guerrilla solution to media hegemony in which the receiver plays an active role in transforming the medium, a "guerrilla warfare involving the constant correction of perspectives, the checking of codes, the ever-renewed interpretation of mass messages."[29] In a sense, *Overdrawn* adheres to this line of reasoning by exploring the possibilities of both "ever-renewed interpretation" and intervening at the source of the messages. By contrast, *Videodrome* succumbs to the folklore that technology and late capital are one and the same, and that there is no escape from the now-global dimensions of media.

Epilogue: The Tenacity of Folklore

In exploring representations of science and technology in science fiction films, I remain—as does Fredric Jameson—skeptical of critical formulations that adopt either apocalyptic or celebratory attitudes concerning

208 postmodernism.[30] I remain committed to a Gramscian position stressing the contradictory nature of contemporary cultural articulations, rather than seeing the readings of the film texts, their pastiche effects in particular, their cavalier treatments of history, and their assumption of the complete assimilation of the spectator into spectacle as yet more instances of common sense in the guise of modern folklore. A common-sense analysis requires that distinctions be made between description and analysis as well as between effects and their causes in order to enable a better understanding of the residual dimensions of cultural production and its emergent aspects.

This discussion of science fiction films does not deny that a number of changes have in fact taken place in representations of science from the 1930s to the present. There is no doubt that the image of the pure scientist—the inspired, misunderstood, and lonely genius—has given way to more pragmatic images of scientists and technologists, images much less ambivalent than in earlier films. There is no doubt either that biology, especially biotechnology, along with electronic forms of communication, has usurped the place of physics as a locus of anxieties about power. There is also no doubt that these films seek links between economics, politics, and subjectivity in ways that are more pronounced than earlier science fiction, and that the politics of vision, linked to media technology, is a central concern. What is not so clear, however, is whether the films are indicative of a totally new phase of culture known as the "postmodern condition." The fact that postmodern discourses recapitulate totalistic concerns about mass culture should alert the cultural critic to the presence of a monolithic assessment of "the masses" which ascribes to them passive submission to power emanating from above in the guise of new and more beguiling dimensions of the "consumer society."

This postmodern assessment stands in direct contrast to Gramscian notions of the complexity of consensus that stress the importance of steering clear of univalent notions of coercion. Though opposition may not be revolutionary, it is also not predictable, and the films do address an array of cultural antagonisms. Science fiction films address contradictions and antagonisms that cannot be easily read and determined but that are desperately in need of less totalizing and deterministic forms of analysis. The distaste for mass culture, the eagerness to assess it as all-encompassing, is not new. New and worth examining, however, are the numerous signs of a breakdown in consensus rather than a uniformity. The persistence of anxieties about technology should not be considered to express uniformity of belief or a consensus but to be a sign of malaise that requires careful analysis to test the persistence of folklore and the presence of difference.

Identifying characteristics of commercial science fiction filmmaking have been its protean quality, its eclecticism, and its acute sensitivity to audience reception. Rather than being static, genre production has undergone numerous changes from early cinema to the present. Change seems to be its driving force. These changes, however, which cannot be denied, seem most often to be quantitative rather than qualitative and seem to be governed by economic, political, and demographic exigencies to meet contemporary conditions. The continuous nature of innovation makes it difficult to assess a decisive moment of rupture marking a radical break in ideological formations. Although sensitive to new forms of expression, I am reluctant at present to see them other than in terms of new folkloric permutations.

From a Gramscian perspective, I take issue with film critics who find that many contemporary science fiction films are expressions of a new, drastic, and unitary permutation of mass culture. As expressed in contemporary science fiction cinema, the particular nature and directions of the contemporary disregard for history; the fusion of high and mass culture; the identification of science with corporate life; the abandonment of individualism; and the privileging of science, technology, and the role of media as major instruments of a new world order are yet to be analyzed and evaluated.[31] These films are not uniform nor are their concerns unique in the history of the genre. In their tone, affect, and celebratory or denigratory treatments of a seemingly new state of affairs, these films maintain time-honored motifs of the genre — space travel, scientific and technological research, mutation, ecological disaster, imagined worlds — though, as might be expected in genre production, the conventions are modified to suit contemporary exigencies and ideologies. The films are familiar as sites for the intersection of generic modes, including melodrama, adventure, history, biography, and autobiography, indicative of the eclecticism and mutability of commercial filmmaking. Alive to the sights and sounds of the contemporary urban landscape, the films portray, in various ways, both the residual and the changing faces of gender, sexual, race, familial, economic, and class relations. And despite their semblances of articulating new discourses, the films are mired in familiar contradictions concerning continuity and change. Postmodern explanations are too linear and depend on technological reductionism. In valorizing material determinations to the exclusion of residual cultural

210   factors as expressed through common sense, in its neglect of existing cultural antagonisms, and in its cavalier treatment of memory, postmodernist description is antithetical to Gramscian analysis of folklore (especially as elaborated in British cultural studies). The tendency of the postmodern discourse is, like the tendencies of fictions of science and science fiction, too dependent on univalent and familiar notions of scientific salvation (or damnation) that are themselves imbricated in the folklore of modernity.

Chapter 9

"Gramsci beyond Gramsci" and the Writings of Antonio Negri

Defending their positions on contemporary politics and culture, Félix Guattari and Antonio Negri have written:

> This is the new politics: the need to recharacterize the fundamental struggles in terms of a continuous conquest of (new) arenas of freedom, democracy, and creativity. And, whatever the militants and the individuals who have "given up on all that" may say, there is nothing anachronistic or retrograde or anarchist in this way of conceiving things; indeed, the new politics attempts to understand contemporary social transformations—including their contradictions—on the basis of the productive activities, the desires, and the real needs that regulate them. What is entirely irrational and mad is the power of the State as it has evolved since the 1960s.[1]

What is the "new politics?" How congenial are Guattari's and Negri's assessments of politics to those of Gramsci?

The impetus of this chapter arises from a need to rethink Gramsci's work in the context of Toni Negri's challenging analyses of the conditions that characterize late capitalism, specifically in relation to existing and alternative conceptions of the state and civil society, of the role of intellectuals, of cultural production, and of the potential for revolutionary struggle. Gramsci's writings in his preprison articles and in the *Prison Notebooks* are situated in the development of what he himself described as Americanism and Fordism. This question arises: Can his political and cultural analyses be brought into alignment with Negri's formulations concerning post-Fordism and its production of new subjectivities conducive to radical social and economic transformation? Can such a comparison validate Negri's analyses of the potential for contemporary political struggle?

The writings of Gramsci and Negri can be compared in ways beyond their concern with Marxism and revolutionary struggle. The most obvious further connection is that both were prisoners of the Italian state and both have much to say on the nature of the modern state and its repressive functions, functions that are intimately tied to the nature of modern capital and its protean forms. If Gramsci's writings are animated by the need to elaborate on the nature of an emergent social subject during the first phases of Fordism, Negri's work seems dedicated to bringing this subject into the arena of contemporary capitalism, which has been termed post-Fordism, and into the forefront of political cultural struggle.

In his writings, Negri himself seems most reluctant to invoke the name of Gramsci for reasons related perhaps to the ways in which Gramsci has been historically institutionalized not only by the Communist Part of Italy (PCI) but also by critics such as Ernesto Laclau and Chantal Mouffe who, in their reformist and culturalist interpretations of Gramsci's notion of hegemony, bypass important questions relating class to conceptions of a political party, and to the nature of radical contestation. Nonetheless, it is my contention that a fruitful reading of Negri entails attention to the ways in which his work extends many Gramscian concerns. Such a reading might also mitigate the general sense in which Negri's work is often identified as vanguardism, anarchism, or wild militancy and is therefore largely ignored, despite his important contributions to a rethinking of Marxism.

The Nature of Political Struggle

Gramsci's writings cover more than the letters from prison and the *Prison Notebooks*. We also have the reviews, correspondence, and other journalistic work prior to his arrest. The work reveals a number of abiding motifs but highlights, in particular, the question of the revolutionary potential among workers and peasants. Gramsci involved himself in organizational work, education, and militant activities in the unions and in the Socialist and (later) the Communist parties. Like Negri, Gramsci was most concerned to describe and examine existing and alternative forms of political engagement in order to assess the nature of collective struggle. Over the course of his life, Gramsci was to develop progressively complicated notions about the nature and possibility of assaults against the state and to raise increasingly complicated questions about culture and class formations. He was consistently aware of and resistant to economism: to the notion that it was possible to produce economic changes without the proper assessment of the level of knowledge on the part of workers and the conditions of force that held sway. He was critical of reformism and sought to identify and combat the various guises in which it appeared.

Like Negri, Gramsci was writing at a time characterized by what he termed a "crisis of authority," that is, "a crisis of hegemony or general crisis of the State."[2] The development and institutionalization of Fascism constitute a major impetus for his work. Imprisonment became a source for his reassessment of the nature of and possibilities for revolutionary struggle in the face of Fascism, which had produced what Gramsci described as a "passive revolution," a "revolution without revolution," or the restoration of hegemony on the part of the traditional vested interests. Though he recognized the imperative to combat this "revolution," he was as suspicious of spontaneism as he was of vanguardism; both seemed to him to be short-term, if not counterproductive, modes of action. Later, in his notes written from prison, he was to examine the failures of many of his colleagues to understand the nature of modern capitalism and to identify the strategies and tactics necessary to bring about communism.

Although Gramsci's notes are obscured by the language necessary to pass the prison authorities, it is still possible to see from his analysis of Italian history, his notes on the "Modern Prince," on civil society and the state, and especially his writings on Americanism and Fordism, that the mode of political analysis required was one that necessitated an orchestrated philosophical, historical, economic, and cultural treatment of prevailing conditions. In similar fashion, Negri's explorations of hegemony and of the possibilities for counterhegemony require such a multivariate type of analysis. Many readings of Gramsci's work slight his conceptions of the political as economic and of the impossibility of severing politics from culture. A characteristic of Fascism, one acknowledged by Walter Benjamin and more recently by Negri, is precisely the way in which politics under Fascism is aestheticized. Culture does not exist apart from questions of domination, nor does it exist apart from the various social groups involved in maintaining existing hegemonic conditions or in opposing them. As Gramsci wrote:

> The methodological criterion on which our own study must be based is the following: that the supremacy of a social group manifests itself in two ways, as "domination" and as "intellectual and moral leadership." A social group dominates antagonistic groups, which it tends to "liquidate," or to subjugate perhaps even by armed force; it leads kindred and allied groups. A social

group can, and indeed must, already exercise "leadership" before winning governmental power (this is indeed one of the principal conditions for the winning of such power); it subsequently becomes dominant when it exercises power, but even if it holds it firmly in its grasp, it must continue to "lead" as well.[3]

These comments indicate that a rethinking of power is a prerequisite to any assessment of politics. Since power is a matter of both consensus and force, it is necessary to identify those elements of consensus that function along with coercion to produce or impede the transformation of forms of leadership. Since domination of the people includes control by existing social/state apparatuses, the struggle for power is institutional, not reducible to a melodramatic conflict among individuals. Moreover, it is not sufficient to identify the struggle as only *between* those traditional groups that exercise leadership and those seeking to gain power. The analysis must extend to identifying antagonisms *among* emergent social groups. An indispensable element in considerations of power is an analysis of economic and social production.

Negri's detailed analyses of Marx's writings in *Capital* and in the *Grundrisse* provide him the means to understand and rethink the nature of the perpetual crises generated by capital. In particular, his lengthy examination of Marx's theory of value as well as classical interpretations of it provides, as we shall see, the basis for his assessment of the potential for revolution under late capitalism. Gramsci's writings are not antagonistic toward economic analysis, and his notes on work and workers constantly stress the interrelatedness of production and politics. His war on Marxist economism was waged in the face of attempts on the part of other Marxists to reduce social and political problems to the realm of money and wages, which can lead one to assume that he was sympathetic to linking economic considerations to questions of ideology and was concerned more for qualitative than quantitative economic considerations. Gramsci is unambiguously in agreement with Marx's assertion in the *Critique of Political Economy* that "it is on the level of ideologies that men become conscious of conflicts in the world of the economy."[4] Since for Gramsci the essential element in political transformation is the reappropriation of civil society by the workers, politics is inextricable from questions of production.

A major distinction between Gramsci's and Negri's positions in relation to the political mobilization of subjectivity, knowledge, and power resides in the nature and level of the productive forces and of the historical antagonisms they generate. In Negri's terms, the potential for the recognition of the "autonomy of the political" is dependent on the "complete restructuring of social relationships produced in late capitalism as exemplified in the post-1968 moment." The socialized worker is the result of "a very impetuous historical process which has pushed the dialectic between autonomy and institutions to the point of an explosion—to the point of an irreversible break."[5] Hence the traditional notions of politics as distinct from the social arena have undergone transformation. Social life, Negri claims, is in effect now pervasively political through the antagonisms generated by new social/economic relations relating to the contemporary state of information technologies and communication.

For Negri the autonomy of the political is not something that is willed into existence. The "self-recognition of the subject" is the consequence of conditions that are constitutive, created out of the particular conditions of social development, conditions that can no longer be factored in terms of purely economic measurements, as we shall see in examining Negri's discussions of value. Furthermore, the constitution of subjectivity and struggle are dependent on militancy and organization, but militancy and organization are now severed from traditional corporative institutions. He also rethinks notions of success and defeat in political struggle: "Sometimes indeed, when one lives through phases of overt struggle, the memory may be one of defeat and of the thousand-and-one underhand or mistaken methods which the clandestine struggles involved."[6]

Negri asserts that what appears to be political defeat may not be so in the long run. Apparent defeat can become the basis for new antagonisms, a position that also seems to echo Gramsci's complex notions of political struggle. Negri links the concept of the clandestine to notions of transgression and subversion: the undermining of the social in its present forms toward the ends of reincorporating the political into the social. In Gramsci's terms, it seems that here we move from the war of siege to the war of maneuver. What is uppermost in Negri's writing as he contemplates revolution is its possibility, and, in terms that are suited to his political purposes, he alludes to "utopia" and "dystopia," concepts that he derived from his discussion of Spinoza:

> Utopia is thus accompanied by the certainty that reality is oppressive though under control. Let us call this situation "dystopia." This means that we have reached the threshold of victory and that the causes which inspire us are irresistible. It also means, however, that victory will require the employment of new and terrible forms of violence, that it will require the direct organization of the social, the reappropriation of production, and the establishment of a new social and productive order.[7]

216   In constructing his politics of subversion, Negri, while sharing certain
notions associated with such poststructuralist thinkers as Deleuze, Guattari, and Lyotard, seems to be more closely linked to specifically Marxist
and materialist conceptions of social revolution and to ways of understanding what he terms "countervailing power." In examining the
potential for subversion in contemporary society, Negri identifies his
conception of subversion with Spinoza's thoughts on power, especially
the notion of countervailing power, which is

> a subversion of all existing structures, or rather, of all those aimed at
> exploitation either in the first or second instance, directly or indirectly.
> Subversion is the destruction of the violence that is inherent in exploitation
> and which runs through society, indirectly, massively and terribly:
> subversion is *countervailing power*. The more the labour force, as the working
> subject, becomes intellectual and social, the more the violence inherent in
> exploitation acquires an intellectual and social character.[8]

The terms that stand out in this particular quotation—power, violence,
exploitation, and intellect—are not only reminiscent of his discussion of
Spinoza concerning power but also of ways in which Gramsci sought to
chart his own notions of social transformation, specifically of the need to
appropriate power that has accrued to the state. The important dimension of power that Negri distinguishes is its negative aspect. According
to Negri, it "can be defined in only one way: against Power."[9] Negri juxtaposes the power of the collectivity as a multiplicity against the notion
of a unified and quiescent mass. Gramsci's concern for the necessary
constitution of organic intellectuals also embeds the notion of building
alternative forms of power that are active rather than quiescent, aimed at
providing a constitutive and informed sense of social conditions, not a
given, one that provides rather than inhibits deliberation. Hence Gramsci is preoccupied with education, history, and philosophy as avenues to
explore the "intellectual and social character" of politics.

Negri too, in seeking to identify the nature of political power, orchestrates historical and philosophic analysis. In an effort to escape the massive, prophetic, and totalizing dimensions of Hegelian thought, he turns
to Spinoza's thought to forge a relationship between politics and imagination:

> Politics is the metaphysics of the imagination, the metaphysics of the human
> constitution of reality, the world. The truth lives in the world of the
> imagination; it is possible to have adequate ideas that are not exhaustive of
> reality but open to and constitutive of reality, which are intensively true;
> consciousness is constitutive; being is not only something found (not only a

possession) but also activity, power; there is not only Nature, there is also second nature, nature of the proximate cause, constructed being. These affirmations, which the interpreters have difficulty squaring with the static image of Spinozism and the immobile figure of cosmic analogy, are instead adequately situated within this new opening in his philosophy. Imaginative activity reaches the level of an ontological statute, certainly not to confirm the truth of prophecy but to consolidate the truth of the world and the positivity, the productivity, the sociability of human action.[10]

This quotation corroborates the ways in which Negri, through his readings of Spinoza, wants to overturn the notion of a given nature of truth and reason deemed requisite to prevailing analyses of human behavior and change. Through his strategic tracing of his conceptions of the constitutive nature of reality to Spinoza, Negri wants to identify countervailing notions of philosophy that are integral to undermining the naturalism characteristic of bourgeois thought. By means of his stress on the importance of social production, Negri seeks to reintroduce the notion of imagination, which can break the stranglehold of conceptions of the state and of existing institutions and the passivity to which they give rise.

The State and Civil Society

Gramsci's discussions of the state and civil society are among the most innovative aspects of his thought. In Gramsci's examination of Italian history, particularly the conditions leading to the rise of Fascism, the state comes to assume a dominant and repressive role. According to him, the state and civil society are not antithetical but acquire different relations in terms of given historical circumstances. The issue of power is closely tied to the condition of civil society and the encroachments of the state. In his discussion of passive revolution that constitutes the restoration of the ruling groups at a time of crisis, the state plays a formidable role in relation to civil society.

In their introduction to the section of the *Notebooks* entitled "State and Civil Society," Quintin Hoare and Geoffrey Nowell-Smith assert that Gramsci seems to put forward several conflicting conceptions of these relations between civil society and the state. He seems to suggest that the two are in conflict with each other; he also seems to see them as reciprocal; yet he seems also to see civil society as subsumed by the state. Because writings on this subject are not unified but are found in different contexts, it seems reasonable to assume that Gramsci sees the relations between state and civil society not as stable but as fluid, and as

218 dependent on specific political, economic, and social conditions within specific historical conjunctures.

Certainly, in his various attempts to describe the nature of Fascism, Gramsci suggests that a process of state assimilation of civil society was taking place; that is, Fascist society draws on the apparatuses of civil society — the church, unions, schools, leisure organizations, and economic activities to consolidate its power. Describing the nature of the relationship of the state to civil society, particularly the notion of the state as a policeman (*veilleur de nuit*), he writes, "The fact is glossed over that in this form of régime, (which anyway has never existed except on paper, as a limiting hypothesis) hegemony over its historical development belongs to private forces, to civil society — which is 'State' too, indeed is the State itself."[11]

In his discussions of Italian history, however, Gramsci indicates that the distinction between civil society and the state is "a methodological one." The "bourgeois class," Gramsci says, "poses itself as an organism in continuous movement, capable of absorbing the entire society, assimilating it to its own cultural and economic level. The entire function of the State has been transformed; the State has become an 'educator', etc."[12] The state subsumes civil society in the ways that it appropriates economic-corporative activities, assumes the role of pure force, and intervenes in the cultural sphere. Because the cultural sphere plays an important role in legitimizing the reigning hegemony, intellectuals cannot be divorced from conceptions of the state. Beginning with the assumption that the conquest of power is intimately tied to the "assertion of a new productive world" and that the hegemony of the dominant class can be located in its linking of economic and political power, traditional intellectuals are neither neutral nor outside of existing power relations.

Gramsci writes that

> since the state is the concrete framework of a productive world and since intellectuals are the social element that identifies itself most closely with governmental personnel, it is characteristic of the function of intellectuals to present the state as an absolute, thus the historical function of intellectuals is conceived as absolute, and their existence is rationalized.... And whenever intellectuals seem to "lead," the concept of the state in itself appears with all the "reactionary" retinue that usually accompanies it.[13]

Gramsci is well aware of the dangers of the absolutist state and of the need in the struggle against "Enlightenment thought" to rethink the nature of civil society from the vantage point of the subaltern. In his essay on the "Southern Question," Gramsci challenges the notion that the workers will have to tie their fates to that of the state. He projects that such an affiliation would result in their becoming mere appendages of the "bourgeois state."[14]

Unlike Gramsci, in relation to questions of power and to the role of the state in bourgeois society Negri uses Spinoza to challenge expressions of natural-right philosophy and especially notions of a social contract, which are usually at the base of the legitimation of the state. Negri points to an important implication of the notion of natural right and social contract: the "dialectical transfer from the individual to the universal to the absolute [is] the political miracle (and mystification) of the bourgeois ideology of the State."[15] Against the notion of a contract and its relation to the power of the state, Negri counterpoises the figure of Machiavelli, invoked by Spinoza, who calls on resistance for an alternative conception of collective will and sovereignty. It is significant too that Machiavelli provides both for Negri and for Gramsci, alternative conceptions of the state. Although there is no question about Negri's resistance to the Hegelian conception of the state, Gramsci's position seems more ambiguous: at times Gramsci adheres to some ideal notion of the state; at other times he is critical of "statolatry."

In order to circumvent the resurrection of the bourgeois state, Negri projects theories of federalism as a possible model in the creation of an alternative to the bourgeois state. He does not reject constitutionalism but seeks to envision an alternative involving the stabilization of conflicting interests in the creation of a classless society. He postulates that such an alternative would contribute further to the growth of collectivity and concomitantly enhance revolutionary subjectivity. The objective is ultimately to achieve the devolution of all the functions of the state to the community but in terms of the hegemony of the proletarian, not the bourgeois, collectivity. These comments seem strange from someone who has insisted on the radically different nature of contemporary society. Yet his groping for precedents and new formulations seems to be generated by his explorations of historical precedents, as exemplified by his work on Spinoza charting alternative forms of hegemony.

The important element for Negri in his analysis of contemporary politics is the power of the state in its numerous forms as expressed in the subsumption of civil society within global capital, and "this phenomenon normally manifests itself in the form of the state.... [Real] subsumption reveals the social dichotomy not simply within civil society, which in any case is impossible to isolate in this situation: rather, it reveals the dichotomy to us within that determinate complex which is constituted by the new composition of civil society and the state."[16] As a conse-

220 quence of real subsumption, the familiar relationship between state and civil society and between "subject and sovereign" is replaced by, in Negri's terms, the existence of "power and countervailing power."

For example, in his examination of the deleterious effects of state power, Negri discusses the threat of nuclear war in relation to communication and expropriation by the state. He posits that "fixed social capital appears as nuclear capital ... [and] must be destroyed."[17] His argument is based not only on the actual threat of extermination but on the nuclear threat as a pervasive form of political control that arises from the fact that *"The nuclear state is a state founded on secrecy."*[18] Such secrecy destroys any possibility for social cooperation, and the nature of expropriation resides in the way the secret becomes the mystified basis for control. The mystification, a major strategy in the perpetuation of government secrecy, resides particularly in the appearance of openness and democratic procedures. Norberto Bobbio in *The Future of Democracy* also expresses concern about democracy's future in the face of state secrecy. In order to counteract the repressive state, Bobbio seeks to strengthen liberal democracy.[19] For Negri, the future of democracy is intertwined with the fate of capital, particularly with exposing connections between fixed social capital and the state machinery in order to revise the notion of the expropriation of the workers' labor and to see it, in contemporary terms, as a "genuine productive process" that can lead to antagonism and change.

The alternatives are now war or revolution: War is the terrain of the state, and revolution is hence the terrain of the socialized worker. It follows that reformism or revolution are not matters of choice but are consequences of prevailing social and political conditions. Reformism in the face of these new global conditions—the nature of the nuclear state and the perpetual warfare of the state against workers—is no longer possible. Revolutionary action would seem to be an outgrowth of the recognition of numerous and varied antagonistic relations toward the state, relations involving the increased knowledge of contradictions concerning work and social identifications. Hence a redefinition of consensus involves a rethinking of not only the nature but also the role of knowledge and the intellectual.

The Formation of Intellectuals, Conditions of Knowledge, and New Subjectivities

With the development and expansion of communications technologies, global consumerism, and the onset of deregulation, what has become apparent (manifested particularly in political struggles since 1968) is the nature of existing antagonisms between the state, the economy, and the worker. Deregulation has brought corporatist strategies of the postwar era to a halt. It has also been instrumental in reintroducing "the ideology of the market to the centre of the political stage."[20] Workers are implicated in local and global issues. They are aware of the manipulation of money, of the numerous antagonisms generated by the ideology of the market and spread by the media, and of the possibilities of subversion.

In contrast to earlier Marxist notions of class struggle, Negri's conceptions of political struggle are more diverse. Class consideration is no longer the sole basis of organization and conflict. He no longer focuses exclusively on the enclosed environment of factory as the place of struggle. Work permeates the entire society in a multitude of ways. Negri acknowledges the various social movements that have arisen in the last few decades and sees them as contributing to new social and political organization. He does not disparage the differences attendant on gender, sexual, environmental, and anticolonial politics, although he does see the different social movements as being in need of a singularity of focus: as a basis of agreement and without sacrificing diversity, they need to arrive at a "molar" consensus about the centrality of exploitation. Exploring the nature of exploitation on the part of the state as well as the nature of capitalist control, Negri remarks that even the bosses now recognize a new state of affairs in the power of the socialized worker. Hence what we have been witnessing for the past few decades is a massive effort to "destroy proletarian and working-class hegemony" through the planning of poverty and social exclusion and through the attack on inflation, which is inextricably tied to "the worker's force, power, and desire." He describes the existence of a "dual society" as the outcome of exacerbated antagonisms. He finds these antagonisms insoluble through the reestablishment of reformist practices, either in Keynesianism or socialism:

> The reformist revolution of the thirties was sustained by political, trade union, and capitalist alliances involving *big labour, big capital, and big government.* If these have come to an end, and if the values which they expressed are now exhausted, today it is perhaps possible to perceive new alliances and new values. New alliances have been constitued in the dynamic of the power/knowledge (or vice versa) of the socialized worker, of the feminist movement and of new groups of revolutionary intellectuals.... It is a fact that, at the stage we have now reached, reformism is now impossible, and that every new form of social cooperation in work, directed at constitutive objectives, represents a catastrophic, revolutionary, and ontologically innovative transformation.[21]

In his critique of value and his invocation of the new subjectivities at work in contemporary society, Negri has gone beyond Gramsci in his analysis

222 of the basis and nature of revolutionary change. No longer advocating a war of position, Negri seems to see greater room for maneuver. The bases for this assessment are derived from his contemporary reading of Marx on value, which aids him in mapping economic transformations from the inter-war era to the present and in projecting a notion of the possibility of revolutionary struggle. Despite differences from Gramsci in his reading of Marx, Negri shares Gramsci's inclination toward communism, not socialism, with radical transformation, not reformism.[22]

Negri's thinking assumes a much more global perspective than Gramsci's though it is clear that Gramsci — in his comments on Americanism and Fordism, and in his speculations on the global implications of capital and of revolutionary action — was aware of the relationship between national and international issues. For Negri, the terrain of the socialized worker *is* global. Earlier varieties of Fascism and imperialism have been transformed in ways that he describes as "more terrible and widespread: *Value has everywhere escaped capitalist control. Or rather, it has overflowed and its presence is fully and widely felt: it circulates among the factories and in the metropolises, and even in the tropical areas hitherto untouched by industrialisation.*"[23]

The politics of world capital is now more uniformly expressed. Automation and computerization are the instruments of contemporary global politics. This technology enhances new forms of control, as well as initiating new forms of social knowledge and cooperation. Although countries captive to neocolonialism have adopted forms of "peripheral Fordism," or, as he modifies it, "peripheral Taylorism" that have become Fordism, they "have become full members of the economy of the socialized worker." He writes further:

> Just as there coexist within the metropolitan countries two levels of existence — one of integration, another of exclusion — so in the world economy there is the level of internal integration and a boundary of exclusion. Counterposed to the capitalist countries (including the ones that have recently joined this category) and to the world market as an organised structure, there is the world of the excluded — a world of hunger and desperation. In short, the "third world" as such no longer exists, and after the accession of a large part of the latter to the "first world," there followed the *discovery of "another world"* which lives on the margins and is built on lower, more wretched conditions than those of the first world.[24]

From these premises, Negri extends the notion of crisis to a global level by indicating some of its manifestations in terms of the international debt, international monetary policies, and new forms of war. Negri is not suggesting that the global situation will produce the demise of capitalism automatically. Rather, his argument is designed to chart the ways in which the situation holds the potential for "overthrowing that domination theoretically and making it problematic and insustainable."[25]

For both Gramsci and Negri, no political transformation can be conceived without an understanding of the conditions of knowledge available to subaltern groups. With respect to the nature of collective organization, Gramsci saw the absolute necessity of linking the urban proletariat to the peasant masses and of rethinking the role of the organic intellectual in effecting this union. Gramsci recognized that to be a traditional intellectual in Italy has signified different things in the North and in the South. Historically, traditional intellectuals have played significant roles in the cultural formation of regional and national identity. Recognizing that in Southern Italy the traditional intellectual has been the intermediary between the landowners and the peasants, Gramsci was insistent on the need to develop new types of intellectuals.

In relation to conventionally disseminated notions of Marxism, the emphasis on the role of intellectuals has several wide-ranging implications. First of all, Gramsci's notion of cultural change, especially with respect to the role played therein by organic intellectuals, needs to be seen in terms of the formation of new intellectual groups (not individuals), groups that cannot speak for the subaltern but with subalterns. Moreover, the need to recapture civil society is also implicit in his comments about the role of the state and its connection to traditional intellectuals. Insofar as the state is legitimated by traditional intellectuals, the role of opposition is to create new intellectual blocs and to weaken the power of the existing ones. The objective of organic intellectuals is to make a "conquest of state power." Given Gramsci's conception of new organizational groups and especially his conception of the party, he is no longer talking of the absolutist state but of the state as civil society.

Gramsci was at pains to elaborate the notion that there is no such thing as a nonintellectual: "although one can speak of intellectuals, one cannot speak of non-intellectuals, because non-intellectuals do not exist.... There is no human activity from which every form of intellectual participation can be excluded."[26] In his discussions of Fordism, Gramsci insists that he is not describing forms of mindless activity but the ways in which this system of production has introduced new possibilities of knowledge through the work process. Moreover, as he discusses

224 common sense, Gramsci is not relegating this proverbial, clichéd, and formulaic mode of describing the world to the limbo of false consciousness. His conception of the intellectual terrain of the worker is more tentative than Negri's.

Like Gramsci, Negri insists on the nature of work as an experience that is social in character. He differs from Gramsci in his emphasis on the workers' greater knowledge of their social conditions and on the contradictory nature of capitalist crisis itself as a producer of new forms of knowledge and antagonism. Negri speaks, of course, from a position that takes into account transformations in late capitalism, particularly those concerning the nature of labor and money. On the basis of his rereadings of Marx, and his awareness of Marx's discussion of the crisis nature of capital, the tendency of the rate of profit to fall, and the impossibility of resolving the inherently antagonistic nature of value and labor, Negri elaborates on the existence for socialized knowledge under late capitalism. He finds that "in Marx's outline of the successive stages of subsumption, the idea of the socialized worker is only merely hinted at and described as a possibility; we, on the other hand, experience the actuality of the concept."[27]

The socialized worker in Negri's terms is characterized by a different relationship to power and knowledge and is no longer dependent on political centralization of state regimes, on control by the clock, on the power of the "boss," and on the capitalist emphasis on pure monetary considerations. In terms that are familiar to readers of Deleuze and Guattari, he writes:

> All this, in the perspective of the socialized worker, corresponds to: a time which is diffuse, articulate, and manifold; a body of knowledge which tends to a maximum of diversity because it is localized and territorialized (without thereby becoming parochial and corporatist, however). What this amounts to is that the socialized worker identifies the nature of the antagonism in the universality of his/her own social being and in the indefinite microphysics of his/her powers.[28]

As Quintin Hoare and Geoffrey Nowell-Smith comment, Gramsci was dealing with the retrenchment of the revolutionary working-class movement.[29] Gramsci's notion of passive revolution needs to be reexamined in the light of the dramatic economic and political changes that have taken place since the 1960s. The radical cultural, political, and economic impetus of the 1960s in Europe and in the United States seems to have vanished in the face of the reorganization of global capital, deregulation, monetarism, and the large-scale proletarianization of sectors of the work force. Yet for Gramsci, passive revolution did not constitute the absence of antagonism, a failure of Marxist analysis in the face of the seeming vitality and protean nature of capital. Rather, the condition he described as passive revolution was a sign that a rethinking of existing forms of cultural and political knowledge was imperative for an understanding of how the antagonisms of subaltern groups have been combated or contained, though not necessarily always successfully. Not one to exalt tradition, Gramsci always examines history in order to learn from past failures, not to enshrine old methodologies. For Negri, the new social and economic exigencies thrown up in the face of the restructuring of capitalist formations have produced new antagonisms affecting gender, sexuality, ethnicity, race, and class, which require new modes of analysis compatible with present conditions and present forms of knowledge. If in Gramsci's time, especially under the powerful grip of Fascism, the possibilities for exploiting antagonisms against the state were a matter for speculation, for Negri they are real.

In Negri's terms, the reality is produced by the nature of new forms of knowledge made available through transformed economic and social conditions. For example, instead of productive labor being confined to the factory, it is diffused, and it permeates the entire society. The arena of production of the worker has expanded through "such infrastructures as communications networks, semi-manufactured information systems ... and so on."[30] Negri uses a spatial metaphor, territoriality, to describe the terrain of the socialized worker. This terrain is now that of technology, particularly communications technology. The crisis for Negri resides in rethinking traditional interpretations of use value, exchange value, and surplus value in such a way that one can allow for the transformation from a quantitative notion of labor power as a producer of wealth to one that takes into account "new objective possibilities of subjective coordination and cooperation." In the past, notions of value were tied to measurements of labor power. In the present, "cartography" is his way of reconfiguring new dimensions of value in the face of shifting sites of production.[31] Elaborating on the notion of value, he asserts:

> We could not but appreciate (as we still do and to an even greater extent) the significance of the theory of value. But though we appreciate and are willing to reaffirm the theory of value on this level [as a producer of wealth and as a drama], we find it less useful as a theory of measurement, of current measurement and—inevitably—of mediation. Value exists wherever social locations of working cooperation are to be found and wherever accumulated and hidden labour is extracted from the turgid depths of society. This value is not reducible to a common standard. Rather, it is excessive.[32]

226 Consonant with his notion of the pervasiveness of the productive process, Negri's reformulation of the theory of value seeks to map—not measure—the various ways in which the new "social machines" are productive of value. The socialized worker is capable of making manifest the ways in which technology is involved in expropriation and exploitation as well as how real potential for the liberation of the worker resides in it.

In his discussion of Marx's conception of the money form, Negri reformulates the question of value, of "money as material representative of wealth." The key to understanding this issue is not inherent in the notion of money as such but in the emphasis on representation. In linking money as representation to questions of social production, Negri is not reducing the question of value to monetary equivalence, a reduction that Marx recognized as a mystification of capitalist economics. Quite the contrary, following Marx, Negri emphasizes that:

> the money form cannot any longer ... simply act as mediation between the costs of production and the general value of social labour. It must become a general function of social production, the means of production of the wage relation in an extended, global dimension. The productive role of money leaves its imprint on capital development in the form of a continuous struggle to liberate itself from its functions of mediation in exchange, taking on its true capacity of domination over wage labour, outside and between the petty transactions of the market place.[33]

No longer does value constitute the specific nature of labor time as a measure. In contemporary capitalist society, money still exists in relation to the circulation of commodities, but money has merged with "the problem of a new and extremely radical kind of crisis over the capitalist domination over the mode of production." In her "Scattered Speculations on the Question of Value" Gayatri Spivak, too, is concerned to find ways that address the question of affective value in qualitative as well as quantitative terms to locate new forms of subjectivities, and to see these as an indication of crisis. She finds that "since the production and realization of relative surplus-value, usually attendant upon technological progress and the socialized growth of consumerism, increase capital expenditure in an indefinite spiral, there is the contradictory drive within capitalism to produce more absolute and less relative surplus-value as part of its crisis management."[34]

Money, in Negri's terms, continues to represent domination, but he is not reiterating the common-sense and reductive notion of "money as the root of all evil" and the need to abolish the money form. His objectives, following Marx, are to understand the nature of value and the ways in which money unproblematically constitutes measurement. Rather, Negri is concerned to rethink the money form in complex terms as constituting value and of rethinking how that value has been represented so as to occlude questions of subjectivity. In the present conditions when all forms of production are "socialized" beyond the confines of the factory, money no longer appears as a "rationale" but as a "radical antagonism, a function of pure domination, as a powerful enemy force, which is no longer recuperable to any mere function of mediation."[35] Hence, the state itself serves as the instrument of tyranny and force. Negri traces the "intermediary" form of this domination to Keynesian economics, in which money served in contradictory fashion to enable the development of socialized labor and, at the same time, served both "to measure labour and as the means of controlling development."[36] Thus the rethinking of value is necessary for predicating the existence of new subjectivities.

Of Americanism, Gramsci notes that it "requires a specific environment, a specific social structure (or at least a determined intention to create it) and a certain type of State. The State is the liberal State, not in the sense of a liberalism in trade but in the more essential sense of free initiative and of economic individualism which, by spontaneous means, through its own political development, succeeds in establishing a régime of monopolies."[37] Gramsci was aware of the contradictory changes being wrought by this new regime, of the need to identify both its new possibilities and the new dangers it creates. In Americanism Gramsci locates the appearance of "a new type of man," a worker whom he identifies in complex terms as involving heretofore unknown psychic, social, and political elements. Again, Gramsci seems to be suggesting, as he does in his discussions of intellectuals, that the term designates characteristics far beyond professional considerations and also far beyond merely economistic concerns. The notion of modernization, in the sense in which Walter Benjamin identified it (as in the *Arcades* project and in his writings on Baudelaire) with psychology and physiology, with new responses to time and space, is also present in Gramsci in more diluted fashion. Discussing the character of men, of the "new woman," and of cinema and other mass entertainments, Gramsci is aware of the role of the technology and of its transformative potential. In some instances, though he is critical of aspects of Taylorism and mechanization, he sees Taylorism as a necessary stage in the creation of new forms of consciousness and behavior.

His comments on education underscore the importance of an awareness of technology — of both its positive aspects and its threats. This

228 aspect of his thinking gives credence to the notion that, given his insistence on the importance of historicizing and of assessing change in relation to new developments in capital and technology, his ideas would certainly have taken appropriately new directions in his attempt to identify new subjectivities, much as Negri's work has. Gramsci's awareness of the city and its effects on the lives of inhabitants is certainly in keeping with his modernist concerns, but he does not, as he indicates in a diatribe against Giovanni Papini, set the city up as the sole criterion of modern life. In a discussion of "supercountry" (*Strapaese*) and "supercity" (*Stracittà*), he is critical of ideologies that set one up over the other. The city, associated with internationalism, and the country, associated with nationalism, have driven trends in determining Italian politics. Gramsci seems more concerned to sweep away instances of analysis that are indicative "of the polemic between parasitic conservatism and the innovating tendencies of Italian society."[38]

Gramsci finds the interrelationship between city and country characteristic of the relationship between the North and the South in Italy. This division constitutes a problematic in capitalist development still evident in differential analyses of relations between the developed northern industrial countries and the so-called periphery where a goodly share of the labor force now resides. Hence, to talk of the city, to talk of the metropolis, without talking of the periphery is to identify oneself with one or another of the ideologies that constitute modernism in relation to capital as represented by Europe in the 1920s and 1930s.

Also characteristic of Americanism and Fordism, as Gramsci develops it, is the trend toward corporativism. In Europe, what he saw was the static treatment of the working classes and the peasant populations, which contributed to disease, malnutrition, chronic unemployment, and the preying of one segment of the parasitic population on another. In his description of Americanism, he sees the development of forms of corporatism, new forms of "rationalisation," that have produced "the need to elaborate a new type of man suited to the new type of work and productive process."[39] This new type of worker, fostered under Taylorism, "is the consequence of more perfect forms of automation and more perfect technical organisation."[40] Along with technological changes have come juridical changes that have altered the socioeconomic structure.[41] In analyzing these changes, it is clear that Gramsci is describing new mentalities that address questions of sexuality, reproduction, ethics, and cultural representations, including the cinema. He is not valorizing modernization, Fordism, or corporatism, but, like Negri in his discussion of "socialized work," he is identifying the contradictory nature of the changes that modernization brings. Both Gramsci and Negri focus on utilizing these changes to move toward massive social and political restructuring.

Describing the nature of Fordism, Gramsci focuses on the nature of the mental activity that is involved in work. He describes the difference between printers and compositors and scribes. Instead of becoming nostalgic about the loss of the scribe's artisanship, he points to the fact that not only were many errors perpetrated by these workers, but their involvement with the text led them to revise, interpolate, and introduce many new elements that led to the "remaking" of the text. By contrast, he finds that the compositor "has to be much quicker; he has to keep his hands and eyes constantly in movement, and this makes his mechanisation easier."[42] Rather than arguing that this latter kind of work is conducive to spiritual death, however, Gramsci sees it as liberating. He suggests, in a fashion that runs contrary to aspects of Russian formalism, that automation permits new and freer forms of thought. One can be distracted now, dissociated from the specific task.

Gramsci does not seek to make mechanization and the economism of the worker the measure by which to understand the nature of modern capitalism, but he seeks to underscore the question of technology as having an important effect on conditions of work and on the degree of knowledge accessible to individuals. In a sense, he anticipates the notion of the socialized worker. One of the arguments he introduces in order to develop his description of Fordism entailing the question of the worker's nonconformity is the boss's fear of the worker, which leads to the educative emphasis characteristic of Fordism. Central to Taylorism (other than its regulatory dimensions, its automatization of movement, and its rationalization of work), according to Gramsci, are its tendencies toward higher wages, the development of workers skilled in the special-.ized work processes that inhibit competition, a continuing reserve army of unemployed, and also forms of state intervention by means of protectionism, state investment, and new modes of worker controls.

Thus Gramsci seems aware of profound changes affecting the nature of work and the socialization of workers. It is clear that he is struggling to describe a key moment in the transition of capitalism from one phase to another much as Negri moves to describe the three phases of industrial work. The transition from semifeudal relations of production to Fordism is certainly a central theme in Gramsci's notes on Americanism and Fordism, and it is intimately tied to his sense of changes exemplified in Fascism and also in opposing capitalism. In Gramsci's discussion of sex, psychoanalysis, and legal prohibitions on leisure activities, he is particularly concerned to describe the socializing dimensions of Fordism: both the instruments available and the antagonisms generated to meet the threat of that socialization.

Discussing sexuality, he indicates how this issue has now come to the forefront as a concomitant of Americanism and Fordism and been subjected to "regulation." He describes the way in which sex can be viewed as "spectacle," as "sport," and ascribes this to "a new sexual ethic suited to the new methods of production and work."[43] In his analysis of the relations between "animality" and industrialism, Gramsci explores two dimensions of this new "problematic": There is a growing "libertinism" that he identifies with these new forms of work and that takes several forms: prominently in the brutalization of women and more subtly in an emphasis, on the part of managers and of the state, on forms of puritanism that seek to regulate these new forms of behavior. What is interesting about Gramsci's comments is the emphasis he places on this connection between social, economic, and political conditions. Moreover, he is not suggesting any univalent prescription but is concerned to identify the potential components of what can now be termed "deterritorialization" of the worker.

Gramsci asserts, with respect to the "sexual field," that it is the upper classes, those not engaged in "productive work," who observe "libertarian" practices. These "enlightened" attitudes are spread by the upper classes to the working classes, who "are no longer subject to coercive pressure from a superior class." Hence Gramsci foresees a crisis developing "in which there is an inherent conflict between the 'verbal' ideology which recognizes the new necessities and the real 'animal' practice which prevents physical bodies from effectively acquiring the new attitudes."[44] Gramsci also sees, in the relationship between these new forms of work and new attitudes toward the body and sexuality, attitudes that can provoke new forms of coercion.

Although Gramsci's comments are quite brief and cryptic and though one may question the basis of some of his generalizations about sexuality, in the larger picture it is clear that he understands that sexuality has become a force to be acknowledged and examined in relation to issues of coercion and consent. These brief comments on sexuality and gender in relation to Fordism and Americanism are a further invitation to understand the increasing incursions of the state, especially the Fascist state, into civil society, traditionally conceived as the sphere of private life. The question of sexuality raises broader questions about the ways in which notions of public and private have been co-constituted, albeit they have been conceived in common-sense terms as separate spheres in the interests of "laissez-faire capitalism."[45] Gramsci's discussion calls attention to the need to elaborate on this relationship for historicizing and understanding the creation of the conditions for new subjectivities, topics that given his own circumstances, training, and background are only rudimentarily addressed but that point to his recognition of changing subjectivity.

Questions of Americanism and Fordism cannot be restricted to purely economic issues but are inevitably tied to questions of social and political import as they involve an understanding of the role played by the state and civil society. Moreover, one cannot discuss these issues in Gramsci without invoking questions involving cultural production— the role of intellectuals, the role of literature, journalism, cinema, and folklore—and these, in turn, cannot ever be considered apart from Gramsci's abiding concern to assess the conditions for change.

Similarly, Negri says, "Let us be clear about this, it is an *intellectual* subject but also a *productive* one. This means that the productive side of work is now apparent principally on the intellectual level."[46] Among other characteristics he attributes to this intellectual subject are that it is "central to society ... ethical ... rebellious."[47] In contrast to Gramsci, Negri here seems to situate these workers at the center rather than at the margins of society, and rather than seeing the workers as passive and contained, he sees them as aware of and responsive to antagonisms. Not only does he see the workers as ethical; he regards them as potentially central and capable of rebelliousness. By contrast, Gramsci, in his prison writings on the nature of passive revolution, indicates that the conditions of workers under Fascism had blunted their rebelliousness. Judging, however, from his comments on organic intellectuals, Gramsci does see the workers as intellectual subjects and as possessing the potential of intellectualism as a consequence of the nature of Fordism, though the nature of the work itself may not in itself be intellectually productive.

Because of the nature of contemporary work, Negri carries his analysis of this intellectual productivity much further than does Gramsci. In his discussion of the significance of "Paris, 1986, 26 November—10 December," Negri identifies a "new class composition and a new political subject." The struggles during these two weeks of 1986 exposed a number of important political problematics: the violence of the state, the reappearance of the political dimensions of struggle that had seemed to have been submerged, and the identification of new political alignments. These "problematics" too revealed the failure of the traditional Left workers' movements.[48] His writings in prison make clear that Gramsci

232 too was critical of the ways in which traditional workers' movements had tended toward syndicalism, corporativism, and economism.

The basis of Negri's analysis of new political alignments derives from his readings in philosophy, particularly his writings in prison on Spinoza in *The Savage Anomaly* as well as his challenging writings on the *Grundrisse* in *Marx Beyond Marx*. Negri's insistence on the link between knowledge and productive forces is traced in *The Savage Anomaly*: "Spinoza's mature thought is a metaphysics of productive force that rejects the critical rupture of the market as an arcane and transcendental episode, that instead interprets (immediately) the relationship between appropriative tension and productive force as the fabric of liberation. Materialistic, social, and collective."[49] The thematics of the Spinoza study are to be understood as an exploration of many of the terms employed by Negri in relation to his conceptions of social production, the nature of antagonism and crisis, and notions of power and collectivity. The emphasis on the liberation of productive forces—its appropriation by the people, and its "antithesis to the capitalist mode of production"—is central to Negri's thought.

Unlike many of the poststructuralists, he does not seem to want to endorse the notion of the "process without a subject." It seems evident from his comments on power and countervailing power that a subject is necessary for revolution. His notion that the new forms of capital have released new forms of subjectivity and that these subjectivities are produced through antagonism is, however, not dependent on substantialist ideologies and does not depend on "foundations which go beyond experience."[50] His emphasis on and reiteration of "experience" is reminiscent of Gramsci's reliance on this notion. For example, Gramsci states, "One may say that no real movement becomes aware of its global character at once, but only gradually through experience—in other words when it learns from the facts that nothing which exists is natural (in the nonhabitual sense of the word), but rather exists because of the existence of certain conditions, whose disappearance cannot remain without consequences."[51]

In these terms, for Gramsci as for Negri, subjectivity is constituted, not given and expressed as *agencements:*

> I believe that the subjective point of view is basically constitutive and that this constitutive process can be interpreted in ontological terms according to an hermeneutic of real determinations. By this I mean that points of view are counterposed in real terms, that the conflict between subjects is something tangible, and that points of view and points of conflict give shape to contexts and frameworks having material importance.[52]

The key terms here are determinations, tangible (or concrete) subjects, and the notion that subjectivity is produced. It is dynamic, not static, and multifarous, not binary or Manichean. Most particularly, the notion of subject is to be examined from the machinic, not organic, and social, not individual, perspectives. The individual subject as the agent of determination has no place in Negri's thinking; subjectivity is collective, social, and "collectively singular."

Drawing on Deleuze's and Guattari's distinctions between molar and molecular notions of subjectivity, Negri sees the importance of acknowledging the plurality of individual and group conflict. Multiplicity is the major feature of the new forms of subjectivity emerging from changes in social production as opposed to old molar notions of class. Negri, however, does not remain at the level of seeing the molecular as the determining factor of social struggle. He asserts that these conflicts are also molar, involving how "one passes from microconflicts to molar conflicts," but he does not see this as affecting the "complexity of antagonisms." His notion of radical subjectivity, in its emphasis on plurality and recognition of antagonistic alternatives, can coexist with molar or dual conflict. The molar and oppositional elements are not static or idealist. They are dynamically constituted in the face of existing antagonisms, and they do not need to be seen as overriding individual and specific group conflicts. This subjectivity is not free-floating but constituted within specific historical formations; and it is produced by and productive of determinate antagonisms. In relation to these specific historical moments, we see that Negri, like Gramsci before him, is seeking to make a correlation between social subjects as formed and formative. To develop this correlation, Negri creates a historical trajectory.

Negri identifies three phases in the development of modern capital and its relation to the state and the concomitant production of new subjectivities: from 1917 to 1929, from 1929 to 1968, and from 1968 to the present. The first period is exemplified by the October Revolution and the consolidation of the working class, which slowly generated responses on the part of capitalist class. The interwar period was characterized by the development of industrialization and, hence, the development of working-class antagonism as exemplified most dramatically in the development of Taylorization, which, Negri argues, both "accelerated the injection of new proletarian forces into production" and also determined the ways that "capital once again turned to the technological path of repression."[53]

The crisis of 1929 "destroyed the political and state mythologies of a century of bourgeois domination" by heralding the appearance of the

234 interventionist state, the appearance of Keynesian economics, and the disappearance of free markets. Contrary to other interpretations, for Negri Fascism was not an exceptional state of affairs but a manifestation of the new "historical form of the capitalist state, the sign of the nature of state intervention in the market. The new form of the planner state created forms of control of the working class through penetration into forms of civil society. The major contributions of Keynesian economics and its political effects are summed up in the word 'regulation,' which describes the attempt to produce equilibrium through a "balanced economy." The welfare state, then, in the form of scientism, assumed the role of planner:

> Juridical and indirect forms of state intervention will not suffice. It is not sufficient for the state to guarantee the fundamental economic convention that links present and future. Something further is required. The state has, itself, to become an economic structure, a productive subject.... In guaranteeing the convention that links the present to the future, the state is still a structure at the service of capitalists; but when it poses itself directly as productive capital, the state seeks also to overcome the structural frictions which a market economy and its indirect relationship with individual capitalists brings about. Thus it becomes a new form of state: the state of social capital.[54]

In its various expressions in Britain and in the United States, Keynesianism served as a means of containing the working classes and as a preliminary phase in the development of the socialized worker. It was not until 1968, however, that the phenomenon of the socialized worker emerged. If the term "mass worker" characterizes productive/political relations until 1968, the term "socialized worker" becomes most applicable to the economic and political situation prevailing after 1968. It is at this moment that the crisis of the planner state became evident and exploitable. The mass worker had set in motion demands relating not only to questions of social mobility but also to wage expectations, to the regulation of both working and nonworking time, and to subjective conditions concerning social values.

Taken together, the elements of this situation produce a crisis in relation to capital and its management of labor. The weapons used against these workers after 1968 include deregulation, unemployment, the creation of poverty, competition for labor on the world market, new forms of technological control, and literal state terror. Negri's mapping is fluid: one phase overlaps another, but the consistent motif is the growing antagonism and the growing social subjection and subjectivity of the

workers, the increasing awareness of the futility of reformism and of   **235**
accommodation, and the increasing violence on the part of the state.

If we adopt the general argument that Negri advances to identify the
present nature of the crisis of capital and the production of antagonistic
subjectivity, we can see that he has followed in significant ways some of
the problems advanced by Gramsci, specifically his concerns with corporatism and with the contradictory manifestations of Americanism and
Fordism. Negri has reconsidered Gramsci's notion of passive revolution
in a contemporary context by insisting on the need to confront possible
ways to produce revolutionary struggle. One could argue from Negri's
vantage point that Gramsci's analysis was suited to the particular conjuncture of the 1917–29 period. Certainly, Gramsci saw the restructura-
tion of capital both as necessary and as productive of conflict. Moreover,
Gramsci's emphasis on the relations between state and civil society as
central to an understanding of the new conditions seems also to be in the
spirit of the *Grundrisse* and of Negri's thinking.

In broad strokes, numerous parallels appear between Gramsci's and
Negri's insistence on the relationship between the nature of productive
forces and their appropriation by the state. For example, when Negri
states that "appropriation is here a constitutive key, and not the basis of
the legitimation of a norm of domination,"[55] his comments are not that
removed from Gramsci's insistence on the tendency to crisis in capitalism, the need to capitalize on these antagonisms, and especially on the
importance of the element of constitutiveness residing in the appropriation of the forms of civil society against the regulating tendencies of the
state. This is where the notion of the party assumes centrality.

The Party

For both Gramsci and Negri the party is an instrument for change; their
idea of it differs from other prevailing conceptions of party. Gramsci is
aware of ideas of the party that are totalitarian and inextricably linked to
existing state structures. He is careful to distinguish his sense of party
from reformist conceptions, which he deems corporative and economistic. His notion of the party contains the germs of a new society, the
seeds of new cultural and political organization. "Clearly," he says, "it
will be necessary to take some account of the social groups of which the
party in question is the expression and the most advanced element. The
history of the party, in other words, can only be the history of a particular social group. But this group is not isolated; it has friends, kindred
groups, opponents, and enemies. The history of any given party can

236 only emerge from the complex portrayal of the totality of society and state (often with international ramifications too)."[56]

As this description suggests, he conceives of the party in terms of process, in terms of organizing rather than as an organization and as heterogeneous rather than as a unified will. The social group is identified not by any absolute markers but through its connections to a notion of history as a process of ongoing constitutiveness on the part of individuals and groups. Social classes are identified by different skills, orientations, and forms of education. The question of singularity and difference seems to be an all-important consideration in his conception of the "modern prince." In relation to the problematic relationship between state and civil society characteristic of his moment of capitalism, he writes:

> The political party, for all groups, is precisely the mechanism which carries out in civil society the same function as the State carries out, more synthetically and over a larger scale, in political society. In other words, it is responsible for welding together the organic intellectuals of a given group — the dominant one — and the traditional intellectuals.... This function of a political party should emerge more clearly from a concrete historical analysis of how both organic and traditional intellectuals have developed in the context of different national histories and in that of the development of the various major social groups within each nation, particularly those groups whose economic activity has been largely instrumental.[57]

This note indicates the complexity that he attached to the notion of party. The party is not a bureaucratic structure based on an identity of interests. His use of the term "welding" suggests that the party serves as a site for the formation of organic intellectuals and implies also the existence of diverse histories as well as the need to develop into a social group. The party seems to assume the role of the state but it is not the state; nor does it assume the same functions as the state. The party is linked to the notion of the resurrection of civil society from its cannibalization by the state.

Gramsci is explicit in differentiating the party and the organic intellectuals that come to comprise it from the relationship of traditional intellectuals to the state. He says: "Indeed it happens that many intellectuals think they *are* the State, a belief which, given the magnitude of the category, occasionally has important consequences and leads to unpleasant complications for the mental economic group which *really* is the State."[58] It must be remembered that he seeks to articulate a notion of the state that is distinguished from economistic and absolutist conceptions.

His reconsideration of the state in terms of the party is, first of all, dependent on new class formations, not on the restoration of old class alliances. Second, Gramsci's explorations are dependent on trying to understand the nature of the new subjectivities that are forged in the process of struggle.

In her discussion of the connections between the party and the state, Anne Showstack Sassoon distinguishes Gramsci's notion of the state from corporativism by citing his claims, on the one hand, "that State and that party which claims moral, ethical leadership in the absence of a pluralism of political and cultural forces, remains on the terrain of coercion and economic corporativism." On the other hand, and in contrast to prevailing forms of corporativism, Sassoon points out Gramsci's suggestion that in "the expansion of civil society and the absorption by civil society of the political realm ... State and society become reunited."[59] Thus Gramsci's notion of the state takes on a different configuration, the opposite of the case in which civil society is absorbed by that state.

Gramsci's concern with the formation of the party is associated integrally with his delineation of the concept of conjuncture, both strategic and organic, since conjuncture involves theory and practice as well as the assessment of possibilities for revolutionary struggle. Above all, his mistrust of spontaneism leads him to link the role of the *condottiere,* spontaneism, and forms of action that lead to restoration and to reorganization. In effect, Gramsci is exploring, in another way, the possibility of passive revolution as opposed to the creation of "new national and social structures." In terms of collective action, there is no such thing as pure spontaneity, he argues; but he does see aspects of spontaneity as conducive to long-range change. Like his notions on common sense, however, his comments on spontaneity are not monolithic or rigidly binary. He finds that "every 'spontaneous' movement contains rudimentary elements of conscious leadership, of discipline."[60]

Likewise, Negri's position in relation to struggle does not valorize spontaneity. He constantly emphasizes the notion of organization, and, in that context, he refers to the party. Like Gramsci, for whom the notion of party animated so much of his writing, Negri believes that circumstances do not change without intervention, no matter how antagonistic the elements. The present celebration of indeterminacy and difference will not in itself bring about the "new social and productive order." Commenting on the nature of the present crisis in relation to the power of the state, Negri asserts that it is in the interests of the proletariat to create a period of stabilization that will serve the interests of enhancing the "reciprocal regulation of subjects."

238   Gramsci was explicit in his advocacy of a collective, rather than individual, notion of leadership. Hence, in his notes as in his earlier writings, the idea of a "party" was crucial. It is the party that is the "modern prince" and not the *condottiere*. He indicates that the "modern prince" is not a single individual, not a "real person," but "can only be an organism, a complex element of society in which a collective will, which has already been recognized and has to some extent asserted itself in action, begins to take concrete form."[61] The prince is not a charismatic leader. The party itself is the integral element in Gramsci's thought as it is in the writings of Antonio Negri and with the same emphasis on its collective character in both writers. Issues of hegemony, conceptions of state and civil society, notions of strategic and organic conjuncture are inextricable then from his notion of the "collective will," which is the party. In discussing the Gramscian notion of the party, it is essential, however, to understand that the emphasis is not on uniformity of character, affect, and thought but on will to struggle.

In describing the nature of subaltern groups, Gramsci says:

> The history of subaltern groups is necessarily fragmented and episodic. There undoubtedly does exist a tendency to (at least provisional stages of) unification in the historical activity of these groups, but this activity is continually interrupted by the activity of the ruling groups; it therefore can only be demonstrated when an historical cycle is completed and this cycle culminates in a success. Subaltern groups are always subject to the activity of ruling groups, even when they rebel and rise up: only "permanent" victory breaks this subordination, and that not immediately. In reality, even where they appear triumphant, the subaltern groups are merely anxious to defend themselves.... Every trace of independent initiative on the part of subaltern groups should therefore be of incalculable value for the integral historian.[62]

In his analysis of the nature of subalternity, Gramsci is careful to consider several crucial elements: subaltern groups are not unified merely by virtue of their subaltern status; whatever unity they achieve is fragile and subject to antagonisms originating from the ruling elements; therefore, their failures are as important to assess as their victories.

Although he sees the existence of a "sediment" of leadership, and hence the need, if not the ability, to distinguish between organicity and strategic conjuncture, spontaneous and planned forms of action, he also sees that spontaneous movements are "accompanied by a reactionary movement of the right-wing of the dominant class."[63] Such movements exist due, in part, to the "objective weakening of the State," but "in the modern world, the regressive examples are more frequent."[64] Again, it is evident that Gramsci attaches great importance to the weakening of the state and to the proper strategies required, via the party, for exploiting that weakness rather than producing the conditions for eliminating it.

The aspects of Gramsci's thought that have intrigued contemporary cultural critics reside particularly in his explorations of hegemony. His notion of hegemony is not of a coalition organized merely on short-range and limited economic and political interests. Gramsci was not advocating simplistic notions of populism that obliterate differing fundamental economic and political interests, nor, by the same token, do his comments seem to suggest forms of "*trasformismo*" against which he had written in his notes on Italian history. His conception of alignments, though more flexible than that of many of his Marxist contemporaries, was based on the shared objective of revolutionary transformation.

Negri's conception of the party and its necessity may also seem to carry negative associations from the development of bourgeois political parties, but, for him as for Gramsci, the party becomes a far different entity in the service of alternative modes of political organization. Negri's comments on the party seem generally aligned with Gramsci's notions of equating the party with civil society. It is a party that operates against and not within the state. Invoking Gramsci's notion of passive revolution, that is, revolution from above in the face of the passivity of the masses, Negri inverts the concept. "Today, it is perhaps appropriate," he writes, "to use the concept 'passive revolution' to indicate a passive process of sectional movements of the masses which imposes a revolution from below."[65]

Since it is no longer possible to generate reforms in Keynesian terms as a means toward allowing workers some measure of wealth, the passive revolution should be waged in terms of the temporal well-being of society, and this cannot take place until proletarian power can consolidate itself. Since the nuclear state operates in imaginary terms to "reinforce the pure image of power" to contain resistance, no democracy is possible within it. No form of democracy can be asserted until the power of the state is destroyed. Moreover, although culture is an important force for producing hegemony and counterhegemony, it cannot be divorced from political considerations, namely, from his notion of the necessity of the party and its connection to the defeat of the state.

Epilogue: Culture, Politics, and Postmodernity

A great deal of Gramsci's writings turn on connections between the political and the cultural. His writings on hegemony, his views of the

240 party, and his conceptions of the relations between state and civil society are inextricable from his concerns about culture, education, and intellectuals. His writings on literature, folklore, and (to a lesser extent) cinema are meaningful in the attempt to understand the nature of consent. His conception of folklore is not static. He sees it, as he sees common sense, as containing the seeds of alternative modes of thought, the sedimentary elements of notions contributing to new cultural forms. Gramsci does not seem to be promoting the creation of new forms *ex nihilo* but rather the creation of new forms out of the pool of existing forms that are embedded in common sense and the folklore of a group. He never writes condescendingly of the subaltern's level of knowledge as degraded and mindless. Although common sense is not "good sense," by the same token, it is not bad sense; and it is also philosophical in that it is based on the intellect, on knowledge of the world. His emphasis on the subaltern's access to knowledge, including his descriptions of the potential for thinking and action available to the Fordist worker, seems to me to be a harbinger of the contemporary socialized worker, though there remain many questions about the forms and nature of the knowledge available to Negri's workers, questions that are linked to new meanings of communication that are very much in contention in discussions of postmodernity.

In discussing the potential of this socialized worker, Negri particularly focuses on what he terms the "expropriation of communication." If the "mass worker" under Fordism produced commodities, Negri asks, what is the commodity produced by the socialized worker? His answer lies in the nature of new communication technologies. To arrive at a critical understanding of communication as a means of repression and as a means to enable socialized workers to appropriate the means of production, one should presumably understand the obvious and subtle forms of political control that emanate from the state and from the media under contemporary capitalism. In language reminiscent of Walter Benjamin, Jean Baudrillard, and Jürgen Habermas, Negri distinguishes between information and modes of "communicative action." He suggests that because communication is the basis for community, the role of information is to negate and then to mystify relationships. In this context, he is more explicit about the nature of socialized work. Distinguishing his position on capital from more idealized and utopian conceptions of cultural value, Negri is insistent on tying his discussion of communication and information to orchestrated analyses of economic and cultural value, circulation, domination, and hence politics:

Is communication as such, then (as value) a pure and simple utopia? No, on the contrary, it constitutes the basic essence of the production of the socialized worker. Precisely for this reason, however, it is to be seen as permeating and enlivening every real determination and as distributing itself widely on the horizon of human artificiality. On the other hand, is information then pure, empty repetition, a residual fact, an inert substance, a simple detritus? For the same reason that communication is not utopia, the answer is obviously, "No." It is within this complex structure, then, that expropriation takes place.[66]

In his discussion of the nature of control involving communication and information, Negri returns to the nature of value. Once again, he suggests that communication must be seen in terms of the social process of production—production of, in this case, information. Challenging and repudiating classical notions of measurement, he is concerned with the "social dimensions of money" that represent another form of control but through mystifying the abstract relations of social production. Cultural capital circulates both as actual money and as a means of social control through its representation and through its mystification in forms of communication. Invoking Spinoza, Negri insists on the materialist nature of communication in relation to social cooperation as integrally related to new forms of social production.

Negri's comments on cultural capital seem, once again, to be in the vein of Gramsci's cultural writings, though tempered and altered by the nature of expanded contemporary technology. Although Negri does not posit a form of "national/popular culture" as Gramsci did, he does point to the absolute necessity of alternative cultural processes, which he sees as even more accessible than did Gramsci. The question of language and culture, the need to consider the nature of cultural articulation, was everywhere present in Gramsci's concern for workers' organization and appropriation of the means of production. The major difference is, of course, that Gramsci did not identify communication explicitly within the circuit of value, though one can extrapolate from his political to his cultural comment his concern with the roles of literature, film, and journalism in forming modern society.

For example, Gramsci's emphasis on the language question, on its collectivizing potential; his concern with "truth rather than legislation" and his emphasis on reason and ethics—all seem convergent with the concerns that Negri articulates through his discussion of Spinoza's writing. Both Negri and Gramsci express a radical desire to understand the nature of knowledge and its appropriation and to struggle against notions of the individual subject's autonomy and of institutional tyranny.

242   The new subject envisioned by Negri is not the isolated individual restricted to the workplace but a member of the community. In relation to Spinoza's explorations of power, Negri comments that "thought experiences the affections of being in their individuality and transforms them into ideas—confused ideas but still real ones. This is an expansion of the space of knowledge in comparison to simply true knowledge; it is a basis and a project for a cognitive and operative process in the world of passions; it is the definitive closure of every 'descending path' (from the absolute to the modes) and a hint toward an 'ascending path,' a constitutive path."[67]

The paradox of Spinoza's thought seems to reside in the "ontological identity of things, attributed to the world, revealed by the world, in its singular plurality." It is the ethical nature of knowledge and its constitutive character that are at the basis of Spinoza's thinking about power and that are so crucial to Negri's development of notions of rebellion and freedom. In Negri's terms, illusion and imagination are central to the ways in which truth functions, and rather than dealing in binary terms with illusion and truth, he wants to reinforce the fluid and constitutive nature of perception and constructions of reality. Negri's emphasis on illusion and imagination and his allusion to "confused ideas but true ones" are not far from Gramsci's notions of common sense.

Negri's critique of culture and politics is related to the work of others who have developed the concept of the "postmodern condition." Although he acknowledges the contributions of Baudrillard and Lyotard in relation to their critiques of present cultural formations, he asserts that the notion of the postmodern can be developed differently and more fully. First of all, he suggests that postmodernism is "a new form of romanticism."[68] This romanticism is marked by a recognition that culture is in a state of crisis; everything has become commodified. He validates the idea of a break between modernism and postmodernism. In postmodernism he sees the succumbing to consumerism and its role in the abdication of meaning. The communications industry has served to sever boundaries between the real and the imaginary. The modernist celebration of production and technology (also inherent in Gramsci's comments on Americanism and Fordism) must be seen as inadequate. Linked to Fordism, this form of thinking belongs to that earlier period; it is no longer viable, given the way the state has expropriated all forms of production.

He acknowledges, with an indebtedness to Paul Virilio, that "postmodernism ... lies in the awareness of this circularity of being, in this continuous circulation of commodities (which is so fast as to become indescribable), in this complete divorce between the sense and meaning of propositions and actions, and finally in the absence of any possible way out of this."[69] He asserts that there is a "positive moment" to this condition. He sees that the situation offers new possibilities for the restructuring of society through its identification of "contradiction, conflict, and new power." Unlike the German systems theorist Niklas Luhmann, Negri's theory does not advocate the proposition of "a social ideology of full circulation, of absolute flexibility, and of radical simplification of the complex ... to save the workings of the Western democracies from the conflict of organized interests and to ensure governability and the forging of instruments and strategies adapted to the attainment of these goals."[70] He does not see that problems can be resolved within the terms formulated by most theorizers of postmodernism.

Negri cannot endorse liberal economic forms of intervention based on postmodernist analysis, because he sees these strategies as only exacerbating economic and social contradictions. In effect, he sees postmodernism itself "as the mystified ideology of the new collectivities or as a primitive but effective allusion to the scientific determination of new subjects in the Marxian phase of real subsumption (or more simply, in the phase of general circulation and communication)."[71] Relying on Marx's observations from the *Grundrisse*, Negri takes the position that, for all of the descriptive adequacy of the effects of real subsumption, analysis of postmodernism does not take into account the formation of revolutionary subjectivities but continues to operate nonanalytically either as apocalypse or as celebration. The theorists of postmodernism are not attuned to the antagonisms generated by these new forms of state power but in one form or another succumb to them.

In elaborating his different, more economically driven and less grandiose, version of postmodernity, Negri identifies two important directions in Marx's formulations for contemporary political struggle. First of all, he stresses the inevitability of crisis deriving from the law of the fall of profit:

> Capitalist growth may indeed urge the compression of its quantity, it can indeed multiply the productive force of labor, but after all the surplus value that can be extorted is limited: there is still the rigidity of necessary labor (necessary part of the labor day) to constitute the limit to valorization.... The sum of necessary labor is rigid and it is precisely on this rigidity that are based the possibilities for a higher valorization on the part of the class, *for a*

self-valorization of the working class and proletariat.... The law of the tendency
to decline represents, therefore, one of the most lucid Marxist intuitions of
the intensification *of the class struggle* in the course of capitalist
development.[72]

Thus one response to the quietism and reformism generated by much of
postmodern thinking is this graphic reminder of the inherent tendency
of capital to crisis, one form of which is manifested in the antagonisms
produced by this rigidity, which has been and is productive of class
struggle. The issue is, of course, the direction of this struggle.

Another source of antagonism identified by Negri in his invocation of
Marx by way of the *Grundrisse* is the social character of surplus value.
Negri writes that "the more *labor is objectified into capital* and capital is
increased; in other words, the more labor and productivity have become
capital, *all the more living labor* opposes this growth in an *antagonistic fashion.*"[73] Again, we can see that we are not confronting a passive response
to the absorption of labor into capital, the subsumption of civil society
into the state, but a situation seething with inherent antagonisms;
though it does not necessarily follow that these antagonisms will necessarily produce revolution. This is not a situation that is automatically
productive of revolution, but it does provide the basis for an alternative
to capital's increasingly totalizing and coercive power.

In discussing circulation, Negri comments that "the social conditions
of production are formed, organized and dominated by the organization
of circulation, by the impulse capital gives to it. Therefore *circulation* is,
above all, *the expansion of the potency of capital;* and for the same reason, it
entails the *appropriation* of all the social conditions and their placement
in *valorization.*"[74] Thus Negri advances another powerful argument for
the socialization of capital and concomitantly for the nature of class
struggle, while exploring the possibilities of subversion. Capital must
seek to overcome time and space as barriers. Both totalizing and disunifying, enabling and also limiting, the process of expansion becomes part
of a permanent revolution: "The expansive, imperialistic process of capital and its tension toward the constitution of average terms of world
exploitation are then simultaneously the result and the premise for the
conditions of revolutionary subjectivity."[75]

The important qualification in Negri resides in the terms of these
"conditions of subjectivity." There is no doubt that Negri is intent on
challenging prevailing notions of the inevitability of postmodern
despair, simplistic notions of reformism and of individual agency. His
"optimism (not pessimism) of the intellect" leads him to chart alterna-

tives to prevailing assessments of postmodernity. His readings of "Marx beyond Marx" lead him to reformulate the conditions of contemporary culture and society in terms that take into account the nature of cultural capital, the existence of new forms of knowledge and new subjectivities, and changing relations of state and civil society. In these respects, it seems that he has not only read "Marx beyond Marx" but "Gramsci beyond Gramsci." Negri is working in ways that elaborate on the earlier work of Gramsci, and is moving toward a productive analysis of contemporary politics.

Like Gramsci, Negri seeks to bring history to bear on an assessment of the possibilities for social change in ways that do not reproduce past authoritarian structures. Negri's redefinition of the nature of collectivity, his emphasis on the importance and availability of knowledge, his discussions of the relations between state and civil society, and his rethinking of the nature of the party constitute serious interventions in the circulation of notions of postmodernity that have become the new "folklore" of cultural politics. This new folklore can be identified, on the one hand, by the celebration of new cultural forms of reading and creativity as intrinsically political and, on the other hand, by the pronouncements of apocalyptic prophecies based on the belief in the totalizing dimensions of information and communications systems. Through his rethinking of Marx, of taking "Marx beyond Marx," Negri avoids both extremes. He resists traditional and reductive economistic and continuist readings of Marxism. In many ways, his analysis of contemporary culture and politics—the nature and role of intellectuals, of knowledge, the state, the party, and mass culture—can be read in such a way as to take Gramsci beyond Gramsci to reinforce the other critical work that has been done to make observations in *The Prison Notebooks* germane to the last decades of the twentieth century.

Notes

Abbreviations for Commonly Cited Works

SPN: *Selections from the Prison Notebooks*
SCW: *Selections from the Cultural Notebooks*
Quaderni: refers throughout to the Gerratana editions of the *Notebooks*
GP: *Gramsci's Politics*
WS: *Which Socialism?*
FD: *The Future of Democracy*

Foreword

1. Antonio Gramsci, *Selections from the Prison Notebooks*, ed. and trans. Quintin Hoare and Geoffrey Nowell-Smith (New York: International Publishers, 1971), p. 276.

Preface

1. Stuart Hall, *The Hard Road to Renewal: Thatcherism and the Crisis of the Left* (London: Verso, 1988), p. 161.

1. Gramsci, "'Knowledge Claims and Knowing Subjects"

1. Donna Haraway, *Simians, Cyborgs, and Women: The Reinvention of Nature* (New York: Routledge, 1991), p. 187; Mary Kaldor, "After the Cold War," *New Left Review*, no. 180 (March/April 1990): 25–40.
2. Gayatri Chakravorty Spivak, *In Other Worlds: Essays in Cultural Politics* (New York: Routledge, 1988), p. 117.
3. For a careful analysis of the importance of Gramsci in relation to contemporary cultural studies, see Jim McGuigan, *Cultural Populism* (London: Routledge, 1992), especially pp. 61–75. See also Graeme Turner, *British Cultural Studies: An Introduction* (London: Unwin Hyman, 1990).
4. Michel Foucault, *The History of Sexuality, Vol. I* (New York: Vintage, 1980), pp. 58–68.
5. Gayatri Chakravorty Spivak, *The Postcolonial Critic: Interviews, Strategies, Dialogues* (New York: Routledge, 1990), p. 31.
6. Mas'ud Zavarzadeh and Donald Morton, *Theory, (Post)Modernity, Opposition: An "Other" Introduction to Literary and Cultural Theory* (Washington, D.C.: Maisonneuve Press, 1991).

7. Fredric Jameson, *The Geopolitical Aesthetic: Cinema and Space in the World System* (London: BFI Publishing, 1992), p. 212.

8. Stuart Hall, *The Hard Road to Renewal: Thatcherism and the Crisis of the Left* (London: Verso, 1988), p. 242.

9. Antonio Gramsci, *Selections from the Prison Notebooks*, ed. Quintin Hoare and Geoffrey Nowell-Smith (New York: International Publishers, 1971), p. 106. Hereafter referred to as *SPN*; see *Quaderni*, ed. Valentino Gerratana (Turin: Einaudi, 1975), 3: 1374.

10. Antonio Negri, *The Politics of Subversion: A Manifesto for the Twenty-First Century* (Cambridge: Polity Press, 1989), pp. 75–88.

11. Gramsci, *SPN*, p. 337; also *Quaderni* 2: 1388.

12. In this context, the notion of "diseducation" seems preferable to that of education. Since the 1960s, pedagogical concerns have been largely contained within the reigning neoliberal consensus. For an elaboration of the concept of diseducation within Italian thought, see Mario Serenelli's *I diseducatori: Intelletuali da Gramsci a Pasolini* (Bari: Edizioni Dedalo, 1985).

13. Joseph A. Buttigieg, "Gramsci's Method," *boundary 2* 17, no. 2 (Summer 1990): 60–81.

14. Antonio Gramsci, *Selections from the Cultural Writings*, ed. David Forgacs and Geoffrey Nowell-Smith (Cambridge: Cambridge University Press, 1984), pp. 382–83, hereafter referred to as *SCW*; *Quaderni* 3: 1891.

15. Immanuel Wallerstein, *Historical Capitalism* (London: Verso, 1984), p. 63.

16. Stanley Aronowitz and Henry Giroux, *Education under Siege* (South Hadley, Mass.: Bergin and Garvey, 1985), p. 63.

17. See David Forgacs, "National-Popular: Genealogy of a Concept," in *Formations of Nation and People* (London: Routledge & Kegan Paul, 1984), pp. 83–97.

18. Gramsci, *SCW*, pp. 420–21.

19. Raymond Williams, *Problems in Materialism and Culture: Selected Essays* (London: Verso, 1980), pp. 40–42. See also Evan Watkins, *The Critical Act: Criticism and Community* (New Haven: Yale University Press, 1978), p. 144.

20. Gramsci, *SPN*, p. 333; *Quaderni* 2: 1385.

21. Gramsci, *SPN*, p. 178.

22. Mary Kaldor, "After the Cold War," *New Left Review*, no. 180 (March/April 1990): 25–40. See also Robin Blackburn, "Fin de Siècle: Socialism after the Crash," *New Left Review*, no. 185 (January/February 1991): 6.

23. Etienne Balibar and Immanuel Wallerstein, *Race, Nation, Class: Ambiguous Identities* (London: Verso, 1991).

24. Spivak, *The Postcolonial Critic*, especially pp. 67–94.

2. The Gramscian Politics of Culture

1. Joseph Buttigieg, "The Exemplary Worldliness of Antonio Gramsci's Literary Criticism," *boundary 2* 11, nos. 1, 2 (Fall/Winter 1982/83): 21–40.

2. Victoria de Grazia, *The Culture of Consent: Mass Organization of Leisure in Fascist Italy* (Cambridge: Cambridge University Press, 1983); see also Renzo De Felice, *Mussolini*, 4 vols. (Turin: Einaudi, 1965–90).

3. Susan Sontag, "Fascinating Fascism," in *Movies and Methods I*, ed. Bill Nichols. (Berkeley: University of California Press, 1979), pp. 31–43.

4. Alistair Davidson, *Antonio Gramsci: Towards An Intellectual Biography* (London: Merlin Press, 1977), pp. 48–93.

5. Leonard W. Moss, "The Passing of Traditional Peasant Society in the South," **249** and Denis Mack Smith, "Regionalism," in *Modern Italy: A Topical History Since 1861* (New York: New York University Press, 1974), pp. 125–46, 147–70; see also Dante Germino, *Antonio Gramsci: Architect of a New Politics* (Baton Rouge: Louisiana State University Press, 1990), pp. 1–24.

6. Ousmane Sembène, *Man Is Culture*, Sixth Annual Hans Wolf Lecture, March 5, 1975, Bloomington, Ind., African Studies Program.

7. Anne Showstack Sassoon, "Gramsci's Subversion of the Language of Politics," *Rethinking Marxism* 3, no. 1 (Spring 1990): 14–25.

8. Ernesto Laclau, *Politics and Ideology in Marxist Theory* (London: NLB, 1977), pp. 81–142.

9. Theodor Adorno, "Commitment," *Aesthetics and Politics*, ed. Fredric Jameson (London: NLB, 1977), pp. 177–95.

10. For example, see *Selected Subaltern Studies*, ed. Ranajit Guha and Gayatri Chakravorty Spivak (New York: Oxford University Press, 1988); and Partha Chatterjee, *Nationalist Thought and the Colonial World: A Derivative Discourse* (Minneapolis: University of Minnesota Press, 1993).

11. Antonio Gramsci, "Ai margini della storia (Storia del gruppi sociali subalterni)," *Quaderni* 3: 2283.

12. Antonio Gramsci, "Noterelle sul Machiavelli," *Quaderni* 3: 1568.

13. Anne Showstack Sassoon, *Gramsci's Politics* (Minneapolis: University of Minnesota Press, 1987).

14. Gramsci, "Noterelle," *Quaderni* 3: 1630.

15. Edward Tannenbaum, *Fascism In Italy: Society and Culture, 1922–1945* (London: Allen Lane, 1973).

16. Mas'ud Zavarzadeh and Donald Morton, *Theory, (Post)Modernity, Opposition: An 'Other" Introduction to Literary and Cultural Theory* (Washington, D.C.: Maisonneuve Press, 1991), p. 125.

17. Antonio Gramsci, "Appunti e note sparse per un gruppo di saggi sulla storia degli Intelletuali," *Quaderni* 3: 1513–18.

18. Gramsci, "Noterelle," *Quaderni* 3: 1579.

19. Walter Adamson, *Hegemony and Revolution: A Study of Antonio Gramsci's Political and Cultural Theory* (Berkeley: University of California Press, 1980), p. 141.

20. Raymond Williams, *Marxism and Literature* (Oxford: Oxford University Press, 1977), pp. 121–28.

21. Gramsci, "Noterelle," *Quaderni* 3: 1578–89.

22. Tom Nairn, "Antonu su *Gobbu*," in *Approaches to Gramsci*, ed. Anne Showstack Sassoon (London: Writers and Readers, 1982), p. 161.

23. Gramsci, "Appunti e note sparse per un gruppo di seggisulla storia degli intellettuali," *Quaderni* 2: 1516.

24. For a discussion of the precursors for Gramsci's notion of common sense and his relation to them, see Edmund E. Jacobitti's "From Vico's Common Sense to Gramsci's Hegemony," in *Vico and Marx: Affinities and Contrasts*, ed. Giorgio Tagliacozzo (Atlantic Highlands, N.J.: Humanities Press, 1983), pp. 367–88.

25. Gramsci, "Note per una introduzione allo studio della grammatica," *Quaderni* 3: 2345.

26. Alberto Marla Cirese, "Gramsci's Observations on Folklore," in *Approaches to Gramsci*, ed. Sassoon, pp. 214–15.

27. Adamson, *Hegemony and Revolution*, p. 128.

28. Gramsci, "Introduzione allo studio della filosofia," *Quaderni* 2: 1385.

29. Susan Sontag, "Fascinating Fascism," pp. 31–44.

30. George Mosse, *Masses and Man: Nationalist and Fascist Perceptions of Reality* (New York: Howard Fertig, 1980), pp. 159–96.

31. Gramsci, "Miscellanea e appunti di filosofia," *Quaderni* 2, pp. 812, 820–82, 962–64.

32. Alberto Maria Cirese, "Gramsci's Observations on Folklore," in *Approaches to Gramsci*, ed. Sassoon, pp. 212–15. See also David Forgacs, "National-Popular: Genealogy of a Concept," in *Formations of Nations and People*, ed. Formations Collective (London: Routledge & Kegan Paul, 1984).

33. Gramsci, "Miscellanea," *Quaderni* 3: 1676–77.

34. Paul A. Bové, *In the Wake of Theory* (Hanover, N. H.: Wesleyan University Press, 1992), p. 36.

35. Gramsci, "Americanismo e fordismo," *Quaderni* 3: 2149–50.

36. Ibid., 2163.

37. Gramsci, "In principio era il sesso (Feb. 16, 1917)," *Letteratura e vita nazionale*, (Rome: Riuniti, 1979), p. 337.

38. Gramsci, "Critica Letteraria," *Quaderni* 3: 2193–95.

39. Gramsci, "Glornalismo," *Quaderni* 3, Gerratana, pp. 2259–75.

40. Gramsci, "Per la storia degli intellettuali," *Quaderni* 2: 1530–51.

41. Gramsci, "Noterelle," *Quaderni* 2: 1602–16.

42. Paul Piccone, *Italian Marxism* (Berkeley: University of California Press, 1983), p. 200.

3. Socialism and/or Democracy: Politics, Culture, and the State

1. *New Left Review* 150 (Mar.–April, 1985): 1.

2. Stanley Aronowitz, *The Crisis of Historical Materialism: Class, Politics, and Culture in Marxist Theory* (New York: Praeger, 1981), p. 121.

3. Chantal Mouffe, "Introduction: Gramsci Today," in *Gramsci and Marxist Theory*, ed. Chantal Mouffe (London: Routledge & Kegan Paul, 1979), p. 1.

4. Anne Showstack Sassoon, *Gramsci's Politics* (Minneapolis: University of Minnesota Press, 1987), p. xviii, hereafter cited as *GP*.

5. Ibid.

6. Perry Anderson, "The Antinomies of Antonio Gramsci," *New Left Review* 100 (Nov. 1976–Jan. 1977): 6.

7. Sassoon, *GP*, p. 22

8. For a discussion of the Sorelian elements in Gramsci's thought, see Nicola Badaloni, "Gramsci and the Problem of Revolution," in *Gramsci and Marxist Theory*, ed. Mouffe, pp. 86–98.

9. For a discussion of the distinction between "dialectical" and "naturalistic" approaches, see Maurice A. Finocchiaro, *Gramsci and the History of Dialectical Thought* (New York: Cambridge University Press, 1988), p. 161.

10. Sassoon, *GP*, p. 32.

11. Ibid., p. 48.

12. Ibid., p. 51.

13. Ibid., p. 67.

14. Ibid., p. 81.

15. Ibid., p. 109.

16. Ibid., p. 119.

17. Gramsci, *SPN*, pp. 11–12, 71–75, 93–95.   **251**

18. Sassoon, *GP*, p. 155.

19. Ibid., p. 193.

20. Ibid., p. 204.

21. Christine Buci-Glucksmann, "Hegemony and Ideology in Gramsci," in *Gramsci and Marxist Theory*, ed. Buci-Glucksmann (London: Routledge & Kegan Paul, 1979), pp. 207–8.

22. Sassoon, *GP*, p. 205.

23. Ibid., p. 209.

24. Buci-Glucksmann, "Hegemony and Ideology," p. 224.

25. Sassoon, *GP*, p. 210.

26. Ibid., p. 212.

27. Ibid., p. 214.

28. Ibid., p. 230.

29. Alan Carling, "Rational Choice Marxism," *New Left Review* 160 (Nov.–Dec. 1986): 26–27.

30. Perry Anderson, "The Affinities of Norberto Bobbio," *New Left Review* 170 (July–Aug. 1988): 12–13.

31. Ibid.

32. Norberto Bobbio, *Which Socialism? Marxism, Socialism, and Democracy*, trans. Roger Griffin, ed. Richard Bellamy (Minneapolis: University of Minnesota Press, 1987), p. 31; hereafter cited as *WS*.

33. Ibid., p. 37.

34. Ibid., p. 163.

35. Ibid., p. 53.

36. Ibid., p. 139.

37. Ibid.

38. Ibid., p. 141.

39. Ibid., p. 142.

40. Ibid., p. 147.

41. Paul Piccone, *Italian Marxism* (Berkeley: University of California Press, 1983).

42. Bobbio, *WS*, p. 158.

43. Ibid., p. 161.

44. Norberto Bobbio, *The Future of Democracy*, trans. Roger Griffin, ed. Richard Bellamy (Minneapolis: University of Minnesota Press, 1987), pp. 21–22; hereafter cited as *FD*.

45. Ibid., p. 24.

46. Ibid., p. 25.

47. Ibid., p. 28.

48. Ibid., p. 31.

49. Ibid., p. 32.

50. Ibid., p. 33.

51. Ibid., p. 39.

52. Ibid., p. 42.

53. Ibid., pp. 52–53.

54. Ibid., p. 48.

55. Ibid., p. 55.

56. Ibid., p. 56.

57. Ibid., p. 57.

58. Ibid., p. 58.

59. Ibid., p. 68.

60. Ibid., p. 69.
61. Ibid., p. 70.
62. Ibid., pp. 72–76.
63. Ibid., p. 81.
64. Ibid., p. 82.
65. Ibid., p. 83.
66. Ibid., p. 91.
67. Ibid., p. 104.
68. Ibid., p. 102.
69. Ibid., p. 105.
70. Ibid., p. 107.
71. Ibid., p. 110.
72. Ibid., p. 111.
73. Ibid., p. 113.
74. Ibid., p. 117.
75. Ibid., p. 135.
76. Ibid., p. 136.
77. Ibid., p. 137.
78. Ibid., p. 143.
79. Ibid., p. 144.
80. Ibid., p. 145.
81. Ibid., p. 156.
82. Ibid., p. 71.
83. Anderson, "The Affinities of Norberto Bobbio," p. 28.
84. Ibid., p. 30.
85. Ibid., p. 26.
86. José Nun, "Elements for a Theory of Democracy," in *The Legacy of Antonio Gramsci*, ed. Joseph A. Buttigieg, *boundary 2* 14 (Spring 1986): 225.
87. Toni Negri and Félix Guattari, *Communists Like Us* (New York: Semiotext[e], 1990), p. 27.

4. Cultural Politics and Common Sense

1. Andreas Huyssen, "Mass Culture as Woman: Modernism's Other," in *Studies in Entertainment: Critical Approaches to Mass Culture*, ed. Tania Modleski (Bloomington: Indiana University Press, 1986), pp. 188–207.
2. See Edmund E. Jacobitti, "From Vico's Common Sense to Gramsci's Hegemony," in *Vico and Marx: Affinities and Contrasts* (Atlantic Highlands, N.J.: Humanities Press, 1983), pp. 367–88.
3. Stuart Hall, "In Praise of the Particular," *Marxism Today* 31 (April 1987): vii.
4. Stuart Hall, "Cultural Studies: Two Paradigms," *Culture, Media, Language* (London: Hutchinson, in association with the Centre for Contemporary Cultural Studies, University of Birmingham, 1980), p. 3.
5. Jean Baudrillard, *Selected Writings* (Oxford: Polity Press, 1988), p. 210.
6. Zavarzadeh and Morton, *Theory, (Post)Modernity, Opposition: An "Other" Introduction to Literary and Cultural Theory* (Washington, D.C.: Maisonneuve Press, 1991), p. 124.
7. Antonio Gramsci, *SPN*, p. 235.
8. Gramsci, *SPN*, p. 235.

9. Sassoon, *GP*, p. 112.   **253**

10. Renate Holub, *Antonio Gramsci: Beyond Marxism and Postmodernism* (London: Routledge, 1992), pp. 69–93.

11. Hall, "Cultural Studies: Two Paradigms," pp. 28–30

12. Gramsci, *SPN*, p. 324.

13. Ibid., p. 9.

14. Ibid., p. 327.

15. For a discussion of Gramsci's uses of language, see "On Gramsci's Language," in *Approaches to Gramsci*, ed. Anne Showstack Sassoon (London: Writers and Readers, 1982), pp. 180–85.

16. José Nun, "Elements for a Theory of Democracy: Gramsci and Common Sense," *boundary 2* 14, no. 3 (Spring 1986): 199.

17. Ibid., p. 201.

18. Ibid.

19. Gramsci, *SPN*, p. 327.

20. Gramsci, *SPN*, p. 333.

21. Stuart Hall, "Gramsci and Us," *Marxism Today* 31 (April 1987): 20.

22. Bobbio, *WS* , p. 154.

23. Joseph A. Buttigieg, "Gramsci's Method," *boundary 2* 16 (Summer 1990): 60–81.

24. Antonio Gramsci, *Selections from Cultural Writings,* ed. David Forgacs and Geoffrey Nowell-Smith (London: Lawrence and Wishart, 1985), p. 205; hereafter cited as *SCW.*

25. Ibid., p. 421.

26. Ibid., p. 189.

27. Ibid.

28. Ibid., p. 195.

29. Ibid., p. 209.

30. Ibid., p. 343.

31. Ibid., p. 344.

32. Ibid.

33. Fredric Jameson, "Reification and Utopia in Mass Culture," *Social Text* (Winter, 1979): 133–34.

34. Gramsci, *SPN*, p. 423.

35. See Dominick LaCapra, "Bakhtin, Marxism, and the Carnivalesque," in *Rethinking Intellectual History: Texts, Contexts and Language* (Ithaca: Cornell University Press, 1983), pp. 291–324; Myriam Diaz-Diocaretz, "The Bakhtin Circle Today," in *Critical Studies: A Journal of Critical Theory, Literature and Culture* 1, no. 2 (1989), ed. Myriam Diaz-Diocaretz; Robert Stam, "Mikhail Bakhtin and Left Cultural Critique," in *Postmodernism and Its Discontents: Theories, Practices,* ed. E. Ann Kaplan (London: Verso, 1988), pp. 116–45.

36. Mikhail Bakhtin, *The Dialogic Imagination: Four Essays,* ed. Michael Holquist (Austin: University of Texas Press, 1981), pp. 271–72.

37. Gramsci, *SCW*, p. 13.

38. Ibid., p. 291.

39. Gramsci, *SPN*, pp. 294–95.

40. Ibid., p. 306.

41. Ibid., p. 296.

42. Gramsci, *SCW*, p. 349.

43. Terry Eagleton, *Literary Theory: An Introduction* (Minneapolis: University of Minnesota Press, 1983), p. 193.

44. James Joll, *Antonio Gramsci* (Harmondsworth: Penguin, 1977), p. 129.

45. The English Studies Group, 1978–79, "Recent Developments in English Studies at the Centre," in *Culture, Media, Language*, p. 266.

46. Ibid., p. 267.

47. Ibid.

48. Ibid.

5. *They Were Sisters*: Common Sense, World War II, and the Woman's Film

1. Peter Brooks, *The Melodramatic Imagination: Balzac, Henry James, and the Mode of Excess* (New York: Columbia University Press, 1984).

2. See, for example, Wayne Koestenbaum's *The Queen's Throat: Opera, Homosexuality, and the Mystery of Desire* (New York: Poseidon Press, 1993).

3. See Christine Gledhill, ed., *Home Is Where the Heart Is: Studies in Melodrama and the Woman's Film* (London: BFI, 1987); Jackie Byars, *All that Hollywood Allows: Re-reading Gender in 1950s Melodrama* (Chapel Hill: University of North Carolina Press, 1991); Jean-Loup Bourget, *Le mélodrame hollywoodien* (Paris: Stock, 1985); Lucy Fischer, *Imitation of Life: Douglas Sirk, Director* (New Brunswick, N.J.: Rutgers University Press, 1991); Marcia Landy, *Imitations of Life: A Reader on Film and Television Melodrama* (Detroit: Wayne State University Press, 1991).

4. Landy, *Imitations of Life*, pp. 68–93, 268–75; Christine Gledhill, ed., *Home Is Where the Heart Is*, pp. 75–83.

5. Gledhill, "Introduction," *Home Is Where the Heart Is*, p. 13.

6. Ibid.

7. Mollie Haskell, *From Reverence to Rape: The Treatment of Women in the Movies* (Harmondsworth: Penguin, 1979).

8. Linda Williams, "Something Else Besides a Mother," in *Home Is Where the Heart Is*, pp. 299–325; and Tania Modleski, *The Women Who Knew Too Much* (New York: Methuen, 1988). In her study of the woman's film of the 1940s, Mary Ann Doane argues that "there is a strong temptation to find in these films a viable alternative to the unrelenting objectification and oppression of woman in the mainstream Hollywood cinema. The recent focus on issues surrounding female spectatorship and the woman's film is determined by a desire to shift the terms of an analysis of fantasy and history in favor of the woman and away from a paternal reference point. Yet the woman's film does not provide us with an access to a pure and authentic female subjectivity, much as we would like to see it do so. It provides us instead with an image repertoire of poses — classical feminine poses and assumptions about the female appropriation of the gaze. Hollywood films of the 1940s document a crisis in subjectivity around the figure of the woman — although it is not always clear whose subjectivity is at stake." In *The Desire to Desire: The Woman's Film of the 1940s* (Bloomington: Indiana University Press, 1987), p. 4.

9. Jane Gaines, "Women and Representation: Can We Enjoy Alternative Pleasure," in *American Media and Mass Culture*, ed. Donald Lazere (Berkeley: University of California Press, 1987), pp. 359–60.

10. Christine Gledhill and Gillian Swanson, "Gender and Sexuality in World War Two Films," in *National Fictions: World War Two in Film and Television* (London: BFI, 1984), p. 57.

11. Gramsci, *SPN*, p. 423.   **255**

12. Tania Modleski, *Loving with a Vengeance: Mass Produced Fantasies for Women* (London: Methuen, 1985); and Ien Ang, *Watching Dallas: Soap Opera and the Melodramatic Imagination* (London: Methuen, 1985).

13. Pam Cook, "Melodrama and the Woman's Picture," in *Gainsborough Melodrama*, ed. Sue Harper and Robert Murphy. Dossier 18 (London: BFI, 1983), p. 21.

14. See Janice Winship, "Nation before Family: Woman, The National Home Weekly, 1845–1953," in *Formations of Nation and People* (London: Routledge & Kegan Paul, 1983), pp. 188–212.

15. Marcia Landy, *British Genres: Cinema and Society, 1930–1960* (Princeton: Princeton University Press, 1991), pp. 140–237.

16. Michael Renov, "Leave Her to Heaven: The Double-Bind of the Post-War Woman," *Journal of the University Film and Video Association* 35 (Winter 1983): 28–36. For a discussion of Hollywood narratives in the war years, see Dana Polan, *Power and Paranoia: Narrative and the American Cinema, 1940–1950* (New York: Columbia University Press, 1986), p. 140.

17. Pam Cook, "Melodrama and the Woman's Picture," *Gainsborough Melodrama*, p. 22.

18. "Filmography," Ibid., p. 74.

19. Sue Harper, "Historical Pleasures: Gainsborough Costume Melodramas," in *Home Is Where the Heart Is*, p. 182.

20. Sue Harper, "Sexuality in Costume Melodrama," in *Gainsborough Melodrama*, p. 22.

21. Harper, "Historical Pleasures," *Home Is Where the Heart Is*, p. 180.

22. "Interviews," *Gainsborough Melodrama*, p. 65.

23. Robert Murphy, "A Brief Studio History," in *Gainsborough Melodrama*, p. 6.

24. Aspinall, "Sexuality in Costume Melodrama," in *Gainsborough Melodrama*, p. 33.

25. Antonio Gramsci, *Quaderni* 2: 1660–61.

26. Gramsci, *SPN*, p. 423.

27. "Filmography," *Gainsborough Melodrama*, p. 71. One critic, commenting on *They Were Sisters*, lamented the film's lack of subtlety: "No sentence is left unfinished, no door unslammed, no head untossed. Instead of the camera uncovering hidden emotion casually, all characters treat it as a psychoanalyst. 'I know I am a bore,' says one. 'No one understands me,' moans another. And all the time whether they sob, or bully or merely cope, the pretence of ordinariness is kept up."

28. Lucy Fischer, *Shot/Countershot: Tradition and Woman's Cinema* (Princeton: Princeton University Press, 1989), pp. 172–216.

29. Tania Modleski, *Loving with a Vengeance*, p. 79.

30. Walter Benjamin, 'The Storyteller," *Illuminations* (New York: Schocken Books, 1976).

31. Pam Cook, "Melodrama and the Woman's Picture," in *Gainsborough Melodrama*, p. 25.

32. Janice A. Radway, *Reading the Romance: Women, Patriarchy, and Popular Literature* (Chapel Hill: University of North Carolina Press, 1984), p. 129.

33. Doane, *The Desire to Desire*, p. 62.

34. Gledhill and Swanson, "Gender and Sexuality in Second World War Films," p. 57.

35. Gramsci, *SPN*, p. 323.

6. Looking Backward: Versions of History and Common Sense in Recent British Cinema

1. Marc Ferro, *Cinema and History*, ed. Naomi Greene (Detroit: Wayne State University, 1977); Anton Kaes, *From Hitler to Heimat: The Return of History as Film* (Cambridge, Mass.: Harvard University Press, 1989); Pierre Sorlin, *The Film in History: Restaging the Past* (Totowa, N.J.: Barnes & Noble Books, 1980); Gilles Deleuze, *Cinema 1: The Movement Image,* and *Cinema 2: The Time Image* (Minneapolis: University of Minnesota Press, 1989); Maureen Turim, *Flashback in Film: Memory and History* (New York: Routledge, 1989); Tim Corrigan, *A Cinema without Walls: Movies and Culture after Vietnam* (New Brunswick, N.J.: Rutgers University Press, 1991); and Geoffrey Nowell-Smith, "On History and the Cinema," *Screen* 31, no. 2 (Summer 1990): 160–72. These texts and the work on common sense by the Birmingham Centre for the Study of Popular Culture, based on Gramsci's writings, are central to this rethinking of historical representations.

2. Gilles Deleuze, *Cinema 2: The Time Image*, p. 264.

3. Marc Ferro, *Cinema and History*, p. 29.

4. See George F. Custen for a discussion of the Hollywood biopic, in *Bio/Pics: How Hollywood Constructed Public History* (New Brunswick, N.J.: Rutgers University Press, 1992).

5. Graham Dawson and Bob West, "Our Finest Hour? The Popular Memory of World War II and the Struggle Over National Identity," in *National Fictions: World War II in British Films and Television* (London: BFI, 1984), p. 11.

6. Homi K. Bhabha, "DisseMiNation: Time, Narrative, and the Margins of the Modern Nation," in *Nation and Narration*, ed. Homi K. Bhabha (London: Routledge, 1990), p. 294.

7. Friedrich Nietzsche, "On the Uses and Disadvantages of History for Life," *Untimely Meditations* (Cambridge: Cambridge University Press, 1991), p. 12.

8. Ibid., p. 41.

9. Walter Benjamin, "Theses on the Philosophy of History," *Illuminations* (New York: Schocken Books, 1976), p. 255.

10. Doris Summer, "Irresistible Romance: The Foundational Fictions of Latin America" in *Nation and Narration*, ed. Bhabha, p. 85.

11. Jean Gili, "Film storico e film in costume," *Cinema italiano sotto il fascismo* (Venice: Marsilio, 1979), pp. 129–30.

12. John Walker, *National Heroes: British Cinema in the Seventies and Eighties.* (London: Harrap, 1985), pp. 119–20.

13. Gramsci, *SPN*, p. 423. For a discussion of folklore in Gramsci's writings, see Moyra Byrne, "Antonio Gramsci's Contribution to Italian Folklore Studies," *International Folkore Review* 2 (1982): 70–75.

14. Leonard Quart, "The Thatcherism of the Market: Thatcherite Politics and the British Film of the 1980s," in *Fires Were Started: British Cinema and Thatcherism*, ed. Lester Friedman (Minneapolis: University of Minnesota Press, 1993), pp. 15–34.

15. Stuart Hall, *The Hard Road to Renewal: Thatcherism and the Crisis of the Left* (London: Verso, 1988), pp. 150–61.

16. Ibid., p. 8.

17. Ibid.

18. Geoffrey Nowell-Smith, "But Do We Need It?" in *British Cinema Now* (London: BFI, 1985), p. 149.

19. Ibid., p. 152.

20. Sheila Johnston, "Charioteers and Ploughmen," in *British Cinema Now*, p. 109.　**257**
21. Ibid., p. 110.
22. Thomas Elsaesser, "Images For Sale: The New British Cinema," in *Fires Were Started*, ed. Friedman, p. 62.
23. Peter Wollen, "The Last New Wave: Modernism in the British Films of the Thatcher Era," in *Fires Were Started*, ed. Friedman, p. 49.
24. Johnston, "Charioteers and Ploughmen," p. 104.
25. Hall, *The Hard Road to Renewal*, p. 167.
26. Andrew Higson, "Re-presenting the Past: Nostalgia and Pastiche in the Heritage Film," in *Fires Were Started*, ed. Friedman, p. 113.
27. Nietzsche, "On the Uses and Disadvantages of History for Life," p. 70.
28. Richard Attenborough, *In Search of Gandhi* (Piscataway, N.J.: New Century Publishers, 1982).
29. John Walker, *National Heroes*, p. 175.
30. Shahid Amin, "Gandhi as Mahatma," in *Selected Subaltern Studies*, ed. Ranajit Guha and Gayatri Chakravorty Spivak (New York: Oxford University Press, 1988), p. 289.
31. Geoff Hurd, "Introduction," *National Fictions*, p. iv.
32. Mary Desjardins, "Free from the Maternal Apron Strings: Representations of Mothers in the Maternal British State," in *Fires Were Started*, ed. Friedman, pp. 130–43.
33. Susan Torrey Barber, "Insurmountable Difficulties and Moments of Ecstasy: Crossing Class, Ethnic, and Sexual Barriers in the Films of Stephen Frears," in *Fires Were Started*, ed. Friedman, pp. 226–28.
34. Higson, "Re-presenting the National Past," p. 124.
35. Slavoj Zizek, *The Sublime Object of Ideology* (London: Verso, 1989), pp. 40, 42.
36. Sue Harper, "Historical Pleasures: The Gainsborough Melodrama," in *Home Is Where the Heart Is: Studies in Melodrama and the Woman's Film*, ed. Christine Gledhill (London: BFI, 1987), p. 191.
37. Jacqueline Rose, "Margaret Thatcher and Ruth Ellis," *New Formations* 6 (Winter 1988): 10.
38. John Hill, *Sex, Class and Realism: British Cinema 1956–1963* (London: BFI, 1986).
39. Jacqueline Rose, "Margaret Thatcher and Ruth Ellis," in *New Formations* 6 (Winter 1988): 11–14.

7. Language, Folklore, and Politics in the Films of the Taviani Brothers

1. Edmund E. Jacobitti, "From Vico's Common Sense to Gramsci's Hegemony," in *Vico and Marx: Affinities and Contrasts*, ed. G. Tagliacozzo (Atlantic Highlands, N.J.: Humanities Press, 1983), p. 370.
2. Gramsci, *SPN*, p. 206.
3. Etienne Balibar and Immanuel Wallerstein, *Race, Nation, Class, Ambiguous Identities* (London: Verso, 1991), p. 96.
4. Wallace P. Sillanpoa, "Pasolini's Gramsci," *MLN* 96 (1981): 123.
5. Ibid., pp. 133–37.
6. Gramsci, *SPN*, p. 178.
7. Gary Crowdus, " 'We Believe in the Power of Cinema': An Interview with Paolo and Vittorio Taviani," *Cineaste* 3 (1983): 34.
8. Ibid., p. 31.
9. Millicent Marcus, *Italian Film in the Light of Neorealism* (Princeton: Princeton University Press, 1986), p. 361.

258   10. Gilles Deleuze, *Cinema 2: The Time Image* (Minneapolis: University of Minnesota Press, 1989), p. 247.

11. Marcia Landy, *Fascism in Film: The Italian Commercial Cinema, 1930–1943* (Princeton: Princeton University Press, 1986).

12. Peter Bondanella, *Italian Cinema* (Bloomington: Indiana University Press, 1983), p. 34.

13. Marcus, *Italian Film in the Light of Neorealism*, p. 23.

14. Crowdus, "'We Believe in the Power of Cinema,'" p. 31.

15. Peter Brooks, *The Melodramatic Imagination: Balzac, Henry James, Melodrama and the Mode of Excess* (New York: Columbia University Press, 1988); Christine Gledhill, ed., *Home Is Where the Heart Is: Studies in Melodrama and the Woman's Film* (London: BFI, 1987); Marcia Landy, *Imitations of Life: A Reader on Film and Television Melodrama* (Detroit: Wayne State University Press, 1991).

16. Gramsci, *SPN*, 129.

17. Bondanella, *Italian Cinema*, pp. 176–77.

18. R. W. Witcombe, *Italian Cinema: From Dance to Despair* (New York: Oxford University Press, 1982), pp. 201–2.

19. Tony Mitchell, "Towards Utopia: By Way of Research, Detachment and Involvement," *Sight and Sound* 47, no. 3 (1979): 176.

20. Crowdus, "'We Believe in the Power of Cinema,'" p. 32.

21. Ruth McCormick, "The Tavianis: War and Remembrance," *American Film* (Jan.–Feb. 1983): 13.

22. Crowdus, "'We Believe in the Power of Cinema,'" p. 34.

23. Mitchell, "Towards Utopia: By Way of Research, Detachment and Involvement," p. 178.

24. Gramsci, *SPN*, pp. 53–54,

25. James Joll, *Antonio Gramsci* (Harmondsworth: Penguin, 1977), p. 29. See also Dante Germino, *Antonio Gramsci: Architect of a New Politics* (Baton Rouge: Louisiana State University Press, 1990).

26. Germino, *Antonio Gramsci*, p. 6.

27. Robert Phillip Kolker, *The Altering Eye: Contemporary International Cinema* (Oxford: Oxford University Press, 1983), p. 119.

28. Mitchell, "Towards Utopia," p. 178.

29. Gramsci, *SPN*, p. 9.

30. Kolker, *The Altering Eye*, p. 117.

31. Witcombe, *Italian Cinema*, p. 213.

32. Marcus, *Italian Film in the Light of Neorealism*, p. 367.

33. Gramsci, *SPN*, p. 420.

34. Walter Benjamin, "The Storyteller," in *Illuminations* (New York: Schocken Books, 1976).

35. Millicent Marcus, *Filmmaking by the Book: Italian Cinema and Literary Adaptation* (Baltimore: Johns Hopkins University Press, 1993).

36. Gavriel Moses, "L'altro viaggio dei Taviani (Or What Luigi Missed)." Paper presented for the Society for Cinema Studies Conference, Montreal, May 21–24, 1987.

8. Postmodernism as Folklore in Contemporary Science Fiction Cinema

1. Annette Kuhn, ed., *Alien Zone: Cultural Theory and Contemporary Science Fiction Cinema* (London: Verso, 1990); Vivian Sobchack, *Screening Space: The American Science Fiction Film* (New York: Ungar, 1987); Andrew Tudor, *Monsters and Mad Scientists: A*

Cultural History of the Horror Movie (London: Basil Blackwell, 1989). See also Pam Ros- **259**
enthal, "Jacked In: Fordism, Cyberpunk, Marxism," *Socialist Review* 21, no. 1 (Jan-
uary/March 1991): 79–103; and Marc Angenot and Darko Suvin, "A Response to Professor Fekete's Five Theses," *Science Fiction Studies* 46, vol. 15, part 3 (November 1988):
324–32.

2. Jean Baudrillard, *Selected Writings*, ed. M. Poster (London: Polity Press, 1988);
Jean-François Lyotard, *The Postmodern Condition: A Report on Knowledge* (Minneapolis: Uni-
versity of Minnesota Press, 1985); Fredric Jameson, *Postmodernism, Or the Cultural Logic of
Late Capitalism* (Durham: Duke University Press, 1990); Fredric Jameson, *The Ideologies of
Theory: Essays, 1971–1986*, 2 vols. (Minneapolis: University of Minnesota Press, 1988); Paul
Virilio, *War and Cinema: The Logistics of Perception* (London: Verso, 1989). For a critical
assessment of these writers' positions, see Alex Callinicos, *Against Postmodernism: A Marxist Critique* (London: St. Martin's Press, 1990).

3. Sandra Harding, *The Science Question in Feminism* (Ithaca: Cornell University
Press, 1986); Donna Haraway, *Simians, Cyborgs, and Women: The Reinvention of Nature* (New
York: Routledge, 1991).

4. Baudrillard, *Selected Writings*, p. 167.

5. Gramsci, *SPN*, p. 189.

6. Gramsci, *SPN*, pp. 189–90.

7. Anne Showstack Sassoon, "Gramsci's Subversion of the Language of Politics,"
Rethinking Marxism 3, no. 1 (Spring): 14–25.

8. Richard Wolff, "Gramsci, Marxism, and Philosophy," *Rethinking Marxism* 2, no.
2 (1989): 45–46.

9. Paul Feyerabend, *Science in a Free Society* (London: NLB, 1978), pp. 89, 91.

10. Louis Althusser, *Philosophy and the Spontaneous Philosophy of the Scientists and
Other Essays* (London: Verso, 1990).

11. Gramsci, *SPN*, p. 467.

12. Michel Foucault, *The Birth of the Clinic: An Archaeology of Medical Perception* (New
York: Vintage Books, 1975), p. 35.

13. Georges Canguilhem, *Ideology and Rationality in the History of the Life Sciences*
(Cambridge, Mass.: MIT Press, 1988), p. 118.

14. Tudor, *Monsters and Mad Scientists*, pp. 135–41.

15. Canguilhem, *Ideology and Rationality in the History of the Life Sciences*, p. 122.

16. Marcia Landy, *British Genres: Cinema and Society, 1930–1960* (Princeton: Princeton University Press, 1991), pp. 389–431.

17. Jeffrey Weeks, *Sex, Politics, and Society: The Regulation of Sexuality Since 1800*
(London: Longman, 1986).

18. Virilio, *War and Cinema*, p. 4.

19. Gramsci, *Selections from the Cultural Writings*, ed. D. Forgacs and G. Nowell-
Smith (Cambridge, Mass.: Harvard University Press, 1985), p. 189.

20. Brian Aldiss, *Frankenstein Unbound* (New York: Warner Books, 1973).

21. Barbara Creed, "Gynesis, Postmodernism, and the Science Fiction Horror Film,"
in *Alien Zone*, ed. Kuhn, pp. 214–19.

22. Haraway, *Simians, Cyborgs, and Women*, p. 7.

23. Ibid., p. 35.

24. Scott Bukatman, "Who Programs You? The Science Fiction of the Spectacle," in
Alien Zone, ed. Kuhn, pp. 199, 207.

25. J. P. Telotte, "The Tremulous Public Body: Robots, Change, and the Science Fiction Film," *Journal of Popular Film and Television* 19, no. 1 (Spring 1991): 15.

26. Claudia Springer, "The Pleasure of the Interface," *Screen* 32, no. 3 (Autumn, 1991): 323.

27. Wolfgang Fritz Haug, *Critique of Commodity Aesthetics: Appearance, Sexuality, and Advertising in Capitalist Society* (Minneapolis: University of Minnesota Press, 1986), p. 134.

28. Umberto Eco, *Travels in Hyperreality: Essays* (San Diego: Harcourt, Brace, Jovanovich, 1986), p. 142.

29. Ibid., p. 144.

30. Jameson, *Postmodernism*, pp. 399–404

31. Scott Bukatman, "Who Programs You?" pp. 196–214; J. P. Telotte, "The Tremulous Public Body," pp. 14–23.

9. "Gramsci beyond Gramsci" and the Writings of Antonio Negri

1. Félix Guattari and Toni Negri, *Communists Like Us: With a Postscript by Toni Negri*, trans. Michael Ryan (New York: Semiotext[e] Foreign Agents Series, 1990), p. 36.

2. Gramsci, *SPN*, p. 210; *Quaderni* 3: 1603.

3. Gramsci, *SPN*, pp. 57–58; *Quaderni* 3: 2010.

4. Gramsci, *SPN*, p. 162; *Quaderni* 3: 1592.

5. Antonio Negri, *The Politics of Subversion: A Manifesto for the Twenty-First Century* (London: Polity Press, 1989), p. 144.

6. Ibid., pp. 148–49.

7. Ibid., p. 152.

8. Ibid., p. 59.

9. Antonio Negri, *The Savage Anomaly: The Power of Spinoza's Metaphysics and Politics*, trans. Michael Hardt (Minneapolis: University of Minnesota Press, 1991), p. 191.

10. Negri, *The Politics of Subversion*, p. 98.

11. Gramsci, *SPN*, p. 261; *Quaderni* 3: 2302.

12. Gramsci, *SPN*, p. 260; *Quaderni* 2: 937.

13. Antonio Gramsci, *Prison Notebooks*, vol. 1, ed. Joseph A. Buttigieg (New York: Columbia University Press, 1992), pp. 229–30. *Quaderni* 1: 132–33.

14. Antonio Gramsci, *The Modern Prince and Other Writings*, trans. Louis Marks (New York: International Publishers, 1978), p. 40.

15. Negri, *The Savage Anomaly*, p. 113.

16. Negri, *The Politics of Subversion*, p. 171.

17. Ibid., p. 125.

18. Ibid.

19. Norberto Bobbio, *The Future of Democracy*, trans. Roger Griffin, ed. Richard Bellamy (Minneapolis: University of Minnesota Press, 1987).

20. Negri, *The Politics of Subversion*, p. 99.

21. Ibid., p. 101

22. Henri Weber, "In the Beginning Was Gramsci," *Italy: Autonomia. Post-Political Politics. Semiotext(e)* 3, no. 3 (1980): 88.

23. Negri, *The Politics of Subversion*, p. 105.

24. Ibid., p. 109.

25. Ibid., p. 114.

26. Gramsci, *SPN*, p. 9; *Quaderni* 3: 1550.

27. Negri, *The Politics of Subversion*, p. 84.

28. Ibid., p. 87.

29. Gramsci, *SPN*, p. 278.

30. Negri, *The Politics of Subversion*, p. 89.   **261**
31. Ibid., p. 92.
32. Ibid., p. 91.
33. Antonio Negri, *Revolution Retrieved: Writings on Marx, Keynes, Capitalist Crisis, and New Social Subjects (1967–1983)* (London: Red Notes, 1988), p. 100.
34. Gayatri Chakravorty Spivak, *In Other Worlds: Essays in Cultural Politics*, p. 166.
35. Negri, *Revolution Retrieved*, p. 101.
36. Ibid., p. 103.
37. Gramsci, *SPN*, p. 222; *Quaderni* 1: 125.
38. Gramsci, *SPN*, p. 289; *Quaderni* 3: 2151.
39. Gramsci, *SPN*, p. 286; *Quaderni* 3: 2156.
40. Gramsci, *SPN*, p. 292; *Quaderni* 3: 2156.
41. Gramsci, *SPN*, p. 292; *Quaderni* 3: 2168–69.
42. Gramsci, *SPN*, p. 309; *Quaderni* 3: 2170.
43. Gramsci, *SPN*, p. 296; *Quaderni* 3: 2150.
44. Gramsci, *SPN*, p. 300.
45. Nancy Fraser, "Rethinking the Public Sphere," *Social Text: Theory/Culture/Ideology*, nos. 25/26 (1990): 56–80.
46. Negri, *The Politics of Subversion*, p. 47.
47. Ibid., p. 48.
48. Ibid., p. 49.
49. Negri, *The Savage Anomaly*, p. 218.
50. Negri, *The Politics of Subversion*, p. 128.
51. Gramsci, *SPN*, p. 158; *Quaderni* 3: 1760.
52. Negri, *The Politics of Subversion*, p. 128.
53. Negri, *Revolution Retrieved*, p. 11.
54. Ibid., p. 26.
55. Negri, *The Savage Anomaly*, p. 221.
56. Gramsci, *SPN*, p. 151; *Quaderni* 3: 1630.
57. Gramsci, *SPN*, pp. 15–16; *Quaderni* 3: 1522.
58. Gramsci, *SPN*, p. 16; *Quaderni* 3: 1522.
59. Anne Showstack Sassoon, *Gramsci's Politics*, p. 234.
60. Gramsci, *SPN*, p. 197; *Quaderni* 1: 329.
61. Gramsci, *SPN*, p. 129; *Quaderni* 3: 1558.
62. Gramsci, *SPN*, pp. 54–55; *Quaderni* 1: 299–300.
63. Gramsci, *SPN*, p. 199; *Quaderni* 1: 331.
64. Gramsci, *SPN*, p. 200; *Quaderni* 1: 332.
65. Negri, *The Politics of Subversion*, p. 186.
66. Ibid., p. 119.
67. Negri, *The Savage Anomaly*, p. 80.
68. Negri, *The Politics of Subversion*, p. 201.
69. Ibid., p. 202.
70. Ibid., p. 205.
71. Ibid., p. 206.
72. Antonio Negri, *Marx Beyond Marx: Lessons on the Grundrisse* (London: Autoitalia, 1991), pp. 101–2.
73. Ibid., p. 90.
74. Ibid., p. 112.
75. Ibid., p. 121.

Bibliography

Adamson, Walter. *Hegemony and Revolution: A Study of Antonio Gramsci's Political and Cultural Theory.* Berkeley: University of California Press, 1980.

Adorno, Theodor. "Commitment." In *Aesthetics and Politics,* ed. Fredric Jameson. London: NLB, 1977, pp. 177–95.

Aldiss, Brian. *Frankenstein Unbound.* New York: Warner Books, 1973.

Althusser, Louis. *Lenin and Philosophy and Other Essays.* New York: Monthly Review Press, 1971.

———. *Philosophy and the Spontaneous Philosophy of the Scientists and Other Essays.* London: Verso, 1990.

Amin, Shahid. "Gandhi as Mahatma." In *Selected Subaltern Studies,* ed. Ranajit Guha and Gayatri Chakravorty Spivak. New York: Oxford University Press, 1988, pp. 288–351.

Anderson, Perry. "The Affinities of Norberto Bobbio." *New Left Review* 170 (July–Aug. 1988): 3–37.

———. "The Antinomies of Antonio Gramsci." *New Left Review* 100 (Nov. 1976–Jan. 1977): 5–78.

Ang, Ien. *Watching Dallas. Soap Opera and the Melodramatic Imagination.* London: Methuen, 1985.

Angenot, M., and Suvin, Darko. "A Response to Professor Fekete's Five Theses." *Science Fiction Studies* 46, vol. 15, part 3 (Nov. 1988): 324–32.

Aronowitz, Stanley. *The Crisis of Historical Materialism: Class, Politics. and Culture in Marxist Theory.* New York: Praeger, 1981.

——— and Henry Giroux. *Education under Siege.* South Hadley, Mass.: Bergin and Garvey, 1985.

Arrighi, Giovanni, Terence K. Hopkins, and Immanuel Wallerstein. *Antisystemic Movements.* London: Verso, 1989.

Aspden, Peter. "In sole anche di notte (Night Sun)," *Sight and Sound* 1, no. 1 (May 1991): 63–64.

Aspinall, Sue. "Sexuality in Costume Melodrama," *Gainsborough Melodrama,* ed. Sue Aspinall and Robert Murphy. London: BFI, 1983, pp. 29–40.

——— and Robert Murphy, eds. *Gainsborough Melodrama.* London: BFI, 1983.

Attenborough, Richard. *In Search of Gandhi.* Piscataway, N.J.: New Century Publishers, 1982.

Bibliography

264   Badaloni, Nicola. "'Gramsci and the Problem of Revolution." In *Gramsci and Marxist Theory*, ed. Chantal Mouffe. London: Routledge & Kegan Paul, 1979, pp. 80–109.

Bakhtin, Mikhail. *The Dialogic Imagination: Four Essays*, ed. Michael Holquist. Austin: University of Texas Press, 1981.

Balibar, Etienne, and Immanuel Wallerstein. *Race, Nation, Class: Ambiguous Identities*. London: Verso, 1991.

Barber, Susan Torrey. "Insurmountable Difficulties and Moments of Ecstasy: Crossing Class, Ethnic, and Sexual Barriers in the Films of Stephen Frears." In *Fires Were Started*, ed. Lester Friedman. Minneapolis: University of Minnesota Press, 1993, pp. 221–37.

Baudrillard, Jean. *Selected Writings*, ed. M. Poster. London: Polity Press, 1988.

Benjamin, Walter. "The Storyteller." In *Illuminations*. New York: Schocken, 1976.

———. "Theses on the Philosophy of History." In *Illuminations*. New York: Schocken, 1976.

Bhabha, Homi K. "DissemiNation: Time, Narrative, and the Margins of the Modern Nation." In *Nation and Narration*, ed. Homi K. Bhabha. London: Routledge, 1990.

———, ed. *Nation and Narration*. London: Routledge, 1990.

Blackburn, Robin, "Fin de Siècle: Socialism after the Crash." *New Left Review*, no. 185 (January/February, 1991).

Bobbio, Norberto. *The Future of Democracy*, trans. Roger Griffin, ed. Richard Bellamy. Minneapolis: University of Minnesota Press, 1987.

———. *Which Socialism? Marxism, Socialism, and Democracy*, trans. Roger Griffin, ed. Richard Bellamy. Minneapolis: University of Minnesota Press, 1987.

Boggs, Carl. *Gramsci's Marxism*. London: Pluto Press, 1976.

Bondanella, Peter. *Italian Cinema*. Bloomington: Indiana University Press, 1983.

Bourget, Jean-Loup. *Le mélodrame hollywoodien*. Paris: Stock, 1985.

Bové, Paul A. *In the Wake of Theory*. Hanover: Wesleyan University Press, 1992.

Brooks, Peter. *The Melodramatic Imagination: Balzac, Henry James, and the Mode of Excess*. New York: Columbia University Press, 1984.

Buci-Glucksmann, Christine. "Hegemony and Consent." In *Approaches to Gramsci*, ed. Anne Showstack Sassoon. London: Writers and Readers, 1982.

———. "Hegemony and Ideology in Gramsci." In *Gramsci and Marxist Theory*, ed. Christine Buci-Glucksmann. London: Routledge & Kegan Paul, 1979, pp. 168–204.

Bukatman, Scott, "Who Programs You? The Science Fiction of the Spectacle," *Alien Zone*, 196–214.

Buttigieg, Joseph A. "Gramsci's Method." *boundary 2* 17, no. 2 (Summer 1990): 60–81.

———. "The Exemplary Worldliness of Antonio Gramsci's Literary Criticism." *boundary 2* 11, nos. 1 and 2 (Fall, Winter 1982–83), pp. 21–40.

Byars, Jackie. *All that Hollywood Allows: Re-reading Gender in 1950s Melodrama*. Chapel Hill: University of North Carolina Press, 1991.

Byrne, Moyra. "Antonio Gramsci's Contribution to Italian Folklore Studies." In *International Folklore Review* 2 (1982): 70–75.

Callinicos, Alex. *Against Postmodernism: A Marxist Critique*. London: St. Martin's Press, 1990.

Cammett, John M. *Antonio Gramsci and the Origins of Italian Communism*. Stanford: Stanford University Press, 1967.

Canguilhem, Georges. *Ideology and Rationality in the History of the Life Sciences*. Cambridge, Mass.: MIT Press, 1988.

Carling, Alan. "Rational Choice Marxism." In *New Left Review* 160 (Nov.–Dec. 1986): 24–63.

Chatterjee, Partha. *Nationalist Thought and the Colonial World: A Derivative Discourse*. Minneapolis: University of Minnesota Press, 1993.

Cirese, Albert Maria. "Gramsci's Observations on Folklore." In *Approaches to Gramsci*, ed. **265**
Anne Showstack Sassoon. London: Writers and Readers, 1982, pp. 212–49.

Cook, Pam. "Melodrama and the Woman's Picture." In *Gainsborough Melodrama*, ed. Sue
Aspinall and Robert Murphy. Dossier 18. London: BFI, 1983, pp.14–29.

Corrigan, Tim. *A Cinema without Walls: Movies and Culture after Vietnam.* New Brunswick,
N.J.: Rutgers University Press, 1991.

Creed, Barbara. "Gynesis, Postmodernism, and the Science Fiction Horror Film." In *Alien
Zone: Cultural Theory and Contemporary Science Fiction Cinema*, ed. Annette Kuhn. London: Verso, 1990, pp. 214–19.

Crowdus, Gary. "We Believe in the Power of Cinema: An Interview with Paolo and Vittorio Taviani." In *Cineaste* 3 (1983): 31–34.

Custen, George F. *Bio/Pics: How Hollywood Constructed Public History.* New Brunswick, N.J.:
Rutgers University Press, 1992.

Davidson, Alistair. *Antonio Gramsci: Towards An Intellectual Biography.* London: Merlin
Press, 1977.

Dawson, Graham, and Bob West. "Our Finest Hour? The Popular Memory of World War II
and the Struggle Over National Identity." In *National Fictions: World War II in British
Films and Television*. London: BFI, 1984, pp. 8–14.

De Felice, Renzo. *Mussolini*, 4 vols. Turin: Einaudi, 1965–1990.

de Grazia, Victoria. *The Culture of Consent: Mass Organization of Leisure in Fascist Italy.* Cambridge: Cambridge University Press, 1983.

Deleuze, Gilles. *Cinema 2: The Time Image* (Minneapolis: University of Minnesota Press,
1989), p. 247.

———— and Félix Guattari. *Communists Like Us.* New York: Semiotext(e), 1990.

Derrida, Jacques. *Dissemination.* Chicago: University of Chicago Press, 1981.

————. *Glas.* Paris: Editions Galilee, 1974.

————. *The Ear of the Other: Otobiography, Transference, Translation.* Lincoln: University of
Nebraska Press, 1985.

————. *Writing and Difference.* Chicago: University of Chicago Press, 1978.

Desjardins, Mary. "Free from the Maternal Apron Strings: Representations of Mothers in
the Maternal British State." In *Fires Were Started*, ed. Lester Friedman, pp. 130–43.

Diaz-Diocaretz, Myriam, ed. "The Bakhtin Circle Today." In *Critical Studies: A Journal of
Critical Theory, Literature and Culture* 1, no. 2 (1989).

Doane, Mary Ann, *The Desire to Desire: The Woman's Film of the 1940s.* Bloomington: University of Indiana Press, 1987.

Eagleton, Terry. *Literary Theory: An Introduction.* Minneapolis: University of Minnesota
Press, 1983.

Eco, Umberto. *Travels in Hyperreality: Essays.* San Diego: Harcourt, Brace, Jovanovich, 1986.

Elsaesser, Thomas. "Images For Sale: The New British Cinema." In *Fires Were Started*, ed.
Lester Friedman, pp. 52–70.

Fekete, John. "The Stimulations of Simulations: Five Theses on Science Fiction and Marxism." In *Science Fiction Studies* 46, vol. 15, part 3 (Nov. 1988): 312–23.

————, ed. *Life After Postmodernism: Essays on Value and Culture.* New York: St. Martin's
Press, 1987.

Femia, Joseph. *Gramsci's Political Thought: Hegemony, Consciousness and the Revolutionary
Process.* Oxford: Clarendon Press, 1981.

Ferro, Marc. *Cinema and History*, ed. Naomi Greene. Detroit: Wayne State University Press,
1977.

Feyerabend, Paul. *Science in a Free Society.* London: NLB, 1978.

Bibliography

266

Finocchiaro, Maurice A. *Gramsci and the History of Dialectical Thought.* New York: Cambridge University Press, 1988.

Fischer, Lucy. *Imitation of Life: Douglas Sirk, Director.* New Brunswick, N.J.: Rutgers University Press, 1991.

———. *Shot/Countershot: Tradition and Woman's Cinema.* Princeton: Princeton University Press, 1989.

Forgacs, David A. "National-Popular: Genealogy of a Concept." In *Formations of Nation and People.* London: Routledge & Kegan Paul, 1984.

Foster, Hal, ed. *The Anti-Aesthetic: Essays on Postmodern Culture.* Port Townsend, Wash.: Bay Press, 1983.

Foucault, Michel. *The Birth of the Clinic: An Archaeology of Medical Perception.* New York: Vintage Books, 1975.

———. *The History of Sexuality,* vol. 1. New York: Vintage, 1980.

———. *Language, Counter-Memory, Practice: Selected Essays and Interviews.* Ithaca: Cornell University Press, 1977.

Fraser, Nancy. "Rethinking the Public Sphere." In *Social Text,* Theory/Culture/Ideology, nos. 25/26 (1990): 56–80.

Friedman, Lester, ed. *Fires Were Started: British Cinema and Thatcherism.* Minneapolis: University of Minnesota Press, 1993.

Gaines, Jaine, "Women and Representation: Can We Enjoy Alternative Pleasure." In *American Media and Mass Culture,* ed. Donald Lazere. Berkeley: University of California Press, 1987, pp. 357–72.

Germino, Dante. *Antonio Gramsci: Architect of a New Politics.* Baton Rouge: Louisiana State University Press, 1990.

Gili, Jean. "Film storico e film in costume." In *Cinema italiano sotto il fascismo.* Venice: Marsilio, 1979.

Gledhill, Christine, ed. *Home Is Where the Heart Is: Studies in Melodrama and the Woman's Film.* London: BFI, 1987.

——— and Gillian Swanson. "Gender and Sexuality in World War Two Films." In *National Fictions: World War Two in Film and Television.* London: BFI, 1984, pp. 56–63.

Golding, Sue. *Gramsci's Contributions to a Democratic Theory: Contributions to Post-Liberal Democracy.* Toronto: University of Toronto Press, 1992.

Goodman, Jonathan, and Patrick Pringle. *The Trial of Ruth Ellis.* Newton Abbott: David & Charles, 1974

Gramsci, Antonio. *The Modern Prince and Other Writings,* trans. Louis Marks. New York: International Publishers, 1978.

———. *Prison Notebooks,* vol. 1, ed. Joseph A. Buttigieg. New York: Columbia University Press, 1992.

———. *Quaderni,* 3 vols, ed. Valentino Gerratana. Torino: Einaudi, 1975.

———. *Selections from the Cultural Writings,* ed. D. Forgacs and G. Nowell-Smith. Cambridge: Cambridge University Press, 1984.

———. *Selections from the Prison Notebooks,* ed. Quintin Hoare and G. Nowell-Smith. New York: International Publishers, 1978.

Guattari, Félix, and Toni Negri. *Communists Like Us: With a Post Script by Toni Negri,* trans. Michael Ryan. New York: Semiotext(e) Foreign Agents Series, 1990.

Guha, Ranajit, and Gayatri Chakravorty Spivak, eds. *Selected Subaltern Studies.* New York: Oxford University Press, 1988.

Hall, Stuart. "Cultural Studies: Two Paradigms." In *Culture, Ideology, and Social Process.* London: Open University Press, 1980.

————. *The Hard Road to Renewal: Thatcherism and the Crisis of the Left*. London: Verso, 1988.   **267**

————. "In Praise of the Particular." In *Marxism Today* 31 (April 1987): vii.

————, et al. *Culture, Media, Language: Working Papers in Cultural Studies, 1972–79*. London: Hutchinson, in association with the Centre for Contemporary Cultural Studies, University of Birmingham, 1980.

Haraway, Donna. *Simians, Cyborgs, and Women: The Reinvention of Nature*. New York: Routledge, 1991, p. 187.

Harding, Sandra. *The Science Question in Feminism*. Ithaca: Cornell University Press, 1986.

Harper, Sue. "Historical Pleasures: Gainsborough Costume Melodramas." In *Home Is Where the Heart Is*, ed. Christine Gledhill, pp. 167–97.

————. "Sexuality in Costume Melodrama." In *Gainsborough Melodrama*, ed. Sue Aspinall and Robert Murphy, pp. 40–53.

Haskell, Molly. *From Reverence to Rape: The Treatment of Women in the Movies*. Harmondsworth: Penguin, 1979.

Haug, Wolfgang Fritz. *Critique of Commodity Aesthetics: Appearance, Sexuality, and Advertising in Capitalist Society*. Minneapolis: University of Minnesota Press, 1986.

Higson, Andrew. "Re-presenting the Past: Nostalgia and Pastiche in the Heritage Film." In *Fires Were Started*, ed. Lester Friedman, pp. 109–30.

Hill, John. *Sex, Class and Realism: British Cinema 1956–1963*. London: BFI, 1986.

Holub, Renate. *Antonio Gramsci: Beyond Marxism and Postmodernism*, London: Routledge, 1992.

Hurd, Geoff. "Introduction." In *National Fictions: World War Two in British Films and Television*, ed. Geoff Hurd. London: BFI, 1984.

Huyssen, Andreas. "Mass Culture as Woman: Modernism's Other." In *Studies in Entertainment: Critical Approaches to Mass Culture*. Bloomington: Indiana University Press, 1986, pp. 188–207.

Jacobitti, Edmund E. "From Vico's Common Sense to Gramsci's Hegemony." In *Vico and Marx: Affinities and Contrasts*, ed. Giorgio Tagliacozzo. Atlantic Highlands, N.J.: Humanities Press, 1983, pp. 367–88.

Jameson, Fredric. *The Geopolitical Aesthetic: Cinema and Space in the World System*. London: BFI, 1992.

————. *The Ideologies of Theory: Essays, 1971–1986*, 2 vols. Minneapolis: University of Minnesota Press, 1988.

————. *Postmodernism, Or the Cultural Logic of Late Capitalism*. Durham: Duke University Press, 1991.

————. "Reification and Utopia in Mass Culture." In *Social Text* (Winter 1979): 130–48.

Jardine, Alice, and Brian Massumi. "Interview with Toni Negri." In *Copyright* 1 (1987): 74–89.

Johnston, Sheila. "Charioteers and Ploughmen." In *British Cinema Now*, ed. Martin Auty and Nich Roddick. London: BFI, 1985, pp. 99–110.

Joll, James. *Antonio Gramsci*. Harmondsworth: Penguin, 1977.

Kaes, Anton. *From Hitler to Heimat: The Return of History as Film*. Cambridge, Mass.: Harvard University Press, 1989.

Kaldor, Mary. "After the Cold War." In *New Left Review*, no. 180 (March/April 1990): 25–40.

Knightley, Phillip, and Caroline Kennedy. *An Affair of State: The Profumo Case and the Framing of Stephen Ward*. London: Jonathan Cape, 1987.

Koestenbaum, Wayne. *The Queen's Throat: Opera, Homosexuality, and the Mystery of Desire*. New York: Poseidon Press, 1993.

Kolker, Robert Phillip. *The Altering Eye: Contemporary International Cinema*. Oxford: Oxford University Press, 1983.

268   Kuhn, Annette, ed. *Alien Zone: Cultural Theory and Contemporary Science Fiction Cinema.* London: Verso, 1990.

LaCapra, Dominick. "Bakhtin, Marxism, and the Carnivalesque." In *Rethinking Intellectual History: Texts, Contexts and Language.* Ithaca: Cornell University Press, 1983.

Laclau, Ernesto. *Politics and Ideology in Marxist Theory.* London: NLB, 1977.

Landy, Marcia. *British Genres: Cinema and Society, 1930–1960.* Princeton: Princeton University Press, 1991.

———. *Fascism in Film: The Italian Commercial Cinema, 1930–1943.* Princeton: Princeton: Princeton University Press, 1986.

———. *Imitations of Life: A Reader on Film and Television Melodrama.* Detroit: Wayne State University Press, 1991.

Lyotard, Jean-François. *The Postmodern Condition: A Report on Knowledge.* Minneapolis: University of Minnesota Press, 1985.

Macciocchi, Maria-Antonietta. "Female Sexuality in Fascist Ideology." In *Feminist Review* 1 (1979).

———. *Per Gramsci.* Bologna: Il Mulino, 1974.

Malpezzi, Frances. *Italian-American Folklore.* Little Rock, Ark.: August House, 1992.

Marcus, Millicent. *Filmmaking by the Book: Italian Cinema and Literary Adaptation.* Baltimore: Johns Hopkins University Press, 1993.

———. *Italian Film in the Light of Neorealism.* Princeton: Princeton University Press, 1986.

Marx, Karl. *Capital.* 3 vols. New York: International Publishers, 1977.

———. *The Eighteenth Brumaire of Louis Bonaparte.* New York: International Publishers, 1990.

———. *Grundrisse: Foundations of the Critique of Political Economy.* New York: Vintage Books, 1973.

McCormick, Ruth. "The Tavianis: War and Remembrance." In *American Film* (Jan.–Feb. 1983): 12–13.

McGuigan, Jim. *Cultural Populism.* London: Routledge, 1992.

Mitchell, Tony. "Towards Utopia: By Way of Research, Detachment and Involvement." In *Sight and Sound* 47, no. 3: 173–78.

Modleski, Tania. *Loving with a Vengeance: Mass Produced Fantasies for Women.* London: Methuen, 1985.

———. *The Women Who Knew Too Much.* New York: Methuen, 1988.

Moe, Nelson J. "Production and Its Others: Gramsci's 'Sexual Question.'" In *Rethinking Marxism* 3, nos. 3–4 (Fall/Winter, 1990): 218–37.

Moses, Gavriel. "L'altro viaggio dei Taviani (Or What Luigi Missed)." Paper presented at Society for Cinema Studies Conference, Montreal, May 21–24, 1987.

Moss, Leonard W. "The Passing of Traditional Peasant Society in the South." In *Modern Italy: A Topical History Since 1861.* New York: New York University Press, 1974, pp. 125–46.

Mosse, George. *Masses and Men: Nationalist and Fascist Perceptions of Reality.* New York: Howard Fertig, 1980.

Mouffe, Chantal, ed. "Gramsci Today." In *Gramsci and Marxist Theory.* London: Routledge & Kegan Paul, 1979.

Murphy, Robert. "A Brief Studio History." In *Gainsborough Melodrama*, ed. Sue Aspinall and Robert Murphy. London: BFI, 1983, pp. 3–14.

Nairn, Tom. "Antonu su Gobbu." In *Approaches to Gramsci*, ed. Anne Showstack Sassoon. London: Writers and Readers, 1982, pp. 159–79.

Negri, Antonio. *Marx Beyond Marx: Lessons on the Grundrisse.* London: Automedia, 1991.

——.*The Politics of Subversion: A Manifesto for the Twenty-First Century.* Cambridge: Polity Press, 1989.

——. *Revolution Retrieved: Writings on Marx, Keynes, Capitalist Crisis, and New Social Subjects (1967–1983).* London: Red Notes, 1988.

——. *The Savage Anomaly: The Power of Spinoza's Metaphysics and Politics,* trans. Michael Hardt. Minneapolis: University of Minnesota Press, 1991.

Nietzsche, Friedrich. "On the Uses and Disadvantages of History for Life." In *Untimely Meditations.* Cambridge: Cambridge University Press, 1991.

Nowell-Smith, Geoffrey. "But Do We Need It?" In *British Cinema Now.* London: BFI, 1985, pp. 147–58.

Nun, José. "Elements for a Theory of Democracy." In *The Legacy of Antonio Gramsci,* ed. Joseph A. Buttigieg. *boundary 2* 14 (Spring 1986): 197–231.

Piccone, Paul. *Italian Marxism.* Berkeley: University of California Press, 1983.

Polan, Dana. *Power and Paranoia: History, Narrative and the American Cinema, 1940–1950.* New York: Columbia University Press, 1986.

Quart, Leonard. "The Thatcherism of the Market: Thatcherite Politics and the British Film of the 1980s." In *Fires Were Started,* ed. Lester Freidman, pp. 15–34.

Radway, Janice A. *Reading the Romance: Women, Patriarchy and Popular Literature.* Chapel Hill: University of North Carolina Press, 1984.

Renov, Michael. "Leave Her to Heaven: The Double-Bind of the Post-War Woman." In *Journal of the University Film and Video Association* 35 (Winter 1983): 28–36.

Rose, Jacqueline. "Margaret Thatcher and Ruth Ellis." In *New Formations* 6 (Winter 1988): 3–29.

Rosenthal, Pam. "Jacked In: Fordism, Cyberpunk, Marxism." In *Socialist Review* 21, no. 1 (Jan.–March 1991): 79–103.

Said, Edward. *Musical Elaborations.* New York: Columbia University Press, 1991.

——. "Opponents, Audiences, Constituencies and Community." In *The Anti-Aesthetic: Essays in Postmodern Culture.* Port Townsend, Wash.: Bay Press, 1983.

——. *The World, the Text, and the Critic.* Cambridge, Mass.: Harvard University Press, 1983.

Sassoon, Anne Showstack. *Gramsci's Politics.* Minneapolis: University of Minnesota Press, 1987.

——. "Gramsci's Subversion of the Language of Politics." In *Rethinking Marxism* 3, no. 1 (Spring 1990): 14–25.

——, ed. *Approaches to Gramsci.* London: Writers and Readers, 1982.

Sembène, Ousmane. *Man Is Culture.* Sixth Annual Hans Wolf Lecture, March 5, 1975, Bloomington, Ind., African Studies Program.

Serenellini, Mario. *I diseducatori: Intelletuali d'Italia da Gramsci a Pasolini.* Bari: Edizioni Dedalo, 1985.

Sillanpoa, Wallace P. "Pasolini's Gramsci." *MLN* 96 (1981): 120–37.

Smith, Denis Mack. "Regionalism." In *Modern Italy, A Topical History Since 1861* (New York: New York University Press, 1974), pp. 147–70.

Sobchack, Vivian. *Screening Space: The American Science Fiction Film.* New York: Ungar, 1987.

Sontag, Susan. "Fascinating Fascism." In *Movies and Methods,* ed. Bill Nichols. Berkeley: University of California Press, 1979, pp. 31–43.

Sorlin, Pierre. *European Cinemas: European Societies, 1939–1990.* London: Routledge, 1991.

——. *The Film in History: Restaging the Past.* Totowa, N.J.: Barnes & Noble Books, 1980.

Bibliography

270 Spivak, Gayatri Chakravorty. *In Other Worlds: Essays in Cultural Politics.* New York: Routledge, 1988.

———. *The Postcolonial Critic: Interviews, Strategies, Dialogues.* New York: Routledge, 1990.

Springer, Claudia. "The Pleasure of the Interface." In *Screen* 32, no. 3 (Autumn 1991): 303–23.

Stam, Robert. "Mikhail Bakhtin and Left Cultural Critique." In *Postmodernism and Its Discontents: Theories, Practices*, ed. E. Ann Kaplan. London: Verso, 1988, pp. 116–45.

Summer, Doris. "Irresistible Romance: The Foundational Fictions of Latin America." In *Nation and Narration*, ed. Homi K. Bhabha.

Tagliacozzo, Giorgio, ed. *Vico and Marx: Affinities and Contrasts.* Atlantic Highlands, N.J.: Humanities Press, 1983.

Tannenbaum, Edward. *Fascism In Italy: Society and Culture, 1922–1945.* London: Allen Lane, 1972.

Telotte, J. P. "The Tremulous Public Body: Robots, Change, and the Science Fiction Film." In *Journal of Popular Film and Television* 19, no. 1 (Spring 1991): 14–23.

Tudor, Andrew. *Monsters and Mad Scientists: A Cultural History of the Horror Movie.* London: Basil Blackwell, 1989.

Turim, Maureen. *Flashbacks in Film: Memory and History.* New York: Routledge, 1989.

Turner, Graeme. *British Cultural Studies: An Introduction.* London: Unwin Hyman, 1990.

Vacca, Guiseppe. "Intellectuals and the Marxist Theory of the State." In *Approaches to Gramsci*, ed. Anne Showstack Sassoon. London: Writers and Readers, 1982, pp. 37–69.

Virilio, Paul. *War and Cinema: The Logistics of Perception.* London: Verso, 1989.

Walker, John. *National Heroes: British Cinema in the Seventies and Eighties.* London: Harrap, 1985.

Wallerstein, Immanuel. *Historical Capitalism.* London: Verso, 1984.

Watkins, Evan A. *The Critical Act: Criticism and Community.* New Haven: Yale University Press, 1978.

Weber, Henri. "In the Beginning Was Gramsci." In *Italy: Autonomia. Post-Political Politics. Semiotext(e)* 3, no. 3 (1980): 88.

Weeks, Jeffrey. *Sex, Politics, and Society: The Regulation of Sexuality since 1800.* London: Longman, 1986.

Williams, Linda. "Something Else Besides a Mother." In *Home Is Where the Heart Is*, ed. Christine Gledhill, pp. 299–325.

Williams, Raymond. *Marxism and Literature.* London: Oxford University Press, 1977.

———. *Problems in Materialism and Culture: Selected Essays.* London: Verso, 1980.

Winship, Janice. "Nation before Family: Woman, The National Home Weekly, 1845–1953." In *Formations of Nation and People*, ed. Formations Editorial Collective Staff. London: Routledge & Kegan Paul, pp. 188–212.

Witcombe, R. W. *Italian Cinema: From Dance to Despair.* New York: Oxford University Press, 1982.

Wolff, Richard. "Gramsci, Marxism, and Philosophy." In *Rethinking Marxism* 2, no. 2 (1989): 41–54.

Wollen, Peter. "The Last New Wave: Modernism in the British Films of the Thatcher Era." In *Fires Were Started*, ed. Lester Friedman.

Zavarzadeh, Mas'ud, and Donald Morton. *Theory, (Post)Modernity, Opposition: An "Other" Introduction to Literary and Cultural Theory.* Washington, D.C.: Maisonneuve Press, 1991.

Zizek, Slavoj. *The Sublime Object of Ideology.* London: Verso, 1989.

Index

Index

Index

Marcia Landy is professor of English and film studies at the University of Pittsburgh. She is the author of several books, including, among others, *Fascism in Film: The Italian Commercial Cinema 1921–1943* (1986) and *British Genres: British Cinema and Society* (1992). She has also published numerous articles on postmodern folklore, women and iconography, neorealism and politics, narratives of conversion, politics and style, and the politics of engaged cinema.